PRAGUE
Eleven Centuries of Architecture

PRAGUE

Eleven Centuries of Architecture

Jaroslava Staňková, Jiří Štursa, Svatopluk Voděra
Illustrated by Jaroslav Staněk
Translated by Zdeněk Vyplel, David Vaughan

Reviewers: Prof. Dr. Marie Benešová, DrSc.
Prof. Ing. arch. Karel Kibic, CSc.
Prof. Dr. Ing. arch. Miroslav Korecký
Dr. Dobroslav Líbal
Dr. Emanuel Poche, DrSc. (†)

ISBN 80-900003-1-2

The present day is characterized by a need for reliable and readily accessible information and data in any particular field of specialization. This book aims to acquaint the reader with the unique cultural and material legacy of old Prague and with the buildings of the present day. The book is in fact an indirect dialogue between three authors, teachers at the Czech Technical University with the same field of interest, but different specializations: Ing. arch. Jaroslava Staňková, CSc., Prof. Ing. arch. Jiří Štursa and Prof. Ing. arch. Svatopluk Voděra, CSc.

A very positive feature of the work is the way the particular topics are presented. The book aims at a concise presentation of information in a number of relatively short chapters, illustrated with drawings, i.e., a combination of graphic representation and of literary explanation covering the circumstances in which buildings were produced, the value of a whole complex in the town, and even the small architectural details.

The publication is not only intended as a textbook presenting all the available data. It also provides the reader or sightseer with more profound information about the sights and monuments of the city and explains their context, as any architectural discussion requires. It is clear that the book was conceived, written and edited by architects.

Prof. Ing. arch. Dr. Miroslav Korecký

Introduction

If you look at the wide spectrum of literature devoted to Prague in the last fifty years you will fail to find a publication that introduces the reader through words and pictures to selected buildings and the complexes of which they form part from each stage in Prague's architectural history. It is very difficult to get detailed information; one has to search through general surveys, monographs on particular styles, periods and architects.

Therefore, we decided to write a book with a sequence of chapters devoted to particular historical periods, which would give the reader basic information about the most important buildings and make him familiar with the main architectural types, with the development of the city and the changes in its appearance at each stage in its architectural evolution. In addition to dating the structures and to giving information about their authors, architects and style, we wished to explain their significance as well as their urban and historical context.

With most of the examples of Prague architecture selected we shall look at the way they have been renovated at different times since 1850 when state-subsidized conservation was introduced. By doing so we hope to show that due to the often extensive reconstructions of historic monuments and to changes in their function they begin to play a different role in the organism of the town and in the life of its society. This approach will enable the reader to get acquainted with the recent history of Prague's monuments and with the architects of recent renovations.

Prague's historic centre, where most of the buildings here described can be found, is a huge complex whose renovation and regeneration will require much effort at every level of society if it is to be preserved for future generations. The great wealth of historic buildings accumulated in Prague, their charm and beauty make this challenging task worthwhile.

We convey our thanks to Dr. D. Líbal, Dr. M. Benešová, Prof. K. Kibic and, in particular, to Dr. E. Poche (†) for their valuable remarks and recommendations. We also express our gratitude to Prof. M. Korecký for his kind foreword.

The authors

Beginnings

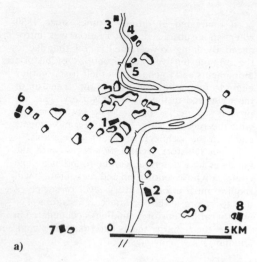

a) **Settlements in the territory of Prague between the 4th and 10th century, fortified settlements from the 8th century:** 1 Prague Castle, 2 Vyšehrad, 3 Levý Hradec; fortified settlements from the 9th—10th centuries: 4 Bohnice, 5 Podhoří, 6 Šárka, 7 Butovice, 8 Hostivař

b) **Reconstruction of Slav settlement, 10th—11th century, in Prague Castle:** 1 St. Vitus' rotunda, 2 St. George's Basilica and Convent, 3 Bishop's House and St. Moritz' Chapel, 4 Royal Palace, 5 timber houses of nobles and their domestics, 6 settlements outside the castle, 7 Church of Our Lady

c) **Prague around 1230:** 1 market-place and Ungelt, 2 Prague Castle, 3 Vyšehrad, 4 settlements outside the castle, 5 Strahov and Pohořelec, 6 settlement Obora, 7 settlements under the castle (with churches of SS. Wenceslas, Andrew, Martin and Michael), 8 settlement Na písku, 9 Bishop's Palace, 10 Monastery of the Knights of St. John and the settlement Trávníček,

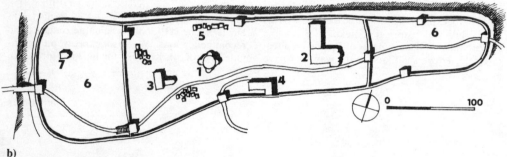

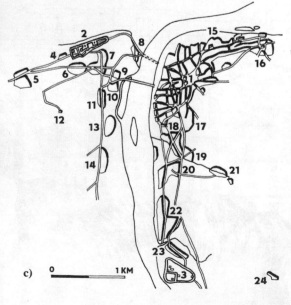

11 Nebovidy, 12 Church of St. Lawrence on Petřín Hill, 13 Újezd, 14 south part of Újezd in Smíchov, 15 Újezd, St. Castulus', 16 Poříčí with a farmstead of German Knights, 17 Újezd, St. Martin's, 18 Opatovice, 19 settlement at St. Lazarus', 20 Zderaz with a monastery and a royal farmstead, 21 Rybník village with a farmstead by St. John's Church "On the Battlefield", 22 Podskalí, 23 settlements under Vyšehrad, 24 Nusle

Beginnings

The area which Prague now occupies was quite densely populated as early as the Paleolithic Age. Archaeological findings show that from the very beginning the left bank of the Vltava was more densely populated than the right bank, which until the late Middle Ages suffered from frequent floods. At the turn of the 5th and 6th centuries Slavs started penetrating into Bohemia and gave the country a new character. Traces of the first Slav settlements go back to the 7th century. There were quite a lot of settlements under Hradčany Hill and on the left bank of the Vltava River, which was then continuously populated. Population concentrated on the sites of old settlements along old roads that had existed here since prehistoric times. In the 8th century quite a dense network of fortified settlements already existed in the region proving that there was a concentration of Slav population in the vicinity of Prague prior to the foundation of Prague Castle. Fortified settlements flourished from the late 8th century to the end of the 11th century. Some of them later became centres of particular tribes and seats of princes.

The Levý Hradec was the immediate predecessor of Prague Castle. It was the main seat of the Přemyslid Prince Bořivoj (died approx. 889), who built the very first Christian church here, dedicated to Saint Clement and already made of stone. By the end of the 9th century its political role weakened as the new Prague Castle became the centre of the country, and later of the great and powerful empire of the Přemyslids. The Castle was initially a fortified settlement controlled by the Přemyslids, quite large, with wooden houses and stone churches, and surrounded by banked walls with three gates. In its eastern part, where now the chancel of St. Vitus' Cathedral is, there was a stone throne where the princes of Bohemia were inaugurated. Prague Castle in the north and Vyšehrad Castle in the south (which was probably a frontier castle of the Zličany tribe), under the Přemyslid rule, defined the area of the future city.

From the 9th century, when the first stone architecture prior to the Romanesque period appeared in this country, only a few structures remain. In addition to St. Clement's Church at Levý Hradec there is the first church within Prague Castle, founded by Prince Bořivoj before 890. The stone church, discovered in 1950 by Ivan Borkovský and identified as Our Lady's, was a simple rectangular building whose foundations can still be seen in the Castle Gallery. We know that it was a sepulchral church, however scientists are still arguing as to its purpose. Another church, St. George's, was founded around 920 by Prince Vratislav (905?—921?). Its original masonry was discovered during archaeological excavations here in 1959—1962 under the eastern part of the later tribune of today's basilica. Architecture in 10th century Bohemia corresponds to the pre-Romanesque art of the late Carolingian and Ottonian era. It was at that time that a systematic development of Bohemian architecture started with the construction of St. Vitus' Rotunda, begun by Prince Wenceslas (assassinated in 935) in 925. The rotunda, which was later replaced by Spytihněv's basilica, was rebuilt as a centrally planned structure with four hoof-shaped apses, similar to the elongated apses of Great Moravian rotundas. The first reconstruction showed that it had been a simplified version of Aachen's Palace Chapel with a gallery. We also know that as early as the late 9th century a new type of rotunda came here from Great Moravia. St. Vitus' Rotunda, whose founder, St. Wenceslas, had been buried in its apse, became a model for many later Romanesque rotundas in this country.

In 973, the bishopric of Prague was established at St. Vitus' Church and, as a result, the role of the Castle and of Prague increased and building activity here further intensified. Almost simultaneously, the first convent—of the Benedictine Order—was founded at St. George's Church and the old church of Vratislav was rebuilt as a short basilica, the oldest in Bohemia.

Romanesque Architecture

The new style gets its name from Rome, as this art appeared in the 11th—13th century in countries that had been part of the Roman Empire. The Franks, the Teutons, the Anglo-Saxons as well as the Slavs contributed to the new style whose uniting idea was that of Christianity, which was spreading rapidly at that time. Therefore, Romanesque art followed the example of old Christian architectural forms, particularly the basilica and centrally planned buildings.

The first stage in the development of the new style occurred in the Carolingian and Ottonian era. Bohemia and its architecture in the 10th century were part of that development. The centres of culture and the arts at that time were the monasteries, which were then beginning to emerge.

The Romanesque style developed in Bohemia and Moravia in the 11th century. From the late 11th century to the mid-13th century the new style completely dominated the arts of the region and the way of life. Its form and detail during that period tended to be simple.

The first vaults were tunnel vaults, followed by cross vaults with large separating bands instead of face arches, and had a small span for reasons of stability. They were also very thick, and therefore required very solid supporting structures, such as walls and pillars. The Romanesque buildings exhibited quite a simple ground plan, confined spaces, few details and small narrow windows. The walls and vaults were mostly made of ashlar blocks and bonded with lime mortar to form regular horizontal layers. Findings show that there were not many buildings made of irregular quarried stone. During the Romanesque period (1100—1230), usually clay slate quarried on White Mountain (Bílá Hora) near Prague was used as a construction material after being hewn and shaped to form regular ashlar blocks, characteristic of many buildings from that time. The architecture of religious buildings featured sculpture and painting, as well as other elements, such as semicircular portals decorated with reliefs, or the articulation of the outer surface of the nave or apse walls by means of lesenes continuing a frieze under the cornice. On the inside, which was plastered, frescoes appeared. The new technology was mostly applied to the construction of monasteries and churches, and later also to fortifications and the first castles. These became prominent features of the landscape and transformed the seats of princes, which until that time had mostly been made of timber.

After the fall of the Great Moravian Empire, the centre of the unification process of the Slav tribes in this region moved from Moravia to the intersection of trade-routes at the Vltava Ford. The ruling princes here were those of the Přemyslid dynasty who by the end of the 10th century controlled the whole country. They had always supported the Catholic Church and contributed to the spread of Christianity; as a result, religious buildings are among the first stone structures in Bohemia. Modern archaeological research has shown that the history of Prague Castle goes back to the late 9th century when the Castle became a centre of political power for the Přemyslids. Ibrahim Ibn Ya'qub, an Arab merchant who visited Prague in the years 965—966, described "Fraga" in his report as a stone town with a busy international market-place, with stone houses and surrounded by stone walls. The Castle was already very large at that time, as the place referred to in the report is beyond any doubt Prague Castle. South of here, not far away, is the castle called Vyšehrad which, as archaeologists have proved, dates from the mid-10th century. Between these two main points several small settlements appeared from which a town developed that in the early 13th century exhibited a stable territorial structure with houses made both of timber and stone and with an increasing number of houses and homesteads made of stone.

Romanesque architecture, which was generally adopted here in the 12th century, developed both in form and technology. The style prevailed until the early 13th century when the first signs of the Gothic style appeared in Prague.

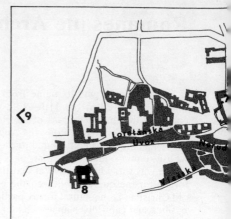

ROMANESQUE ARCHITECTURE

Romanesque houses—remains in the basement of later houses in the Old Town are marked with the number of the respective house (according to D. Líbal)

Prague Castle, Romanesque Part

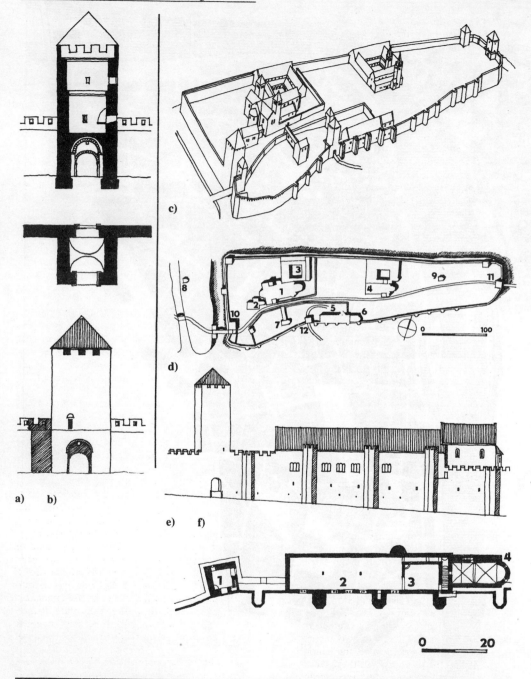

a) b) **Black Tower of Prague Castle**
c) **Romanesque part—reconstruction**
d) **Prague Castle at the end of 13th century:** 1 St. Vitus' Basilica, 2 Bishop's Palace, 3 cloister, 4 Convent and Basilica of St. George, 5 Prince's Palace, 6 All Saints Chapel, 7 Our Lady's (?) Church, 8 cemetery chapel, 9 St. John Baptist's Church, 10 White Tower, 11 Black Tower, 12 south gate
e) f) **Prince's Palace:** 1 south tower and gate, 2 palace, great hall, 3 prince's room, 4 All Saints Chapel

(14)

Prague Castle, which is a symbol of the thousand-year history of the City of Prague, was initially a walled-in site founded by the Přemyslids in the latter half of the 9th century. The pre-Romanesque site, which was already quite large, was protected by clay mounds and a timber palisade. Between the east and the west gates there was a paved road whose remains still exist under the present-day paving of the Third Courtyard. The West Gate was used to get to Levý Hradec, while the East Gate opened the way to the settlement below the Castle. The houses of the prince and of his followers were initially timbered and were situated south of the Castle's east-west axis, while the religious buildings, already made of stone, were concentrated in the larger northern part of the site. The buildings which in the early 10th century dominated the skyline of the Castle were the Prince's Palace, St. Vitus' Rotunda and St. George's Church. In the 970s the tower of a convent adjoining the church and the new bishop's palace were added. In the mid-11 th century, under Prince Břetislav I, the primitive fortification of the Castle was rebuilt and walls made of clay-slate ashlar were erected. The walls, up to five metres high, were reinforced with towers over the West Gate, the South (Palace) Gate, and the East Gate. The Prince's Palace was rebuilt in 1041, probably after a fire.

Under Prince Vratislav II (1061—1092) there were quarrels among the Přemyslids and, as a result, the position of Vyšehrad became stronger while the Castle lost for some time its role as the prince's residence. Although the attention of Bohemian sovereigns focused on the Vyšehrad, construction work went on also in Prague Castle. After the 1091 and 1142 fires the Castle saw several reconstructions, and each time its architecture became more imposing. A particular reason for the large-scale rebuilding work throughout the Castle was the need to reinforce the fortifications and to repair the damage caused during the siege of the Castle in 1142 by the Prince of Moravia.

Around 1100, the Castle had stone walls, and the churches, the convent, the Bishop's Palace and the adjoining St. Moritz' Chapel were all stone buildings too. There was also accommodation for the Prince's entourage, the canonry, the courtiers and the servants, and there were stores and workshops. Another great reconstruction of the Castle took place under Prince Soběslav I (1125—1140) who moved from Vyšehrad back to Prague Castle. He started by constructing new walls here; the construction of strong castle walls with tall towers made of white stone ashlar

began in 1135. At the same time, a large new palace was built, fifty metres long and ten metres wide, with a vaulted hall for the prince and with a chapel to All Saints in the eastern side. The southern wall of the palace, facing the Vltava River, had Romanesque coupled windows and was reinforced with a number of pentagonal towers. This is how Prague Castle was built "following the example of Latin towns".

After 1918, when the Czechoslovak Republic came into being, new renovation works in the Castle started in order to convert the devastated complex into a place worthy to be the seat of the President and of the Government. At the same time, archaeological excavations were carried out during which the foundations of Spytihněv's basilica and St. Vitus' Rotunda were discovered. To make the discoveries accessible to the public Josef Plečnik, the new Architect of the Castle, covered them with a reinforced concrete slab above the level of the Third Courtyard which was at that time on an incline. This brought about a further levelling of the Courtyard in 1928—1932 and it became a plain paved horizontal area.

Another renovation of the Romanesque part of the Castle took place in 1930 during the restoration of the Theresian Wing attached to the Louis Palace. The archaeological findings from the years 1922—1929 were arranged by Otto Rothmayer. The work continued until 1951; Romanesque foundations and early Gothic cellars were exposed and the architect added as new elements blind red-brick arcades whose ground plan corresponds to the masonry discovered by archaeologists.

In the 1960s, František Cubr and Josef Hrubý rebuilt Rudolph's Stable and the adjacent parts as a picture-gallery for the Castle. They succeeded in finding a suitable solution to the problem of connecting and harmonizing spaces of different character and different age and of making accessible to the public what was probably the oldest religious building in the Castle: Our Lady's Church. The Castle Gallery is certainly very impressive with a quality of great harmony. The unusual way of representing archaeological findings through a glass wall, lit as in the theatre, contributes favourably to the general effect.

The last major problem was how to make the remains of the Romanesque convent of Abbess Mlada under the courtyard of today's St. George's Convent accessible to the public. This was solved by František Cubr and Josef Pilař as part of the general reconstruction.

Vyšehrad: Prehistory and Early Middle Ages

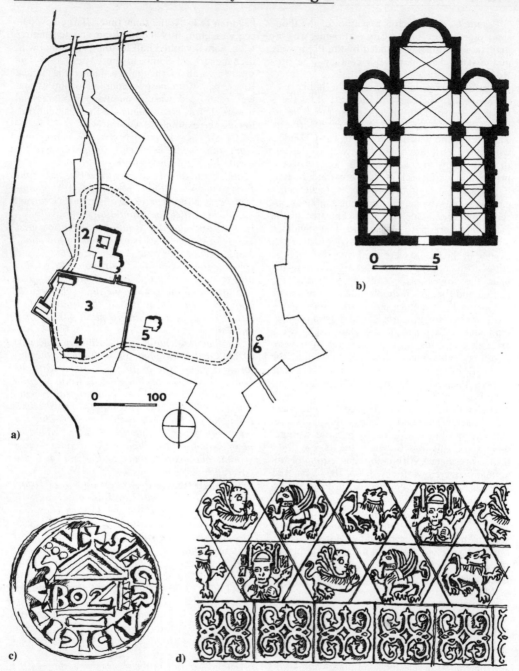

a) **Vyšehrad in 11th century:** 1 Church of SS. Peter and Paul, 2 chapter house, 3 acropolis, 4 palace, 5 St. Lawrence's Church, 6 St. Martin's Rotunda
b) **St. Lawrence's Basilica**

c) **denar, a coin minted by Boleslav II at Vyšehrad with inscription VISEGRAD CIVITAS**
d) **the floor of St. Lawrence's Basilica with animal motifs and the Emperor Nero**

One of the most important historic monuments of the Czech nation is Vyšehrad, whose early history is linked with many legends and myths about the origins of the Czech state under the first Přemyslids. According to the chronicler Cosmas, in whose time the castle was already called Vyšehrad (its initial name had been Chrasten), the early history of the castle goes back to the time of the War of the Czech Amazons. Recent archaeological excavations have shown, however, that Vyšehrad is a little newer than Prague Castle and that its history goes back to the early 10th century.

The strategic position above the confluence of the Vltava and the Botič River on a rocky headland had attracted settlers since prehistoric times. The first settlements had existed here as early as the third millenium B. C. In the late Stone Age Vyšehrad was an important hilltop settlement, one of many known to us within the area of Prague. However, no evidence is available that would confirm the existence of an early Slav settlement here and, consequently, the presence of the first Přemyslids. For a long time, there was no mention of Vyšehrad in written documents. It is not mentioned in the Legends of St. Wenceslas and St. Ludmila from the 10th century, either.

The earliest surviving evidence of Vyšehrad's existence are coins (denars) minted here under Boleslav II (967—999). Vyšehrad at that time was a typical Přemyslid fortified settlement with a palace in the western part of the acropolis and with houses made of stone and wood, protected by walls. From this period the recently discovered foundations of a cruciform pre-Romanesque Ottonian church survive beneath the Romanesque basilica of St. Lawrence. From the same period are also the earliest churches here, St. Clement and the basilica of St. John the Evangelist at the Prince's Palace. We know neither the location of St. Clement's Church nor what it looked like, however this dedication is known to us from many Slav settlements as early as the 9th century.

The few sources of information we have tell us that during the Polish invasion of about 1000 under Boleslav the Valiant, Vyšehrad was loyal to the Přemyslids. In the late 11th century Vyšehrad was the seat of Prince Vratislav II (1061—1092), who later became the first King of Bohemia. He built here a prince's palace, a collegiate basilica to SS. Peter and Paul, and a chapter house. The chapter was established here in 1070 and was directly controlled by Rome. Prior to this basilica,

which was constructed at the same time as Spytihněv's basilica at Prague Castle (1060—1096), two or three other religious buildings are supposed to have existed at Vyšehrad. The acropolis with the Prince's (later King's) Palace was separated from the other buildings at Vyšehrad by a banked wall and a moat. As a result, all the religious buildings, except the old Church of St. John the Evangelist at the Palace, remained outside the citadel, apparently at the request of the sovereign. The complex is supposed to have been surrounded by a Romanesque wall, of stones bonded with mortar, which replaced the original fortification. The stronghold could be entered from the east through a gateway at St. Martin's Rotunda. The main road, which existed for many centuries, ran westwards to the Church of SS. Peter and Paul. Vratislav's church from the late 11th century was extended and generously furnished by Prince Soběslav I before 1129, and later, in the late 13th century, it was rebuilt in the early Gothic style. It was at that time that an elongated presbytery was built, the end of which was discovered by Bořivoj Nechvátal behind the eastern wall of Vyšehrad Cemetery. Starting with Vratislav II, who was also buried here, the Přemyslid princes had their seat at Vyšehrad for seventy years, until the time of Soběslav I (1125—1140). Only at the end of his reign did Soběslav decide to move back to Prague Castle, where he immediately began a large-scale reconstruction of both the walls and the palace. Soběslav II was the last Přemyslid to be buried at Vyšehrad (in 1178).

Of the original works from the Přemyslid period it is mostly buildings outside the citadel that have survived. Of the Palace, only an arch of the stone bridge that connected the chapter house north of SS. Peter's and Paul's Church with the Palace courtyard remains. St. Lawrence's basilica, beneath which archaeologists have discovered remains of the above-mentioned pre-Romanesque building, dates probably from the same time as the mint of Boleslav II. The only building that has survived intact is St. Martin's Rotunda built by Prince Vratislav. We do not know of any other religious buildings, although in 1130 a chapel consecrated to St. Mary Magdalene and St. Margaret is mentioned.

After the mid-13th century, having lost its position as a central stronghold and being far away from the walls of the new towns, Vyšehrad was gradually abandoned, and of the former royal residence only an isolated chapter house remained. However, under Emperor Charles IV it regained its royal splendour.

The Forerunner of St. Vitus' Cathedral

a)

a) **St. Vitus' Rotunda**
b) **St. Vitus' Rotunda**—probable ground plan (according to J. Cibulka)
c) d) **St. Vitus' Basilica**
e) f) **comparison with the present cathedral in size and ground plan**

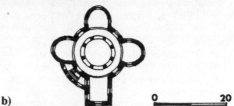

b)

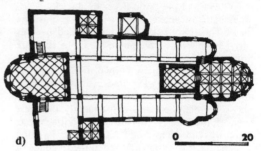

d)

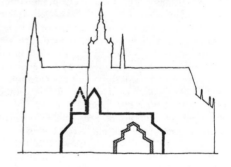

c)

e)   f)

(18)

The churches at Prague Castle are important historic monuments surviving from the early history of the Czech state. Over a thousand years, up to 1929, they have evolved through changing styles and functions and under changing aesthetic demands into an extremely valuable work of architecture.

The original Palace Chapel, the pre-Romanesque rotunda founded by Prince Wenceslas, developed into the collegiate, episcopal, and later archepiscopal basilica, St. Vitus' Cathedral. It is a unique building, and as the role of the Castle increased and the Czech feudal state and the Church became increasingly powerful, important works of art were concentrated here. From the very beginning the Cathedral dominated the Castle and the Vltava Basin due to its situation in the centre of the stronghold, to its architectural beauty and to its importance. It was a symbol and a centre of the Catholic Church in Bohemia and Moravia. St. Vitus' Rotunda, founded by Prince Wenceslas, was completed probably in the third decade of the 10th century. The Rotunda was probably constructed by foreign builders who introduced a new measure of length, the "foot", which was generally equal to the ancient Roman foot. This detail, which is of some importance, shows that the country had relations with and was oriented towards southern countries (Dalmatia).

The remains of St. Vitus' Rotunda were found underground during the completion of St. Vitus' Cathedral between 1911 and 1928. Kamil Hilbert, the architect charged with the completion of the work, found them under the floor paving of Parler's St. Wenceslas' Chapel. The remains can still be seen below the ground. They made it possible to reconstruct the chapel, which was a centralized structure with an internal gallery and tribunes on the upper floor, and with a vaulted interior.

To give an idea of how big the rotunda was we need only mention the inside diameter, which was thirteen metres. Its founder, Prince Wenceslas, was buried in the southern apse of the rotunda. Prince Břetislav (1034—1055) brought here in 1039 the remains of St. Adalbert from Gnezdno in Poland. The rotunda became a place of pilgrimage at that time. The chronicler Cosmas says that on St. Wenceslas' day in 1060 Prince Spytihněv I (1055—1061), Břetislav's successor, saw that there were so many pilgrims coming here that they could not get into the chapel, and he therefore decided to build a big new basilica consecrated to Saints Vitus, Wenceslas and Adalbert above their tombs. We cannot be sure what this basilica looked like and its form is disputed; the same also applies to the suggestion that, prior to its construction, Wenceslas' rotunda had been pulled down as early as 1060. The basilica survived a fire during its construction and was completed under the first Bohemian king Vratislav around 1090 with a crypt to St. Gaudentius.

The building was an unprecedented work in the country. The two-aisle Romanesque church, made of white clay slate and 70 metres long, had in its western part a transept with two impressive towers at the points of intersection of the transept and the aisles. At both ends of this excellent layout there were vaulted crypts. It has been argued that there might have been another lower tower over the crossing of the nave and the transepts, as was the case at Mainz Cathedral, from where both the main religious ideas and the latest aesthetic trends were coming to Bohemia. On the other hand, a drawing of St. Vitus' Basilica is still available which was made before its demolition and which shows, in addition to the two west towers, a third tower at the east end of the southern aisle. There was probably also a tower over the northern part of the chancel.

St. Vitus' Church built by Spytihněv, the white silhouette of which could be seen from afar, was taller than the older church consecrated to St. George. The large and spacious structure with a transept and two tall towers, oriented and constructed so as to surmount and respect the tomb of St. Wenceslas, dominated the Castle for a long time. The two-aisle basilica probably had wooden ceilings. The central nave was separated from the aisles by arcades. It was in this basilica that the first royal coronation took place on 15th June 1085 when Prince Vratislav and his wife Svatava were crowned King and Queen of Bohemia. Other kings of the Přemyslid and Luxembourg dynasty were later also crowned there.

At the early stage of the reign of Charles IV, Prague was still predominantly a Romanesque town, in spite of a few early Gothic buildings. In 1344 the bishopric was raised to an archbishopric, and shortly afterwards the foundation stone was laid of a new Gothic cathedral to replace the old Romanesque basilica which was gradually torn down to make way for the construction of the new church.

The Oldest Monastery

a) St. George's Basilica, interior
b) original appearance
c) St. George's Convent, site
d) basilica, ground plan

The first monasteries and convents (Benedictine and Cistercian) appeared in this country in the 10th century as Christian strongholds and also as the starting points for colonization. Being organized communities of monks and nuns serving a particular order, they soon became centres of culture, and later also of charity.

One of the first was the Benedictine Convent at St. George's Church within the Castle founded in 973 by Boleslav II's sister Mlada, the first abbess of the convent. Daughters of the Bohemian royal dynasty were educated here and among the abbesses there were many royal princesses. The location of the convent within the Castle, its size, and also the fact that it was founded at the same time as the bishopric of Prague (in 973) are evidence of the strong position of the Church in the Přemyslid state and also of the support the Church enjoyed under the Přemyslids. Adalbert (Vojtěch) Slavník, the second bishop of Prague, founded some years later, in 993, the first Benedictine Monastery at Břevnov, on the road leading from Prague to the west. We can get a good idea of what the most beautiful Romanesque monasteries looked like from the Premonstratensian Monastery at Strahov, founded by Vladislav II in 1140 on Mount Zion (Sion), as Strahov Hill was then called.

Monasteries and convents were founded by members of the ruling dynasty. Each monastery had a church, usually a basilica, and a cloister around a square courtyard with a well in its centre. The main rooms adjoining the cloister were the chapter house (for meetings), the refectory (dining-room) and the dormitory (bedroom). The first monasteries and convents were mostly built in isolation and were therefore protected by high walls. Inside, there were outbuildings, workshops, a hospital, and gardens.

St. George's Basilica, the second biggest church within Prague Castle which played an important role at the princes' inauguration ceremonies, was founded prior to 920 by Bořivoj's son, Prince Vratislav (915—921) and was situated near his palace. Large-scale archaeological excavations since 1959 have yielded more information about the first structure built by Vratislav, which was a rhomboidal building with solid walls. Its founder was buried here, as well as other members of the Přemyslid dynasty.

With the founding of a convent here by Abbess Mlada in 973, soon after the bishopric of Prague was established, it became necessary to enlarge the small church. The building was a short basilica, with a nave, two aisles and three choirs, and was technically and architecturally quite advanced. Most of it has survived to the 3present day. A characteristic of the basilica is the narrowness of the aisles compared to the nave.

The church, whose central part with massive piers has survived, was largely rebuilt, probably by the end of the 11th century, being made longer and taller. Galleries were constructed over the aisles and simultaneously the northern tower was built. A large-scale renovation of the basilica was needed after a disastrous fire in 1142. As a result, the church acquired its present-day form. Its large nave has a flat ceiling. A main choir was built ending in an apse, and a crypt was dug under the presbytery. The aisles, which until that time had had flat ceilings, were vaulted over and a second white tower was erected over the south chapel. At the beginning of the 13th century a late Romanesque chapel dedicated to St. Ludmila was attached to the south tower.

In the third quarter of the 14th century the church was given a new façade which, along with an additional storey to St. Ludmila's Chapel, was made by Parler's workshop. The southern entrance of the basilica, in the Renaissance style, was enriched after 1500 by the Court architect Benedikt Ried (Rejt) with a tympanum and a relief representing St. George fighting the dragon. In the Baroque era a new western façade was built in 1671 and, from 1718 to 1722, a chapel dedicated to St. John of Nepomuk was added by František Maxmilián Kaňka or, as recent research has shown, by Filip Spannbrucker.

Thus, the interior of the basilica was rebuilt and enlarged several times. The most valuable late Romanesque sculpture in Bohemia, a three-part relief representing the seated Madonna, King Přemysl Otakar I and Abbess Agnes was kept here; now it can be admired in a department of the Czech National Gallery that is located in the nearby convent. The convent was closed by Emperor Joseph II and converted into barracks. Gradually, both it and the church became derelict.

The renovation and cultural reactivation of the complex of St. George's Convent has been one of the major undertakings of the state-organized ancient building preservation industry since the end of the Second World War. In 1959, Ivan Borkovský started archaeological research that continued until 1962. Simultaneously, stability and hydrogeological surveys continued as the situation in the northern part of the complex was somewhat complicated (at the Stag Moat). The renovation itself was carried out from 1963 to 1974 according to plans by Josef Cubr and Josef Pilař. The plans changed during the work; the complex was initially intended to be a Monu-

ment to the Czechoslovak People. Now there was a new aim to be fulfilled: the installation of the collection of early art from the National Gallery. To cope with the new task technical and architectural interventions were needed and many technical problems had to be solved, such as heating, ventilation, lighting, fire protection, etc. The renovation of this valuable historical complex demonstrates the high standard of ancient building preservation in this country and shows how historic monuments can be reactivated by giving them a new social function. Outstanding works of Bohemian art from the Gothic period to the high Baroque are exhibited here. In archi-

tectural terms, each part of the complex was conceived differently. The large quadrangle was covered so that the archaeological findings here exposed could be seen. The basement and the ground floor, which are the oldest parts of the complex, keep to the original layout. The first floor, which was last rebuilt in the 17th century, has been arranged for the installation of mainly Baroque works. This alteration, which has often been criticized, can be justified by the high standard of architectural work. Thus, the National Gallery acquired excellent exhibition rooms within the most important historic monument in Prague.

Three Romanesque rotundas have survived intact as important architectural monuments. They are all quite small, with a cylindrical nave of 5 to 6 m diameter, vaulted and with an adjoining apse. They all have a conical roof with a lantern. These simple rotundas were among the earliest religious building types in this country.

St. Martin's Rotunda at Vyšehrad is in a place which is now called "V pevnosti" (In the Fortress). It used to be a parish church probably built by Prince Vratislav II in the latter half of the 11th century at the same time as his new palace, and is now the oldest rotunda in Prague and the oldest historic monument at Vyšehrad as well. This centralized structure with its rather unusual parabolic apse still has the original masonry of thin ashlar blocks with lesenes on the apse, a lantern with new posts, a concha, and a dome over the nave. The south portal is neo-Romanesque. The architectural details are mostly new.

The second of the three surviving rotundas is the Chapel of the Holy Cross in the Old Town of Prague at the intersection of Karolina Světlá Street and Konviktská Street, in a small garden surrounded by neo-Romanesque railings. It used to be located on an important road leading from Vyšehrad to the Vltava crossings. The parish (or

manorial) church at a farmstead dating from the early 12th century is also quite a small and plain structure whose circular nave of 6 m diameter is domed and has an opening at the top. There is an apse with lesenes terminating in an arched frieze. The building has a conical roof surmounted by a lantern with coupled windows. Fragments of 14th century wall-paintings of St. Mary's Coronation can still be seen in the nave.

The newest rotunda is that of St. Longinus and its history goes back to the late 11th century. Situated beside St. Stephen's Church in the New Town of Prague it is believed to have been originally consecrated to St. Stephen and to have been identical to the parish church of the village called "Rybníček" mentioned as early as 933. Only later, after the construction of the Gothic church nearby, did its consecration change. The rotunda has a cylindrical nave of some five metres in diameter, domed and covered with a conic roof, and has a lantern which is now Baroque. The lantern, the portal and the brickwork altering the shape of the original apse date from the 17th century when a nave was attached to the rotunda (the nave was later pulled down within the redevelopment of the area).

In 1962 the foundations of a rotunda were discovered in the Old Town at the former monastic

a) b)

c) d)

e) f)

g)

a) b) St. Martin's Rotunda
c) d) St. Longinus' Rotunda
e) f) Rotunda of the Holy Cross
g) Romanesque rotunda, section

church dedicated to St. Ann. It was the rotunda of a Romanesque homestead from the 12th century to which a nave was added around 1230. The Templars, who acquired the church, converted the rotunda into a presbytery for the church of St. Lawrence. The church was later demolished and in its place an aisleless building appeared in 1339 that has survived until now.

There was much debate about all these Romanesque rotundas during the period when modern conservation methods were being established, and their future fate was discussed. Finally, it was decided to preserve and renovate them. Other rotundas are known to us from archaeological findings which are mostly very limited, except in the case of the four-apse rotunda of St. Vitus under St. Vitus' Cathedral.

St. Martin's Rotunda at Vyšehrad is the best known due to its location within a National Historic Monument. In 1782 it was closed, along with St. Longinus' Chapel, and converted into a military storehouse and ammunition works. After 1848, the rotunda was also used for some time as a shelter for the poor. The greatest danger, the threat of demolition came in 1841 when a road was planned from the Botič Valley to Pankrác. Thanks to Count Chotek another solution to the problem was found and the rotunda was renovated by Antonín Baum from 1878 to 1880. The missing and damaged parts were restored or replaced, but in the spirit of a romantic neo-Romanesque style, as can particularly be seen in the windows and the lantern. Then the interior was restored by Josef Helbich and Jan Heřman (ceiling frescoes) and by Karel König (decoration of the walls);

a new altar was made by František Sequens.

Much effort was needed to save the Rotunda of the Holy Cross in the years 1861—1862 when there were plans to demolish it and put a tenement house in its place. Thanks to the members of the Association of Artists the chapel was purchased by the City of Prague and renovated between 1863 and 1869. Leading artists of the Association contributed to the renovation. A new altar was designed by Bedřich Wachsmann in collaboration with the painter Jan Popelík, the wall to the right of the entrance and the triumphal arch were decorated by Petr Maixner. The cast-iron railings separating the rotunda from the pavement were designed by Josef Mánes. The general restoration work was supervised by Ignác Ullmann.

Situated at an important point in the New Town of Prague, St. Longinus' Rotunda has had the most dramatic history of all the Romanesque centrally planned churches. It was closed in 1782 as a church and was threatened with demolition. It was saved thanks to the National Museum Society, particularly to František Palacký. Later on, some renovation was carried out. After the development of its surroundings, the Baroque wall was removed in 1929—1930, the old parts were restored and the large opening connecting the nave of the Baroque church with the rotunda (which was used as a presbytery) was bricked in. Then, between 1934 and 1935, the interior of the chapel was restored and the masonry altar dating from 1720 as well as the Baroque panels that had been removed during the reconstruction and renovation were returned to the rotunda.

Romanesque Houses

Romanesque stone houses were built below Prague Castle during the reign of Vladislav, mainly in what is now the Old Town. In the mid-12th century they lined the streets now known as Celetná, Karlova, Husova and Jilská, and around the market-place (now Old Town Square). They were often the main stone building of a homestead. Their siting was determined particularly by the uneven and irregular ground, which also played an important role in their conservation. The ground floors were partly below ground level and have often survived in good condition as the cellars of the houses that were later built in the Gothic style on the same site. This was due to the fact that in the latter half of the 13th century large-scale flood-protection measures were undertaken and the groundlevel was raised. Thanks to the new groundlevel (two to four metres higher), these houses of considerable architectural value could be conserved. The street level in the Old Town is now at the same height as the ground floor ceilings of the original houses.

The first of them was discovered in 1893 during the rebuilding and demolition of a part of the Old Town. Since the 1960s, surveys have brought to light about seventy houses of great historical interest. Romanesque houses were often located in the middle of walled-in homesteads, where there were also outbuildings, probably of wood, or lined busy roads. They had up to three storeys with excellent tunnel and groin vaults supported by massive Romanesque masonry. The construction material was white clay slate. The ground floor, which was half-sunk, was usually not used for living, but for crafts and trade. The upper floor was in fact an elevated ground floor which could be entered by means of external stairs at the back or stairs built into the masonry. A feature of the Romanesque houses in the Old Town is the variety of types. The simple type had a rectangular ground plan, as for instance in the cellar beneath today's palace No. 12/558 in Celetná Street. Another type had a more complex layout with an additional space attached to the main part (house No. 12/53, Celetná Street). A less frequent type had two bays of groin vaulting separated by a band. The most ambitious Romanesque houses had groin vaults with one (exceptionally two) support, as in the house No. 21/156, Husova Street, or the house No. 21/156, Husova Street, or the house No. 10/16, U radnice Street, and the house No. 3/222 in Řetězová Street.

Prague's early feudal secular architecture culminates in the house of the Lords of Kunštát and Poděbrady No. 222, Řetězová Street in the Old Town. The house, which is accessible to the public, is an oblong two-storey palace with a pitched roof and a big external staircase at the longer side. The central vaulted hall with a portal in the centre has two adjoining rooms with fireplaces. The original feudal homestead from the late 12th century still exists at its full height, although the subsequent historical periods and, in particular, its neo-Classical reconstruction have left many traces. Now it is integrated with the neighbouring house No. 3/946, Řetězová Street, which stands on the site of its former outbuildings.

In the house No. 16, in the cellar of the new town-hall built in 1928, parts of a needlessly demolished tower-house from the mid-12th century still exist, particularly a complete vaulted hall with a central column.

Thanks to a thorough architectural and historical survey and to the registration of all buildings in the historic centre of Prague dozens of Romanesque houses are already known to us that have survived, in spite of many reconstructions, as part of later buildings.

Full renovation of these houses is largely impossible, and the remains are therefore preserved as part of the renovation and reconstruction of particular buildings. As much as possible, they are made accessible to the general public. In the following text the most interesting examples from the wide range of houses are mentioned.

The oldest Romanesque relic is the house No. 16 which was part of a block of medieval houses demolished at the beginning of this century to clear a plot of land needed for the construction of a new town-hall between the streets Platnéřská and Kaprova. A sketch still exists that was made by Kamil Hilbert during the demolition work. Although it was known that the house was a unique ancient building with three surviving storeys, it was hastily demolished and through the intervention of prominent cultural figures, members of the Old Prague Protection Club, only the ground floor could be saved (now the basement under the pavement at the entrance to the new town-hall). The Romanesque remains were preserved and made accessible from the interior of the town-hall. In 1939, the original central column of the vault was replaced by a replica. In 1962, the Monument Preservation Centre worked to preserve the masonry, together with the remains of the neighbouring house No. 31, Kaprova Street.

Another example is the renovation and rehabilitation of the house No. 222, Řetězová Street,

Romanesque Houses

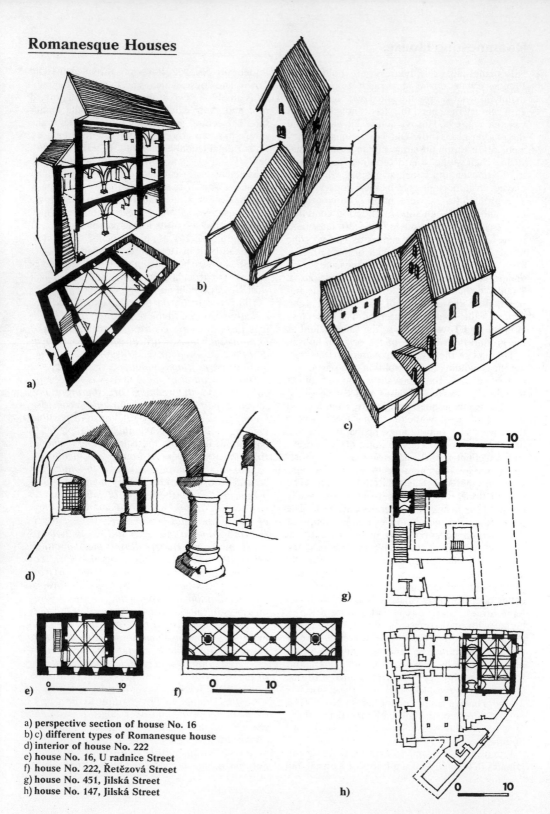

a) perspective section of house No. 16
b) c) different types of Romanesque house
d) interior of house No. 222
e) house No. 16, U radnice Street
f) house No. 222, Řetězová Street
g) house No. 451, Jilská Street
h) house No. 147, Jilská Street

Romanesque Houses

which is a unique surviving example of a feudal walled-in homestead. Now it is called the House of the Lords of Kunštát and of Poděbrady. The house has been thoroughly surveyed and as much of what remains as possible has been preserved and restored. The house has been adapted to accommodate a permanent exhibition to King George of Poděbrady and has become his memorial. The work done here since 1950, including research, has brought very positive results. Thus, the unique remains of a 12th century palace could be conserved.

Other Romanesque houses are gradually being integrated into the respective buildings being restored in the historic centre of Prague to suit changes of function, as for example during the most recent renovation of the Old Town Hall, whose sight-seeing tour now includes also the Romanesque and Gothic cellars of the house called "U kohouta" (At the Cock), or during the large-scale adaptation of the houses Nos. 156 and 229, Husova Street, as exhibition rooms for the Central Bohemian Gallery.

Many other Romanesque houses, for instance those in Jilská and Michalská streets, are still to be adapted.

GOTHIC ARCHITECTURE

GOTHIC CHURCHES AND MONASTERIES

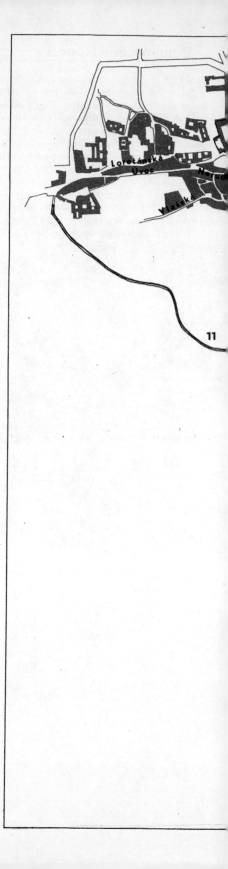

11

0　　　　　　　　　　1km

Gothic Architecture

In the 12th century, in the late Romanèsque period, new and more decorative elements were applied in the Ile de France. From there the new architectural features spread to England, still in the 12th century, and later on also to Germany, Italy and Spain. Early Gothic art appeared in Bohemia around 1230.

The name of the new style is not as old and was used for the first time in the Renaissance period in Italy. It was believed to have been invented by the Germanic Goths, although it had in fact originated in France, where it was called "stil ogival", i. e., the lancet style.

The Gothic style is based on the ribbed vault which improved the stability of the vaulting system by raising and pointing the arch at its top, and by neutralizing the lateral pressure through a system of buttresses. This made it possible to abandon the massive block-like construction and to make the structure lofty and seemingly light by giving a finer form to both the main structure and the details. With growing technical courage and experience vaults of greater span were built and the form as well as the bearing structure became more sophisticated.

The main construction material of the Gothic era was stone, mostly sandstone. It was less solid and less durable than granite (which was also used), but was more easily workable, which was its main advantage. Ceramic material, usually brick, was also widely used, especially in secular buildings, as it facilitated the production of shaped elements and the vaulting of spaces between the ribs.

With the evolution of the style and its technology the bearing structure of stone buildings changed, too, particularly the layout; the dimensions of spaces increased and the windows became larger with rich stone tracery and often with stained glass.

The outer structure, the architectural forms and the use of sculpture combined to create rich ornamentation like a lacework. This combined effect and the synthesis of decorative and architectural elements can best be observed in those buildings that most represent the Gothic era — the cathedrals — the culmination of all the architectural and technical skills of the time.

Stone was also used for the construction of other religious and secular buildings, rich middle-class houses, town-halls, hospitals, as well as fortifications and works of engineering. The Gothic era was an important historical period in which revolutionary changes in the structure of settlements took place. Particularly in the 13th and 14th century, many new villages and dozens of towns appeared that had been carefully planned according to a new rational formula. Many important early medieval settlements, such as the sites of markets, settlements below castles, at fords and on important roads were converted into towns. Because of these new settlements even the large forests on the edge of the country were considerably reduced in size.

The above processes also had a major effect on Prague. The early medieval, rather loose agglomeration of a number of settlements between the two castles of Prague was given a new order. In 1230, Wenceslas I (1230—1253) allowed the town to erect walls around what is now the Old Town with a total area of some 140 hectares. The town-walls were completed in 1241 and gave shelter to several older settlements. The areas between them, also protected by the walls, immediately became centres of significant new building activity. Of these new settlements Havelské Město with its regular plan should be particularly stressed. The Lesser Quarter of Prague was founded in 1257 by Přemysl Otakar II by uniting several old settlements under the Castle. Prague rapidly developed again under Charles IV who made Bohemia the centre of the Empire and started building Prague as its capital. Thanks to his monumental town-planning decision to build a New Town of Prague, the city became the biggest town in Europe. Charles also started a fundamental reconstruction of the Castle and of Vyšehrad. In the Castle, at the point which dominates Prague, he began a cathedral to represent the newly founded archdiocese.

He also founded a university in Prague and invited many religious orders to build their monasteries here. At the same time as the construction of religious and public buildings under his reign, also the building activity of the townspeople also reached a peak both in the Old Town and, in particular, in the New Town in accordance with the new grand plan.

Building activity in the high Gothic style continued after the death of Charles IV for some two decades until it was interrupted by the tragic economic, political and military events of the Hussite period. However, in spite of these dramatic events that also had material consequences for Prague, and in spite of economic and building stagnation, Prague was, even after the end of the Hussite Wars in 1434, one of the most imposing towns in Europe.

After the reign of George of Poděbrady, Vladislav II of the Polish dynasty of Jagiello was enthroned in 1471 and, in more favourable economic conditions, he encouraged new architectural activity here. The arts and architecture of Bohemia again came to the forefront in Europe and many works were made then at the final stage of the late Gothic period that anticipated new philosophical ideas and changes in the field of the arts. The local architects showed a new artistic orientation towards the secular and sought new sources of inspiration. Their example was the Renaissance which had already become deeply rooted in southern Europe.

The Old Town and Its Walls

With the advent of Gothic architecture in the early 13th century the appearance of Prague significantly changed. The area around the old market-place on the right bank of the Vltava developed into a new administrative and economic unit limited and protected by walls. Between 1232 and 1234, the old urban settlement in Prague (civitas pragensis), which concentrated around today's Old Town Square, further developed by building the first of Prague's pre-planned quarters, Havelské Město, in the area of the Fruit Market (Ovocný trh), Coal Market (Uhelný trh), Rytířská and Havelská Streets. The regular plan of the new district, which was constructed at the same time as the Agnes Convent, was the work of King Wenceslas I's (1230—1253) master of the mint, Eberhard, "locator" and the first magistrate of the district. For the Bavarian settlers here, he also built St. Gallus' parish church on the site of its predecessor in the middle of the New Market with the Royal Magistrate's Office. The townsmen's houses here had compact street façades and their rear walls respected the existing patterns of yards and gardens. The regular system can still be seen in the plan of the town. Dominating Havelské Město were also massive rectangular towers whose remains have been discovered in several houses in the south-eastern part of the market-place. One of them still survives at its full height, No. 16/403, Rytířská Street. Wenceslas I, soon after his inauguration, as his chronicler reports, allowed the Town of Prague and other market towns to be walled-in, as the right to build town-walls was one of the main privileges granted when a town was given the status of borough. This status was granted by the sovereign and it was also the king who was the owner of the town-walls, although the towns themselves had to bear the expenses related to their construction and reconstruction.

Part of the fortification system were bulwarks and ramparts, and also a moat with a drawbridge. Within the bulwarks there was a gatehouse with a heavy portcullis moving in a frame.

According to a contemporary chronicler, the Old Town walls were built from 1230 to 1253. At that time, in the reign of Wenceslas I, the long process of transformation of Romanesque Prague into a Gothic town was completed. Gothic reconstruction concentrated in the area of the Old Town and the construction of town-walls is closely linked with this development. The Old Town was naturally protected by the Vltava, and the first walls were therefore built not along the river, but in the north-eastern part of the town.

The erection of town-walls started around 1234, probably at the place called now "Na Františku" and remains of the original fortification system were discovered here during the construction of an administrative building, No. 1039. To offer the best protection the new town-walls did not follow the exact boundaries of the old settlements under the Castle. In some places the walled-in area was much larger, and there were therefore some undeveloped areas between what is today the lower part of Wenceslas Square and the Powder Tower (Prašná brána). On the other hand, there were some settlements

The Old Town and Its Walls

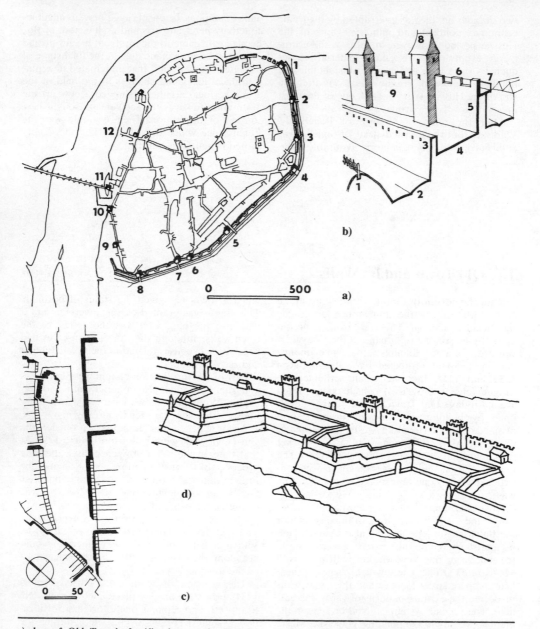

a) **plan of Old Town's fortifications:** 1 St. Francis' Gate opposite Klimentská Street, 2 gate in Dlouhá Street, 3 St. Benedict's Gate, Královdorská Street, 4 "Odraná" (St. Ambrose's) Gate, Celetná Street, 5 St. Gallus' Gate, na Můstku, 6 gate in Perlová Street, 7 Zderaz Gate, na Perštýně, 8 St. Stephen's Gate, Karoliny Světlé Street, 9 gate in Betlémská Street, 10 gate in Na Zábradlí Street, 11 Old Town Bridge Tower, 12 gate at the end of Kaprova Street, 13 gate "za Židy"

b) **plan of Gothic fortifications:** 1 mound with palisade, 2 ditch, 3 wall with arrow-slits, 4 moat, 5 wall, 6 battlements, 7 gallery, 8 tower bastion, 9 "courtine" wall

c) **plan of Havelské Město**

d) **comparison of Gothic and Baroque fortifications**

The Old Town and Its Walls

that remained outside the walled-in area, as for instance the settlement called "Na Poříčí" and parts of the later New Town.

The Old Town walls were 10 to 12 metres high and crenellated. The main bulwark was about two metres wide and consisted of two stone walls filled with rubble and mortar. In front of the bulwark, there was a lower banked rampart, 15 to 20 m wide, a moat 25 m wide and 8 m deep, and a mound. There were bridges, initially of wood, over the moat leading to the gateways controlling the town entrances. Today's street called "Na příkopě" (On the Moat) reminds us of the ditch once separating the Old Town and the New Town. The fortification system followed the streets Revoluční, Na příkopě, and Národní.

All the entrances to the town were controlled by gates. Rectangular towers, up to 30 m high, were erected along the town-walls at a distance of some 60 m from each other, according to the particular needs of the town. Two of them still survive in the block between the streets Národní and Bartolomějská, Nos. 10, 12, 4/310, 313. Of the original gates only "Havelská brána" (Gallus Gate) still exists, as high as the second floor of the house No. 12/404, Rytířská Street. There were altogether thirteen gates and towers. The Old Town walls were never taken or destroyed in battle. The fortification system, high Gothic in conception, was completed before 1310.

One hundred years later, Charles IV founded the New Town of Prague adjoining the Old Town. The high and massive New Town walls with battlements, almost three kilometres long, were constructed within two years, by 1350. Almost all the remaining settlements on the right bank were now walled-in. Vyšehrad was also integrated into the fortification system of the town.

Twenty-five years after the constitution of the Old Town (in 1257), Přemysl II founded on the left bank of the Vltava another town, which was later called the Lesser Quarter of Prague, and protected it with walls whose remains have been discovered in several places (for instance in the first courtyard of the Wallenstein Palace). The walls were two metres thick and were dressed in ashlar.

Middle-Class Houses

The transformation of Romanesque settlements and homesteads took place gradually, under the reign of Přemysl Otakar II. The typical Gothic town plan consists of a regular network of streets with plots for middle-class houses. This was also the case in Havelské Město, the plan of which strongly influenced the organism of the Old Town. The regularly planned streets and blocks of houses at the south-eastern side of the market-place were certainly "built on open ground." It was at that time that the first middle-class houses built both as a home and a workshop for a single family came into being.

The new, compact character of the town placed new demands on the middle-class house. Houses were built on narrow and deep plots, perpendicular to the town square or the street, so that as many houses as possible could face the square or the street. The houses were therefore very narrow, just three bays, and quite tall and deep. Being all of practically the same width, they created rhythmical façades that were often enriched with arcades. Some of these fine houses also have an oriel or a turret. From the 14th century on, the houses had house signs. Their main walls were at right angles to the street and their courtyards, which stretched back as far as the street behind, were enclosed with walls whose height reached almost the first floor. In the early years after the foundation of the town, houses were mostly built of wood; only the town-walls, churches and monasteries were made of stone.

Until the third quarter of the 13th century all buildings were at the old Romanesque ground level. However, because of frequent floods the ground level was raised by two to three metres and the ground floors of the Romanesque and early Gothic houses became basements. An example of an early Gothic house built in the late 13th century already on the raised ground of the Old Town is a house in the northern part of Týnská School (No. 14/604, Old Town Square).

Middle-Class Houses

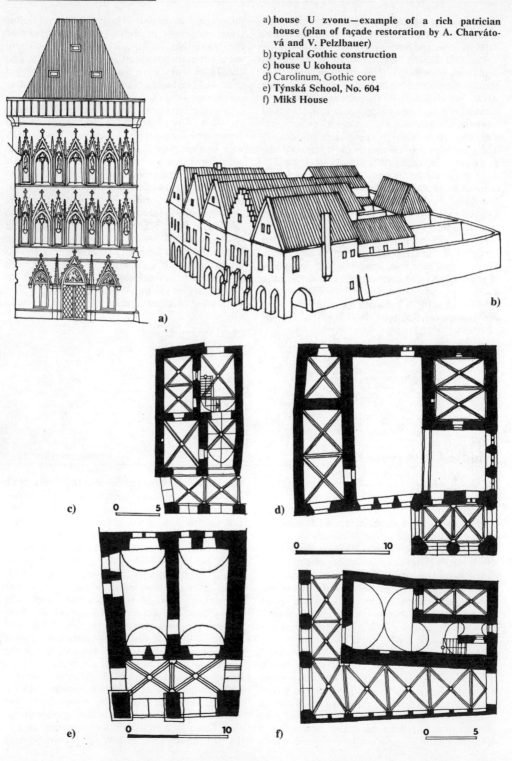

a) **house U zvonu — example of a rich patrician house (plan of façade restoration by A. Charvátová and V. Pelzlbauer)**
b) **typical Gothic construction**
c) **house U kohouta**
d) Carolinum, Gothic core
e) **Týnská School, No. 604**
f) **Mikš House**

a)

b)

c)   0   5

d)   0   10

e)   0   10

f)   0   5

(34)

It has the oldest vaulted arcade known to us in this country. The other buildings of that time, already built at the level of today's streets, have been rebuilt many times, which is why there are not many houses with early Gothic vaults still standing in Prague. The oldest examples can be seen in Celetná Street and around Old Town Square. The oldest house of purely Gothic plan known to us is the ground floor of the house called "U kohouta" (At the Cock) in the south wing of the town-hall.

More houses built around the end of the century have survived. After a fire in 1316 many new stone houses were built in the Old Town. It was at that time that the simple houses Nos. 20/400—22/401, Rytířská Street, at the former New Market of Havelské Město were constructed. Their plan is less deep and quite wide. One of the important houses is that known as "Volflin od kamene" and which later (in 1338) became the central part of the town-hall of the Old Town. In addition to houses with a carriage-way more ambitious houses with a large hall were built, such as the Rotlev House. The hall was in the centre of the ground floor, where both work and trade took place. If the house was granted the privilege of beer-brewing, beer was also served here. From the hall, one descended into a cellar where there was usually also a well, and climbed the stairs to the living floor in whose centre there was an upper hall or a palace, usually with a joist ceiling. From there the living rooms in the front part and the bedroom in the rear part could be reached.

At the end of the 14th century there was a great variety of house types. There were houses made of stone, plastered and with painted façades, as well as red-brick houses with vaulted arcades and portals, with pointed lancet windows or with windows of rectangular shape with carved decoration.

In spite of great changes over subsequent generations, hundreds of Gothic houses have survived. However, many of them were later given a Renaissance, Baroque or neo-Classical façade, as in the case of the rebuilt impressive tower-house "U zvonu" (At the Bell) No. 13/605, Old Town Square, whose history probably goes back to the late 13th century. It underwent major rebuilding in the second quarter of the 14th century and on the old site a palace was then constructed with a richly decorated main façade facing west, which was clad with hewn ashlar blocks. As old engravings show, the house had a Gothic hipped roof. In addition to many architectural elements, Gothic wall paintings were discovered during the renovation of the house.

Although a great many middle-class houses have Gothic parts, there are only a few examples where the Gothic plan and style are preserved to a larger extent. An excellent example of this is the house called "U zvonu" (At the Bell) on Old Town Square opposite the Týnská School. Sadeler's engraving of Prague shows here a fine stone house in the style of Jagiello Gothic. However, until the 1961 technical and historical survey nobody believed that the house could be an adapted Gothic palace as it shared a façade with the Kinský Palace. The 1965 thorough survey revealed the most surprising fact: behind the Baroque façade a fine stone Gothic front was found, and enclosed in the brick of the Baroque refacing even the major part of the stone carving and sculpture was discovered. The wide range of studies and renovation plans related to the house were concluded by Ladislav Pelzlbauer and Alena Charvátová, SÚRPMO (State Institute for Renovation of Historic Towns and Buildings) architects, whose plan was then carried out. The front part of the house was returned back to its Gothic state so that the old façade could be restored. The building was given a new staircase and a new slate roof. The hipped roof and, in particular, the new gallery are disputed. In order to conserve the beautiful Baroque galleries supported by consoles in the courtyard it was decided that the number of storeys in the northern part should remain. The layout of the building was adapted to house social events and exhibitions. To restore the façade, the conservation method was finally applied and the fragments of the decoration discovered behind the Baroque façade were restored. (For further Gothic houses see page 43).

Agnes Convent

The Agnes Convent is the oldest early Gothic complex not only in Prague, but in the whole of Bohemia. It is composed of several buildings of considerable architectural and historical value built between 1233 and the late 1280s. The Convent of the Poor Clares on the right bank of the Vltava in the north-western part of the Old Town was founded by King Wenceslas I and his sister Agnes who was later beatified and, in 1989, canonized by the Church. She became the first abbess of the new convent. For many years the convent enjoyed considerable favour with the royal court and from the very beginning it was a centre of Gothic architecture in Bohemia.

The architecture of this very first Gothic building in the country was of very high quality, although due to the long time of construction the style was not quite pure. The first parts were still made of Romanesque ashlar, but later bricks were used. The buildings made during the first half of the 13th century correspond fully to the Cistercian style of Burgundian Gothic which was spreading in this country through building workshops.

The main part of the complex is the long eastern wing of the Convent, made mainly of brick, whose narrow northern side reaches the high town-wall which was built at the same time, as well as St. Francis Church. This hall-church without presbytery has often been regarded as one of the early Minorite buildings. It was completed around 1240. From the late 16th century to 1981 it was just a ruin where practically only the outer walls survived. Initially, the convent was connected with St. Castulus Hospital, which later separated from the convent and moved to Křižovnické (Knights of the Cross) Square near the Judith Bridge. It was at that time, prior to 1240, that the other part of the complex, a monastery was constructed. When the Minorite Monastery was built right next to the Clares, a new church had to be built for the nuns, as the Minorites had taken over their church, St. Francis'. Around 1250, the Minorites added to the church a presbytery with a pentagonal apse which was attached to the southern side of the new rectangular church of the Clares. The new church was low, without a presbytery, and had a gallery for the nuns in the western part. On the northern side the two-storey chapel to St. Mary Magdalene was built on. The building of the Minorite Monastery started in the 1240s; the Minorites remained here until 1419 when the Monastery was closed and never again re-established.

In the third phase of construction starting in the mid-13th century a cloister and a large vaulted kitchen were constructed here. The monastery was protected by a high wall, the western part of which has survived. The main period of early Gothic building at Agnes Convent ended around 1260.

In the 1270s a presbytery at the women's Church of St. Saviour was built. The vault of the presbytery was much higher than the nave of the older church with which it was connected by a crescent with rich early Gothic profiles. The presbytery completed the construction of the complex in the 1280s, along with the building of a mausoleum for the Přemyslids and the tomb of St. Agnes, founder of the convent.

With the first popular riots in Prague in 1420 the convent and the monastery were abandoned, until the Dominicans came here in 1556. After 1626, the Clares returned and stayed here until the convent was closed by Joseph II. Then, the convent became derelict and was occupied by the poor.

When dealing with the history of the complex it appears that its greatest threat came in 1782 when the monastery was closed, poor people came to live here and workshops were installed in the complex, and then again in the 1890s when it was threatened with demolition as part of the Old Town slum clearance. To save this unique historic monument the Association for the Renovation of Agnes Convent was established in 1892 and had several studies made that were primarily concerned with renovating the churches here. One of the plans, prepared by Antonín Cechner, was carried out, and as a result both churches as well as a part of the convent and monastery buildings were restored. After Cechner's death the renovation work was interrupted until 1940. Then, Oldřich Stefan restarted the surveying and planning work, and gave a new impetus to the renovation. He also organized some construction and reconstruction work. In 1941 and 1942, and from 1953 to 1955 detailed archaeological, technical and historical research took place here, which continued in 1960 and made it possible to prepare a new masterplan for the renovation of the complex.

The respective plans were prepared at the State Institute for the Renovation of Historic Towns and Buildings (SÚRPMO) by Josef Hyzler who continued the reconstruction and renovation in the spirit of Stefan's restitution method. Important changes both in the concept and the methodology came after 1965 as the new investor, the National Gallery, formulated a new programme for the use of the complex. A competition was organized to deal with a complicated conservation task: reroofing the collapsed hall-nave church of St. Francis. The competition resulted in

Agnes Convent

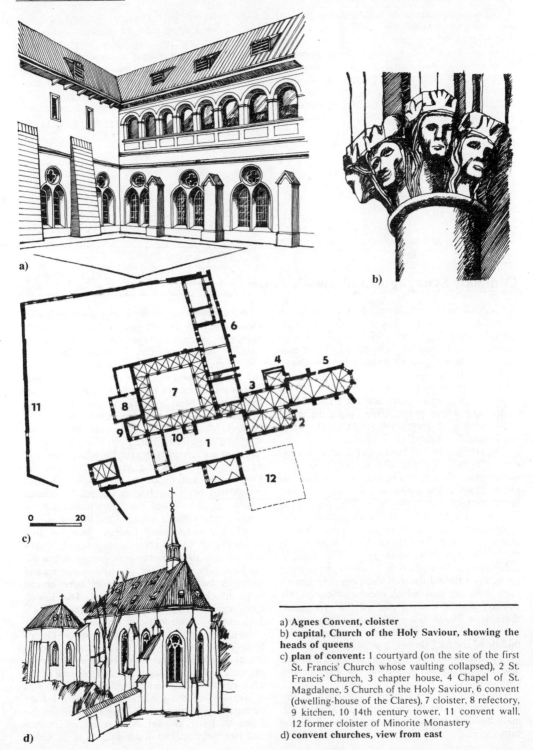

a) **Agnes Convent, cloister**
b) **capital, Church of the Holy Saviour, showing the heads of queens**
c) **plan of convent:** 1 courtyard (on the site of the first St. Francis' Church whose vaulting collapsed), 2 St. Francis' Church, 3 chapter house, 4 Chapel of St. Magdalene, 5 Church of the Holy Saviour, 6 convent (dwelling-house of the Clares), 7 cloister, 8 refectory, 9 kitchen, 10 14th century tower, 11 convent wall, 12 former cloister of Minorite Monastery
d) **convent churches, view from east**

the significant decision to build a dominant roof and complete the western wall of the church. The respective plans, as well as the renovation plans for the whole complex were prepared by Josef Hlavatý and Karel Kunca. In 1978, the complex was designated a National Cultural Monument. The first phase of renovation was completed in 1981 and the renovated sections, i. e., the square monastery building, the kitchen, the new entrance hall, the old garden and the houses along the street U milosrdných, which *were adapted as technical departments and a café, were opened to the public. Most of the convent rooms are used as exhibition halls where Czech 19th century paintings are displayed. A second phase of conservation continued until 1986 and several projects have been realized: St. Francis' Church has been roofed, both adjoining churches restored and their surroundings adapted, including the conservation of the former monastery.*

Old-New Synagogue and Jewish Town

The Old-New Synagogue, which is one of the best conserved medieval synagogues in Europe, ranks among the oldest architectural sights of Prague. It is still used for worship and is the oldest of the seven synagogues that have survived in Prague. It used to be a centre not only of the religious, but also of the social life of the Jewish Ghetto. It was a sanctuary and a school, as well as a place where public affairs were discussed until the Jewish Town-Hall was constructed in the late 16th century.

The synagogue was built around 1280 on a vacant, elevated site. Because of this, it has survived intact, although to enter it we now have to climb down a few stairs. The synagogue is entered through one of the oldest portals in Prague, with beautiful carved decoration in the tympanum; then we come into a space that is conceived, as in the case of Agnes Convent, in the Cistercian-Burgundian style. The vaulted hall-nave has two pillars in its centre supporting six bays of ribbed five-cell vaulting, nine metres high in its top part, which is quite unique in this country. In the eastern part of the synagogue there is a Torah box containing a parchment scroll on which the Pentateuch is written. In the middle of the hall, there is a pulpit (almemar) behind a late 15th century Gothic lattice. There are also several chandeliers from the 16th to the 19th century.

The outer tall brick gables date back to the 14th century, and the low annexes around the main building date from the 14th to the 18th century.

We should also mention here the old Jewish Cemetery with almost twenty thousand tombstones of which many are of great historical value. The tombstones date from the 15th to the 18th century. To this cemetery, which is one of the most important Jewish burial-places, tombstones were brought from the original old cemetery that had been in today's Vladislavova Street in the New Town and was closed in the 15th century. Most of the best preserved and most interesting tombstones date from the 17th century. The famous cemetery is now being restored and renovated. In 1893, the Municipal Council of Prague decided to demolish Josefov District, which had been the Jewish Ghetto of Prague. The reconstruction of the district was accomplished in two decades, and of the former ghetto, which had been called Josefov since the 18th century and where there were altogether 288 houses, only the monuments of great cultural value have survived. Today, very old municipal and religious buildings can be found here amidst large blocks of tenement houses. The Jewish Congregation is now based in the former, late 16th century town-hall that was rebuilt in 1765.

Neither the Old-New (also New or Great) Synagogue nor many other outstanding monuments of medieval architecture escaped the romantic purification trends in the latter half of the 19th century. This unique building, which was a synthesis of the evolution and changes over centuries, was puristically "made clean" in the 1880s by Josef Mocker. As a result, its interior and internal decoration are known to us today

a) b) **Old-New Synagogue**
c) **vaulting**
d) **Jewish Town in 1791:** Old-New Synagogue, 2 Town-Hall, 3 High Synagogue, 4 former Ceremony Hall, 5 Klaus Synagogue, 6 Old Jewish Cemetery, 7 Pinkas Synagogue, 8 Maisel Synagogue, 9 Old Town Square

(39)

only from paintings by Czech painters of the early 19th century. Due to the reconstruction of Josefov, and particularly due to the elevated position of Pařížská Street, the original intimate scale has disappeared.

Of the other Jewish monuments the first we should mention is the synagogue called Pinkasova (Pinkas Synagogue) which is beside the Jewish Cemetery. The synagogue was founded in 1479 by Rabbi Pinkas. In 1535, it was rebuilt and enriched with excellent reticulated vaulting and rich architectural elements. Another alteration followed in 1625 (the southern wing was added and a gallery for women was built), then in the 18th century, and finally around the mid-19th century. During the adaptations in the 1950s it was converted into a Memorial to the Victims of Fascism.

Other Jewish sanctuaries survived the demolition of Josefov, but they were more or less affected by the 19th century alterations, as for instance the Spanish Synagogue (called Old School) which was given its present form in 1864 by Ignác Ullmann. The last restoration took place in the years 1958—1959 and the synagogue now houses a public exhibition of Jewish textiles, a collection that ranks among the best in Europe.

Another sanctuary, the Maisel Synagogue, is also used for exhibition purposes. The synagogue, designed by the Jewish architects Josef Wable and Juda Goldschmid, was built in the late 16th century and rebuilt several times in the latter half of the 19th century: first in 1864 by Josef Wertmüller, and then from 1893 to 1913 by Antonín Gerstl. In 1961, the State Jewish Museum installed here an exhibition of liturgical silver vessels, which was called Silver from Czech Synagogues. Another late Gothic sanctuary, the Klaus Synagogue, was rebuilt at the end of the 17th century in the early Baroque style and was given an excellent tunnel vault decorated with rich stuccowork. In 1884 further alterations, in a rather romantic vein, were carried out. Now, part of the collection of the State Jewish Museum is displayed here and occasional exhibitions are organized. The last synagogue, called Vysoká (i.e., Tall) or Radniční (Town-Hall) Synagogue from the latter half of the 16th century was rebuilt in 1693. The alterations carried out at the end of the 19th century resulted only in some simplifications of the façade. Today, selected textiles ranging from the Renaissance to the 19th century are concentrated there.

The last building in this short survey of Jewish monuments is the Jewish Museum, which is quite a new building constructed in 1906 by Antonín Gerstl in a neo-Romanesque style and was initially intended as a mortuary of the Jewish Cemetery. After some alterations it is used now, together with other buildings, to display collections of artefacts brought here since the German occupation from 153 Jewish congregations. The collection, which now contains objects dating as far back as the 15th century, is hardly paralleled anywhere in Europe.

Town-Hall of the Old Town   GOTHIC ARCHITECTURE

The Town-Hall of the Old Town (Staroměstská radnice) as it appears today developed from several middle-class houses, gradually purchased or donated, and many times rebuilt over the centuries. In spite of this, the group of houses with elements dating from the Romanesque era constitutes a remarkable architectural complex.

The central part of the town-hall, built with the consent of King John of Luxembourg, was Volflin's two-storey stone house from the second half of the 13th century situated in the middle of the market-place (now adjoining the tower in the southern wing of the town-hall). The house was adapted after 1338 to the needs of the Municipal Council and of the Court, and one storey was added. In Volflin's time there were draper's shops nearby that belonged to the house, and other workshops and stalls continued towards St. Nicholas Church. This was probably the very first trading centre of Prague. The Volflin House, however, proved not to suit all the needs of the capital's town-hall, and was therefore extended westwards. As a result, many shops in its vicinity were closed in 1360 and moved to the former market-place of Havelské Město.

In 1387, the neighbouring house owned by the shop-keeper Kříž was purchased, where today there is a fine Renaissance window, and rebuilt together with the town-hall. The Volflin House then lost its initial form and only some fragments and the Gothic doorway have survived. Some time after 1338 the construction of a massive, almost 60 m high town-hall tower began. On the first floor of the tower a chapel with an oriel window was built in 1348. The present-day chapel of the town-hall, consecrated in 1381,

Town-Hall of the Old Town

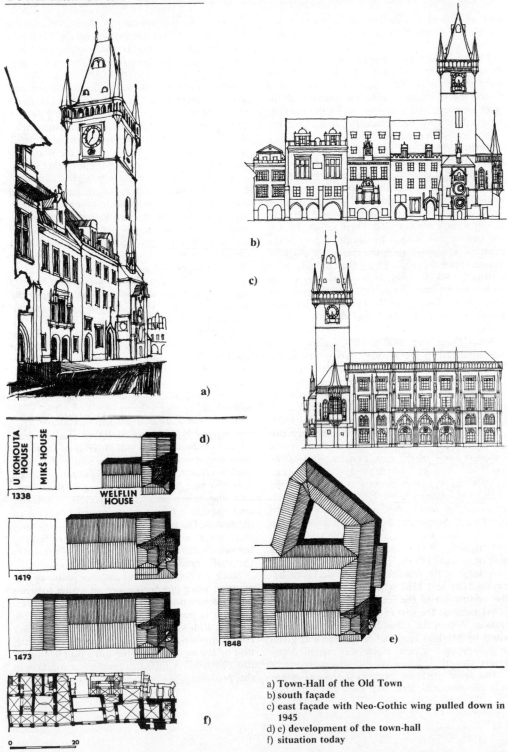

a) Town-Hall of the Old Town
b) south façade
c) east façade with Neo-Gothic wing pulled down in 1945
d) e) development of the town-hall
f) situation today

(41)

with its fine carved decoration seems to reflect the beauty of the architecture of Prague Castle at that time.

The town-hall was finished when the Hussite Revolution started. The most important rooms were those on the first floor, with the Council Room, the Community Hall, the chapel with the oriel window, the archives, and other official rooms. The town-hall retained its initial form until the mid-15th century.

Further major changes took place after 1461, soon after George of Poděbrady had been elected King of Bohemia (in 1458). Part of the late Gothic rebuilding was the chapel (1481) and the beautifully decorated doorway with a vestibule, made probably by the architect and sculptor Matěj Rejsek around 1480. Then, the annex dating from about 1400 in the southern part of the tower was adapted to house the tower-clock by Master Hanuš (1490). There had already been a tower-clock as early as the beginning of the 15th century, installed in 1402 and followed by a bell seven years later. In 1548, the neighbouring house owned by the furrier Mikš was incorporated.

Much later, from 1830 to 1834, another house was attached to the western part of the town-hall. It was the house called "U kohouta" (At the Cock), a remarkable early Gothic building with a vault from the late 13th century. Its façade was rebuilt in the neo-Classical style. In spite of all the adaptations, the houses attached to the western part of the town-hall have retained their original character. To the north of the tower, where only the ruins of the new eastern wing of the town-hall damaged during the 1945 uprising can be seen today, a large house was built at the end of the 15th century in the late Gothic style with an excellent meeting-hall and a beautiful reticulated vault. Some time before 1618, another storey was built over the Community Hall in the eastern wing of the town-hall. The eastern wing was demolished in the 1830s.

A large-scale rebuilding was undertaken between 1784 and 1787 when the town-hall, after the unification of the four towns of Prague (in 1784), became the seat of the municipal administration. Within the rebuilding, which was supervised by Mathias Hummel, the tower was given a gallery and a new clock was installed (by Franz Heger).

The large northern wing, in a somewhat unsuitable romantic style, was built from the late 1830s onwards according to plans prepared by Pietro Nobile and finished between 1844 and 1848 by Paul Sprenger. This part of the town-hall was totally destroyed during the Prague Uprising in May 1945.

In 1865 the historic tower-clock was restored and was given a circular plate with medaillons representing the twelve months by Josef Mánes. The original is now preserved in the Museum of the City of Prague. In 1962, the clock was partially renovated and on that occasion the plate was replaced with a replica by Bohumil Číla.

A rather ill-informed architectural intervention took place in 1879 when the municipal council invited Antonín Baum to rebuild the former Mikš House in the neo-Renaissance style as part of the construction of a Town Council Chamber. It was again rebuilt in 1911 by Josef Chochol. In the subsequent period a number of minor changes took place, such as the redevelopment of the Mayor's Hall by Jan Kotěra in 1912 and the reconstruction of the staircase and the entrance hall in 1938—1939 by a group of architects headed by Pavel Janák, with Zdeněk Wirth as a technical advisor. In the entrance hall large mosaics were carried out from designs made in 1904 by Mikoláš Aleš. From 1938 to 1940 the original arches in the Mikš House and in the neighbouring house (At the Cock) were restored and became part of the exhibition rooms of the town-hall.

Major renovation work was necessary after the Second World War. The truss was repaired, as well as the staircase and the roof of the tower, including the corner bartizans above the tower gallery. The damaged oriel of the tower chapel was restored, which was quite a difficult task, and the tower-clock was repaired, renovated, and given new figures of the apostles by Vojtěch Sucharda. The burnt out neo-Gothic 19th century wing was removed and only two window bays of the original structure remained as a memorial to the 1945 uprising.

Since 1st February 1984 another phase of restoration work has been going on which focusses on the tower and the town-hall façade. The restoration is part of a general renovation of the famous King's Way. At that time, the last of six competitions took place, aimed at the reconstruction of the west wing of the town-hall. However, this competition failed to produce a solution to this problem.

Where the Rudolfinum Building now stands there was once a very old settlement with a market-place, where a very old trade-route forded the river. The very first market-place in the Old Town was located in the area where now Široká Street is. As the Old Town was enclosed and fortified with walls the market-place moved to today's Old Town Square (Staroměstské náměstí), where an important trade-route passed through from the north-east to the customs-house (Ungelt) and then on to Judith Bridge. It was here that as early as the late 12th and the early 13th century Romanesque building concentrated, around the large market-place. The dense concentration of stone buildings, including some thirty churches, constituted the real basis of a large town. In connection with the urbanization policy of the last Přemyslids, the market-place at St. Nicholas Church and Ungelt, where a hospital with Our Lady's Church had stood as early as the 10th century, became the centre of the settlements on the right bank protected by the Vltava and, as of the 1230s, also by town-walls. When the level of the Gothic streets in Prague was raised due to the canalization of the river, the remains of the old Romanesque houses were buried for centuries, and were rediscovered in the basement of today's houses during the recent technical and archaelogical research.

Examples of the early Gothic architecture on the square are the patrician Volflin House (now at the corner of the town-hall tower), the house "U kohouta" (At the Cock) with newer arcades, and the Týnská School from the mid-13th century. The Old Town was not allowed to build its first town-hall until quite late, in 1338, with the consent of John of Luxembourg, although it had been granted the status of borough much earlier, in 1232—1234.

In the main centres of the Old Town and Havelské Město arcades were built that were often projecting from older houses. Apart from the town-hall of the Old Town, which is discussed in a separate chapter (see page 40), another symbol of the Old Town is the Church of Our Lady before Týn, the main church in the town since the Hussite Revolution. The church was founded at the end of the reign of John of Luxembourg and built from 1380 by Peter Parler's workshop. The typical gable of the church dates from 1463, and bears a golden statue of the Madonna from 1626 which replaced the original golden chalice from the era of George of Poděbrady. The northern tower of the church, built in the years 1463—1466, burned down in 1819 and was given a new roof in 1835; the southern tower was built from 1506 to 1511.

A large-scale restoration of the church was undertaken following a survey in 1976, and a general renovation of the roof, the towers, their spires, and the façade started in 1980. The respective plans were prepared by the State Institute for Renovation of Historic Towns and Buildings, and are being carried out by the Pražský stavební podnik (Prague Building Enterprise) and the Pražský průmysl kamene (Prague Stone Industry).

In front of the church there is an early Gothic building called "Týnská škola" (Týnská School), No. 2/604, Týnská Street which, in its current form with Venetian-type gables, dates from the mid-16th century. From the late 14th century to the mid-19th century there was a parish school here, where Matěj Rejsek, the architect of the Powder Tower, worked as a teacher at the end of the 15th century. Next to the school is an early medieval house called "U bílého jednorožce" (At the White Unicorn), No. 15/603, Old Town Square, which was later rebuilt in the Gothic and Renaissance styles. In the late 18th century it was given a late Baroque façade that added another storey, but to the detriment of the beautiful early Baroque gables. Under the corner of the house a Romanesque room from the turn of the 12th and 13th centuries was discovered. We owe all this information to the thorough technical and historical survey of the east front of the square carried out in the 1960s.

On the other side, next to Týnská School is an interesting Gothic corner house "U zvonu" (At the Bell), No. 605. Behind its Baroque façade an excellent example of secular architecture from about 1340 was found (for more information see the chapter "Gothic Houses", page 33). The Golz-Kinský Palace on the square was built from 1755 to 1765 by Anselm Lurago and designed by Kilian I. Dientzenhofer. The Kinskýs possessed the palace until 1786. The typical Rococo façade of the excellent late Baroque house is the work of Ignaz F. Platzer.

The palace underwent a partial rebuilding in the 1830s when it received a new staircase in the Empire style by Heinrich Koch, and again in 1893 when the palace became a German grammar school. During the Prague Uprising in May 1945 the allegories of the Four Elements in the attic of the house were damaged and in 1946 they were replaced by replicas.

Today, the palace houses a department of the National Gallery and a collection of engravings. Part of the building is also the neighbouring house that was rebuilt in 1835 by Heinrich Koch for Duke Kinský in the neo-Rococo style. The other houses on the east side of the square were

Old Town Square

a)   b)

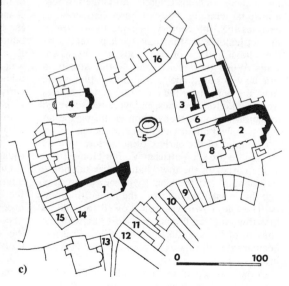

a) b) **Church of Our Lady before Týn**
c) **plan of square:** l town-hall, 2 Church of Our Lady before Týn, 3 Goltz-Kinský Palace, 4 St. Nicholas' Church, 5 Hus Memorial, 6 house U zvonu, No. 605, 7 Týnská School No. 604, 8 U jednorožce No. 603, 9 U kamenného stolu No. 550, 10 U bílého koníčka No. 548, 11 U modré hvězdy No. 479, 12 Na kamenci No. 478, 13 U vola No. 462, 14 U minuty Nos. 2—3, 15 Petzold House No. 4, 16 Monastery of the Pauline Order, No. 930
d) **view of the square in 1743** (by J. J. Dietzer)

c)

d)

Old Town Square

rebuilt between 1904 and 1905, during urban renewal.

The façades of the houses on the southern side of the square, whose plans best conform to the square's historical layout, are mostly Baroque, but they conceal much older, predominantly Gothic architecture. Most of them were damaged during the uprising in May 1945 and therefore had to be restored after the war at great cost. Starting with the east corner the following houses are worth mention: "U kamenného beránka" (At the Stone Lamb; 16/551, Old Town Square) with a Renaissance portal from about 1520 and with a late Renaissance gable from the early 17th century, which was seriously damaged as well as the neighbouring house "U kamenné P. Marie" (At the Stone St. Mary), No. 552, which was built in the spirit of Bohemian neo-Renaissance for Štorch's Publishing House and decorated with frescoes by Mikoláš Aleš. Both houses were renovated in 1949.

The corner house of Železná Street, No. 548, called "U jednorožce" (At the Unicorn) or "Bílý koníček" (The White Horse) is renowned for its Romanesque core with an early Gothic tower-like superstructure from the 13th century. The house was rebuilt in 1496, extended, and was given beautiful reticulated vaulting in the carriageway by Matěj Rejsek.

The front part of the house was renovated in 1966, including the parts facing Železná Street. The opposite houses Nos. 483, 482 and 481 were severely damaged by fire in May 1945 and were completely restored in 1951. The houses were connected, and No. 482 was incorporated in the others. No. 481 contains a traditional watchmaker's shop.

Near the end of Melantrichova Street is the house No. 462, called "U vola" (At the Ox), with a statue by Lazar Vidmann from about 1760 and a steep early Baroque gable. The house was rebuilt in 1835—1836 by Karel Roštík for the tradesman Kyncl.

The house projecting in front of the town-hall, called "U minuty" (At the Minute), No. 3, has a late Gothic core from the late 16th century. It was rebuilt in 1564, and after 1603 gradually decorated with figural sgraffiti which were then covered over with a late Baroque façade. In 1896 the house came into the hands of the Municipal Council.

During the rebuilding in 1905 the Renaissance sgraffiti were discovered which were later, in 1919, restored by Jindřich Čapek. From 1940 to 1945, the house "U minuty" (At the Minute), together with the neighbouring house No. 4, was rebuilt for administration purposes. The last changes were made in 1963 when a luxury glass shop was created here.

The entire south side of the square was again renovated in 1986 as part of the renovation of the King's Way. The restoration work included a number of projects, and the parterres of all the adjoining houses will be renovated. For the first time in the historic core of the town the system of mains and drainage was renovated by concentrating all the networks in special tunnels.

A prominent Baroque building in the square is St. Nicholas' Church built by the younger Dientzenhofer between 1732 and 1735, which was initially part of the Benedictine Monastery. The outstanding quality of its architecture, including sculptures by Anton Braun, was hidden behind the big Krenovský House until the demolition of a part of the Old Town and Josefov. In 1787, the church was closed and converted into a storehouse. In the 1860s it was used as a concert hall and in the 1870s it was put at the disposal of the Russian Orthodox Church.

The interior was restored from 1914 to 1918, and since 1920 the church has been used as a place of worship for the Czechoslovak Church. The last renovations were made in the late 1970s.

The Royal Palace at the Castle

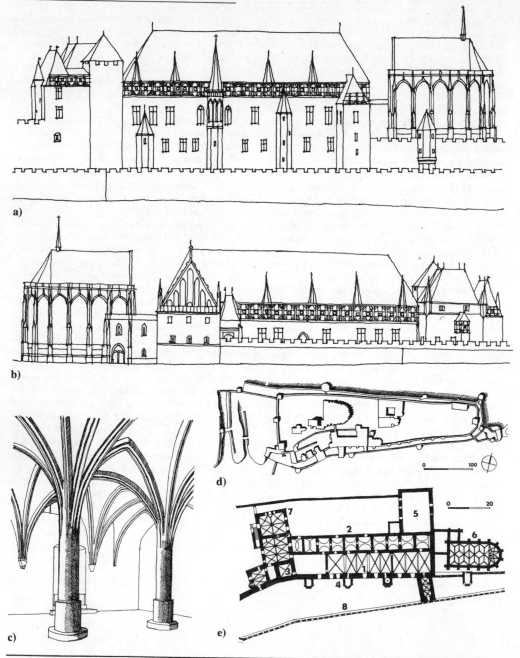

a) **reconstruction of the south façade under Wenceslas IV**

b) **reconstruction of the north façade under Wenceslas IV**

c) **Column Hall**

d) **the Castle in the late Gothic period, reconstruction
(about 1520)**

e) **ground plan of Gothic palace:** 1 Charles' royal palace, 2 arcaded corridor, 3 Romanesque south tower,
4 remains of Romanesque turrets, 5 Land Archives
wing, 6 All Saints Chapel, 7 Column Hall wing, 8 fortification from the time of Charles IV

The great rebuilding of the Castle under Soběslav and Vladislav was followed by another major rebuilding in the reign of Přemysl Otakar II (1253—1278), the most powerful and most internationally respected king of the Přemyslid dynasty. The rebuilding focused on the fortifications and on alterations to the royal palace as a residence and seat of administration. Přemysl concentrated in the first years of his reign on improving the fortification system by constructing massive walls and digging ditches. Deep ditches were dug particularly in the west where the Castle was quite vulnerable, across the whole ridge, separating the Castle from what is now Hradčany District. In the vacant area to the west of the ditch a large settlement appeared. In the east part of the Castle, the gate in the Black Tower was closed and another gateway was constructed in the wall leading to the road called Na Opyši. The original Romanesque palace was enlarged by attaching new buildings and by increasing the height of the old palace. Evidence of this lies in the late Gothic Vladislav Hall, under which, deep beneath the level of the Third Courtyard today, the ground floor and a part of the upper floor of Soběslav I's Romanesque stone palace from 1135, a massive 50 m long structure can still be seen. It stood on the site of the very first wooden palace from the 9th century and the earlier palace that had existed here from the 10th to the early 12th century. The Přemyslid Palace was destroyed by a fire around 1303, soon after its rebuilding by Přemysl Otakar II. And soon afterwards, in 1306, the Přemyslid dynasty died out with the death of Wenceslas III. After a short interregnum John of Luxembourg was elected King of Bohemia and his dynasty then ruled in the country for three generations. With Charles IV, John's son and successor, the country entered a new era which gave both the old and the new important buildings in the Castle and in the town their final form. With King Charles IV high Gothic came to the country. Soon after his return from France in 1333, Charles started a large-scale rebuilding of the Castle as the first stage of his plans for Prague. Prague Castle, the seat of his ancestors, was deserted and derelict at that time. Under Charles IV, a large and sumptuous palace of the French type, with two halls on the upper floor and a Chapel of Our Lady was built on the old Romanesque foundations by reconstructing and enlarging the old building on the site, to the north of the old Romanesque gate which had been closed. The main building of the palace had nine lancet arcades on the ground floor opening onto the courtyard in the north. The arcades were bricked-in under Charles's son and successor Wenceslas IV, and only three of them have been discovered as yet. Much later, in the 1370s, soon after the completion of the beautiful choir vault in St. Vitus' Cathedral, Peter Parler constructed the All Saints Chapel attached to the palace. The chapel was seriously damaged by the 1541 fire; nevertheless, some details have survived that prove the high quality of Parler's workshop.

Together with the palace, the walled-in area of today's Third Courtyard was reconstructed and could be entered from the west through a gateway in a rectangular tower. In 1369, the fortification system of the Castle was strengthened with an additional wall and a ditch in the south. The White Tower and the Black Tower were given new gilded lead roofs.

Charles IV's building activity at the Castle was developing to keep pace with his political achievements, such as, for instance, the establishment of the archbishopric of Prague. The old episcopal church did not meet the new needs, and one of Charles' first decisions was therefore to construct a new and more splendid church. The old basilica of Spytihněv, which was still standing here, gave way to the new cathedral. The construction and rebuilding activity at the Castle was supposed to last several decades; however after Charles' death the role of the Castle in European politics declined.

Another rebuilding of the Castle started after Wenceslas IV decided in 1383 to leave the Castle and move to the Royal Court in the Old Town. It was at that time that the main south wing of the palace was rebuilt, the arcades in the north were bricked-in, new rooms with tunnel vaults were added and the adjoining single-storey part in the south was given cross vaults. A new transverse wing was attached to the main palace. Excellent examples of the architecture of that time are two colonnaded halls with vaults from about 1390 on the ground floor of the west wing, from where you can now enter the excavations under the Third Courtyard.

The Cathedral

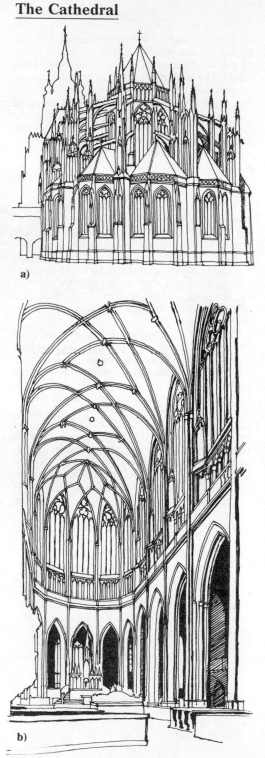

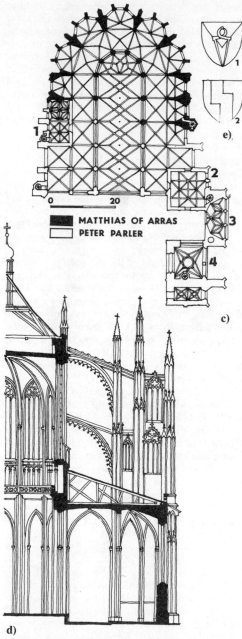

a) Gothic chancel

b) nave

a)

b)

c)

d)

e)

MATTHIAS OF ARRAS
PETER PARLER

0   20

1
2
3
4

a) **Gothic chancel**
b) **nave**
c) d) **ground plan and section:** 1 sacristy, 2 St. Wenceslas' Chapel, 3 Golden Gate, 4 tower with the belfry
e) **signs of Matthias of Arras and Peter Parler**

St. Vitus' Cathedral at the Castle, which is the biggest of Prague's churches, a mausoleum for the kings of Bohemia, a gallery of their sculptures and portraits, and a treasure-vault where the country's crown jewels are preserved, was founded by Charles, when still the Duke of Moravia, together with his father, King John of Luxembourg, when the bishopric of Prague was promoted to an archbishopric.

Charles IV was enthroned in 1346, and from the very beginning of his reign he followed through his plans to make Prague a great centre of the Empire with fine architecture and high culture. Charles' providence was ingenious and set the pattern for the development of the town for centuries ahead. Charles also strongly influenced the form of the cathedral by choosing two outstanding architects of different schools: Matthias of Arras and, after his death in 1352 (Matthias was buried in St. Anne's Chapel in the cathedral), Peter Parler.

The chancel of the cathedral and the pair of pillars of the choir reaching the arcades under the triforium prove that Matthias conceived the church as a basilica of the cathedral type. In eight years he had built eight chapels; the ninth chapel, dedicated to the Holy Cross, was finished by Peter Parler. The concept of the interiors, linear and largely without decoration, complies with the principles of French architecture of the mid-14th century.

In 1348, still before Parler came to Prague, Charles ordered the removal of St. Wenceslas' relics from his tomb in the Romanesque basilica. He already planned an imposing chapel for the tomb of the nation's patron saint. Probably in the years 1352—1356 the construction of a sacristy and a treasure-chamber on the upper floor started.

Peter Parler from the Swabian town Gmünd was summoned in 1356 by King Charles to Prague to head the local building workshop. In Gmünd, he worked together with his father, Master Heinrich, on the presbytery of the local Church of the Holy Cross.

Due to a number of quite unusual conditions, many special features were needed both inside and outside the structure which made the cathedral exceptional. The atypical features of Parler's structure can best be seen on the south front due to the fact that the main entrance facing the Royal Palace and St. Wenceslas' tomb were here.

The first plan realized by the young Parler was the completion of the Chapel of the Holy Cross in 1356 (initially consecrated to SS. Simon and Judah), where the skill and original art of the young architect can best be seen in the window tracery. Also the next six-light window of St. Andrew's Chapel (also known as Martinic Chapel) with its flowing tracery signalled a new development of the style in this country. By 1366, Parler had completed the Chapel of St. Wenceslas started by Matthias of Arras, and soon afterwards also the main south portal and the treasury on the upper floor intended to house the crown jewels. The vault of the chapel, whose interior was finished in the early 1370s, is another master-piece by Parler. The chapel was intended to be a parallel to the Chapel of the Holy Cross at Karlštejn Castle. Simultaneously, a festival gate called the Golden Gate was constructed in the south that opened into the Castle courtyard through three pointed arcades. The façade was enriched in 1370—1371 with a mosaic of the Venetian type representing the Last Judgment. The intricate vault of the antechamber was intended to reflect its significance, and anticipated the outstanding vault by Parler covering the presbytery.

The outer wall of the east choir, which crowns all his work, was deliberately concealed from view by Parler. He created a construction skeleton with just small supporting piers remaining in the interior between the windows with rich tracery. Compared to other similar buildings in Europe, St. Vitus' Cathedral exhibits a very rich system of buttresses. The extreme complexity of the outer walls contrasts with the calm atmosphere of the interior, with its remarkable reticulated vault in the choir reaching a height of 30 metres. This type of vault had been tested by Parler in advance in the Old Town Bridge Tower. The consecration of the choir in 1385 required a provisional wall to separate the choir from the two-aisled nave under construction. This provisional measure, however, survived for five centuries.

Of the sculptural work in the church, the remarkable statue of St. Wenceslas made by Parler's nephew Heinrich in 1373, and the gallery of portraits of the Přemyslid dynasty, archbishops, architects and supervisors of the cathedral construction in the triforium are to be particularly stressed. It is a unique feature in Europe, with twenty-one sandstone busts from 1374—1385 made at Parler's workshop. At the outer triforium, there are figures representing Jesus Christ, the Virgin Mary, and various saints.

Peter Parler died in 1399, and his sons Václav (Wenceslas) and Jan (John) continued realizing his bold plans for twenty years. The great south tower, whose foundation-stone was laid in 1392 and which was never completed, was the last stage in the building of the cathedral under the Luxembourgs.

The huge quantity of stone pillars and arches of the cathedral, crowned with pinnacles forty metres above the pavement of the Third Courtyard, prove the great art of their creators. (For more information about the completion of the cathedral see page 215).

Vyšehrad Castle in the Reign of Charles IV

Another high point in the history of Prague's other castle started with the enthronement of Charles IV. Wishing to pay due tribute to his ancestors and predecessors on the Bohemian throne, the Emperor Charles wanted to revive the old Přemyslid tradition and give Vyšehrad a new purpose and function. Still as Duke of Moravia, preparing his coronation he drew up the rites for the coronation ceremony of the kings of Bohemia. One of the stipulations was a pilgrimage to Vyšehrad to be made by the future king on the eve of his coronation. And Charles was the first to make the pilgrimage, on 1st September 1347.

Charles' plan was to convert Vyšehrad, still deserted at that time, into a sumptuous royal residence. In place of the derelict Romanesque homestead a new royal palace was constructed which, as research at Vyšehrad has shown, was located amidst the vacant area near the elongated building in the south-western part of the castle, parts of which still exist. Sadeler's engraving (1618) shows the palace already as a big ruin with high arcades. During research here before the Second World War the foundations of the palace as well as remains of some other structures were discovered.

Vyšehrad was attached to the newly founded New Town of Prague and a new fortification system was built here from 1348 to 1350 with battlements, towers and two gateways, of which one, the legendary east gatehouse called Špička that crowned the complex, existed in its original form until the mid-17th century when a new massive Baroque system of fortifications was constructed at Vyšehrad and, as a result, the last medieval structures and constructions here disappeared. The form of the gatehouse is known to us now only from some contemporary engravings and from a reconstruction made in 1903 by Antonín Wiehl. The construction of a Gothic fortification system was a large-scale building scheme within the general town-planning activi-

ty of King Charles in Prague. The fortification of Vyšehrad, which at that time became a stone fortress, corresponded in its main features and scale to the New Town walls. Some thirteen, or even fifteen rectangular towers, more than seven metres wide, were erected at the bulwarks at a distance of approximately sixty metres from each other. A major new building at Vyšehrad was the royal palace with a ground plan that corresponded to the earlier princes' palace. Its architecture, as proved by historical documents, was certainly as fine as that of Prague Castle. Servants' quarters were constructed at the palace, an aqueduct was built, as well as a school.

After 1364 a major rebuilding of the collegiate Church of SS. Peter and Paul took place, and today's nave with two aisles and lateral chapels as well as a new shorter choir were built. In subsequent centuries the church saw many other alterations. It was rebuilt in the 15th century and received a new choir at the end of the 16th century to which a sacristy was attached in 1607–1610. An early Baroque belfry was constructed at the church in 1678. Major alterations were made in the first half of the 18th century and the Gothic vault was replaced by a new one, of Baroque type. Between 1723 and 1729, F. M. Kaňka, following a plan by G. Santini-Aichel, completely rebuilt the church. In this form, with its dynamic undulating façade, the church survived until 1885 when it was rebuilt by Josef Mocker in a neo-Gothic style.

In 1420, almost all buildings at Vyšehrad were destroyed in a battle between the Hussite Army and Emperor Sigismund. Except the rebuilt collegiate church and the rotunda, which is the oldest in this country, most of the religious buildings here disappeared. The same applies to the hospital with the Church of Our Lady under Vyšehrad dating from 1364. Thus, the fame of Vyšehrad, which was primarily due to Charles IV, did not last long.

Much of the information we have about Vy-

Vyšehrad Castle in the Reign of Charles IV

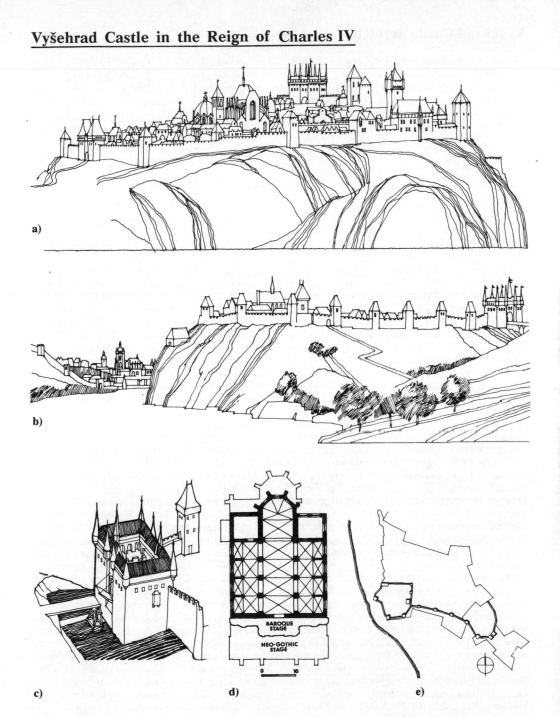

a)

b)

c)

d) BAROQUE STAGE / NEO-GOTHIC STAGE / 0 — 10

e)

a) Vyšehrad in the reign of Charles IV—reconstruction, view from the Vltava
b) reconstruction, view from the south

c) reconstruction of the south gate (Špička)
d) plan of the Gothic Church of SS. Peter and Paul and its further development
e) Gothic fortifications of Vyšehrad

šehrad as a Přemyslid and Carolingian castle is the result of systematic archaeological research carried out over the last two decades. East of the church the remains of another sanctuary were discovered, some 110 m long, with a Romanesque core and a later presbytery of elongated heptagonal shape. An apse was then constructed to close the chancel in the west part, which was rebuilt during the neo-Gothic renovation. (For more information about the rebuilding of Vyšehrad see pp. 253—255).

Lesser Quarter

As archaeological findings show, the territory of the Lesser Quarter (Malá Strana) was colonized a long time before modern history began. Recent research has shown that the first marketplace with a settlement existed under the headland with the castle as early as the 8th century and was closely linked with the history of Prague Castle. A painting representing the Lesser Quarter at the end of the Romanesque era informs us about the network of streets as they had developed by the early 13th century. There were two main roads, one coming from the west and one from the south. The road coming from western Bohemia went through Břevnov to Strahov Hill and from there, through Loretánská Street, to the Castle or, through Nerudova Street, to Judith Bridge. The south road from Košíře passed through Újezd, Karmelitská Street, the Lesser Quarter Square to Sněmovní Street, where the original settlement probably had its centre, and climbed up to the south gate of the Castle. The first settlement under the Castle was apparently situated in the area of what is now Sněmovní Street.

One of the first buildings here was the Bishop's Court founded by Bishop Jindřich Břetislav, nephew of King Vladislav II, at the end of the 12th century near the north end of Judith Bridge. Until the end of the 12th century the bishops had their seat at the Castle, and then moved to the new residence. Around 1263 the Court was protected by fortifications and later, under Bishop Jan IV of Dražice, was rebuilt and decorated. Opposite the Court and south of it, also near the bridge, a monastery of the Knights of St. John and a Church of Our Lady were built in the 12th century. The church was a basilica, whose remains were discovered early in this century.

The first churches in the Lesser Quarter were confined to the territory of the early feudal settlement here. They were as follows: St. Wences-las on the Lesser Quarter Square (predecessor of St. Thomas), St. Andrew and St. Martin in Sněmovní Street, Our Lady under the Chain at Velkopřevorské (Grand Prior) Square, St. Lawrence on Petřín Hill, St. Lawrence under Petřín Hill, St. Mary Magdalene at Nebovidy, St. John "Na prádle" at Újezd, St. John the Baptist at Obora, SS. Peter and Paul at Rybáře, St. Matthew at Obora, and possibly also St. Michael under the Castle and St. John at Újezd. Some still stand, some have been rebuilt and some were demolished long ago. From the very beginning of its history, the development and growth of the Lesser Quarter were limited by its territory closed in by the slopes of Petřín Hill, Hradčany, and the Vltava River. South of the walls built by Přemysl Otakar II there was a large plain with scattered settlements (Obora).

The development of the territory accelerated at the end of the reign of Wenceslas I, who in 1253, having learned about the importance of fortified towns, started constructing fortifications around the end of Judith Bridge. His son Přemysl Otakar II, crowned in the same year, continued the work started by his father. He built banked walls and towers around the Bishop's Court and around the opposite commendam of the Knights of St. John. Walls enclosed the space between the Castle and the bridge. Přemysl expelled the local population and invited new colonists to settle here, mostly Germans. Thus, by force, the continuity of the local population in the Lesser Quarter, as the new town was later called, was interrupted. Even before the foundation of the royal borough here in 1257, town-walls were constructed, traces of which can still be seen in the plan of the Lesser Quarter. Simultaneously, a new central marketplace was created and a parish church of St. Nicholas was built in the middle of it and consecrated in 1283. As the role of the new market-

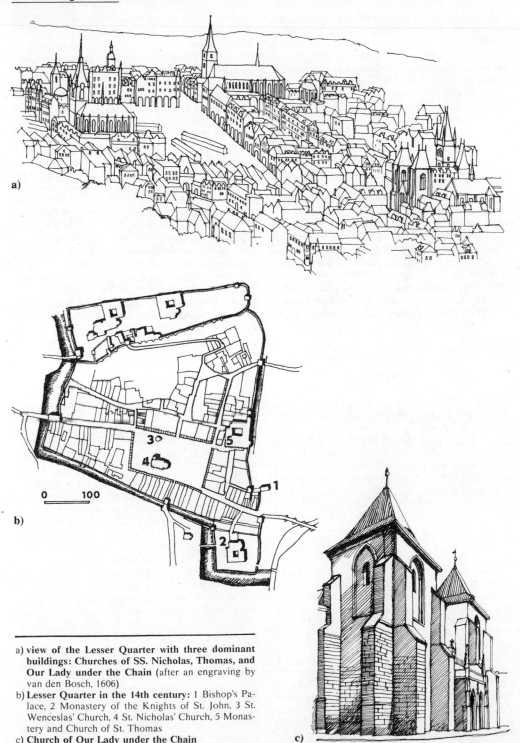

a) **view of the Lesser Quarter with three dominant buildings: Churches of SS. Nicholas, Thomas, and Our Lady under the Chain** (after an engraving by van den Bosch, 1606)

b) **Lesser Quarter in the 14th century:** 1 Bishop's Palace, 2 Monastery of the Knights of St. John, 3 St. Wenceslas' Church, 4 St. Nicholas' Church, 5 Monastery and Church of St. Thomas

c) **Church of Our Lady under the Chain**

place (now Malostranské náměstí—Lesser Quarter Square) was increasing, that of the earlier centre of the settlement in the area of today's Sněmovní Street was decreasing, and the old market-place finally disappeared in the reign of King Charles as the earlier important south gate of the Castle was closed.

One of the most important architectural complexes in the new town (i.e., the Lesser Quarter) was the Augustinian Monastery with St. Thomas' Church, whose presbytery was consecrated in 1315. The Augustinians at St. Thomas' acquired a large area for their monastery within the town-walls.

In the vicinity of Judith Bridge Tower a great merchant's house had been built, and its importance increased with the construction of Charles Bridge. Charles IV gave the house to his courtier, Duke of Saxony Rudolph I, who had a sumptuous Gothic palace built here, the original façade of which was discovered in 1959 under the plaster of the first and second floors. The most important of these structures, the old Romanesque Bishop's Court, was rebuilt and decorated in the 14th century in the French style. However, its original shape and size can today only partly be determined. In the 14th century the old Romanesque basilica of Our Lady at the Monastery of the Knights of St. John was largely rebuilt and its masonry is now part of the Grand Prior's Palace. Together with the construction of New Town walls, which was completed in 1360, the fortification system of the Lesser Quarter was rebuilt. The new fortification system also covered the commendam of the Knights of St. John and a major part of Újezd in the south, and Strahov Abbey in the west. Thus, the territory of the town considerably increased under Charles IV and with the construction of new town-walls the old Přemyslid fortification system lost its role. Of the fortification system built by Charles, the Hunger Wall, six metres high and two metres wide, with rectangular towers has survived intact. Along the wall, on its inner side a gallery protected with battlements was built. Further constructions in the Lesser Quarter prior to the Hussite Wars are not clear. The medieval architecture of this—now typically Baroque—district of Prague almost disappeared in 1420, and particularly after the great fire in 1541.

New Town of Prague

Charles IV started to carry out his plan of enlarging the towns of Prague soon after his coronation, after the construction of a new royal palace. One of the reasons for the plan was the fact that the Old Town of Prague with its new university could not accommodate all the new population. The unprecedented scale of the broadly conceived plan of the New Town amazes us even today. The New Town, whose foundation-stone was laid by Charles IV on 26th March 1348, was the fourth historic town of Prague.

The New Town founded by Charles and surrounded by an arch of town-walls almost 3.5 kilometers long from Vyšehrad to Těšnov covered an area of some three hundred and sixty hectares, which was three times as much as that of the Old Town of Prague. The fact that the area of Charles' town was big enough for the following five centuries shows how provident and well conceived his plans were. The old trade roads were fully respected, which led from the old centre (Old Town Square) to the New Town through three gates: St. Ambrose's Gate (now Powder Tower), St. Gallus' Gate (now the lower part of Wenceslas Square), and St. Martin's Gate (Na Perštýně). Streets planned in the New Town were quite broad: from 18 to 27 metres, and from them the modern major roads have developed. There were three central points (the Cattle Market, the Horse Market, and the Hay Market) lying on the axis of the New Town. The Horse Market (today Wenceslas Square) was the main transverse axis dividing the New Town into the lower and the upper parts. The walls, whose foundation-stone was solemnly laid in Charles' presence and which enclosed the large area, were built within an extremely short time-span of two years, which was a remarkable technical achievement. It is supposed that the walls were constructed uninterruptedly by some one thousand workmen. Calculations have shown that about 27 thousand wagons of quarry stone were needed to construct the walls that were five metres wide and ten metres high, with all their towers and gates. The line followed by the walls proves that the boundary of the New Town's territory was fixed at the very beginning. The walls enclosed the old early medieval settlements around the Old Town. Not only the walls, but also the whole New Town was constructed very quickly. From written documents we learn that the construction of the New Town was completed as early as 1372 and that at that time

New Town of Prague

a)

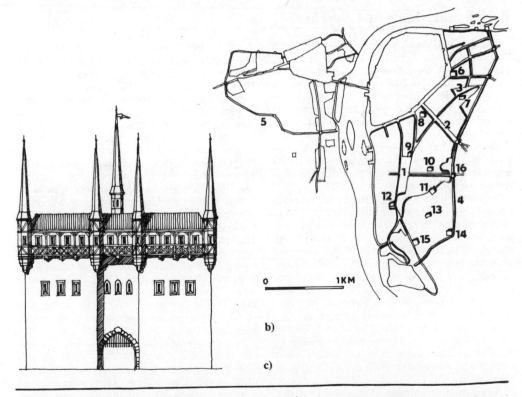

b)

c)

a) **dominant buildings of New Town** (after an engraving by van den Bosch, 1606), from left to right: 1 Town-Hall, 2 St. Stephen's Church, 3 Sow Gate, 4 Corpus Christi Chapel, 5 St. Catherine's Church, 6 Karlov monastery, 7 Slav monastery (Emmaus)

b) **plan of Prague after the construction of New Town:** 1 Cattle Market with the Chapel of Corpus Christi, 2 Horse Market, 3 Hay Market, 4 New Town fortifications, 5 Hunger Wall, 6 St. Ambrose's Monastery, 7 St. Henry's Church, 8 Monastery of Our Lady of the Snows, 9 Town-Hall of the New Town, 10 St. Stephen's Church, 11 St. Catherine's Church, 12 Slav Monastery, Emmaus, 13 St. Apollinaire's, chapter house, 14 monastery, Karlov, 15 monastery, na Slupi, 16 St. John's Gate (Sow Gate)

c) **reconstruction of the former Sow Gate** (now end of Ječná Street)

most of the streets were already lined with houses.

Churches and monasteries standing in the original settlements were preserved, and new dominant buildings were located on elevated parts of the uneven territory of the New Town, these buildings being the churches of St. Stephen, St. Henry, St. Apollinaire, St. Charles, St. Catherine, and the Emmaus Abbey. The Town-Hall, too, was situated on an elevated dominant site.

There were four gateways in the new walls opening into the country: Poříčská Gate, Horská (Mountain) Gate, Horse Gate, and Sow Gate (al-so called St. John's). The general conception of the town discloses that Charles wanted to re-build Prague as a huge fortress protected by the Castle in the north and by Vyšehrad in the south. He therefore also enlarged the walls of Hrad-čany and of the Lesser Quarter (the Hunger Wall), and Vyšehrad Castle was integrated into the consistent fortification system (1351). The result was a unique work of town-planning with a number of architectural masterpieces, which had no equivalent in Europe at that time.

Parish and Monastic Churches

The oldest Gothic church that has survived is St. Francis in the Agnes Convent (see page 36). There was an early Gothic parish church, St. Lazarus, in the New Town of Prague, mentioned in 1281 and demolished in 1900. The little church was built before the mid-13th century; the carved tympanum of the entrance portal is preserved in the lapidary. The same applies to the Dominican church of St. Clement which later gave way to new structures built by the Jesuits and whose presbytery is now part of the presbytery of St. Saviour's.

Remains of the monastic Church of the Holy Cross in the Old Town were removed in 1890 in connection with the demolition of Josefov District. No information is available about what the church at Strahov Abbey looked like after the 1258 fire, however remains of its Gothic masonry still exist in the Renaissance twin-towers. Connected with the Agnes Convent was also a church belonging to the Knights of the Cross with Red Star who settled in 1252 in the Old Town near Judith Bridge. The church was of considerable architectural interest, but only its foundations have survived. It was quite a short church with a nave and two aisles and a shallow presbytery.

Apart from the number of monastic churches, municipal churches were also built, however at a much slower rate. They included today's churches of St. Gallus, Our Lady before Týn, St. Nicholas in the Old Town and St. Nicholas in the Lesser Quarter. However, their initial form has gone, as they have all been rebuilt and replaced several times. After 1300, two-aisled churches were built of considerable size and bold plan.

A similar new concept was also applied in rich monasteries, such as the Augustinian two-aisled basilica of St. Thomas in the Lesser Quarter. However, except for the general plan with a rather long presbytery, typical for the churches of some religious orders, not much has remained here of the original structure. The church has been rebuilt several times. The monastery of the Augustinians (Eremites) was founded by King Wenceslas II at the older small church of St. Thomas after 1285. The presbytery was consecrated in 1315. A similar plan can be seen in St. James' Church and the monastery of Minorites whose construction was initiated by John of Luxembourg and Queen Elisabeth after the 1316 fire. The queen also built a large new refectory for the monastery in 1319. Here, too, there was a long and high choir, of which some traces have remained in the exterior of the church, which was a typical basilica. The last rebuilding took place in the Baroque period (after 1689). The vaults of the church were over thirty metres high.

In the reign of John of Luxembourg aisleless churches were also built, such as St. Anne's Church built by the Dominican nuns in the place of an earlier church from the 13th century, at a former commendam of the Templars where they moved at that time. The new church, whose nave was built around 1329, also had a long choir. This type of long, aisleless church architecture, unique in Prague, then became typical of the monastic churches of the medieval women's orders. This church, whose hall was 17 metres high, was rebuilt in the 17th and the 18th centuries, and was closed in 1782, together with the

Parish and Monastic Churches

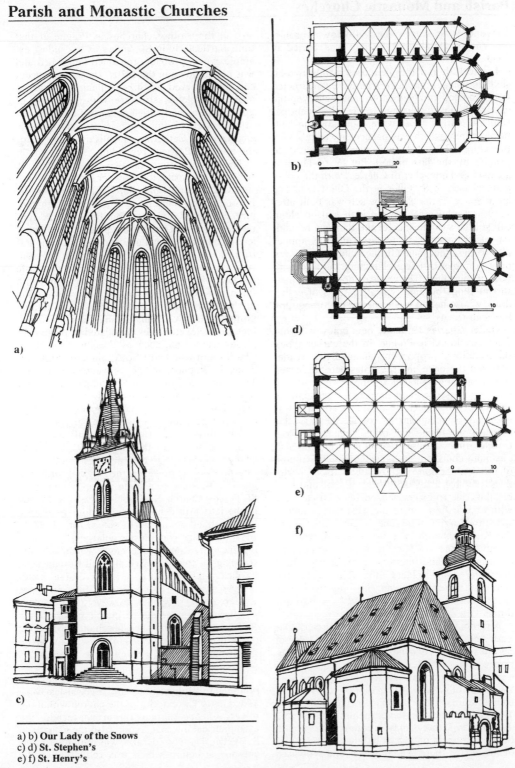

a) b) **Our Lady of the Snows**
c) d) **St. Stephen's**
e) f) **St. Henry's**

convent. At St. Anne's, the well-known chronicler Václav Hájek of Libočany was buried in 1553.

In the 13th and 14th centuries mainly two-aisled churches of basilican type were constructed that had deep and high choirs, particularly in the case of monastic churches. In the subsequent period, the earlier types were joined by the hall-nave church, which was particularly suitable for preaching. The last type was introduced in Prague by the last bishop, Jan IV of Dražice, a friend and a teacher of Charles', with the collegiate church of St. Giles in the Old Town. The large space of the church, which was built after 1310 and whose centralized plan had no choir, can still be seen, in spite of the Baroque rebuilding of its interiors. Its towers—and this applies also to the other main Gothic buildings—are not only examples of fine architecture, but also symbols of their time. The verticals dominating their surroundings became typical features of cathedrals, whose height was a matter of competition between towns.

Under Charles IV, many new types of layout were developed in Prague. In the earlier types, the traditional proportions changed, the arcades between the nave and the aisles became larger, the separating function of the triumphal arch was suppressed and, in particular, the depth of the nave was reduced. St. Vitus' Cathedral was intended as a culmination of all these Gothic aspirations. However, other buildings from Charles' time are also important, such as the Augustinian church in the New Town. The Church of the Assumption of Our Lady and of Charles the Great at Karlov built between 1350 and 1377 became, due to its centralized symmetrical nave with arcades in front of the west part, a unique structure for the time. The original interiors of the Karlov church have not survived, which is a pity as the 1575 vault was a remarkable achievement. The interiors from Charles' time disappeared due to late Gothic, Renaissance and Baroque rebuildings. The tall roof with rich Gothic forms was later replaced by a Baroque dome.

A rather unusual building is the Church of Our Lady "Na trávníčku", belonging to the Order of Servites and dating from the 1360s, when a monastery was founded here. The church has a square ground plan and was later roofed with four bays of cross vaulting supported by a central column; its internal space is unusually light. The central idea of this structure, remarkable due to its type and quality, is combined here with the new concept of a short hall-nave. At the axis of the façade there is a tall tower of a type used

also in three other churches in Prague at that time, particularly in St. Anne's as the oldest example, which probably remained unfinished and was pulled down in the 1870s. The same concept can be observed at St. Apollinaire's, which is a simple aisleless structure with two bays of groin vaulting and with a polygonal chancel. Another tower of this type is at the monastic Church of St. Catherine which is now, except for the tower, a Baroque rebuilding.

The Gothic form of the two-aisle church of St. Ambrose opposite the Powder Tower has not survived, either, as the church was rebuilt in the Baroque period and later, in the early 19th century, converted into a custom-house in the Empire style (now in Hybernská Street). The Benedictine Church of Our Lady and the Slavonic Patron Saints "Na Slovanech" (see page 60) constructed between 1348 and 1372 is a two-aisle basilica of the so-called preaching type with three polygonal apses. During the construction of the New Town of Prague many outstanding Gothic structures commanding their surroundings from elevated sites or located in prominent places were built, such as the churches of St. Charles and Our Lady, St. Apollinaire, St. Catherine, St. Stephen, and Na Slovanech (Emmaus). The municipal Church of St. Stephen (1350) has rather heavy proportions and an impressive mass. Parish and municipal churches were often extended, particularly by attaching another aisle, which indirectly illustrates the growth of population. This was also the case of St. Adalbert's Church which was given a new aisle and a separate presbytery; however, the original form was lost in a Baroque rebuilding in the 18th century. St. Peter's Church Na Poříčí was also extended in the late 14th century and an additional aisle was attached to its north side. From 1382 to 1411, the space was further enlarged by removing the old Romanesque nave, which was still standing, so that the original small Romanesque basilica was replaced by a larger Gothic building. As a result, a homogeneous internal space was created. The façade, however, still displays its original Romanesque form and the size of the Romanesque towers. The Church of St. Martin in the Wall was also extended in this way and given a new Gothic vault as well as a tower at its southwest corner.

St. Castulus' Church was extended northwards in the late 14th century and two aisles were added here. The exterior of the church with a big tower reflects, particularly in its façade, the asymmetrical internal layout. Also the Church of St. Wenceslas "Na Zderaze" was initially a Romanesque structure which was rebuilt after the

Parish and Monastic Churches

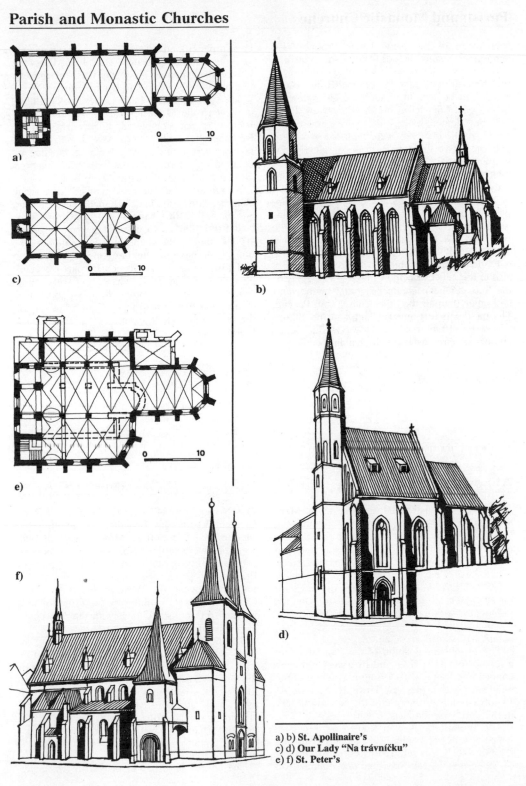

a)

c)

e)

f)

b)

d)

a) b) **St. Apollinaire's**
c) d) **Our Lady "Na trávníčku"**
e) f) **St. Peter's**

foundation of the New Town. Probably for economic reasons, the old Romanesque masonry was incorporated in the new Gothic structure, so that here in the façade the original Romanesque tower can be seen in its entirety. The same applies to St. Michael's Church in the New Town and St. Clement's Na Poříčí where the earlier Romanesque buildings were replaced by Gothic churches of very simple form. A completely new building was the Church of Our Lady "Na louži", which however is known to us from illustrations only.

The Church of Our Lady before Týn, an important building with tall and narrow Gothic windows, dominates its surroundings. Its façade with two towers is one of the characteristic features of the Old Town Square (see page 43).

Evidence of the ambitions of the architect lies also in the new Carmelite Church of Our Lady of the Snows, unexpectedly large and intended to be bigger than all the other churches in Prague. The nave was forty metres high and the church was to be 110 metres long. However, due to unfavourable circumstances the building could not

be completed and its new and lower reticulated vaulting was not built until after 1606. The very long choir remained as just a torso of the big two-aisle basilica that had been planned.

The Church of Our Lady Under the Chain belonging to the Monastery of the Knights of St. John was not completed, either. The earlier Romanesque church here was demolished to give way to a new Gothic building, but due to unfavourable circumstances only two massive Gothic towers and a portico were built.

A remarkable, centrally-planned octagonal church with adjoining chapels on Charles Square, called the Chapel of Corpus Christi, was built from 1382 to 1393 (see Fig. page 68). The ground plan of the chapel was a simplified version of the nave of Our Lady in Trier from the mid-13th century. Over its central part a rectangular tower was built where holy relics and crown jewels were shown to the public. The church was demolished in 1791, and thus one of the most remarkable examples of Luxembourg Gothic was lost.

Abbey "Na Slovanech"

The new monastery, consecrated to St. Mary and to Slavonic patron saints, was founded by Charles IV at an old parish church to SS. Cosmas and Damian in Podskalí and was intended for south European Slav monks. The monastery, which was called by contemporaries "a wonderful work", was built in the territory of the Chapter of Vyšehrad and was intended to continue the local tradition of Slavonic divine services, as it was believed that St. Methodius and St. Procopius had stayed at Vyšehrad.

The prominent position of the monastery on a terrace over the river and by a very old road connecting Prague with Vyšehrad was one of the main sites within the New Town. Its position also corresponds to the role of the new monastery in the purely Czech New Town.

The monastery is also known as Emmaus, which is a newer name. In medieval documents the monastery was referred to as the Monastery of St. Jeronimus the Slav, and was founded on

21st November 1347 with the consent of Pope Clement VI for Slav Benedictines coming from Mediterranean countries. Monks from all Slav countries were supposed to concentrate here to cultivate the religious life in the Slavonic parts of Prague, and probably also to overcome the distinction between the Western and the Eastern Christian Church. In this way the Emperor also wanted to establish contacts with the Slav countries in southeast Europe.

The new monastery, which was therefore initially called "Na Slovanech", was finished in 1372. On the day of its consecration the part of the Gospel speaking about the disciples going to Emmaus was read, and for that reason the monastery was later also called Emmaus. Until the Hussite Wars the monastery was a centre of culture and art. In 1419 the Hussites founded a consistory here, and in 1446 it became a unique Utraquist monastery.

The church here had a nave with two aisles,

Abbey "Na Slovanech"

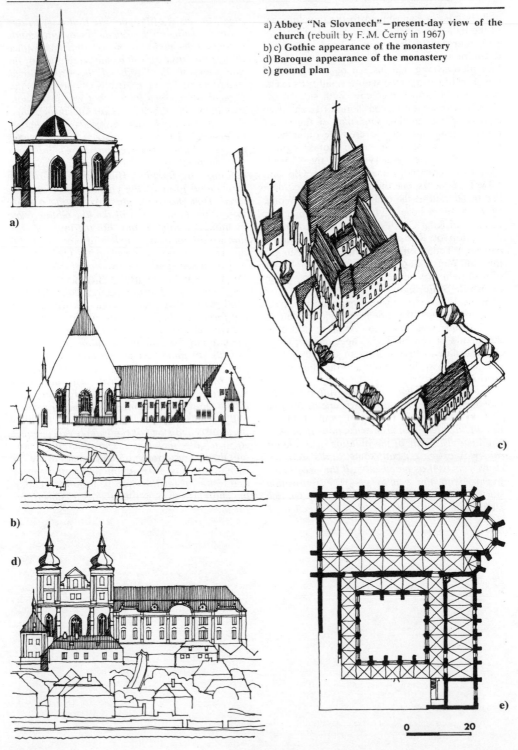

a) **Abbey "Na Slovanech" — present-day view of the church** (rebuilt by F. .M. Černý in 1967)
b) c) **Gothic appearance of the monastery**
d) **Baroque appearance of the monastery**
e) **ground plan**

a)

b)

c)

d)

e)

0   20

and its interior contributed to the development of the hall-type of church. It was one of the biggest churches in Prague completed before the death of the Emperor. The interior was some fifty metres long and instead of towers it had a high roof surmounted with a small turret. The monastery is attached to the south side of the church, with a cloister consisting of twenty-two bays of groin vaulting. One part of the set of frescoes that reputedly covered the outer walls of all four sides of the cloister to a total length of about 130 metres has survived. Of the 85 wall-paintings depicting scenes from the Old and New Testaments, one third were destroyed during an air raid at the end of the Second World War, and other beautiful frescoes made by court painters of King Charles IV who worked on the decoration of Karlštejn Castle were seriously damaged. Today, only fragments can be seen, yet they still represent one of the most valuable sets of wall-paintings not only in this country, but in the whole of Europe.

In the 17th century, while inhabited by Spanish Benedictines, the monastery was rebuilt in the Baroque style. Two towers were added to the façade of the building. The monastery was closed as late as 1941. During an air raid on 14th February 1945 it burned out and the church was destroyed.

The reconstruction and renovation of the monastery and of its church was one of the first and most important tasks in Prague after the war in the field of the preservation of ancient buildings. The state of the building after the air raid was extremely bad; some vaults were destroyed as well as practically all the neo-Gothic façade with the twin-towers. The renovation started in 1946 and was supervised by Oldřich Stefan and Bedřich Hacan from the Czech Tech-

nical University of Prague. The first stage of renovation, lasting until 1956, included stabilization of the vaults, their completion and the renovation of the truss, as well as the adaptation of the monastery to the needs of the Czechoslovak Academy of Sciences. At the second stage, disagreement emerged as to what was to be done with the western façade. An architectural competition in two rounds was organized to find an optimum level of harmony between the new spires and the Gothic structure, and also a harmony with the neighbouring group of interesting office buildings by Bohumil Hübschmann. First, the neo-Gothic form of the church was to be restored. Then, however, Jan Sokol made a study suggesting a renovation of the late Gothic gable by making it hipped, and showing that the solution would not mean any loss of monumentality and could be a good starting point. Owing to this new argument, the second round of the competition was won by František M. Černý who suggested giving a new form to the west gable by using shell plates of reinforced concrete, whose modern form would echo both the original gable and the compact form of the twin-towers with which the mass of the church had culminated.

Thus, an important precedent both in theory and in architectural practice was set: the application of modern architectural form on a large scale to a very important historic building, such as the church of the Emmaus Monastery.

By reconstructing the west façade the most important second stage of renovation was completed, which also included a renovation of the nave and the last restoration of the frescoes in the cloister. At the last stage of modernization, social and technical facilities will be installed to adapt the church to its new function as a concert hall for the city.

In the middle of Prague at the corner of Ovocný trh (Fruit Market) and the streets Železná and Kamzíková a complex of buildings has been standing for six centuries which once was the college founded by King Charles and which has traditionally been called the Carolinum. It is now the rectorate of Charles University, the first university in Central Europe, founded by Charles IV on 7th April 1348 "to increase the fame and glory of the Kingdom of Bohemia". The grandson of King Wenceslas II thus fulfilled the intention of his grandfather to establish a university in Prague.

There were more than thirty universities in Europe at that time, mostly in Italy and France. The new university in Prague followed the example of older universities, particularly of those in Paris (1215) and Bologna. The school in Prague was called "universal", which means that the professors at and graduates from all four faculties (law, medicine, theology and philosophy) were entitled to work in all countries controlled by the Roman Catholic Church.

The new university had no buildings of its own, no rooms for lectures and studies. Lectures were held in monasteries, and also in the dwellings of some of the masters. Ceremonies were held at St. Vitus' or at the Archbishop's Palace. In 1364 the first college of Charles University moved to the house of Lazarus the Jew (Lazar Žid) in the Old Town. Another college, later called Angel's, appeared at the same time and included a large botanical garden founded by Charles IV's doctor, Angelo of Florence, on the site of today's Central Post Office in Jindřišská Street, New Town.

In 1383 the university obtained an appropriate and suitable building, now called the Carolinum, which was the rebuilt patrician house of the mint-master Jan Rotlev. The university was granted the building by King Wenceslas IV. It stood on a site where in the mid-13th century there had been a house with yard, which later, as the ground level of the Old Town was raised, became a basement. The Rotlev House had two dwelling parts: a two-storey wing in the north with rectangular windows in its west façade, and a south wing, also with two floors and with projecting arcades in the west. Two bays of ribbed groin vaulting have survived in the arcades of the house. At its southwest corner there was once a massive tower. In 1378, part of Charles' college was also a two-floor house at the southeast corner, to which brick arcades with pointed arches were later attached. Between the latter and the Rotlev House, there was another middle-class house with brick arcades and ribbed

vaults. Of great importance was the construction of a great assembly-hall and a university chapel, and the creation of an inner court surrounded by very interesting medieval galleries that can still be admired. The general rebuilding of the Carolinum was completed in the early 15th century. Charles College, which was initially called the Great College, was a free-standing building, which was a large, picturesque two- and three-storey structure with a steep Gothic roof and bartizans dominating the area. Inside, there were assembly-halls, classrooms, dwellings for masters and their aides, as well as baths, and even a prison.

Master Jan Hus, rector of the University, stayed in the Carolinum, and after his death the University became one of the centres of the revolutionary movement. Therefore the Jesuits, who in 1623 took possession of the Carolinum, removed from the University all evidence of the Hussite period. The last rebuilding of the Carolinum took place in the early 18th century. In 1711, František M. Kaňka made plans of the existing building and then carried out a Baroque rebuilding which was finished in 1718.

The Carolinum is the oldest university building and its role is still very important. It is the seat of the University Rector and of other central offices of Charles University, and major ceremonies are held here.

Already before the Second World War it was clear that the complex needed renovation. As of 1928, collections of the Postal Museum were housed here, while the other rooms were used as stores and shops. Thanks to Professor Vojtěch Birnbaum a technical, historical and archaeological survey of the complex was made after 1930 which confirmed that under Kaňka's Baroque work there were still many relics of the original medieval architecture. However, the survey conducted by Alois Margold was stopped due to the war and a complex renovation based on detailed surveys and analyses prepared by Academician Václav Vojtíšek could not start until 1946. The renovation project was prepared and realized by Jaroslav Fragner, who later in recognition of his outstanding architectural work was awarded the title of "National Artist". The major and quite bold rebuilding and renovation covered not only the historic University Building itself, but also other houses of the block between Ovocný trh (Fruit Market) and Celetná Street that were intended for the University Administration rooms.

The complicated and important renovation work was divided into several stages. Quite early, in 1949, the Great Assembly-Hall was restored

Carolinum

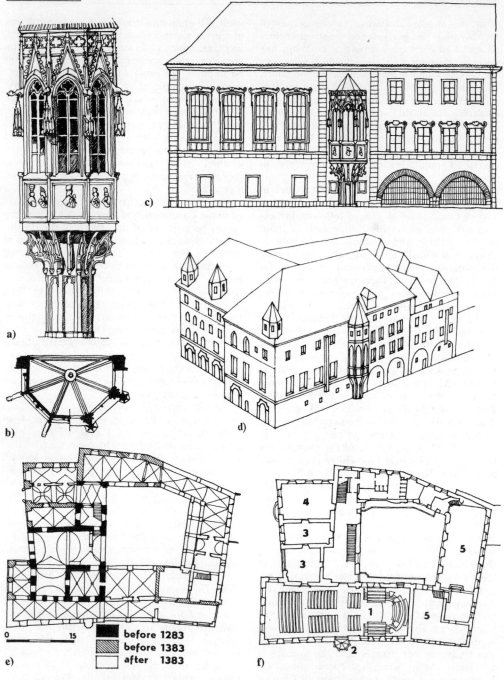

a)

b)

c)

d)

e)

f)

before 1283
before 1383
after 1383

0   15

1
2
3
3
4
5
5

a) b) **Carolinum oriel**
c) **south front, after Fragner's renovation**
d) **appearance before Baroque rebuilding**

e) **plan of ground floor**
f) **plan of first floor:** 1 assembly hall, 2 oriel, 3 cloakrooms for professors, 4 small assembly hall, 5 other
halls

and extended in length by a third, and adjacent ceremonial and meeting rooms, cloakrooms, a foyer and a new main staircase leading to the passage of the Rotlev House were built. The renovation and rebuilding of the ground floor of the east wing with the Hall of Patriots continued, as well as the restoration of the courtyard where a statue of Jan Hus by Karel Lidický was installed. This second stage, which was the most important, was finished in 1959. In the last major phase, which included renovation and rebuilding of the neighbouring houses in Celetná Street, a new building for the University Rector-

ate was constructed east of the old historic building. It offered a new solemn entrance to the whole complex, with a logical sequence of services and functions, and with the necessary administration rooms. The building proves the high working standards and the imagination of Jaroslav Fragner and his team in dealing with this complex task.

The last stage of the Carolinum rebuilding was completed in 1965. As a result, the University and the City of Prague were provided with an excellent complex which combined qualities of history and tradition with the beauty of its new function.

Charles Bridge

Like every large city lying on a river, Prague has many bridges. However, few countries in Europe can boast of an outstanding medieval structure comparable with Charles Bridge and its towers. The stone bridge, which was initially called Prague Bridge, and which since 1870 has born the name Charles Bridge was founded by Charles IV on 9th July 1357 near the remains of the old Romanesque bridge called Judith Bridge (built about 1170), which had been heavily damaged by floods in 1342. The beautiful new Gothic bridge successfully resisted the subsequent great floods in 1496, 1784 and 1890. The bridge was built by Peter Parler and its construction was finished in the early 15th century.

The old Romanesque bridge built by King Vladislav I in the 1170s and named after his wife was used until the first years of Charles' reign. However, it was built at the lower Romanesque level of the Old Town and very soon the bridge could not meet the needs of Prague under Charles IV. Judith Bridge lay a little to the north and had towers at both its ends, parts of which have survived. Its Old Town tower is concealed in the projecting part of the former Generalate of the Knights of the Cross, and one of the Lesser Quarter towers has survived completely. The bridge, following the example of the bridge in Regensburg, was the second in Central Europe and a unique work of engineering; it was also the longest bridge in Central Europe (half a kilometre). Remains of its piers can still be seen in the

Vltava, and also in the cellars of some houses in the Lesser Quarter (Nos. 77, 78, 82 and 85).

Around 1373, Peter Parler finished the construction of a tower controlling access to Charles Bridge on the Old Town bank. The new bridge, which was 520 metres long and 10 metres wide, was four to five metres higher than its Romanesque predecessor and the span of its sixteen massive arches, clad with hewn sandstone blocks, was much bigger.

The bridge, which connects the Castle with the Old Town and forms part of the famous King's Way, was also of great strategic importance. In 1648, the Swedes used the bridge to attack Prague and destroyed some of its decoration as well as the west façade of the Old Town Bridge Tower. In 1723, oil lamps were installed here that were in 1866 replaced by gas lamps. The bridge became an excellent open-air gallery of thirty Baroque sculptures. Most of them date from the years 1683 to 1714, being the work of such fine Baroque artists as Matthias B. Braun, Johann Brokoff, and his sons Michael Johann and Ferdinand Maxmilian.

The bridge can be reached from the Old Town through an extremely beautiful medieval tower, supported by the first pier of the bridge. The tower is also the most impressive building on Knights of the Cross Square (Křižovnické náměstí). The east wall of the Old Town Bridge Tower is decorated with sculpture, and is of great architectural interest. The tower is an out-

Charles Bridge

a)

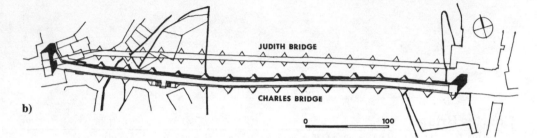

JUDITH BRIDGE

CHARLES BRIDGE

0   100

b)

c)

d)   e)

a) b) Charles Bridge
c) figures of Charles IV, St. Vitus and Wenceslas IV
on the east façade of the Old Town Bridge Tower
d) east façade of the Old Town Bridge Tower
e) east façade of the Lesser Quarter Bridge Tower

standing combination of architecture and sculpture of great artistic value. In the lower part of the tower, above the gate, are the coats-of-arms of the lands possessed by Charles IV and a veiled kingfisher, the heraldic symbol of King Wenceslas IV. At first floor level, where the decorative elements of the façade are accented, there are sculptures of St. Vitus, the patron saint of the bridge, of Charles IV and Wenceslas IV, and, at the top, of St. Adalbert and St. Sigismund, patron saints of Bohemia. The top floor appears light due to a system of arches and piers. The west façade facing the Castle was originally also decorated with statues. However, it was destroyed in 1648 by the guns of the Swedish army besieging Prague. The reticulated vault of the high gateway, made after 1373, anticipated the vaults of St. Vitus' choir. The tower was completed around 1380.

At its other end, entering the Lesser Quarter, Charles Bridge is closed by two quite plain towers flanking the bridge gate and decorated with the coats-of-arms of the lands possessed by Wenceslas IV. The taller tower was built later, in the reign of George of Poděbrady, and probably replaced an older Romanesque tower. The tower imitated Parler's style, as proved by niches in the façade intended for statues which, however, were not installed here. The lower bridge tower was rebuilt after 1591 in the Renaissance style. The tower is of Romanesque origin and was part of the fortification system on the left bank of the river. The original parts date back to the second quarter of the 12th century, so the tower is older than Judith Bridge. The Society for the Protection of Old Prague is now accommodated here.

Charles Bridge, which is a national monument of cultural and technical significance, and a unique gallery of Baroque works of art and of some 19th century works, had to wait a long time before it was renovated. The first step towards its protection was the decision to close it to all traffic, first trams and then automobiles, to keep the bridge, as one of the most important parts of the King's Way, for pedestrians only. After a structural survey, a fundamental renovation of the entire bridge began in the 1970s. Step by step, provisional platforms were installed as each pier and arch was fixed. The clay core of the piers was removed, the foundations were secured by piles, and the masonry was reinforced. Many ashlar blocks that were destroyed or damaged were removed, which was quite a difficult task, and replaced by new ones of a sandstone of the same granularity and colour. Simultaneously, the sculptural decoration was restored. The most valuable sculptures that were endangered by the effects of weathering and of pollution were removed, placed in the lapidary of the Municipal Museum and replaced by replicas. The technical preparation for the work was directed by Leonid Arnautov from the State Institute for the Renovation of Historic Towns and Buildings in Prague. The Institute also made plans of all the technical and architectural work to be done, including new paving, which was now flush, without the former lower central roadway. Consequently, the bridge became even more monumental and its function as a promenade increased. At the same time, the Old Town Bridge was restored, particularly the Great Hall on the first floor with a 16th century ceiling that had been taken from the Old Town Hall and installed here during the renovation of the tower by Josef Mocker in the years 1874—1875. During the restoration of the tower the valuable sculptures were removed from the wall facing the Old Town, placed in the National Gallery and replaced by copies. The ice guards, which are a typical feature of the bridge, were also replaced.

Town-Hall of the New Town

a)

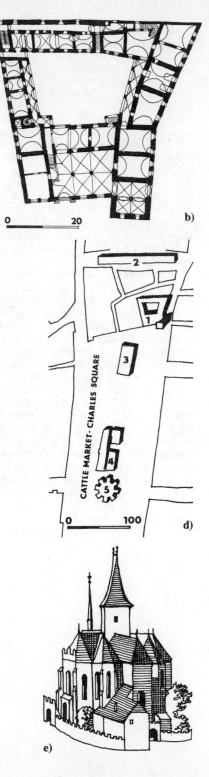

b)

d)

c)

a) **Town-Hall**
b) **plan of ground floor**
c) **main room on the ground floor**
d) **original situation:** 1 town-hall, 2 meat shops, 3 herring shop, 4 shops, 5 Corpus Christi Chapel
e) **Corpus Christi Chapel** (after van den Bosch's engraving, 1606)

e)

Town-Hall of the New Town

One of the most important buildings in the New Town of Prague from the reign of King Charles was the town-hall. It was intended as a centre of municipal administration and law-court, and was built soon after the foundation of the town, certainly prior to 1367. The town-hall witnessed the beginning of the Hussite Revolution, and also later, in the time of revolutionary battles and struggles, it retained its important position in Prague and even competed with the town-hall of the Old Town, from which it differed in that it had been constructed for this particular purpose. The towers of both town-halls exhibit the same late Gothic features. The town-hall of the New Town was built in the Luxembourg era and has survived so to the present day. The northern part of the east wing and the layout of its southern part date from the reign of King Charles.

The dominant site in the corner of the market, at a change in ground level in the vicinity of the former Church of St. Lazarus, was quite suitable for this symbol of an independent royal town which the town-hall became after the separation of the New Town from the Old Town in 1367.

The Cattle Market (Dobytčí trh), now Charles Square (Karlovo náměstí), was planned by the Emperor as an important trade centre and also as a counterpart to the Old Town Square. The local town-hall was therefore to be of much architectural beauty. It was also decided that the route of the coronation procession of Bohemian kings should go from Vyšehrad across the New Town Market to the Castle. Charles IV also wanted to have a centre of religious life here. Therefore, a tower was built in the middle of the Cattle Market and some time later, from 1382 to 1393, a Gothic centralized Chapel of Corpus Christi was also built in this place and the imperial crown jewels and relics of saints were shown to the public here. However, the Cattle Market could not retain its important position for long, and the Horse Market (Koňský trh, now Wenceslas Square) took over its role.

The town-hall was constructed between the last quarter of the 14th century and 1418. A hall-nave with six bays of vaulting supported by two massive cylindrical columns was built from 1411 to 1418, and has survived to the present day. On the first floor of the east wing (facing Vodičkova Street), there is a large hall with a Gothic rib vault supported by Renaissance columns. In the corner of the plan, which now has three wings, there is, as in the town-hall of the Old Town, a tower with a chapel on its first floor. The chap-el was rebuilt in the Baroque style in the early 18th century. The building has been several times rebuilt, particularly when the New Town and the Old Town merged (in 1520—1526). The main façade was then rebuilt in the Renaissance style, with the high gables we know today. Some time later, after a great fire in 1559, a west and a north wing were built around the arcaded courtyard.

Regrettable alterations to the town-hall were made after the unification of all four towns of Prague in 1784 with all administration concentrated in the town-hall of the Old Town. The town-hall of the New Town lost its great importance and was used as a law-court, office, and even as a prison. For the needs of the court, the old part of the town-hall was rebuilt in 1806 in the Empire style. As a result, the main façade facing the square lost its characteristic gables. Attitudes towards the town-hall changed at the turn of this century. Two architects, Kamil Hilbert and Antonín Wiehl, rebuilt the main façade facing Charles Square in 1905—1906 and restored here the large Renaissance coupled windows in the main hall and the Renaissance gables. The 19th century interior of the building has remained.

The first modern alteration took place in the years 1958—1959 when the Gothic hall on the ground floor was adapted as a hall for wedding ceremonies in Prague 2 District. In 1962, the town-hall was declared a national cultural monument.

Proposals were also made to restore the whole building, however the first studies were prepared much later, in 1979 by SURPMO designers, after a survey made in 1976—1977. The latest restoration plans come from Václav Girsa's studio, Centre 08. Plans based on the detailed survey have been prepared that include the renovation of the original Council Hall, which is 23 m long, 11 m wide and 7 m high and is intended for sessions of the District Council. The first floor of the wing facing Vodičkova Street will be adapted for wedding ceremonies and the wing facing the courtyard will house a restaurant. The former prison in the rear part will be converted into a library, and there will also be a solicitor's office and a flat for the warden. New vertical communications are also planned to connect the different departments.

The renovation started in 1973 with the tower, where many stone blocks, particularly in corners and jambs, had to be removed and replaced.

Bethlehem Chapel

a)

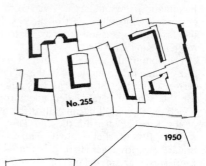

c) 1783

b)

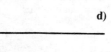

No.255 1950

d)

1954

e)

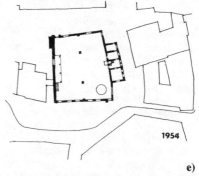

f)

a) **Bethlehem Chapel**
b) **original situation** (engraving by J. D. Huber, 1765—1769)
c) d) **territorial development:** 1 sacristy, 2 pulpit and preacher's house, 3 belfry, 4 cemetery, 5 former church of SS. Philip and James
f) **section—present-day appearance**

(70)

Bethlehem Chapel

In a part of the Old Town of Prague called Bethlehem, where there were no palaces and no monasteries, but where the poor of Prague were concentrated, a chapel was built in 1391 where sermons were to be given in the Czech language. The church, which was called Bethlehem Chapel, later became in some respects the most important church in Prague and played a significant role in the course of European history. It was built by Johann of Milheim, a royal courtier of King Wenceslas IV, and by a shopkeeper named Kříž who had alotted for this purpose a plot of land with a malt-house, a church consecrated to SS. Philip and James (destroyed during the Hussite Revolution), and a cemetery.

The chapel, which was a unique religious building in Prague, featured plain architectural forms so as to proclaim the new ideas concerning the position and role of the Church. Many new and progressive ideas appeared at that time and the Bethlehem Chapel was the first religious building whose layout corresponded to the spirit of the Reformation.

The heyday of the Bethlehem Chapel came with Master Jan Hus, who preached here and was a warden of the house. How successful, popular and effective his sermons were can be demonstrated by the fact that he preached up to seven sermons on feasts and holidays and that the chapel, which was just one third smaller than the big Vladislav Hall in the Castle, could accommodate three thousand people.

For a hundred years, the Bethlehem Chapel was one of the main centres of the Utraquist Church. Its interiors were plain, the presbytery and the pulpit were not prominent, and the walls were decorated with texts from Hus' and Jakoubek's tracts.

The chapel was connected to the warden's house, which was the former malt-house. On the ground floor, there was a sacristy and an entrance to the pulpit. Upstairs, there was accommodation for the preacher, where Jan Hus lived and worked for ten years. In his time, the chapel had a joist ceiling with two supporting posts under the roof valley. The inside space was over ten metres high and the quadrangular ground plan of the chapel covered an area of almost eight hundred square metres.

In the 16th century, the chapel was given a beautiful reticulated vault supported by fifteen octagonal pillars. Although the vault was very sophisticated and the three rows of pillars were arranged so that the lateral arches did not exert too much pressure on the outer walls, it soon started disintegrating and at the end of the 18th century it had to be removed.

Under Joseph II, in 1786, the chapel was closed, as was the cemetery in front of the chapel under the orders of the municipal council. Its location is now marked on the paving of the square. Many important figures in our history were buried in the cemetery, such as Jakoubek of Stříbro (in 1429), a teacher at Charles University, or the book-printer Jiří Melantrich of Aventino (in 1580). The roof and the vault of the chapel were removed, the south wall was pulled down, and between 1836 and 1837 a new dwelling-house in the Empire style was built here.

The loss of the Hussite symbol was a painful event not only in the architectural history of Prague. Long after that, as late as 6th July 1954, the Chapel was reconstructed and solemnly re-opened in a large public ceremony. Thus, the wish of Jan Hus, asking his compatriots before his execution at Constance "to be kind to the Bethlehem Chapel...", was fulfilled.

Today, the Bethlehem Chapel occupies a special position among Prague's monuments, which is due to its eventful past and, in particular, to the form of its reconstruction. In 1869, the year of the 500th anniversary of Jan Hus' birth, the Hussite tradition revived as well as interest in the place where Hus once had preached. Step by step, all available information and documents related to the chapel and to its form were gathered. An important milestone in the development of the idea of reconstruction was the year 1915 when two publications were prepared—about Master Jan Hus and about the Bethlehem Chapel—with an attempt to reconstruct the form of the building. We owe very much to Karel Guth who concentrated all the available information and graphic illustrations related to the chapel, and found a protocol from 1836 where it was said "to construct the house No. 255 the old masonry up to the second floor will be used". Also the initiative of Alois Kubíček is to be appreciated, who before the First World War privately searched for traces of the chapel in the flats of the tenement house and made some very promising findings. In spite of the continuous research and the efforts of many Czech scientists (Zdeněk Nejedlý, Karel Guth, Václav Novotný, František Krejsa, Zdeněk Wirth, and others) and in spite of the fact that the plans of the chapel from the years 1783 and 1661 had been discovered, only little was done until the Second World War to realize the idea of its reconstruction. Only after the war, on 30th July 1948, the Government approved plan to reconstruct the monument which had been so important for the Czech nation and for its history. It was a new and unique task for ancient building

Bethlehem Chapel

preservation theory and practice. The earlier restorations, no matter on which theoretical platform they were based, had always to cope with an existing building, more or less damaged or rebuilt. Now, however, a total reconstruction was planned that required a wide scientific platform in order to avoid any hypothetical approach. Time has shown that this was not possible in some details of the layout and form. The survey made in 1919 and 1920 as well as after the demolition of the house No. 255 showed that the east and west walls had completely survived and that the north wall had survived in part. Foundations of the original central piers supporting the vaults and dating from the mid-17th century

were found, as well as many fragments of window jambs and tracery, portals, window openings, wall paintings, etc. As a result, together with archival documents, there was enough information available to start the reconstruction.

The studio of the Stavoprojekt Company headed by Jaroslav Fragner was charged with the task and Bedřich Hacar from the Czech Technical University of Prague was invited to offer assistance. They, and also many others successfully fulfilled this task and their work considerably contributed to the reputation of Czechoslovak specialists in ancient building preservation.

Powder Tower

One of the most remarkable monuments in Prague dating from the late Gothic era is the Powder Tower, initially called the New Tower, which was built in 1475 by King Vladislav II Jagiello. The expenses were born by the Old Town and the tower was constructed by Matěj Rejsek of Prostějov to replace one of the original thirteen Old Town gates, the dilapidated "Odraná" Gate.

The importance of the gate increased at the end of the 14th century after the Royal Court was built in its vicinity (where the Community House now stands), which became a residence of the Bohemian kings during the Hussite period. Wenceslas IV lived here permanently as of 1383. The Court was later the royal seat of Sigismund, Albrecht, Ladislav Pohrobek (= Posthumous), as well as of George of Poděbrady who lived here after 1454 first as the country's governor and later, as of 1458, as its king until his early death on 22nd March 1471. Vladislav II Jagiello, too, lived here for some time. In 1483, however, concerned for his safety during religious riots, he decided to move back to the Castle, which he had in the meantime repaired at great cost.

Although King Vladislav II himself laid the foundation stone of the New Tower, the citizens, at whose expenses it was built, cut an inscription in the tower saying that it had been built "to pay honour and tribute to the inhabitants of the

town". Thus, the tower was evidence of the growing influence of the town and its patriciate, which after the revolution had got rid of its obligations to the Church and had acquired a great deal of property. As a result, the profits could be used by the town councillors for the benefit of the municipal administration and its policy. The important political role of the middle-class after the Hussite Revolution brought about a higher level of culture here, particularly in the municipal schools. The University of Prague, in spite of its separation from other parts of the world due to its support of the Utraquist Church, did much good work in educating generations of school teachers and municipal scriveners who brought culture and education to towns. The builder of the New Tower (now Powder Tower), too, was a teacher at Týnská School, and contributed to Prague's architecture by having participated in its construction, first as a mason and later as a builder. Rejsek was not the first architect of the Powder Tower, but the tower was his first (although unfinished) work. Its first architect was Master Václav of Žlutice who followed the example of Peter Parler's work. The Powder Tower itself discloses the fact that its model was Parler's Bridge Tower, built a hundred years before. However, instead of the intelligibility of the Bridge Tower the Powder Tower displays an optical playfulness, ignoring the function of par-

Powder Tower

a) b) **Powder Tower**
c) **window in west façade, detail**
d) **original appearance**

ticular elements and exhibiting a superfluity of details.

In 1483, soon after founding the tower, King Vladislav II left the Royal Court and the tower lost its political importance. The fame of the Royal Court vanished and, as a result, the interest in completing the construction decreased. The construction work slowed down, and the tower remained unfinished for centuries, having only a provisional roof. Even the reticulated vault of the gateway is fairly new; it dates from Mocker's 19th century renovation. Of course, it controlled the entrance to the town from the east, i.e., an important road coming from Kutná Hora, once the heart of the country's silver mining area. Its great bulk forms the beginning of the oldest arterial road of Prague leading to the Castle: the King's Way, which was the most renowned street in the Old Town.

In 1757, when Prague was besieged by the Prussian army, the tower was seriously damaged and in 1799 its damaged decoration was removed. For some time it was used as a gunpowder store and since that time it has been called the Powder Tower. The tower as we know it is 65 metres tall and displays both late Gothic and 19th century neo-Gothic features.

The first alterations of the Powder Tower were made in 1823: a tower-clock was installed here and the shape of the Baroque roof changed through the addition of four semicircular dormers.

Like many other ancient buildings in Prague the tower did not escape the romantic atmosphere of the latter half of the 19th century. Josef Mocker was charged with its restoration, and from 1875 to 1886 he converted the building into a romantic neo-Gothic work. He increased the decoration by adding to the earlier masonry and sculptural works by contemporary artists (sculptors Jindřich Čapek, Bernard Otto Seeling, Josef Strachovský, Ludvík Šimek and Antonín Wildt), removed the clock and increased the dominant role of the tower by constructing a tall hipped roof with four bartizans at each corner of the gallery, similar to that of the town-hall tower in the Old Town and to the Lesser Quarter Bridge Tower. However, the romantic restoration was not the last alteration in the history of the tower. In 1911, a sumptuous building, the Community House was constructed in its vicinity and joined to the tower by means of a connecting passageway conceived in the spirit of Mocker's architectural morphology.

The Castle in the Late Gothic Period

GOTHIC ARCHITECTURE

After King Wenceslas IV's death, Prague Castle remained uninhabited for a long time. In the Jagiello dynasty it again became a royal seat.

In 1485, a renovation of the old palace started and, above the Romanesque walls within the former palace of Charles IV, the new Vladislav Wing was constructed in the form known to us now. The new palace is an example of outstanding late Gothic as well as early Renaissance architecture.

First, an annex was built with a room known as the Vladislav Bedchamber above the entrance passage of the palace, with a beautiful stellar vault that was probably made by Hans Spiess of Frankfurt. Spiess also built a bridge-passage leading from the king's rooms to a new Royal Gallery in the Cathedral (1490—1493), built probably by Benedikt Rieth (Rejt) and conceived as a late Gothic double-vault without supports and with a parapet richly decorated with hewn naturalistic motifs and with coats-of-arms of the lands possessed by Vladislav Jagiello. The par-

apet was partly restored by Mocker in 1878. The ribs in the form of drying branches seem to symbolize the final stage of the Gothic.

Like King Charles, Vladislav Jagiello also chose an excellent architect: Benedikt Rieth (Rejt) of Piesting (1454—1534), who was as great a master as Peter Parler, the architect of the Cathedral. Rieth's work in the Castle culminated at the end of the 15th century in the construction of fortifications and three new towers, called Daliborka, Bílá věž (White Tower) and Mihulka, and, in particular, in the construction of the huge Throne Hall. The hall replaced the first floor of Charles' palace and its three large rooms: the hall, the Chapel of Our Lady, and Charles' chamber. The architecture of this 62 m long, 13 m wide and 13 m high hall, which was called the Great Throne Hall or the New Palace, was still Gothic. The bold work was technically very difficult and during its construction one of the vault bays collapsed and had to be rebuilt. On the other hand, the hall survived the great fire at the

The Castle in the Late Gothic Period

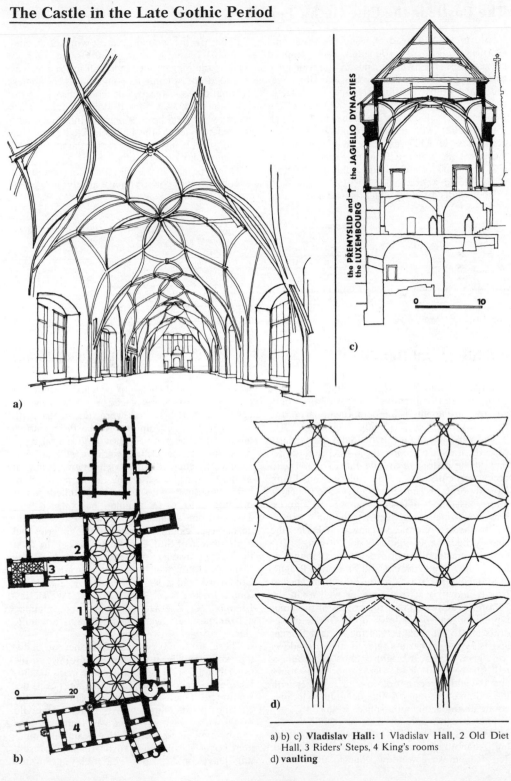

a)

b)

c)

the PŘEMYSLID and the LUXEMBOURG → the JAGIELLO DYNASTIES

0   10

d)

a) b) c) **Vladislav Hall:** 1 Vladislav Hall, 2 Old Diet Hall, 3 Riders' Steps, 4 King's rooms
d) **vaulting**

0   20

Castle in 1541. Instead of using the traditional Gothic straight ribs, Benedikt Rieth applied curved ribs, intertwining and creating an intricate and bold vault. The arches and ribs cover the space almost weightlessly. In the architectural conception and in its effect the spirit of the Renaissance can already be seen. The huge hall (1492—1502), with its large windows, Quattrocento in style, which date the advent of the Renaissance at Prague Castle to exactly 1493, is a unique work of architecture, marking the close of the medieval era.

The Vladislav Hall, which is—after St. Vitus' Cathedral—the second greatest work of art and the most beautiful secular late Gothic room as well as the biggest medieval hall in Prague, was intended for solemn meetings and ceremonies, coronations and feasts, but it was also used for jousts until 1577. Under Rudolph II fairs of art works were held here. When the Imperial Court moved to Vienna, the hall remained empty for a long time, being used for major gatherings and meetings only occasionally.

Now, the hall is used for the most important events in the country, particularly for presidential elections.

Windows and portals are among the most beautiful and impressive architectural details, and they are an important component part of the historical townscape.

The windows of Gothic buildings, particularly of cathedrals are among the most beautiful details in the history of architecture. The tall windows, vertically divided by mullions into lights, have more or less intricate tracery. The tracery is often based on different geometrical figures; however sometimes it seems to be quite irregular. In the late Gothic, starting with Parler, the shapes became elongated and "flowing". The Gothic masters developed a wide range of forms, of which many can still be seen in Prague.

Stained glass was already known in ancient Rome, and it is at that time, as well as in the Romanesque period that the origins of the great fantasy of leaded windows in the Gothic cathedrals are to be sought. Like the ancient Roman artists, Gothic masters glazed their windows with glass plates of bright colours and connected them with lead. The unbroken tones and the wide spectrum of colours, together with the complex layout of the beautiful windows create an unearthly atmosphere inside.

The construction of Gothic windows demonstrates very well the great progress in building technology since the Romanesque period. The Romanesque windows, due to thick walls, were small and their jambs bevelled, even in big buildings. Posts were placed in the window recesses and the doors were decorated with abundant figural sculpture. At the Premonstratensian Monastery on Strahov Hill several types of simple Romanesque windows still survive, such as the coupled windows in the western wall of the chapter house, or the tall narrow rectangular windows with massive bevelled jambs opening into a rectangular hall, which was a storeroom. Coupled windows of the Romanesque type can also be seen in the galleries and in the tower of St. George's Basilica in the Castle. There is also a carved coupled window in the Bishop's House which can be seen in the Third Courtyard, and a similar window is also to be found in the west façade of St. Wenceslas' Church "Na Zderaze", in the part containing a Romanesque tower whose remains are quite clearly visible.

There are not very many Romanesque buildings still standing in Prague. The Gothic, on the other hand, is represented here by many beautiful windows and portals from all stages of its development. One of the earliest examples is the entrance of the Old-New Synagogue in the Old Town with a vestibule separated from the main hall by a moulded portal with a beautiful tympanum covered with naturalistic reliefs representing leaves and grapes. The richly decorated

Architectural Details

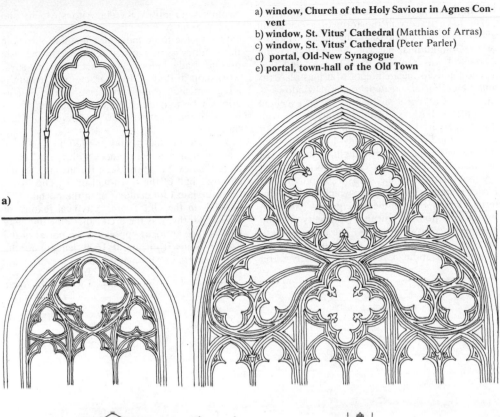

a)

b)

c)

d)

e)

(77)

two-light windows of St. Saviour's from the 1270s have tracery in the form of a cinquefoil above two open trefoils. In the upper windows of the longitudinal part of the presbytery the cinquefoil was replaced by a five-pointed star.

The high Gothic architects, Matthias of Arras and Peter Parler, created beautiful windows in St. Vitus' Cathedral in the Castle. An excellent example of Parler's outstanding art is the window tracery in the Chapel of the Holy Cross. For the first time in Bohemia and Moravia, flowing tracery was applied. The six-light window in the neighbouring Martinická Chapel, too, has tracery that differs from the Arras tradition. In 1362, Parler completed the sacristy which could be entered from the Cathedral gallery through a moulded pointed entrance whose tympanum also features flowing tracery. The forms and colours of the stained glass in the Cathedral are the work of outstanding Czech artists, namely Karel Svolinský, František Kysela, Alfons Mucha and Max Švabinský.

One of the three most monumental portals in this country is the northern entrance to the aisle of Our Lady before Týn, made by the royal workshop in Prague. Its characteristic feature is a big semicircular tympanum, with carved decorations, whose figural relief of the Last Judgment is one of the great works of sculpture from that time.

The late Gothic period has left Prague with many windows and entrances with typical interlaced shapes, as can be seen for instance in the entrance hall of the town-hall of the Old Town from the late 15th century, or in the portal of St. Martin's in the Old Town. A typical feature of the late Gothic was the arch called "the donkey's back" (ogee arch), as applied to the portal of the Riders' Steps from about 1500, leading to the Vladislav Hall in Prague Castle.

Renaissance Architecture

Renaissance means literally "rebirth". In Italy, the word was used in the early 15th century to indicate the return to ancient standards in the arts due to the number of Roman works of architecture and art that attracted the attention of artists and inspired them to follow their example. Such efforts had already existed since the very beginning of the Middle Ages in the mid-8th century in northern Italy and in the Rhineland, being known as a Carolingian and Ottonian Renaissance which, however, did not last long and was not of great influence.

The Renaissance style, which originated in the early 15th century in Italy in the region of Florence spread throughout the country and in the 16th century it reached other European countries beyond the Alps. Of utmost importance among the Renaissance arts was architecture. Buildings were now made for the needs of man. As a result, the character of monumental architecture was changing: instead of spaces complying with the philosophy of the Middle Ages, new spaces, large, comfortable and light were created. The new style featured a plain mass and a simple form, and exhibited a tranquility of architectural rhythm. Unlike the Gothic dynamism and verticalism, a static and horizontal principle now prevailed. Buildings became static, with a horizontal emphasis. The principal units freely applied and combined by the Renaissance architects were the column, pillar, pilaster, architrave, archivolt and vault. From ancient architecture the architrave system was adopted by the Renaissance. By means of the above tools of expression, the wall—in contrast with the Gothic—regained its tectonic role. Of great importance was the new formation of spaces. The imaginary Gothic space was replaced by a compact space, optically and clearly delimited. The architectural mass was plain. As opposed to the Gothic pointed and curved lines, straight lines and right angles were now used.

Construction technology changed in the Renaissance, too. Ribbed vaults and associated supporting systems were abandoned and a new construction system, rapid and economical that had been known here since the Great Moravian Empire was introduced. First, the whole structure was bricked-in and then the surface was finished. In the Renaissance the masonry was plastered, as were also wooden and timber-framed buildings, as proved by a vista of Prague dating from 1562. In addition to the traditional materials some new ones were introduced and applied, in particular, for construction and decoration. An important construction material was mortar, which was used for plaster, sgraffiti, bosses, and for some architectural elements. Since the very beginning of the Renaissance, brick manufacture had been rapidly developing, and not only standard and glazed bricks, but also specially made ceramic window and door jambs were manufactured. Wood was used for the construction of roof trusses, cornices and fine coffered ceilings. Wood was in some cases also applied to the construction of vaults. Widely used were, in particular, tunnel vaults with lunettes, cloister vaults, trough vaults, cavetto vaults with or without lunettes, and melon vaults. These vaults provided large enough surfaces for artistic decoration. In addition to domes, cross vaults (of the Roman type) were also widely applied, usually without ribs, often with ridges at the groins. This is how the typical Renaissance ridge vault originated.

In the late 15th and the early 16th centuries, as the evolution of the Bohemian Gothic was culminating in the Vladislav late Gothic style, Italian Renaissance forms started penetrating into the country. King Vladislav II moved in 1491 to Buda, but he continued the renovation of Prague Castle. Since 1489, the renovation had been in the hands of an outstanding late Gothic artist Benedikt Rieth (Rejt), who was the first to apply elements of the new style. His work in the Castle culminated with the construction of the Vladislav Hall. The year 1493 written in the Renaissance window in its façade is a historic date indicating the beginning of a New Age in the arts of this country. Rieth's creative mind found a harmony between the principles of Renaissance morphology and the Gothic arts, and his person became a symbol of the time. After the tragic death of King Louis Jagiello, Archduke Ferdinand I of the Habsburg dynasty was elected Bohemian King. He lived in the Castle until 1547 when he left Prague and moved to Vienna, and appointed his son Archduke Ferdinand as Governor of Bohemia.

Italian artists bringing the new style from Italy and spreading it through Central and Northern Europe directly influenced artistic life in Prague.

RENAISSANCE ARCHITECTURE

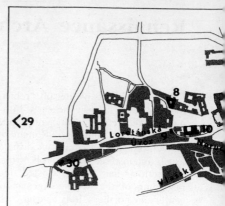

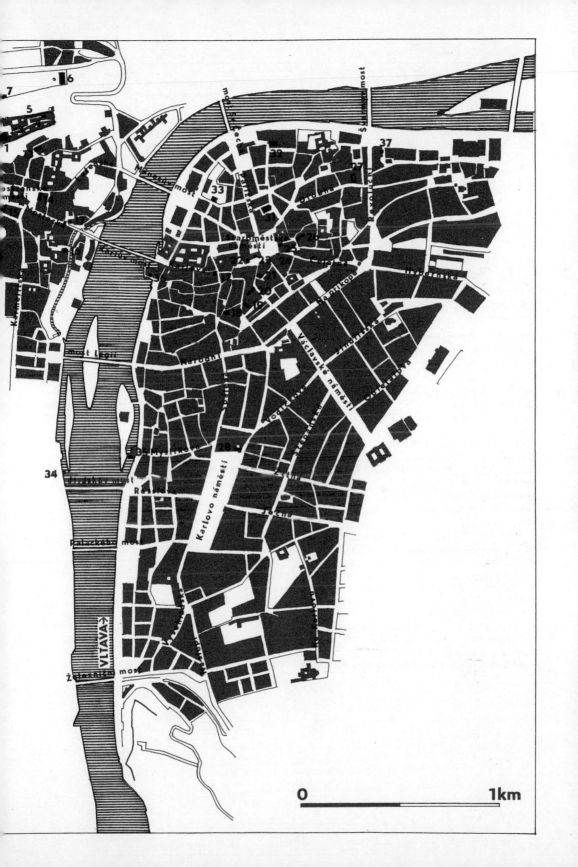

Their stay and work in this country between 1537 and 1576 is considered the peak of the Renaissance here.

The renovation of Prague Castle, started under Ferdinand I by the Court architects Ulrico Aostalli and Bonifaz Wohlmut, continued.

The late Renaissance era (1576—1614) started in Prague with Emperor Rudolph II, who moved in 1584 from Vienna to Prague. His court was one of the main centres of the late Renaissance in Europe, sometimes known as Mannerism. The original Italian style absorbed at that time motifs of Dutch and German art.

There was much tension between Rudolph's successor Matthias and the Estates and, as a result, the sovereign transferred his residence again to Vienna in 1617. On 23rd May 1618 the Estates rose up, which was the beginning of a national tragedy.

The First Renaissance Palace

The Royal Palace fundamentally changed at the turn of the century due to the construction of the unique Vladislav Hall (1486—1502), to which four transverse wings were attached whose upper floors could be reached by means of Gothic spiral stairs. The south-west wing, called the Louis Wing of the Old Palace, is the first Renaissance palace in this country, built between 1503 and 1510. The palace, which was part of the king's private rooms, was also the last major building realized by Benedikt Rieth, Court architect of three kings (Vladislav, Louis and Ferdinand), whose work ingeniously combined late Gothic forms with the rationalism of the early Renaissance.

The Louis Wing is a Renaissance building not only in its details, but also in its general conception. The architect applied here fully the Renaissance principle of having several floors above one another, with large rectangular windows placed vertically on one axis. The window jambs, symmetrically placed and, in addition, moulded as deeply as the thickness of the masonry, seem to have been standardized. The Gothic internal spiral stairs are replaced here by a modern two-flight Renaissance staircase. The palace exhibits genuine Renaissance forms primarily in its exterior, as the ground plan of this first Renaissance palace had to respect the layout of the adjoining buildings, although it is a separate entity.

The main room of the palace, at the same level as the Vladislav Hall, is the former Bohemian Chancellery (second floor of the palace), which was the office of Bohemian governors for two centuries. It was here that the governors Vilém Slavata of Chlum, Jaroslav Bořita of Martinice and their scribe Fabricius were thrown from the window down into the ditch by Protestant noblemen to start the uprising of the Bohemian Estates against the Habsburgs in 1618. Upstairs is the Hall of the Imperial Court where on 19th June 1621 twenty-seven leaders of the revolt against Ferdinand II were sentenced to death. On the first floor of the palace, below the Vladislav Hall is the former Crown Hall (under Rudolph II an office of the Court War Council).

This first Renaissance palace in this country, featuring the new style in its layout as well as in its architectural details, set the example, together with the Royal Palace to which it is attached, for the renovation of the Martinic Palace on Hradčany Square 100 years later (see page 128).

The First Renaissance Palace

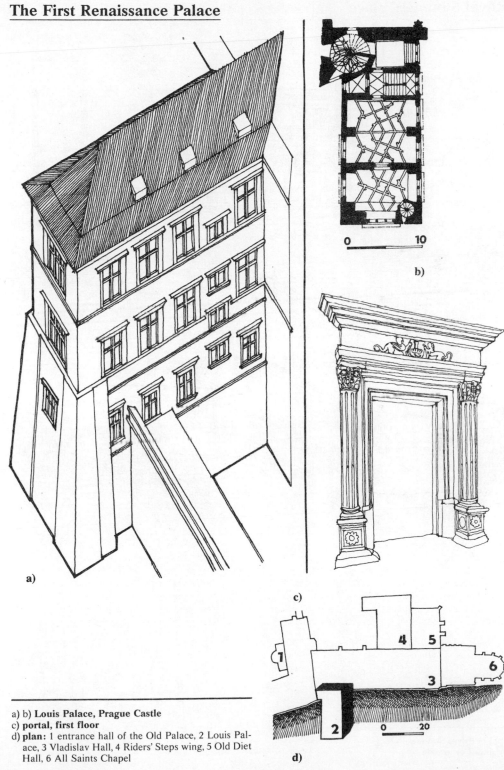

b)

a)

c)

d)

a) b) **Louis Palace, Prague Castle**
c) **portal, first floor**
d) **plan:** 1 entrance hall of the Old Palace, 2 Louis Palace, 3 Vladislav Hall, 4 Riders' Steps wing, 5 Old Diet Hall, 6 All Saints Chapel

Royal Summer Palace

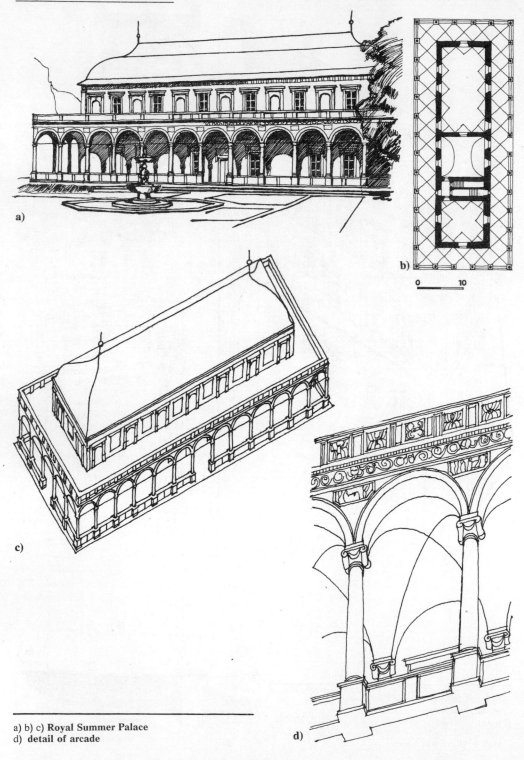

0   10

a) b) c) **Royal Summer Palace**
d) **detail of arcade**

The pleasure palace in Prague Castle, known as the Royal Summer Palace or the Belvedere, was built in the eastern part of the new Royal Garden with exotic plants in the place of former vineyards outside the bulwarks above the Stag Moat. It was the only possible site for extending the Castle, as the narrow terrace of the headland was too small for a large-scale rebuilding in the Renaissance style. Under Ferdinand I the idea of a pleasure palace amidst a decorative garden as in Italy was realized for the first time not only in this country, but anywhere in Central Europe.

In 1535, Giovanni Spazio adapted a terrace sixty metres above the Vltava to a large garden. For that purpose, it was necessary to bridge over the Stag Moat, and so a wooden roofed bridge supported by stone piers, which was mentioned as early as 1536, connected the Castle with the new garden. The Italian gardener Francesco created the first geometrical garden conceived in harmony with a work of architecture, simultaneously with the construction of the palace. As of 1538, J. Mittel continued his work. At that time, exotic trees were planted on the southern slope of the Stag Moat where after 1565 red deer were kept. For the first time in Prague, fig-trees, almond-trees, apricot-trees, orange-trees and lemon-trees were grown in greenhouses. The exotic plants were planted and the "giardinetto" was created by Hugo Vennia. M. and C. Reinhardt created a geometrical garden with beds of colourful flowers in 1548. In the garden, which was extended in the 1550s, the renowned botanist P. O. Matthioli planted many other flowers including some rare tulips. Later, in 1573, a bronze fountain of the Dutch type called the Singing Fountain was installed in the middle of the giardinetto. The fountain was designed by Francesco Terzio and cast—after a model made by G. Ventura and C. Bracco—from 1564 to 1568 by the famous bell founder Tomáš Jaroš. He also cast the biggest bell in Prague, called Sigismund, in the tower of St. Vitus' Cathedral. The fountain ranks among the most important Renaissance sculptures in this country.

The pleasure palace, which is also incorrectly referred to as the Belvedere, was built by Ferdinand I for his wife Anna of Jagiello. The building was also intended to be used for royal ceremonies taking place in the neighbouring garden. It was designed by the Italian mason and architect Paolo della Stella who initially, in 1547, made it in model form, probably after a plan by an important Italian architect. Stella also brought with him from northern Italy models of fine ornamental and figural reliefs with ancient motifs, and he applied them to the arcade walls. This set of Renaissance reliefs covering the walls is one of the biggest in this country. Giovanni Maria and Giovanni Domenico della Stella also contributed to this important architectural work.

The building is characterized by a typical airy arcade carried by tall columns with Ionic capitals, and by rich reliefs in the corners and on the balustrades of the gallery. The windows and doors comply with the theories of Sebastian Serlio, a contemporary theoretician of architecture whose book was published in 1537. The palace, which has an excellent layout and fine architectural details, was paid for by the Bohemian Chamber and constructed by Italian architects, namely Giovanni Spazio and later, as of 1538, by Giovanni Mario Aostalli del Pambio and Giovanni Lucchese. For fourteen years, until his death in 1552, Paolo della Stella conducted construction work, which was often interrupted due to a lack of money. The ground floor with the arcades was completed at that time. The construction was also directed for some time by Hans Tirol who started building the upper floor. In 1555, however, the construction was again interrupted, as it had been many times before, particularly after the great fire in Prague of 1541. Before Ferdinand I could realize his major plans, the fire destroyed a great part of the town as well as of the Castle, and the construction had to be interrupted for many years. It was also at that time that Ferdinand I left Prague and the country and his son Ferdinand of Tirol was appointed governor.

Between 1557 and 1563, the new Castle architect Bonifaz Wohlmut completed the construction of the upper floor and surrounded the structure with a beautiful arched gallery. The final form probably did not fully correspond to the original plan, as the walls in the upper part of the palace were changed. To complete the construction, a unique timber centering of 10 m span was used. An original and unusual roof in the form of an upturned ship's keel was created which is a strong feature of the skyline of the Castle. The interiors of the palace, which included a dancing-hall and a gallery on the upper floor and private rooms on the ground floor, were completed between 1561 and 1563.

At the same time, other facilities for the entertainment of the court in the vicinity of the pleasure palace were constructed: a ball-game court was built between 1563 and 1568 on the transverse axis of the garden, and a field for ball-games was created between the Court and the Belvedere, as well as a maze in the rear part of the garden, a tiltyard in what is now Chotek Park, and a pheasantry with an aviary.

Royal Summer Palace

In 1648, Swedish soldiers destroyed and plundered the rich interiors of the palace which had been much loved by Emperor Rudolph II. However, far worse times came for this beautiful building under Joseph II who converted it into a military laboratory.

The current appearance of the Royal Garden is due to the changes that took place here in the Baroque period. In 1757, the garden was reshaped in the French style and later, in the 19th century the original concept weakened due to the tall trees, and the garden was looking more like a natural landscape. The east part of the garden was converted in the 1830s into an English park called Chotek Garden after its founder.

The pleasure palace was renovated and restored in 1845—1846 as new ceremonial rooms were needed in the Castle. The work was directed by Bernard Grueber who introduced some changes in the layout by making a ceremonial room in the north part with a wide two-flight staircase and by adapting the upper floor for exhibitions. The changes made by Grueber were fully in the neo-Classical spirit and were particularly harmful to the interiors of the palace. Later, between 1851 and 1865, the hall on the upper floor was decorated with fourteen wall-paintings after sketches made by Christian Ruben, director of the Academy of Fine Arts in Prague. The individual paintings with motifs from Czech history were made by Ruben's pupils, particularly by Antonín Lhota, Karel Svoboda, Josef M. Trenkwald, Emil Laufer and Jan Thiele.

Another major renovation of the palace was carried out by Josip Plečnik from 1928 to 1930 in connection with a general renovation of the Castle in the recently founded Czechoslovak Republic. Plečnik made a coffered ceiling over Grueber's staircase. The renovation of the façades unfortunately affected the sandstone surface with rich figural and ornamental decoration due to the application of cement grout. The grout paint gave a unity of style for some time to the building, but brought about a disintegration of the stone. *Just before the Second World War, in 1938, Pavel Janák and the garden architect Otakar Fierlinger restored the giardinetto in front of the western façade of the palace. The four central square fields of the chessboard-like garden were conceived as a labyrinth with shaped boxtrees after an engraving made by Paul Vredeman de Vries.*

The most important renovation of the palace took place from 1953 to 1955 within the framework of a large-scale renovation and social reactivation of the large area to the north of the Castle. The general plan included also a renovation and adaptation of the Ball-Game Court (see page 125) and of the Riding-School (see page 87). A technical survey of the palace disclosed many defects in the structure that were due to insufficient waterproofing of the gallery over the arcades. The greatest defects were found in the Ionic columns of the arcade that were overloaded with the weight of the gallery, and in the roof truss as well as in the copper roof.

The renovation plan was prepared by Pavel Janák in collaboration with Bedřich Hacar and Ladislav Nováček, who dealt with the technical aspects. By means of a sophisticated system of reinforced concrete structural elements it was possible for more of the weight of the gallery to be born by the massive inner walls. The ceiling and the "donkey-back" truss had to be reinforced and the roofing replaced. Thus, a basis for the subsequent restoration of the outer walls was created. The grout layers were removed, the imperfections sealed, the surface restored, and the interiors renovated.

The Renaissance garden in front of the west arcade was redeveloped and the Singing Fountain by Master Jaroš was restored. As a result, "the most beautiful piece of Renaissance architecture north of the Alps" was saved and Prague acquired attractive rooms for exhibitions of painting, sculpture, graphic and decorative art.

The great fire that in June 1541 destroyed the Lesser Quarter and quickly spread to the Castle and to Hradčany District also damaged the Cathedral. The unique vaulting of the Vladislav Hall resisted the fire; however, many buildings in the Castle as well as in Hradčany and the Lesser Quarter were destroyed. The disaster, on the other hand, facilitated the advent of Renaissance architecture.

In the first years after the fire, the fortification system of the Castle was repaired and the recently built wooden bridge (later known as "Prašný", i.e., Powder Bridge) was restored. It stood on stone piers and linked the Castle with the new Royal Garden. At the same time, the ruins of destroyed houses in the main courtyard (now Third Courtyard) were removed; the rubble was used to level the steep slope where now the garden called "Na valech" (On the Ramparts) is, and to raise the ground level in some parts of Kampa Island, which could be easily reached from the Castle. The Third Courtyard was then restored and new houses were built around it.

In connection with the large-scale building activity in the Castle a new construction office was established here whose main task consisted in renovating the Vladislav Hall and the adjoining Old Diet Hall. Reconstruction started in 1559 and four years later the room was vaulted by Bonifaz Wohlmut. Its Gothic-style arches were already quite new in conception and were more or less purely decorative. In the hall a marble-hewn Renaissance cathedra for the Chief Scribe was placed.

The Cathedral was repaired, too, and was given a new roof truss covered with copper. The renovation of the tower, however, required much more time and only later, after twenty years, was it crowned with a new Renaissance cupola. The supporting pillars at the corners of the tower were capped with octagonal turrets, which increased the beauty of the superstructure.

Over a short period a music gallery was built that in 1557 closed the west part of the Cathedral. The façade of Wohlmut's gallery was conceived as a two-floor Renaissance arcade, however, still covered with a Gothic vault. In 1925, when the Cathedral was completed, the arcade conceived in the spirit of Palladian Classicism was displaced to the northern transept.

Bonifaz Wohlmut respected the wish of his clients and made vaults still in the late Gothic style, as in the Old Diet Hall.

The scope and the rate of Wohlmut's work in the Castle show how much creative energy he had and how much authority he enjoyed. His last building, with a very sophisticated plan, was the Great Ball-Game Court, which was completed in 1568 and was a large, 14 m high building containing a hall and covered by a tunnel vault with lunettes. Ball-games were very popular among the aristocracy at that time and such buildings were often constructed. The Ball-Game Court is a rectangular 60 m long building opposite the Castle, and its south wall, which was made rhythmical by massive buttresses, faces the Stag Moat while the arcades on the other side open into the Royal Garden. The northern arcaded façade is articulated by tall Palladian sandstone columns whose roughness contrasts with the fine sgraffiti on the surface between them. The Ball-Game Court was very little used, and was therefore in 1723 converted into stables and later into a military storehouse.

A renovation of the Ball-Game Court, whose excellent Renaissance architecture had long not been recognized, began in 1946. Due to its location and foundation on a thick loess layer, to the lack of maintenance and to insufficient use, the building was slowly settling, the foundations and the longer walls cracked, and finally the tunnel vault with lunettes collapsed.

The first public interest in the building was shown early this century. However, the main reason was not the architecture, but the valuable sgraffiti. In 1917—1918, their first restoration took place and a method was applied which at that time was considered extremely effective, but which proved very harmful to many buildings. In 1925, parts of the masonry, particularly the cornices and entablatures were perfectly restored and the building was given a new wooden roof truss. However, the other work planned inside could not be realized. All the work was destroyed in May 1945 when retreating German soldiers set the Court on fire and the provisional wooden ceiling and truss burned. Fortunately, the outer architecture was not much damaged.

Soon after the war renovation work started. Bedřich Hacar and Ladislav Nováček carried out a structural analysis, Quido Záruba did a geological analysis of the subsoil and the technical criteria for renovation were formulated. Work to make the building structurally sound started in autumn 1946. Pavel Janák, the Castle architect, was charged with the renovation project and with planning its future function. In order to provide ceremonial rooms here, it was necessary to introduce a number of changes and modifications to the structure and form of the building, the most important being a new ceiling separating the lower storey with the service rooms from the ceremonial rooms covered with a new reinforced concrete shell replacing the ori-

The Castle in the Renaissance

a) **Ball-Game Hall**
b) **Renaissance cupola of St. Vitus' Cathedral**
c) **transition from Gothic to Renaissance: Gothic ribs on the south Renaissance pilaster** (Old Diet Hall)
d) **Renaissance tribune, Old Diet Hall**
e) **Wohlmut's gallery in St. Vitus' Cathedral**

ginal vault. The original height of 14 metres was thus divided into 9 and 5 metres, and there was also a new layout in the ground plan: the 60 m long building now had a 40 m long main central part and two end rooms 10 by 10 m each that were initially without lighting. The open arches of the north arcade on the wall facing the garden received new large windows made of steel and wood, with leaded glass. Similar windows were made in the gable walls to illuminate the flanking rooms. The building was equipped with a reinforced concrete roof truss covered with pantiles; at the corners, ornamental gargoyles were installed projecting from the new roof gutters. The ceremonial rooms were given new diagonal, chequered marble pavings, and 18th cen-tury chandeliers from the Castle Depository were installed here. On the south wall, Janák hanged six Brussels tapestries from a 17th century tapestry cycle called Antony and Cleopatra. After the 1952 renovation of the building the sgraffiti were restored and fixed by Josef Wagner.

The renovation of the Ball-Game Court proves the high standard of ancient building conservation in Czechoslovakia in the first years after the war and, in particular, the skill of Pavel Janák.

A further restoration and stabilization of the unique sgraffiti was made in 1972—1973 by the sculptors František Lahoda and Miroslav Kolář. The architectural elements were restored by the cooperative Štuko.

Hvězda Hunting Lodge

Where the hunting lodge "Hvězda" (which means Star) now stands there was once a wood called Malejov that since the 10th century had belonged to Strahov Abbey. In 1574, King Ferdinand I decided to have his game park here, and purchased the wood. From 1541 to 1543, a wall around the wood was built, with two gates: the Břevnov Gate and the Liboc Gate.

As of the early 16th century many country houses and summer palaces were built, the most beautiful certainly being the Royal Summer Palace (Belvedere) in the Castle of Prague. In 1555, before it was completed, the construction of another palace, a hunting lodge in the Břevnov Game Park started. The palace was planned by Ferdinand of Tyrol, son of King Ferdinand I and Imperial Governor of Bohemia. He also suggested the unusual ground plan in the form of a six-pointed star after which the palace was named.

With the appointment of Ferdinand of Tyrol as the country's governor, and after his arrival in Prague, both the quantity and quality of construction changed and a new stage in the development of the Castle and its surroundings started. The Hvězda Palace, designed by this cultivated dilettante, was built from 1555 to 1557 by the Prague Court architects Giovanni M. Aostalli and Giovanni Lucchese under the guidance of the Court architect Hans Tirol and later Bonifaz Wohlmut.

The striking feature of the building is the centralized plan in the form of a six-pointed star. It complies with the Renaissance principle of having a centralized structure above a regular geometric figure. The building originally had a conical roof that in the 17th century was replaced by an onion-like cupola with a lantern, and at the end of the 18th century by a low tent roof. Bonifaz Wohlmut later built here a long sala terrena and surrounded the complex with a wall with bastions, which had not been planned by the Governor.

The interior of the palace had a richly articulated layout with architectural detailing. On the first floor, very luxurious private rooms in the form of elongated rhombuses, with mirrors and rich stuccowork were built and a banqueting hall on the second. The vaults are decorated with stuccowork, with reliefs on motifs from ancient mythology. The stuccowork was made by unknown Italian masters over four years, and is an extremely valuable example of Renaissance art. One of the plasterers was probably the Arch-

Hvězda Hunting Lodge

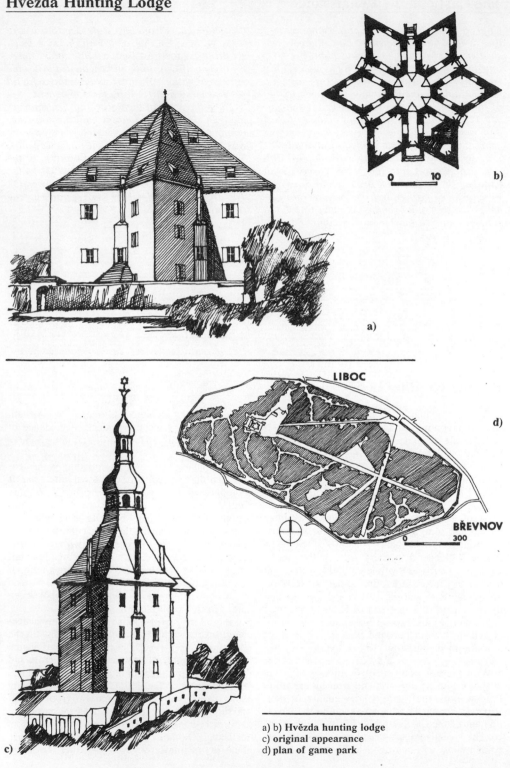

a) b) **Hvězda hunting lodge**
c) **original appearance**
d) **plan of game park**

LIBOC

BŘEVNOV

duke's plasterer G. A. Brocco. The stuccowork was used instead of complicated and more costly stone rib decoration.

After the 1620 Battle of White Mountain the palace and the large game park fell into disrepair, and until the mid-18th century foreign armies often camped here. Under Joseph II a powder magazine was here for many years. The desolate palace had to wait a long time for its renovation. Only after 1918, and particularly after 1945 could it be renovated and White Mountain with the game park and the palace was declared a national monument.

The hunting lodge lost its function after the death of Ferdinand. Due to its location far away from the social focus and to its unusual centrally-planned ornamental layout that could only with difficulty be adapted to new functions, it was never altered and—apart from the two occasions when the roof was replaced—it survived until 1949 in its original form.

When a new use for the monument was discussed with the aim of ensuring its long physical and cultural preservation, it was decided to make it a museum to Alois Jirásek, a writer who very well described the period of national decline that had started with the tragic Battle of White Mountain. Pavel Janák, who at that time was working on the renovation of the Ball-Game Court at the Castle, was invited to prepare the renovation project. The plan was realized from 1949 to 1951, when the museum was opened. Janák's unaffected plain approach to the renovation and to the installation of the museum showed his excellent understanding of historical architecture and the authenticity of the work. The palace was restored with its inner simplicity and outer austerity; a new artistic form was only applied in the new wooden dome surmounting the hall on the second floor. The architecture of the building was very deeply respected, and the necessary administrative rooms and services, including a transformer station were located outside the palace in new buildings near the enclosure wall. Thus, both the exterior and the interior of the palace avoided any apparent modern alteration. The renovation is an example of the due respect of the architect for a historic architecture, and can be regarded as the beginning of a new attitude to its use. In 1964, the exhibition here was extended, and a museum to the national painter Mikoláš Aleš was also installed here.

Bohemian Renaissance

Because of the great fire in the Lesser Quarter and Hradčany in 1541 more houses in the Renaissance style were built there than on the right bank of the river.

The new style was imported by Italian architects, masons, bricklayers and plasterers who came to Prague and settled here. They formed a colony in Prague, traces of which still exist in some names, for instance Vlašská (= Italian) Street, Vlašský (= Italian) Hospital, or Vlašská (= Italian) Chapel at the Clementinum Building. However, their new, mainly Gothic environment influenced them strongly; they adapted themselves to and adopted the local way of life as well as the local architectural traditions. On the other hand, local architects, bricklayers and masons learned much from the Italian masters. As a result, some compromises were made in the construction of new palaces inspired by the Italian example, and a typical Bohemian Renaissance style developed with tall brick gables, adorned by volutes and arches and articulated by cornices and pilasters. This solution was due to the narrow plots for tall houses with steep roofs.

This can be seen in the first palaces in Prague, such as Rožmberk Palace, Lobkovic Palace, or the Old Burgrave's House which is now the House of Czechoslovak Children. The Burgrave's House was built in the reign of Přemysl Otakar II. The Gothic house was destroyed in the 1541 fire, and in its place Giovanni Ventura constructed in 1555—1556 a new house with a staircase turret and Renaissance gables, and with a façade decorated with simple sgraffiti.

However, among the earliest works paving the way to the Bohemian Renaissance style were the east (1546) and west gables of the Vladislav

Bohemian Renaissance

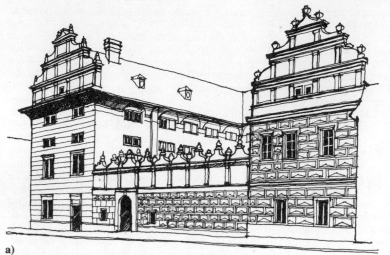

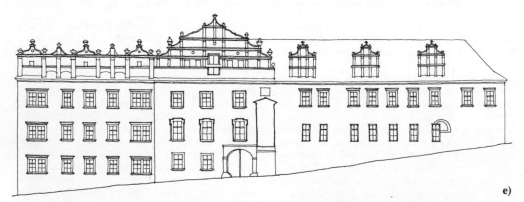

a) Schwarzenberg Palace
b) original east gable of Vladislav Hall—reconstruction
c) Burgrave's House

d) north façade of the former Rožmberk Palace in the Castle—reconstruction of original appearance
e) palace of the Lords of Hradec, No. 193—north façade facing the New Castle Steps

Palace in Prague Castle. The first noble house conceived in this style was that of the Rožmberk Family in Jiřská Street. On the site of the old Rožmberk House destroyed in the Castle fire, a palace was constructed from 1545 to 1573 by Giovanni Fontana (?) and Ulrico Aostalli for Vilém of Rožmberk, which had the oldest arcaded courtyard in Prague. It had many volute gables resembling those of the neighbouring Royal Palace that were built at the same time (1545—1563).

At the same time (1555—1576), Jan of Lobkovic, the Chief Burgrave of Prague, also constructed his monumental palace in front of the Castle on Hradčany Square. The huge building, replacing four earlier noble houses, was constructed by Agostino Galli. This is the most beautiful Renaissance palace in Prague, and was later called the Schwarzenberg Palace. It has a two-wing plan, a courtyard and a gate, and due to its prominent site on a cliff above the slope with the Castle has become an inseparable part of the Hradčany skyline. Its massive structure, articulated by rather small coupled Renaissance windows and covered with sgraffiti, was crowned by a large Central Italian lunette cornice and stepped gables. The painted coffered ceilings from the late 16th century have also survived.

The sgraffiti of the Schwarzenberg Palace on Hradčany Square were restored for the first time from 1871 to 1880 by Josef Schulz. In the present century, the palace housed the National Technical Museum which stayed here until a new building for it had been constructed on Letná Square. The Military Museum has been here since 1945, when the Germans had the collections from the Hospital for Disabled Soldiers (Invalidovna) in Karlín District brought here. During the uprising in May 1945 the palace was severely damaged and two years were needed to renovate its interiors. From 1955 to 1959 its façade was restored by Stanislav Vacek, the sgraffiti were completed and stabilized, the gallery above the Town-Hall Steps was restored and the palace was given a new roof.

In 1958, it was decided to make a House of Czechoslovak Children by adapting the former Burgrave's House. The first study made in 1960 by Josef Hlavatý of SURPMO showed that it was possible to adapt the house provided the neighbouring small Lobkovic House No. 7 was involved in the project. The adaptation started in 1962 according to a new plan and respected the original material and spatial relations between the two houses. Only the necessary connections were made in the enclosing wall and the front wall of the Burgrave's House. An outbuilding at the north wall of the Castle was pulled down as well as an interesting house with a hipped roof by the west wall of the courtyard. As a result, the courtyard of the house lost its original intimacy, but an impressive complex appeared.

The main entrance to the house is in a steel and glass hall in front of the house whose wings embrace a new atrium with a fountain in the middle.

The particular functions were solved with more or less respect for the historic building. On the one hand, there are excellent restorations, such as that of the only painted ceiling from the Rudolphinian era, or the cleaning of Romanesque masonry while, on the other hand, some modernizations were made that were insufficiently justified (particularly the entrance atrium or the Social Hall). The same applies to the interiors. In addition to some simple and variable forms suiting the children's mind there are rooms like museum galleries, with fine artistic decoration.

In spite of the above criticisms, the house is a good example of renovation of two buildings that in the recent history of the Castle had not been at the centre of public interest, which focused on the more attractive buildings. For the first time a building in the Castle had to serve a civic purpose, and a balance between the "official" and the "practical" aspects of the adaptation was sought.

Another important aspect of the renovation, which was completed in 1965, is the solution of technical problems. This is very well done, in terms of lighting, heating, craftmanship, etc. One action that should particularly be mentioned is the removal of the ceiling fresco representing Solomon's Judgment from the Court Room of the Burgrave's House and its installation in the Green Hall in front of the entrance to the Vladislav Hall.

Of Renaissance origin also is the former Lobkovic Palace, No. 3, opposite the Burgrave's House, with beautiful arcades in the inner courtyard. It has been renovated many times; the last rebuilding took place between 1810 and 1813, when it was rebuilt in the neo-Classical style by František Pavlíček, and then in the early 1860s. As of 1977 the palace has been adapted to house some departments of the National Museum, and in 1987 an exhibition called "Monuments of Our Past" was opened here.

Working Buildings

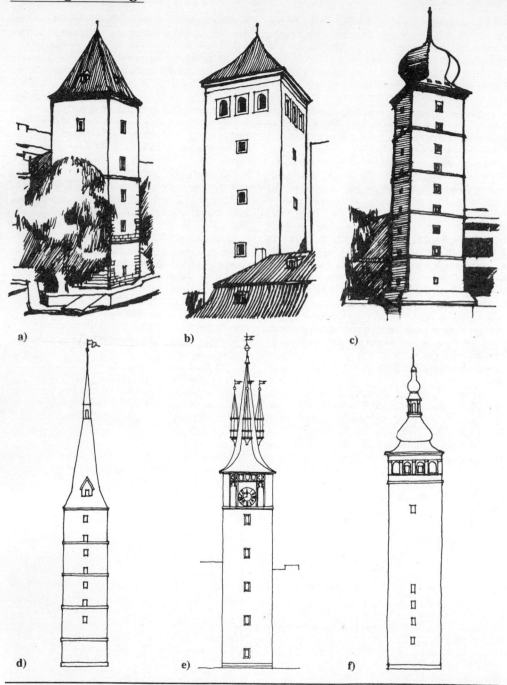

a) water tower, Lesser Quarter
b) lower water tower, New Town
c) water tower, New Town
d) water tower, New Town—original appearance
   (Gothic)

e) water tower, Old Town
f) water tower, Old Town—original appearance
   (Renaissance)

(94)

Renaissance Prague included, in addition to important palaces and middle-class house, also some interesting technical and functional structures, such as mills and water towers, which have contributed to the townscape of Prague since the Middle Ages.

Water-mills existed on the Vltava River as of the 10th century, and even in the 19th century there were still about fifty such mills in Prague, of all sizes. Two of the three mills on Kampa Island still have their mill-wheels. A typical feature of the island is the 8 m high wheel of the Grand Priory Mill dating from the 16th century. The other mill, called "Huťský", for some time belonged to the Renaissance humanist Viktorin Kornel of Všehrdy.

More dominant, however, have been the water towers dating from various periods. The oldest one, called Peter's Tower, stood near the mill at Charles Bridge, and burned down in 1425.

As the town grew and the number of malt houses, workshops and dwelling-houses increased, the consumption of water increased, too, particularly as of the 15th century, as well as the number of water works. The Old Town Waterworks at Charles Bridge, built in 1489, ranks among the oldest plants of this type in Europe. It supplied water from the Vltava to public fountains and houses in the Old Town. Later, probably around 1495, a New Town waterworks was built under Zderaz, and was called "Šítkovská". In 1591, it was restored, as it had been destroyed in 1588 by a fire, together with a number or neighbouring mills. Another renovation took place in 1651. In 1648, the masonry was damaged by Swedish guns, a fire destroyed the roof and the truss. Its tall tower with a Baroque cupola can now be seen next to the Mánes Building which was built in 1930 on the site of the earlier Šítkovské Mills demolished in 1928. It is known, however, that the local mills were mentioned as early as the 12th century, as a property of Vyšehrad Chapter. Water was distributed from the New Town waterworks by gravity to public fountains in both towns of Prague.

In Smíchov District, on the left bank of the Vltava, a water tower belonging to the Lesser Quarter was built in 1562. It is known as "Petržilkovská", after the miller Jan Petržilka who built a mill below the tower in 1483. The tower supplied Vltava water to all fountains in the Lesser Quarter.

In 1602, a tall tower was built in Petrská Quarter. Its current form dates from 1658. The tower is the tallest of all the water works in Prague, and was also the most expensive. It stands near the New Mills, which have been so called since the early 14th century, i.e., before the New Town of Prague was founded. The mills were demolished in 1916. This lower waterworks of the New Town in the vicinity of Šverma Bridge is now far from the river, with which it was once closely linked. Its isolation is due to large river deposits over the centuries. For the same reason several small islands in the river here gradually increased in size and eventually joined to form one large island in the 18th century, now called Slovanský Island which was later, after the 1784 flood, surrounded with an embankment and planted with trees.

The three oldest water towers mentioned above supplied Vltava water to the town until 1912, and now rank among Prague's important historic sights.

Another remarkable technical work, dating from the Rudophinian era should be mentioned here: the tunnel under Letná Square built from 1581 to 1593 to supply water to a new pond in the Royal Game Park. The tunnel, which is 3.5 m wide, 2.2 m high and about 1 km long was driven with much difficulty and initially had wooden supports; in the 18th century the tunnel was lined with brick. It begins at the former Novomlýnský (New Mill) weir (Captain Jaroš Embankment) and ends in the former game park. This remarkable work still serves its original function, being in a relatively good condition. Protection measures are now being prepared to preserve this technical monument.

Technical constructions were included in the ancient building conservation system rather late and their value was therefore mostly considered from the point of view of their practical usefulness. Technically and culturally obsolete structures and installations such as mills, bridges, weirs, etc., were replaced or demolished without any feeling of regret.

A characteristic feature of Kampa Island in the Lesser Quarter is the Grand Priory (Velkopřevorský) Mill on the Čertovka, which is a branch of the Vltava River enclosing the picturesque island. The mill, which has not been working for decades, is maintained and preserved, as it is an important part of the surroundings of Charles Bridge. Its large waterwheel was restored in the 1960s, and now a renovation of the large building is taking place with the aim of adapting it to the needs of Slavoj Vyšehrad Sports Club according to a project prepared by SURPMO. The other two mills on the Čertovka, which are less prominent, will be renovated later.

Water towers constitute another group of technical monuments. Their function is now per-

formed by modern water-supply systems, but they are being renovated, as they are important elements in the Prague skyline. The tower which adjoins the Mánes Building was partly restored in the late 1960s when its cupola received a new copper cladding. The same was done at the Petr-žilkovská Water Tower on the opposite bank of the Vltava. The Novomlýnská Tower and the remaining part of the mill are still awaiting restoration and a new use, in spite of the 1964 contest which resulted in a suggestion to incorporate them into a new hotel here. So far, however, the plan has not been realized.

To conclude this chapter, the most important renovation in this field should be mentioned: the restoration of a group of Old Town mills and waterworks that was carried out from 1972 to 1980. The historic group of mills at Novotného lávka (bridge) have been rebuilt many times. After a disastrous fire in 1848 caused by the Imperial artillery, commanded by General Windisch-grätz, the buildings were rebuilt for other purposes. The malt mill (malt house) was rebuilt according to plans by Josef Bělský, and in 1928 it was converted Into municipal baths. The build-

ings called Šejdovny (Small and Great) and incorporating the water tower changed hands many times and were completely rebuilt in 1935—1936. Another house here, No. 250, to the left of the tower, was called "Hever", and was restored after the fire and rebuilt in 1878. The buildings are supported by piles of different depth. Due to years of erosion, the foundation walls of the canals were damaged, water washed away the watercourse and exposed the pile ends. Due to decay some parts of the masonry sank and cracked, and after 1967 parts of the complex collapsed. After a number of studies and consultations it was decided to renovate the houses and adapt them for the House of Technology. The renovation plan was prepared by Josef Švastal and a team of workers who, together with the building company "Vodní stavby", confronted this technically very difficult and interesting task. As a result, an extremely valuable and picturesque complex could be saved. It is generally known as Novotného lávka and now houses an important scientific and technical centre that for many years has been organizing both scientific and cultural events.

Middle-Class Houses   RENAISSANCE ARCHITECTURE

How the Renaissance style was applied in the towns of Prague can still be seen in many middle-class houses and, of course, in the town-halls, which rank among the most important buildings here.

The town called Hradčany built a Renaissance town-hall from 1598 to 1604, which was quite small, but decorated with sgraffiti and beautiful gables with volutes. The building (1/1973, Loretánská Street) is known to have already been standing in 1498. It was one of the few houses at Hradčany that were not struck by the great fire of the Castle in 1541. Its current form dates from the years 1602—1604, the interiors were renovated in the 18th century. Now it is a dwelling-house.

In the Lesser Quarter of Prague a new town-hall was built from 1617 to 1719 by Giovanni Filippi. The original late Renaissance house has survived in the façade in Letenská Street, where-

as the wall facing Malostranské (Lesser Quarter) Square lost its towers during a renovation in the latter half of the 19th century. The town-hall of the Lesser Quarter was used for its original purpose until 1784.

Some time before 1520, the town-hall of the Old Town was given a beautiful window in the Renaissance style, and also the town-hall of the New Town was rebuilt in the same style in two stages. A vista of Prague from 1662 shows the Renaissance appearance of the Lesser Quarter of Prague, whose central market-place was surrounded by houses with arched gables and attics. Also houses at both ends of what is now Nerudova Street had Renaissance gables. We can get an idea of what they looked like by looking at the gables of Týnská School, No. 14/604, Old Town Square, or at the Renaissance double house of a unique Venetian type in Husova Street that has been renovated

Middle-Class Houses

a) **Town-Hall, Hradčany**
b) **Town-Hall, window, Old Town**
c) d) **house U zlatého stromu, No. 729, Dlouhá Street**
d) **Tynská School, gable, No. 603**
f) **gable of house No. 229, Husova Street**

and now houses the Central Bohemian Gallery.

However, the bearing walls and the interiors of the above house were still Gothic and the Renaissance style was just applied to the new façades—decorated with geometrical and figural sgraffiti, coupled Renaissance windows and portals, and exceptionally with lunette cornices, as well as volute (Lombardian type) and arched (Venetian type) gables—and to the arcaded courtyards.

Some of the earliest sgraffiti (1566) have survived on the façade of the house No. 18/213, Nerudova Street, called St. John of Nepomuk. Under the Renaissance exterior of this middle-class house with rich sgraffiti the Gothic core of the house has survived which, however, was later rebuilt in the Baroque and neo-Classical style. The small arcaded courtyard of the house No. 1/745 called "U dvou zlatých medvědů" (At the Two Golden Bears), Kožná Street, Old Town, was built in 1555 and was probably inspired by the noble houses. The rich Granovský House in Týnský Dvůr also had arcades as early as 1560. There is also a two-storey arcaded courtyard of a former patrician merchant's house "U zlatého stromu" (At the Golden Tree) No. 37/729, Dlouhá Street, dating back to 1608, which was some time later altered by Mayor Krocín. The house has not changed too much since, but it was given a new façade in the 1870s and was heightened in 1927. The houses Nos. 463 (Teufel House) and 465 ("U koruny", i.e., At the Crown) built around 1615 to plans by some important architects rank among the most splendid houses. Also worth mention are the houses "U Brunclíka", No. 5/510, Havelská Street and "U minuty" (At the Minute) on the Old Town Square, as well as the houses Nos. 261, 265 and 266 on Lesser Quarter Square (Malostranské náměstí).

Prague became a genuine Renaissance town in the reign of Emperor Rudolph II (1576—1611). Construction activity at that time concentrated in the Lesser Quarter, Hradčany, and Pohořelec.

The country's metropolis had at that time some sixty thousand inhabitants and 3,300 houses. The imperial seat and court attracted many foreigners. Middle-class houses were therefore often adapted to accommodate tenants. Vacant plots and courtyards were built-up and the territory of the town was densely filled-in.

Late Renaissance

The reign of Rudolph II was the last chapter of the Renaissance for Prague and the Castle. The Castle was an important centre of science and the arts in the Empire, Prague had fine architecture and was an important European town. The Emperor was not only a passionate collector of works of art, but also an enthusiastic builder. His activity in the Castle crowned the development of Renaissance architecture in Bohemia.

When Rudolph II came to power, Ulrico Aostalli was still working in the Castle. He realized plans by other architects, such as B. Wohlmut and G. Gargiolli, but he was also a good technician and carried out many remarkable projects. In 1591, Giovanni Gargiolli of Florence was appointed Imperial Architect; he worked in Prague from 1586 to 1599. There were also many artists from the Netherlands and Germany, and through them the northern Renaissance reached this country, with sculptural forms different from the picturesque Italian and Bohemian Renaissance. An excellent example of the style is the Royal Mausoleum in St. Vitus' Cathedral by the Dutch sculptor Alexander Collin. Around 1600, Giovanni M. Filippi, an architect oriented towards Rome, was called to Rudolph's court and stayed here until 1616.

The first late Renaissance building here was constructed on Hradčany Square. It was the Martinic Palace, built in 1583. The first churches in the Renaissance style were also built here; however, they were not many. In 1611, German Lutherans built their church consecrated to St. Saviour in Dušní Street in the Old Town. In 1626, after the defeat of the anti-Habsburg rebellion, the church passed over into the hands of the Pauline monks in the neighbouring monastery, which was connected with the church by means of a covered passage. The monastery was closed in 1784 and the church was converted into a storeroom of the mint placed in the former monastery (1689) by Paul I. Bayer. The church was reconsecrated in 1863 and has been used since by the Evangelists. The church of the Czech Brethren (SS. Simon and Judah) in the Old Town, built between 1615 and 1620, was in-

Late Renaissance

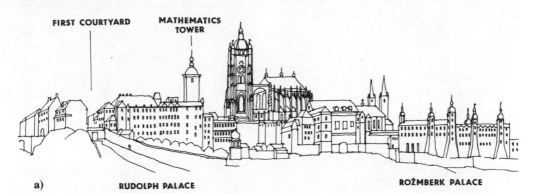

a)

FIRST COURTYARD **MATHEMATICS TOWER**

RUDOLPH PALACE   **ROŽMBERK PALACE**

b)

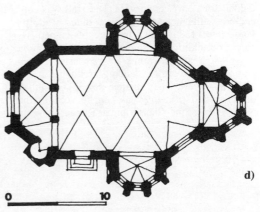

c)

d)

a) **Prague Castle in 1606** (according to van den Bosch)
b) **west part of the Castle (1755):** 1 Rudolph Palace,
2 Paradise Garden, 3 Empress' Palace, 4 Maxmilian's
kitchen, 5 Matthias Gate, 6 White Tower, 7 former
Mathematics Tower, 8 Rudolph Stable with the
Spanish Hall upstairs, 9 Ferdinand I's Stable, 10 Armoury, 11 Chief Chamberlain's House, 12 kitchen,
13 royal construction office, 14 wooden bridge to
Hradčany, 15 steps to the Lesser Quarter
c) d) **St. Roche's Church, Strahov**

tended as a chapel and replaced an earlier chapel with the same consecration that had existed here since 1357 at the latest. After 1620, the church was adapted to the new needs, and rebuilt in the Baroque style in the first half of the 18th century. It became part of the monastery and the hospital of the Brothers of Mercy who came here after 1620.

All these churches, including St. Roche's Church on Strahov Hill which is an excellent example of Rudolphinian architecture built from 1602 to 1612 by the Emperor to thank God for preventing the plague of 1599 from reaching the country, show a remarkable combination of Gothic and Renaissance features. These last religious buildings built in Prague prior to the 1620 defeat of the Bohemian Estates prove the strong tradition of the Gothic in Bohemia and Moravia which continued until the Baroque era. Under Rudolph II the Castle was extended westwards, towards Hradčany. The old Royal Palace was used by the court offices while the Emperor lived in a new long palace in the south wing facing the town. A garden called The Paradise was created in front of the palace replacing the former vineyards here. After 1920, the garden was restored by Josip Plečnik and was given its current form.

A new northern palace was built from 1584 to 1606 with two large halls, namely the Rudolph Gallery, which was originally called the New Hall, and the Spanish Hall above the old and the new stables. Giovanni Gargioli worked here as Court architect. In 1602, Giovanni M. Filippi was appointed Imperial Chief Architect and from 1602 to 1606 he constructed the large almost fifty-metre long Spanish Hall which was intended for court ceremonies. The Hall was connected with the neighbouring older Rudolph Gallery of 1589—1593. In spite of its neo-Baroque rebuilding the Spanish Hall ranks among the most beautiful rooms in the Castle. Filippi and Gargioli were the leading architects at the Imperial Court. They further developed Italian patterns and principles, as can be seen in the New Stables, the Church of St. Roche, the gate of the Imperial Palace, and also the Matthias Gate.

The Church of SS. Simon and Judah remained part of the hospital called "Na Františku" until the end of the Second World War. Then, its future social function was discussed. Its close links with the hospital and the raising of the ground level after the demolition of Josefov considerably complicated any renovation plans. Studies were prepared envisaging a concert and recording studio for Panton Music Publishing House, the last study being prepared in 1984 by Josef Hlavatý. So far, however, only a superficial renovation has been carried out. The church now houses the depository of the Museum of Prague.

The last stage of the renovation of Strahov Abbey also included St. Roche's Church, which was converted into an exhibition hall called Musaion, where many outstanding exhibitions have already taken place, notably the exhibition of decorative glass and of glass sculptures.

Renovation work is concentrating on the late Renaissance buildings in the Castle, which have been systematically restored as part of the Castle renovation plan. First we should mention the Spanish Hall, which underwent a "Second Baroque" renovation between the years 1865 and 1868. In the early 1970s, the hall was completely restored by the cooperatives Štuko and Umělecká řemesla. Under the hall are the Rudolph Stables, and next to it is the Rudolph Gallery, which was converted in 1965 into the beautiful Castle Gallery by František Cubr and Josef Hrubý. They showed a good understanding of the archaeological findings and the remains of the Church of Our Lady, which have been incorporated in the renovation.

Between 1918 and 1938, many rooms in the adjoining wing were renovated and the Matthias Gate was restored. For more information see the Theresian Renovation of the Castle (page 173). Among the major late Renaissance buildings the Michna Palace (now Tyrš House) is particularly worth note. The palace is described in a special chapter (see page 64).

Architectural Details

a)

b)

c)

d)

e)

f)

a) window, north façade of the Vladislav Hall
b) portal of Ungelt, No. 659
c) portal of Old Diet Hall, the Castle
d) portal of the palace of the Mettychs of Čečov, No. 490, Velkopřevorské Square
e) St. George's basilica, south portal
f) portal of the house U dvou medvědů, No. 475, Kožná Street

(101)

Architectural Details

The first Renaissance elements applied in Prague were architectural details, used quite early, in the late Gothic period, apparently as a result of the stylistic exhaustion of Gothic architecture after thriving for centuries in Prague.

Renaissance windows and portals used in the late Gothic Vladislav Hall heralded the new style. This style was applied by Benedikt Rieth (Rejt) around 1500 to the portal of the Riders' Steps as well as to that of St. George's Church (1520). Through Rieth's workshop the new portal set a precedent and was soon applied to the façade of many buildings in Prague, such as the town-hall of the New Town (1526) and the middle-class house called "U jednorožce" (At the Unicorn) on Old Town Square (No. 17/551).

With the contribution of Italian masters to the Summer Palace (Belvedere) in the Royal Garden, the isolated Renaissance elements became generally applied. The theoreticians of the Italian Renaissance, following ancient precedents, were publishing treatises which included patterns of architectural details that were then applied or used as inspiration in countries on the other side of the Alps. Due to the availability of information about Italian 15th century Renaissance portals many beautiful portals were built in Prague that enriched many, often plain, façades. A very good example of this is the portal of the former Melantrich House in the Old Town dating from 1563. The house, which was one of the most important Renaissance buildings here, was demolished in 1895. Fortunately, its portal has been saved and can now be seen in the back façade of the Museum of Prague.

Quite typical in Prague was a type of massive arched portal, with plain or embossed blocks both in the arch and on the sides. One of the earliest portals of this type (from 1560) has survived in Ungelt, No. 639, in the Old Town.

Prague's portals were mostly influenced by the northern Renaissance, for instance that of Hrzán Palace, once the House of the Mettychs of Čečov at Velkopřevorské (Grand Prior's) Square, Lesser Quarter of Prague (1586), and the latest of them, that of the house called "U pěti korun" (At the Five Crowns), No. 11/465, Melantrichova Street, Old Town, dating from 1615, which exhibit traces of the Dutch influence. The most ornamented of all the portals in Prague is that of the house "U dvou medvědů" (At the Two Bears), No. 1/475, Kožná Street, Old Town, dating from about 1580 and combining both the Dutch and the Italian elements.

In the early 17th century the above Dutch elements were eliminated by a new wave of Italian influence. Thus, the spirit of the Italian late Renaissance was applied by a local master following the available examples to the portal of the Old Magistrate's House, No. 12/404, Rytířská Street, Old Town, which once was the seat of the Royal Magistrate of the Old Town.

Baroque Architecture

The name Baroque comes from the Italian word "barocco", which means strange, peculiar, and referred to deviations from the then new Renaissance style in some architectural works of the late 16th century. In the 17th and 18th centuries the Baroque was a dominant style in Europe. Its first traces reached Prague before 1620, and the style underwent three stages of development here. The early Baroque, which was sometimes called Jesuit, prevailed in Prague until the 1690s, and was replaced by the high Baroque that flourished here until the 1740s. Then, the late Baroque period came, whose last stage is called Rococo.

Generally speaking, the Baroque style shows two different trends: the Classical branch including French and Viennese Baroque, which was rather sober and rigorous, and the dynamic Italian branch, full of sensuality, sentiments and animation. The dynamic branch tended towards increasingly complex shapes and volumes, often through the interpenetration of different geometrical figures. The final effect is based on the alternation of convex and concave curves and surfaces, a new Renaissance sense of movement, increased tension between elements, the manipulation of light and shadow, and the effects of painting and plastic arts. Classical Baroque philosophy was based on the Renaissance, whose principles were further developed theoretically and practically. In spite of their contradictory nature, both trends aimed to create monumental and dramatic spaces. In the 17th and 18th centuries, both trends co-existed simultaneously, alternately coming into and going out of fashion.

Baroque architecture continued to apply previous construction technologies. Bricks bonded with mortar were typically used. A massive masonry structure of brick, stone, or both, coated with a thick layer of plaster was the norm. Plaster was richly decorated with architectural elements, moulded both on the inside and outside of the building. Experienced plasterers developed a variety of architectural forms and details. An important architectural element was again the vault, which was however conceived in a new way. Various types of vault were used in the Baroque buildings, for instance the Bohemian vault, dome, tunnel vault with lunettes, cloister vault and groin vault. Baroque architects also often developed new vaults of intertwining type.

After the 1620 defeat of the Estates, a great deal of power came into the hands of the Catholics. As of 1627 only the Catholic faith was allowed in the country. The non-Catholics had to leave their public posts and offices and were no longer granted municipal rights. Those who refused to be converted were ordered to leave the country.

During the Thirty Years' War the appearance of Prague did not change very much, but the town lost a great part of its population. New, foreign nobles came here who had profited from the war, and the Jesuits came to power. At the same time, Prague Castle lost its status as a royal residence and became a secondary seat of the Habsburgs, a provincial town. The population was decreasing and many houses were abandoned as a result of considerable property changes after the 1620 defeat of the uprising. The beneficiaries purchased houses at very low prices, and municipal plots were combined so that very large new houses could be built. Prague was besieged in 1648 by the Swedish army, and the Habsburgs decided to make the town a major Baroque fortress. However, the town had to bear almost all the expenses related to the construction of large new defensive walls. Until the end of the 17th century, middle-class houses seemed very poor compared with the rich and sumptuous religious buildings. Only in the last decade of the 17th century did building activity in the town revive.

The arts started again to flourish in the town thanks to many outstanding artists who contributed to its new appearance, such as the architects Jean B. Mathey, Giovanni B. Alliprandi, Christoph Dientzenhofer, Giovanni Santini-Aichel, Kilian Ignaz Dientzenhofer, František Maxmilian Kaňka, the sculptors Matthias Bernard Braun, Ferdinand Maxmilian Brokof, the painters Petr Brandl, Václav Vavřinec Reiner, and other artists. This integration of the arts transformed the appearance of the town, and the quality of both its intimate and monumental spaces dramatically increased.

In addition to many palaces and gardens, a number of new churches were constructed in the Baroque style and many medieval churches were rebuilt. At the same time, the building activity of the middle-classes was increasing again, mostly within the framework of the old Gothic town plan.

After the death of Charles VI another war broke out, the War of Austrian Succession, which hit Prague again, as so many times before. The town was occupied in the years 1741 and

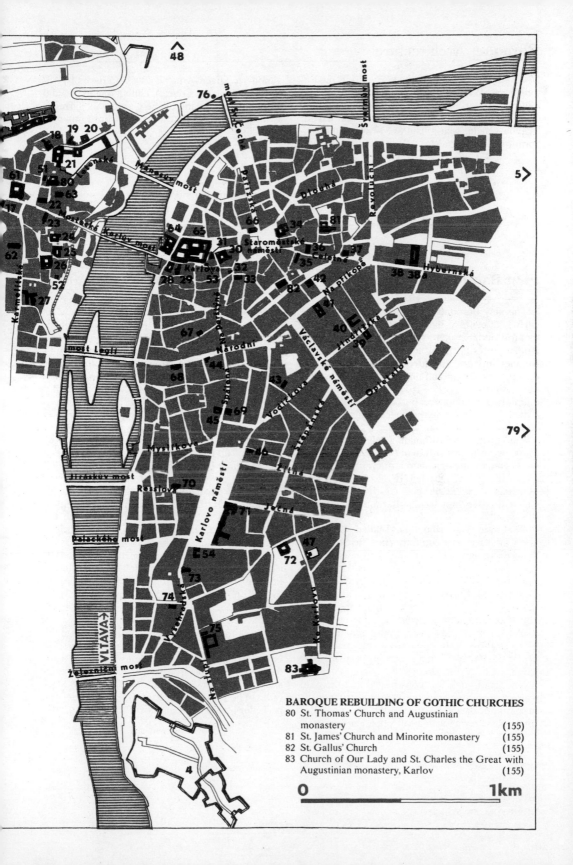

BAROQUE REBUILDING OF GOTHIC CHURCHES

80 St. Thomas' Church and Augustinian
    monastery (155)
81 St. James' Church and Minorite monastery (155)
82 St. Gallus' Church (155)
83 Church of Our Lady and St. Charles the Great with
    Augustinian monastery, Karlov (155)

0   **1km**

1742, and again besieged in 1757 during the Seven Years' War. All this brought devastation and caused irreparable damage to the city. Many houses were destroyed, as well as a great part of Prague Castle. Maria Theresa ordered the restoration of the Castle and its conversion into a modern palace. A project was prepared by Nicolo Paccassi, the Court Architect of Vienna, and the whole south side of the Castle was harmonized and given the late Baroque form known to us today.

First Baroque Buildings

The new Baroque style reached Prague in the early 17th century and was first applied to architectural details, such as gables and portals. The Roman pre-Baroque style, sometimes called Mannerism here, appeared in Prague at the end of Rudolph's reign and under his successor, Emperor Matthias (1612—1619). By 1620, the first buildings heralding the Baroque had been constructed, and the style then became deeply rooted here for a very long time.

Among the earliest buildings, dating from the 1590s, were the oval Italian (Vlašská) Chapel in the Clementinum, the church of German Lutherans in the Lesser Quarter (1611—1613), and the Matthias Gate at Prague Castle dated 1614, which was the first secular Baroque building in this country.

The gate was sometimes called Scamozzi Gate, as it was attributed to Vincente Scamozzi, a north Italian architect and theoretician who spent some time in Prague. Recent research, however, has shown that the gate was built by Giovanni M. Filippi as a new main entrance to the Castle above the ditch at Hradčany Square, and was originally incorporated in the Castle wall, with a rich gable bearing the Imperial coat-of-arms above it. In the 1760s a new renovation of the Castle was begun according to plans prepared by the Viennese architect Nicolo Paccassi. A new front wing was constructed and the gate was incorporated into the new construction. It lost its interior and was converted into a late Baroque passageway with a sail vault. Paccassi's lat-er neo-Classical construction framing the Matthias Gate further stressed its architectural qualities. The gate was probably based on the citadel gate in Mantua by Giulio Romano.

The Church of the Holy Trinity in the Lesser Quarter, which originally belonged to German Lutherans and whose architect was probably Giovanni M. Filippi, was similar in conception to the church in Rome with the same consecration by Domenico Fontana. It had a nave without aisles, lined with chapels, and its original façade faced Petřín Hill. Only its portal has survived and can now be seen in the new façade created in 1644, after the defeat of the Estates when the church was reorientated, renovated and reconsecrated to Our Lady the Victorious. The Emperor personally decided to give the church to the Carmelites, a Catholic order of Spanish origin.

The present-day early Baroque façade, completed in 1644, proves the importance of the Italian Classical Baroque in religious architecture in Prague. To make the church more accessible, two old houses were pulled down and a terrace with three steps in front of the main façade was built instead.

The church was intended to commemorate the victory of the Habsburgs over the country's Estates in 1620. The new façade as we know it today was paid for by Colonel Count Husmann and the Spanish General Don Baltassar de Marradas. The portal and the Matthias Gate set the precedent for many subsequent Baroque portals.

First Baroque Buildings

a)

b)

c)

d)

e)

a) **Matthias Gate**
b) **Vlašská (i.e., Italian) Chapel of the Clementinum**
c) d) e) **Church of Our Lady the Victorious**

Wallenstein Palace

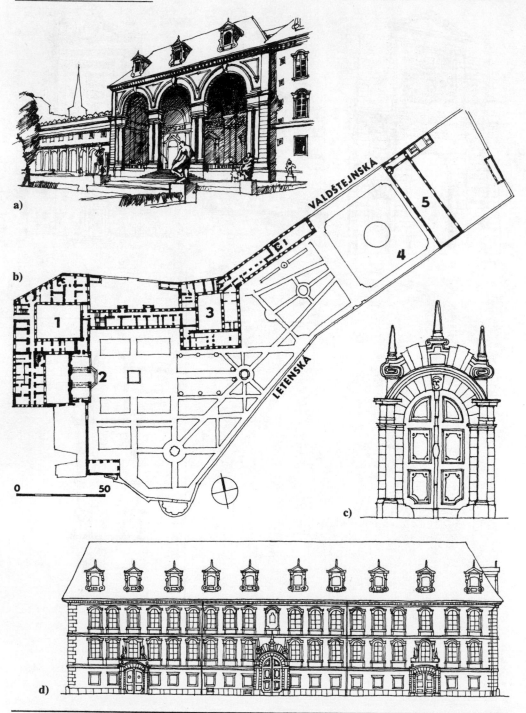

a) b) **Wallenstein Palace:** 1 main courtyard, 2 sala terrena, 3 stable, 4 pond, 5 riding-school

c) **main porch**
d) **façade on Valdštejn Square**

Wallenstein Palace

Two important figures who made their fortune from the war, Wallenstein (also known as Waldstein or, in Czech, Valdštejn) and Michna of Vacínov, built their palaces in Prague. The first, and also the largest, Baroque palace was the Wallenstein (Valdštejn) Palace which was built in the Lesser Quarter of Prague without any regard to the old buildings, streets and fortifications and without any regard to the original owners of the twenty-three houses, three gardens and the brickworks at Písecká Gate that had to be demolished to clear the space needed for its construction. Thus Wallenstein, in 1621 the Imperial Commander of Prague and in 1627 Duke of Frýdlant and Commander-in-Chief of the Imperial Army, dramatically changed the plan of the town and gave a new character to the originally middle-class district where as early as the 14th century an inn and the houses of small artisans had stood.

The colossal palace, constructed by Andrea Spezza and Niccolo Sebregondi under the direction of Giovanni Pieronni and built on combined plots of land, was followed by other similar buildings which, however, were not on the same huge scale.

This construction activity was due to large changes in property ownership which made it possible after the defeat of the Estates for the new nobility, the ecclesiastical institutions and the nouveaux riches of the war to buy houses, particularly those that had been confiscated, at a very low price. The size of the site acquired by Wallenstein and its situation within the built-up area strongly influenced the general layout of the building.

Albrecht of Wallenstein decided to build his monumental palace in the Lesser Quarter of Prague.

He feverishly built his large palace from 1624 to 1630 in stages. The palace was separated from the outside world and concentrated around a landscaped garden and five courtyards. The complex included also a sala terrena, which is architecturally the most valuable part of the palace, designed in the late Italian Renaissance style by Giovanni Battista Pieronni after the portico of a church in Leghorn. There was a riding-school closing the garden in its eastern side, as well as stables and barracks as a necessary part of a general's house. The perimeter of the complex is almost 750 metres.

The garden, which was founded in 1623 according to a plan prepared by Andrea Spezza and finished only four years later, is famed for its sala terrena as well as for a number of bronze statues of ancient gods by Adriano de Vries which were, however, stolen in 1648 by the Swedish army, transported to Sweden and installed in the royal garden of Drottingholm. Bronze replicas of the beautiful sculptures were placed this century in the garden of the Wallenstein Palace to substitute the originals.

The rhythm of the main façade of the Wallenstein Palace, 60 m long and occupying one side of Valdštejn Square, is created by three horizontal unvarying strips of windows (ground floor and two upper floors) and by dormer-windows in the roof. The layout and the articulation of the façade was, however, influenced to a great extent by the Trčka Palace which was incorporated into the new complex. The façade hides the central hall covering two floors, whose decoration was made by the plasterer and painter Baccio Bianco. The large fresco in the ceiling surrounded by a stucco frame glorifies Wallenstein's military art and victories.

The Wallenstein Palace, with both late Renaissance and early Baroque elements, is an exemplary new noble house from the period of the Prague Counter-Reformation.

Renovation of the monumental Wallenstein Palace already started early in this century when Walcher of Moltheim, a Viennese architect, worked here. In 1913, he restored the great sala terrena, and on that occasion replicas of the sculptures by Adrian de Vries taken away by the Swedes were made.

In the Second World War, the east-west wing along Valdštejnská Street was adapted to house offices, and thus the most ruinous part of the palace could be saved. After 1945, the complex came into the hands of the state and housed the Ministry of Education. Therefore, soon after the war it was decided to undertake an overall renovation of the palace. The project was prepared by the Studio R of Stavoproject (later SURPMO), namely by Miloš Vincík and Julie Pecánková.

The palace was adapted to meet the needs of the Ministry of Education and its administration. The sala terrena was again restored, the garden parterres were rehabilitated, and the great pool in front of the riding-school that had been filled for a century was restored.

The riding-school, following to a certain extent the example of the riding-school at the Castle by Janák, was converted into an exhibition hall of the National Gallery where initially 19th century paintings were displayed. Today, the hall is used for important ad hoc exhibitions. In the front (entrance) part and in the rear part of the riding-school separate two-storey rooms were created, and in the rear part also some minor exhibition rooms. A difficult part of the renovation was the stabilization of the damaged truss, which carries by means of rods a coffered ceiling from the 18th century.

The general renovation, whose last stage included a restoration of the interiors and installa-tions in the main building, took place between 1949 and 1954. The main hall of the Wallestein Palace and the adjoining rooms have been used for many years for both municipal and national cultural events.

Baroque Fortifications

The medieval walls dating from the reign of King Charles could not, as the Thirty Years' War had shown, provide sufficient protection for Prague, and therefore, immediately after the war, the Emperor ordered the building of a new defence system.

The new band of town-walls in front of the old Gothic fortifications was reinforced with forty large new, pentagonal bastions, and Prague could be entered through eleven gateways. The Baroque bulwarks surrounded the town systematically according to a plan prepared by the military engineer Giovanni B. Pieronni in collaboration with General Count de Conti. The plan envisaged two citadels adjoining the town that could each be defended separately. The first one was supposed to be at Vyšehrad, whose strategic role proved important during the invasion by the Saxons in 1631, and in particular during the second Swedish invasion in 1648. The other citadel was planned on Strahov Hill or in Prague Castle.

The construction of fortifications that had been planned since 1649 and were supposed to enclose all the settlements on both the right bank and the left bank of the Vltava, including the Castle, started in 1654. The town-walls were quite simple, whereas the citadel of Vyšehrad had a very sophisticated fortification system. Due to new weapons and, in particular, to artillery, the defence system had to be reorganized. Bastions projecting from the fortification walls were built and the earth dug from new ditches was heaped to form mounds, reinforced with masonry and red-brick walls, and the corners were strengthened with sandstone blocks.

Consequently, Prague was enclosed in an armour of large-scale fortifications whose construction was the work of some excellent military engineers as well as of outstanding architects, such as Carlo Lurago, an architect working in the Old and the New Towns, and the Court Architect Santino de Bossi, who worked in the Lesser Quarter and at Hradčany.

Considerable remains of the Baroque fortifications from the 17th and 18th centuries, such as brick-walls and bastions have survived in the Petřín Gardens and on Strahov Hill.

Within the construction of new fortification systems de Bossi also built a new access road to Hradčany, and a ramp leading to the Castle was cut from the end of what is now Nerudova Street to the first gate of the Castle.

Its new role as a modern fortress brought about fundamental changes in Vyšehrad, once a seat of the Přemyslids. Ferdinand III ordered the building of new massive fortifications here, and, as a result, the old walls were demolished. In spite of the large scale of the new fortification system, designed by the Emperor's military advisors, the construction went quite smoothly. In 1656, the Tábor Gate and the armoury were built, and twenty years later, from 1676 to 1678, the bastions. The Citadel of Vyšehrad had six bastions that were named after saints, for instance St. Bernard and St. Ludmila. In the east, the citadel was protected by two bastions forming a corner wall between two gates, the Leopold Gate and the Tábor Gate.

The most impressive structure at Vyšehrad at that time was the Leopold Gate, which was built

Baroque Fortifications

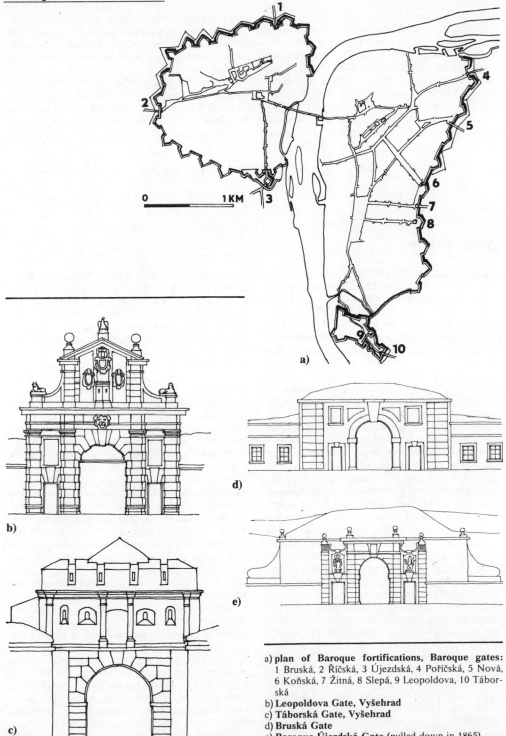

a) **plan of Baroque fortifications, Baroque gates:**
1 Bruská, 2 Říčská, 3 Újezdská, 4 Poříčská, 5 Nová, 6 Koňská, 7 Žitná, 8 Slepá, 9 Leopoldova, 10 Táborská
b) **Leopoldova Gate, Vyšehrad**
c) **Táborská Gate, Vyšehrad**
d) **Bruská Gate**
e) **Baroque Újezdská Gate** (pulled down in 1865)

prior to 1670 and which was also called the French Gate. This second inner gateway to be passed through before entering the Baroque fortress was constructed in the Baroque Classical style of north Italian fortifications. The gate was designed by Carlo Lurago who was apparently inspired by the Matthias Gate at Prague Castle. The gateway is surmounted with a tympanum with a big carved eagle, probably by Giovanni Battista Allio. The newest gateway at Vyšehrad that has survived is the Brick Gate (Cihlová brá-

na) from 1841 which was designed by the military engineer Jiří Weiss upon the initiative of Prague's Governor Karel Chotek. The gate ranks among the best Empire buildings in Prague.

The present-day form of Vyšehrad is therefore due to the Baroque concept of the military citadel and to its subsequent development until the mid-19th century. The fortress ceased to serve its military purpose in 1866.

Clementinum

The Clementinum Building was one of the first Jesuit colleges in this country, and also the greatest building that they constructed here. The Jesuits were invited to Prague in 1556 by Ferdinand I to support his counter-Reformation policy, and they settled in the former Dominican Monastery at St. Clement's near the bridge. This was the first and permanent seat of the Jesuits, and also a centre of the increasingly strong Counter-Reformation policy. Here, replacing a former medieval church which later gave the name to the whole complex, an impressive Baroque church, consecrated to St. Clement, with plain courtyards, was built from 1711 to 1715 by František M. Kaňka. Its nave and Chancel rank now among the most valuable Baroque interiors.

The Clementinum in its size and fortress-like conception became a symbol of the hard Counter-Reformation line of the Jesuits both for contemporaries and for following generations.

It is the third largest historic complex in Prague and was built systematically over decades, with the support of the Habsburgs, until 1773, when the Jesuit Order was abolished here. The complex stands in the Old Town near Charles Bridge, covering an area where once there were over thirty houses, many gardens, three churches, the old Dominican Monastery, and two streets. The Clementinum, the seat of Old Town Jesuits, was constructed over one hundred and fifty years on a large site of almost two hectares, and included a complex of buildings surrounding five courtyards. It also incorporated St. Saviour's Church, once the main Jesuit church in Bohemia, which was founded in 1578 and counstructed in the years 1600, 1638—1640 (by C. Lurago), with a dome by Francesco Caratti

(1648). There was also a church dedicated to St. Clement, and an "Italian" (Vlašská) Chapel. The centralized domed chapel with an oval plan from the end of the 16th century and with a portico facing Charles Street dating from 1715 (by František M. Kaňka) replaced a very old church with the same consecration from about 1240. The complex included also many secular buildings, such as schools, a college and a library, as well as a theatre, an observatory with towers, and a printing shop. The oldest part of the complex adjoined Křižovnické (Knights of the Cross) Square, next to St. Saviour's Church, and from here the Jesuits extended their building eastwards.

The construction of the college started in 1653, its main architect being Carlo Lurago, who was joined by Francesco Caratti (he built, among other parts, the former refectory, now reading-room of the State Library) and Giovanni Domenico Orsi, and was completed in 1726 by František M. Kaňka, who built here the observatory tower (1721—1723) and finished the east wing facing Mariánské Square. From 1724 to 1730, F. M. Kaňka built here also a remarkable Mirror Hall in the former chapel, richly decorated with stuccowork, the Library Hall and the Mathematics Hall. The above architects succeeded in creating a unique building whose massive structure, however, dating mostly from the 17th century, was far from harmonious with the medieval environment and was a strange element among the old houses around. A drawing from 1750 informs us about its appearance at that time; the drawing was made by F. B. Werner, who drew many historic buildings in Prague before the Jesuit Order was abolished in 1773.

Clementinum

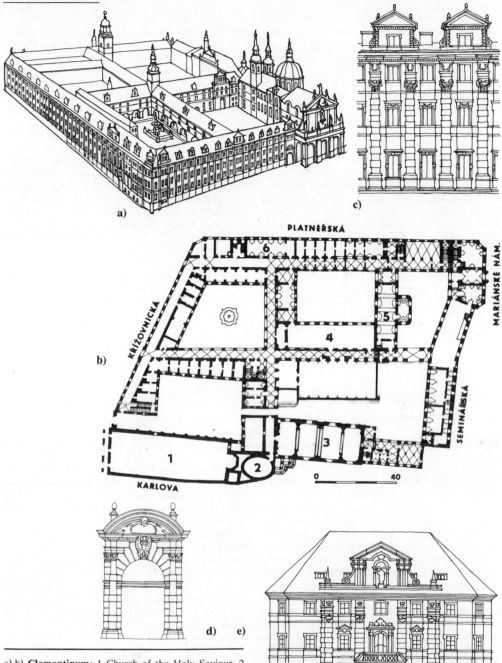

a) b) **Clementinum:** 1 Church of the Holy Saviour, 2
   Vlašská (i.e., Italian) Chapel, 3 Church of St. Clement,
   4 great summer refectory, 5 Mirror Chapel, 6 winter
   refectory
c) **part of façade**
d) **west portal facing Křižovnické (Knights of the
   Cross) Square**
e) **east façade, Mariánské Square**

(113)

Clementinum

After the abolition of the Jesuit College in 1773, the building housed an archbishop's seminary and part of Prague University with the Imperial Library, which has developed into the present State Library. In 1880, the Clementinum was attached to the University which, in turn, located its library here. In the 19th century, there was a Painting Academy here for many years. At that time, the Clementinum became a centre of the national revival movement.

The Clementinum was given a new function in 1923 when it was decided that it should house several public libraries and also the University Library. The architectural design was prepared by Ladislav Machoň, with the help of Zdeněk Wirth in historical and artistic matters. From 1926 to 1930 he realized a very fine and erudite work in several stages, which anticipated, together with Pavel Janák's works, a modern, integrated approach to the renovation of ancient buildings. The Baroque architecture was preserved, while the buildings were equipped with modern installations and services. Even the inevitable architectural changes, such as the construction of an additional floor for library depositories, or of a new reading-room in the first courtyard, were made with much understanding of the historic qualities and environment of the complex. Many excellent artists were invited before the Second World War to contribute to the decoration, for instance Otto Guttfreund (emblems), Jaroslav Horejc (ceramics) and Jaroslav Benda (paintings).

In the 1950s, further parts of the complex were renovated, and the Clementinum is now seat of the State Library of the Czech Republic comprising the National Library, the Slavic Library, the Technical Library, and the University Library, which is the largest. There is also a Historic Manuscript Department. The present-day role of the complex brings about new needs, and further modifications are therefore being made in the Clementinum. We should also mention here the general renovation of St. Saviour's which included a very expensive restoration of the dome drum. The renovation was carried out by the Štuko Cooperative and by ČFVU (Czech Fine Arts Fund) restorers between 1971 and 1984.

Jesuit Buildings

The time following the 1620 defeat of the Bohemian Estates brought about an immediate separation of the country from the Protestant North. This particularly suited the new nobility coming from abroad and, in particular, the powerful Counter-Reformation orders that settled in the country and secured their positions here.

The first seat of the Jesuits was the Clementinum at Charles Bridge in the Old Town (see special chapter, page 112) which, however, soon proved insufficient. They therefore also settled in the heart of the Lesser Quarter, where they strongly influenced the medieval environment (see special chapter, page 137). Almost at the same time they also settled in the centre of the New Town. To fulfil the wishes of the Jesuits, Ferdinand III gave them in 1623 the old Gothic centralized Church of Corpus Christi on the then Cattle Market (now Charles Square), as well as some other buildings and the adjacent plots of land. The chapel was used by the Jesuits until the construction of a new church, and in 1791 it was pulled down. The construction of a noviciate and a Jesuit college in the New Town started in 1656. The first stage of construction was finished in 1665 and then a plan was prepared of a new church of the "Il Gesu" type. The college was completed in 1702, and replaced thirteen gardens and twenty-three plots. The south and central parts were built by Carlo Lurago and Paul Ignaz Bayer, and the rest, up to the church, was finished in 1770 by Johann Georg Wirch. The church was closed in 1773 and converted into a military hospital (now Teaching Hospital). Wirch's building was destroyed in 1945 during an air raid and then restored.

The building acitivity of the Society of Jesus considerably increased after the Thirty Years' War. When they arrived in Prague in 1556 after being summoned by Ferdinand II, the Jesuit community in Bohemia had only six colleges and two residences, whereas in 1653 it already possessed twenty-three colleges, six residences and a profession house, and their building activity

Jesuit Buildings

a) b) **St. Ignatius' Church**
c) **St. Ignatius' Church with Jesuit College**
d) **location of the Clementinum**
e) **location of St. Nicholas' Church and Jesuit College**
f) **location of St. Ignatius' Church and Jesuit College**

a)

0   10   **b)**

c)

d)   e)   f)

0   100

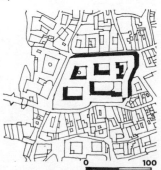

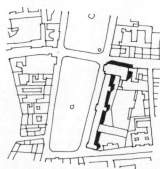

continued until the mid-18th century.

Many architects were invited to build other houses for the Jesuits in Prague, the most renowned and the most in demand being Carlo Lurago (died 1684), who realized not only his own designs, but also a number of other architects' plans. He started working for the Jesuits in the Lesser Quarter, and then contributed to the construction of the Clementinum Building and took part in that of the Jesuit Church of St. Ignatius in the New Town. Another important architect was Francesco Caratti (died 1677) who made the first dome for the Jesuits in this country, the polygonal dome of St. Saviour's Church. The last work of Giovanni Domenico Orsi (died 1679), who also designed the profession house in the Lesser Quarter and made the first plan (unrealized) of St. Nicholas Church, was the northern part of the Clementinum Building. Ignaz Bayer (died 1733) built the tower of St. Ignatius on Charles Square and its projecting portico to complete the construction started in 1665 by Carlo Lurago's workshop. František M. Kaňka (died 1766), too, did a lot for the Jesuits, although he was also a very popular architect among the nobility. Kaňka completed the construction of the Clementinum by creating the front wall facing Mariánské Square, the Mirror Chapel, the Library, and St. Clement's Church. These works reflect his special sense of spatial disposition. In addition to the Clementinum, after 1660, the Old Town Jesuits also used St. Bartholomew College where until 1773 they had a boarding grammar school, as well as St. Wenceslas College in Husova Street. After the dissolution of the order the latter college was used for some time by the Faculty of Philosophy.

The large building was then put at the disposal of the Bohemian Engineering School, from which the present-day Czech Technical University developed. In the course of the 19th century and in this century as well, many changes in the layout have been made to enable the monastery building to be used for education and serve the particular departments. The height of the college was increased by one or, in places, two additional storeys, which has proved a mistake as it had a negative impact on the form and size of the courtyards. Since the new modern complex of the Technical University in Dejvice District was completed the former seminary has housed the Editing Department of the Technical University and various studies are now being prepared for its renovation to make it a ceremonial building for the University, for instance for graduation ceremonies, together with the Bethlehem Chapel, which was closed by the Jesuits.

The last building constructed by the Jesuits to be mentioned here is the house called Konvikt (theological seminary), which is an interesting irregular building, replacing several houses and surrounding a large courtyard between Bartolomějská and Konviktská Streets. The house was used as a religious boarding school until the dissolution of the order in 1773. Since that time, many important cultural, and even revolutionary events have taken place here, particularly in the Great Hall, which is the former refectory, where many outstanding artists appeared, for instance Beethoven, Rubinstein, Wagner, and the violonists Ondříček and František Laub. Also Antonín Dvořák graduated from here and later became director of the Organ School which was located in this building. Many important workers' meetings also took place in the hall. After the war, Jiří Trnka's animated puppet film studio moved in, and has been there up to now. At present, the arcades are being renovated, as well as the parts along Konviktská Street, where remains of the original Gothic architecture still can be seen.

In the mid-18th century the Jesuits built a summer residence near the Vltava, behind what is now Klárov. The residence was pulled down in 1893 and a new palace was built on the site; it is now the Prime Minister's Office.

The uninterrupted large-scale building activity of the Jesuits in Prague ended in 1773.

Černín Palace

A little town called Hradčany was founded in 1321 by the burgrave of Prague Castle, Berka of Dubá, on the site of an old settlement outside the Castle. In 1598 the town was granted the privileges of a royal town, and due to the proximity of the Castle many palaces and residences of prominent nobles were built here.

Humprecht Jan Černín did the same in Hradčany with his palace as Wallenstein in the Lesser Quarter. It was not easy at that time to purchase a plot of land needed for the construction of such a large building as the Černín Palace. Nevertheless, Černín managed to purchase land on the outskirts of the town. One of the highest points in the town was chosen for the site (276 m above sea level), eighteen metres higher than the floor level of St. Vitus' Cathedral. Certainly, for Černín his palace was a matter of prestige and its monumentality was expected to be more impressive than that of the other palaces.

Four generations of the Černíns and a number of outstanding architects worked for many years on this sumptuous building. The palace was originally planned with four wings, a transverse part and two courtyards. The main front, of great architectural quality, faces the east, towards the Castle. The monumental façade, 135 m long, is punctuated by a long line of thirty half-columns. The first sketch is said to have been drawn personally by Giovanni Lorenzo Bernini whom Humprecht Jan Černín of Chudenice, the Imperial Ambassador to Venice, met during his stay in Italy.

Francesco Caratti, the chief architect of the palace, who had also designed the Michna Palace and St. Mary Magdalene's Church in the Lesser Quarter, continued work on the palace until his death in 1683, being followed by Carlo Maderna, Domenico E. Rossi, Giovanni B. Alliprandi and, as of 1718, by František M. Kaňka. Kaňka completed the palace in 1720 by constructing monumental stairs and finishing the comfortable interiors. His contemporary, Václav Vavřinec Reiner, decorated some rooms and the ceiling over the main staircase with frescoes. The garden façade of the palace designed by F. Caratti is in a taste characteristic of its time. It was built between 1669 and 1688 and its two salae terrenae, also conceived in the spirit of northern Palladian architecture, opened into the palace garden. The garden was laid out later, after 1718, by František M. Kaňka. Much later, in 1934—1935, it was restored in its original form.

The palace was plundered by the French army in the 1740s, and then restored by Anselmo Lurago who also completed the main front wall by constructing new porches and a balcony. A garden pavilion was also built in the garden at that time.

After the devastation of Prague in 1757 and after some military campaigns, during which the palace was damaged, the Černíns sold the desolate palace in 1851 to the Imperial Military Administration, which decided to convert it into barracks and invited Anton Wolf to carry out the project. Wolf rebuilt the palace in 1855 and 1856. He divided the space horizontally so as to create an additional storey, bricked-in the beautiful sala terrena, which was then used—together with the neighbouring rooms—as a store and a stable, the garden was converted into a "Befehlsplatz" and a number of ugly sheds and cabins were built along the garden walls.

This shameful situation was reversed after the First World War. After a competition in 1924, Pavel Janák was charged with the renovation of the palace for the Ministry of Foreign Affairs. Caratti's original plans of the palace were found in the archives of Jindřichův Hradec, and they enabled Pavel Janák to renovate the derelict rooms and façades accurately and restore the original concept of the palace. The costly renovation was carried out from 1928 to 1936 and included not only a restoration of the palace itself, but also a modern renovation of the garden in front of the north façade with the sala terrena. Pavel Janák collaborated here with the garden architect Otakar Fierlinger. The new administrative and ceremonial function of the house required many modifications and modernizations within the palace and in its surroundings. Loretánské Square in front of the palace sloped down to Loretto Church and to the Capuchin Monastery, and it was therefore necessary to level the ground in order to make a parking area here. Pavel Janák decided to make a radical change by creating a large elevated terrace with a supporting wall, the effect of which was reduced by steps and by a segmental bastion at its south end, where the site of the Chapel of St. Matthias that had been demolished is marked out on the paving. These changes had a negative effect on the general layout of the square by breaking the immediate visual contact between the front wall of the palace and the Loretto Church.

Černín Palace

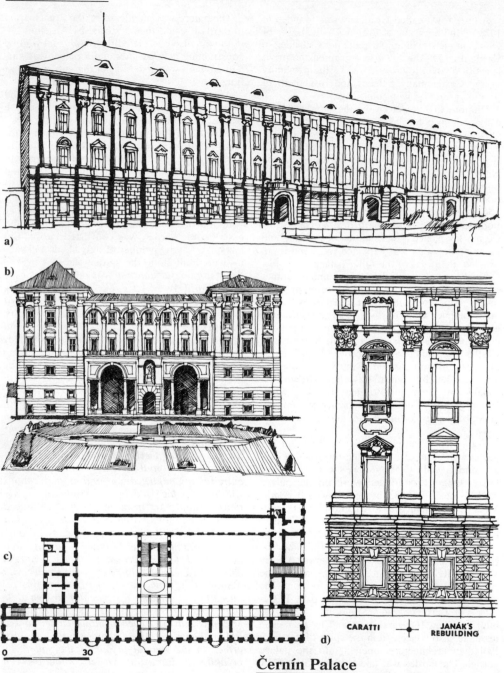

CARATTI ——|—— JANÁK'S REBUILDING

Černín Palace

a) Černín Palace
b) garden façade with sala terrena
c) plan of ground floor
d) part of façade — comparison of the original with Janák's renovation

(118)

Černín Palace

The Ministry of Foreign Affairs, however, needed more office space and these needs became more urgent. Therefore, an administrative red-brick building without any decoration was added to the palace between the years 1930 and 1933. Janák was strongly criticized for the Constructivist form of the new building which spoiled the view of the palace, but he was praised for the fine renovation of the palace.

Today we regard Janák's renovation of the Černín Palace and his approach to the task as a pioneering example of the modern practice of ancient building conservation—a method of saving and conserving ancient buildings by giving them a new social function and admitting the inevitable structural changes in their layout.

Knights of the Cross Square

Knights of the Cross Square (Křižovnické náměstí) is quite small, and its initial medieval form underwent a Baroque redevelopment. The square, which is said to be one of the most picturesque in Europe, has a beautiful view, with a contrast between the Gothic and the Baroque, the Bridge Tower and the churches, and, in particular, between its closed form and the open view of the skyline of Hradčany.

For three centuries the square was dominated by the Old Town Bridge Tower. Only in the late 17th century did the tall and impressive Baroque dome of the neighbouring Church of the Knights of the Cross appear and complete the beautiful view of the Old Town as seen from the Castle.

In the square, the remains of a Romanesque paving can still be seen in front of the Church of the Knighs of the Cross, which in the 12th century was on an axis with the bridgehead of Judith Bridge, the oldest stone bridge in Prague. In 1252, the Monastery of the Knights of the Cross with Red Star was built onto the Church of the Holy Spirit. The order was the only Bohemian religious order, and was founded around 1230. Fragments of the original two-aisled Church of the Holy Spirit still survive in the foundations of the later Baroque church.

The noble building of St. Francis' Church enriched the appearance of the town with its beautiful dome and has been considered the most harmonious of the Baroque churches in Prague. The building, which is characterized by excellent proportions and a purity of form, is architecturally equivalent to the neighbouring Bridge Tower.

The church was built between 1679 and 1689, and was designed by Jean Baptiste Mathey, a Burgundian studying in Rome. He came to Prague with Count Wallenstein, the Grand Master of the Knights of the Cross, who was returning to Prague after being appointed archbishop here.

It was no easy task to build a new Baroque church on such a small site next to the massive Clementinum Building with St. Saviour's Church at its corner.

St. Saviour's Church is a long two-aisle building with galleries and a polygonal cupola, and was once the main Jesuit church in Bohemia. Its three-axis portico is an important architectural element in the square. The dome was erected in 1648 by Francesco Caratti, while the church itself, which still had Gothic foundations, was constructed over many years by Carlo Lurago and Francesco Caratti. The towers at the chancel dating from the late 16th century were completed in 1714 by František M. Kaňka. Thus a church was built that ranks among the most valuable early Baroque buildings in Prague.

As the depth of the square along the axis of Charles Bridge was insufficient, Mathey situated his church along the transverse axis. This is the reason why St. Francis has an unusual north-south orientation. With this church, which is a centralized building with a magnificent dome and an oval plan, the architect introduced to Prague a new type of structural and spatial solution. In 1722—1723, the dome was decorated by Václav Vavřinec Reiner with a fresco representing the Last Judgment.

West of the church is the building of the monastery, originally Gothic, but rebuilt around 1660 by Carlo Lurago in the early Baroque style. The building also incorporated the old 12th century

Knights of the Cross Square

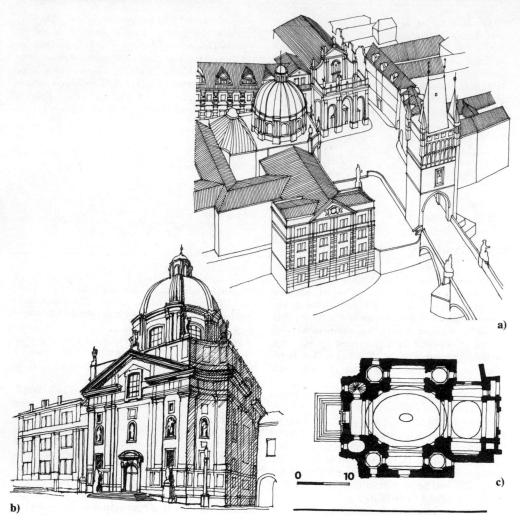

a) Křižovnické (Knights of the Cross) Square
b) c) St. Francis' Church
d) Church of the Holy Saviour

Romanesque tower of Judith Bridge, as proved by a projecting tower-like structure facing the Vltava. This two-storey building of the former Generalate of the Knights of the Cross was renovated and enlarged in 1846 by Johann Brunn. From 1901 to 1911, Josef Sakař enlarged the building by attaching an Art Nouveau wing to the northern side.

The intimate atmosphere of the square also includes a bronze memorial to Emperor Charles IV that was placed here in 1848 on the occasion of the 500th anniversary of Charles University. Its model was made by Ernst J. Hähnel, a sculptor from Dresden.

The square, which leads onto Charles Bridge, was restored together with the bridge in the mid-1970s. The paving of the bridge was continued through the gateway of the Bridge Tower and integrated with the paving in front of the bridge. The Bridge Tower was restored, together with its sculptural decoration, the most valuable sculptures being replaced by replicas and installed in the National Gallery; the same was done with many statues on the bridge. Prior to this, the façades of the houses south of the bridge were renovated.

In 1976, the exteriors of the Church of St. Sav-iour were restored, including a very complicated renovation of the octagonal drum of the main dome over the church crossing. A technical survey showed that its timber-frame was in very poor condition and had to be replaced. The plan was prepared by Josef Švastal of the Faculty of Civil Engineering, Czech Technical University in Prague, the renovation of the façades and interiors was carried out by the Štuko Cooperative and by ČFVU (Czech Fine Arts Fund) restorers.

The north end of the square includes the façades of the church and the monastery of the Knights of the Cross. An extensive renovation of the church façade was carried out from 1982 to 1985, following a restoration of the interiors between 1968 and 1972. The new colour of the dome was strongly criticized both by the general public and technical specialists as soon as the scaffolding had been removed. Although an analysis of the paint and plaster layers showed that the dome had not been colour-painted, the renovation plan was based on a controversial iconographic document from the 19th century showing the dome colour-painted, which however had not been historically verified. The colours of the renovated dome spoil the beautiful architecture of Jean B. Mathey and its details.

Troja Palace

In the 17th century hundreds of vineyards, many villages with manors and farmsteads, farms and peripheral villas surrounded Prague, which was enclosed by its new Baroque walls. The landscape around the town was like a green ring, with many summer houses of noblemen and other rich people.

One of the most important suburban palaces and villas was the summer house of the Sternbergs in the Prague suburb of Troja. The palace, which perfectly fitted into the surrounding landscape, was considered quite remarkable. This was confirmed by the Kurfürst of Saxony, Augustus the Strong, who visited it soon after its completion. The summer palace conceived in the spirit of the Roman suburban villa and built from 1679 to 1691 is believed to be one of the best works of Jean Baptiste Mathey, also called Matheus Burgundus. He was a painter and architect who based his art on Roman Classicism and French Rationalism and contributed considerably to the development of architecture in this country. He introduced many new and inspiring ideas that formed the basis of the Bohemian Baroque, which soon came to rank amongst the best in Europe. Recent historical research has proved

Troja Palace

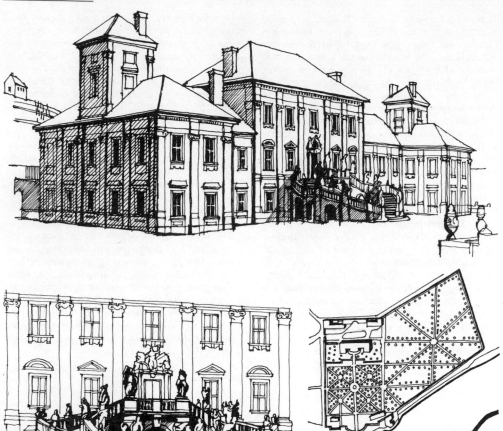

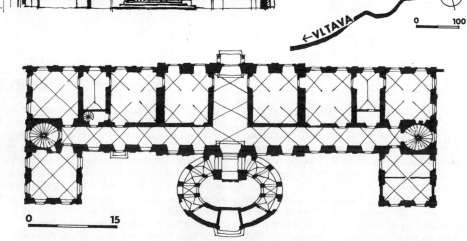

←VLTAVA

0   100

0   15

Troja Palace

that Mathey took part in the construction of the palace as of 1685 and that the building was begun by Domenico Orsi.

The construction of the palace was an example of the new freedom in art, the new attitude to architectural mass and to interior planning, which totally differed from the previous concept of architecture based on block-like compact palaces. An interesting new element in the palace was the external oval staircase from the years 1685—1703, where two sculptors from Dresden, Johann Georg and Paul Herrmann, depicted the victory of the Olympian gods over the Titans. The busts of ancient gods dating from about 1705 were probably made at Johann Brokof's workshop.

Much attention was paid to creating a harmony between the palace and the adjacent French-type garden created by Georg Seemann after 1698. The large garden, enriched with terraces, has a geometrical star-like network of paths with vistas, with the main part of the palace in its centre. The balustrade is decorated with big urns and busts of Roman emperors made of terracota. The palace, together with its outbuildings which also form part of the symmetrical layout, along with the garden and the vineyard, arrived at an architectural unity, as proved by a contemporary illustration of the palace and its surroundings.

The outbuildings behind the rear wall of the palace (Nos. 147—149, Trojská Street) have a staircase in their centre. They have one floor only; the rooms, dating from 1691, are tunnel vaulted, decorated with lunettes, and some of them with paintings. The complex also includes a former beer-brewery (1/4, U Trojského zámku Street) built at the same time as the palace and later rebuilt in the neo-Classical style, a service courtyard (6/68, Povltavská Street), a mill (No. 7/74, Povltavská Street), and a farm (No. 7/8, Pod Havránkou Street).

The Troja Summer Palace, whose interiors were decorated with paintings by Francesco and Giovanni Marchetti, and particularly after 1690 by Abraham and Isaac Godyn, housed collections of modern Czech sculptural works from the National Gallery for a time between the two World Wars.

The Palace of Troja, in spite of its high architectural quality and artistic interest was neglected for a long time both by the conservation bodies and by the public. Being quite a long way from the centre of the town and its main activities, the palace was not given much attention as to its possible social and cultural use, although some ideas were considered. The palace fell into disrepair, particularly its former garden parterre and its sculptural and architectural decoration.

In 1922, the palace came into the hands of the state and some restoration was carried out here before the Second World War: in 1926, the engineer Josef Schwarz and the sculptor Jindřich Čapek restored the beautiful Baroque staircase and its sculptures, and in 1928 a renovation of the façade and the roof truss was begun and the pantiles were replaced. Many restorers took part in the restoration of paintings in the interiors. In 1935, a renovation of the garden parterre started according to a plan prepared by the landscape architect Otakar Fierlinger. The building housed some modern sculpture collections in the National Gallery. Before the end of the war, the ceramic garden urns on the upper garden terrace were renovated.

By the end of the 1950s, the façade of the palace had been renovated again, and in 1976 a plan for detailed renovation of the complex was prepared by the SURPMO (State Institute for Renovation of Ancient Towns and Buildings). The palace was originally intended to serve the Municipal Council of Prague. The plan then changed in favour of the Gallery of Prague. The architectural plan was prepared by Milan Pavlík and Otakar Kuča (renovation of the garden). It anticipated a great number of visitors, for whom many services were included. Many problems, particularly of a technical nature have been solved, such as the fixing of the false vault in the main hall with a fine fresco by Abraham Godyn of Antwerp (1691—1697). The renovation started in 1977 and ended in 1989, including a thorough restoration of the garden. The public is thus able to admire another important building of the Bohemian Baroque.

Riding-School at the Castle

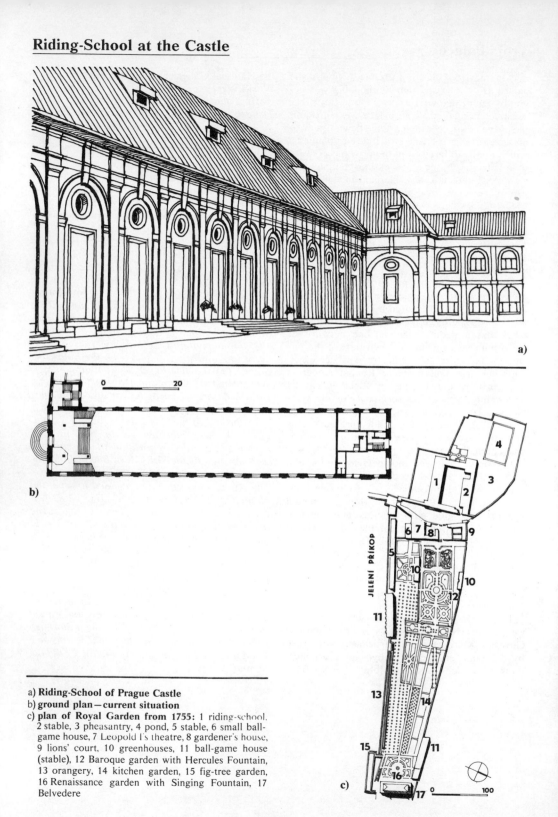

a) **Riding-School of Prague Castle**
b) **ground plan — current situation**
c) **plan of Royal Garden from 1755:** 1 riding-school,
2 stable, 3 pheasantry, 4 pond, 5 stable, 6 small ball-
game house, 7 Leopold I's theatre, 8 gardener's house,
9 lions' court, 10 greenhouses, 11 ball-game house
(stable), 12 Baroque garden with Hercules Fountain,
13 orangery, 14 kitchen garden, 15 fig-tree garden,
16 Renaissance garden with Singing Fountain, 17
Belvedere

(124)

Opposite the entrance to the Royal Garden is the Riding-School with a courtyard, which once housed Rudolph's pheasantry founded before 1600. The new Baroque riding-school replaced an older and smaller riding-school of 1572, whose size and fittings no longer met the new needs. A strong impetus for its construction was probably Wallenstein's new riding-school from 1630. The aim was the same: entertainment of the nobles, for whom other buildings (now we would probably say sports facilities) were also built, such as ball-game courts. Emperor Leopold I decided in the late 17th century to build a new large riding-school in the new area behind the Stag Moat belonging to the Castle.

Jean Baptiste Mathey, the most important architect in Prague, was invited to prepare the plan for a new riding-school at the Castle, together with Antonio Canevalle. They both received detailed instructions. The large 92 m long building with a hipped roof has a rectangular, 40 m wide ground plan. The building has an interesting narrow main façade, punctuated by tall Tuscan columns. The original function of this plain building is revealed by two reliefs depicting horses, high up under the cornice so that one does not now notice them. During the renovation the main front wall lost the great imperial eagle which had been its dominant element.

The large building, whose construction was quite economical due to the use of material from the demolished outbuildings, was finished in 1694. The long south front wall facing the Castle was articulated with false arcades, the interior let in light through small oval windows only. The front wall was colour-painted, as planned by Mathey. The black, ochre and light blue building certainly made a strong visual impression.

The architect did not live to see the completion of the work. In 1693 he left for France where he died soon afterwards. The building was finished one year later. Next to it is an open riding-school with an arcaded gallery.

The Riding-School burned down in 1760 and had to be repaired, particularly the ceiling and the roof. It is from that time that the present-day timber-ceiling dates, which is very well built with massive beams. The huge truss is architecturally very impressive.

The building later ceased to serve its original purpose and was used as a storehouse.

As part of the adaptation and regeneration of the area to the north of the Castle three major buildings here were renovated after 1945: the Royal Summer Palace (Belvedere), the Ball-Game Court, and the Riding-School. The first building to be renovated was the Riding-School. This rather plain, but monumental building by an important Baroque architect slowly lost its original function. The large space of the winter riding-hall, lit only through small elliptical openings in the arches of false arcades, made a gloomy impression. However, it was in good condition. Pavel Janák's conception was much broader and did not concentrate on the building alone. Janák also included in his plan the space beneath the Riding-School forming a terrace above the southern slope of the Stag Moat; he sited the garages of the Castle here, converted the terrace into a garden parterre with excellent views of the Castle, and connected it with the Riding-School by means of tall French windows replacing the false arcades. The floor of the Riding-School was raised to the level of the terrace. He left the original wooden ceiling on the truss beams, and created a gallery in the east part at the same level as the floor of the arcades at the summer riding-school. Windows identical to those opening onto the south terrace were put in the northern façade facing the former service courtyard, which was converted into a flower-bed.

Due to the changes the interior now had fine proportions. The main entrance in the eastern façade remained. The fact that the false arcades were opened did no harm to the architecture of the building; on the contrary, the exhibition hall was thus connected with the terrace and the beautiful northern façade of Prague Castle. With the renovation a new exhibition and social hall was acquired and the alterations proved that even plain service buildings could assume an important social function.

Hradčany Square

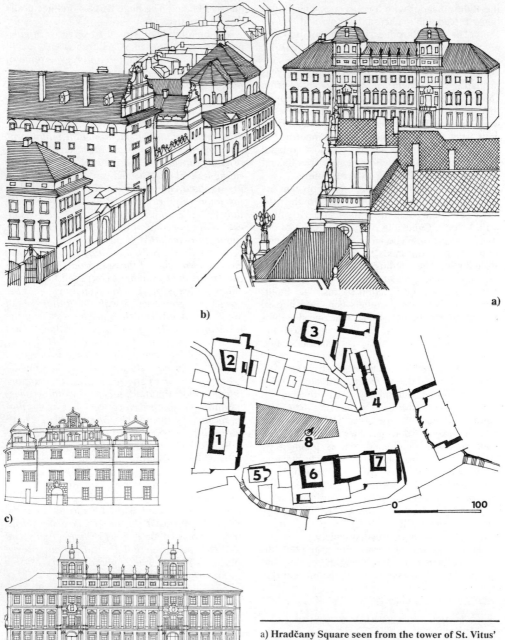

a)

b)

c)

d)

a) **Hradčany Square seen from the tower of St. Vitus'**
b) **plan of the square:** 1 Tuscan Palace, 2 Martinic Palace, 3 Sternberg Palace, 4 Archbishop's Palace, 5 St. Benedict's Church, 6 Schwarzenberg Palace, 7 Schwarzenberg (Salm) Palace, 8 Our Lady's Column
c) **Martinic Palace**
d) **Tuscany Palace**

(126)

Hradčany Square (Hradčanské náměstí) became an important space in front of the Castle in the late 18th century. The square retained its medieval size and plan, but was surrounded by beautiful palaces in the Renaissance and Baroque style. The triangular area had once been the market-place of a feudal small town called Hradčany.

In 1360, increasing the fortification system of the Lesser Quarter, Charles IV also enclosed Hradčany with walls and thus determined its future plan and size. The original inhabitants had to leave their houses around the market-place and move into the adjacent streets so as to vacate the area for new palaces for the clergy and nobility. The town had a parish church consecrated to St. Benedict and later also a town-hall on the square. After the 1541 fire many palaces were built in the area of Hradčany. Although some Renaissance palaces have remained, the present-day appearance of Hradčany District and its square dates from the 17th and 18th centuries. The square, which the old King's Way leading to the Castle entrance over a drawbridge had once crossed at its southern end, acquired its present form in the Baroque period.

After the big fire in the Lesser Quarter and Hradčany in the mid-16th century the area in front of the Castle became a residential district for the nobility where palaces surrounded with gardens were built from the mid-16th to the early 19th century. Consequently, an impressive triangular space developed with palaces, some of which are of great architectural interest.

A focal point of the square is the Baroque Column of Our Lady by Ferdinand M. Brokof and the cast-iron gas lamp-post, one of the few that have survived from the 1860s.

In the last third of the 17th century Count Thun-Hohenstein built his palace here on a dominant site at the west side of the square to rival the Castle. The large early Baroque palace was built from 1689 to 1691, and was later called the Tuscany Palace after its owner, Grand Duchess of Tuscany, who purchased it in 1718. The monumental four-winged building has an interesting symmetrical facade which was quite unusual at that time. It has two remarkable projecting sections crowned with roof galleries, which were typical elements of the Roman Baroque, and portals and columns which make us believe that the palace was built by Mathey. The attic between the galleries is decorated with statues of mythological gods.

Jean B. Mathey had already rebuilt the Archbishop's Palace on the north side of the square next to the Castle. The renovation of the originally Renaissance Gryspek House dating from 1669—1694 is now hidden under Wirch's Rococo façade, but parts of Mathey's original building as known to us from an old engraving from 1720 can still be seen. The building shows the influence of 17th century Roman architecture. Its central part is made prominent by a roof gallery, which was also characteristic of other works by this architect. He adopted here a plan similar to the Tuscany Palace. There are beautiful ceremonial halls from the latter half of the 18th century, decorated with fine wall-hangings. These are in fact the only original public rooms in Prague that have remained intact.

Both the above palaces fully respected their surroundings and actively contributed to the architecture of the town, in spite of their relative isolation. They introduced to the town's architecture a new articulation of shape and mass, as well as a formal discipline and a sobriety of details.

The most beautiful Renaissance palace on Hradčany Square and in the whole city is the Schwarzenberg Palace (see page 93) with the adjacent and much later Salm (or Smaller Schwarzenberg) Palace dating from 1800—1810, which replaced several noble houses in the Renaissance style. The latter forms an important element of the view of the Schwarzenberg Palace (now the Military Museum) from the Castle. Its present-day neo-Classical form is thanks to František Pavíček who, in 1810 and 1811, converted two older residential houses into a palace. The house was initially used for ceremonial purposes, and later it was converted back to a dwelling-house. After 1945, the palace housed the Swiss Embassy.

The Tuscany (or Thun-Hohenstein) Palace well suits the present-day needs of the Ministry of Foreign Affairs which uses it for both administrative and ceremonial purposes. It was rebuilt both inside and outside, and several years ago its façades were renovated and the roof was repaired. The Archbishop's Palace was rebuilt in 1765 according to plans prepared by J. J. Wirch. During the subsequent renovation in 1888, Platzer's sculptures on the attic were replaced by new statues made by Thomas Seidan, and the chapel dating from 1599 was rebuilt. The palace is now the seat of the Apostolic Administration and of the Archbishop, and in the last three decades its exterior has been renovated several times.

Although the Sternberg Palace next to that of the Archbishop does not form part of Hradčany Square, it should be mentioned here due to its proximity. It shares a gate with the Archbishop's

Palace and its four-winged plan was probably part of a larger project, the façade of which was to have faced the square. The building is architecturally remarkable, rebuilt over three years after 1945 for the National Gallery, whose collections were then displayed here, particularly those of old European fine arts and a collection of 19th and 20th century French art.

Baroque Renovation of Martinic Palace

This large palace with a large inner courtyard built on an irregular site stands in the corner of Hradčany Square. Before the 1541 great fire, there were four middle-class houses on the site, one of which was owned by the famed chronicler Beneš Krabice of Weitmille.

After the fire, the ruins were purchased by Ondřej Teyfl who around 1570 started constructing a new house. Jiří Bořita of Martinice, the Royal Governor of the Kingdom of Bohemia, was the next owner and continued the reconstruction of the Renaissance palace. His nephew Jaroslav extended the palace in 1634 by adding other wings towards the Stag Moat and giving the building its present four-winged form. At the same time, a wide early Baroque gable was built above the main front wall facing Hradčany Square. Further analysis by historians would probably reveal that the additions are unique in showing how the architectural principles behind one building were imposed on another one. It is an example of the glorification of one person and his social prestige by means of architecture. We know that Jaroslav Bořita of Martinice, the owner of the palace after the 1620 defeat of the Bohemian Estates and the Royal Governor of the country prior to that defeat, was thrown from the window of the Bohemian Chancellery in the Louis Wing of the Royal Palace during the Prague Defenestration in 1618, together with Vilém Slavata. Both officials survived the fall and escaped, Martinic fled to Munich. The defeat of the Bohemian Estates gave him the chance to return again to this country, where he was soon awarded the title of Count and received back all his property. Vilém Slavata had a statue of himself made, showing him being protected by angels from falling, and Count Bořita of Martinice followed his example by having the famous moment carved in stone for further generations.

Bořita of Martinice completed the palace above the Stag Moat so that its mass and layout resembled the old Royal Palace, although on a smaller scale. Both the horizontal and vertical planning of the Royal Palace, with the Vladislav Hall, the All Saints Chapel and the adjoining Louis Wing, was an example for him to follow. As a former Royal Governor he knew the Royal Palace very well and he conceived the northern wing of his palace to imitate it.

The Royal Palace was oriented along the axis of the Castle, while the Martinic Palace followed the axis of Hradčany Square. The layout was also significant. Being L-shaped, the Martinic Palace has its short wing projecting into the Stag Moat, while the wings of the Royal Palace face the slopes under the Castle.

Not only the layout of the two palaces, but also the articulation of the façades is very similar, as well as the accent put on the third storey. The same applies to the width of the façade, which in the case of the Royal Palace is fifty metres, whereas that of the Martinic Palace is only half that. Also the width of the section projecting from the northern part of the Martinic Palace is only half the width of that in the south façade of the Louis Wing. Another interesting fact is that the height of the symbolically important third floor of the Martinic Palace is exactly half the height of the parapet of the Bohemian Chancellery window.

The main element in the layout of the Royal Palace since the late Gothic period has always been the Vladislav Hall. It is oriented along the east-west axis, the main emphasis being put on the architectural beauty of the east façade connecting the hall with the royal All Saints Chapel. Similar features can also be observed here. The best architecture in the northern section of the Martinic Palace can be seen in the banqueting hall which is in an equivalent position to the Vladislav Hall. The decorated east side, like the Vladislav Hall, has a palace chapel attached. The height of the flat ceiling is again half the height of the Vladislav Hall, although the latter is covered with a unique and extremely intricate late Gothic vault. This shows that there was not a transfer of morphology, but of mass, volume

Baroque Renovation of Martinic Palace

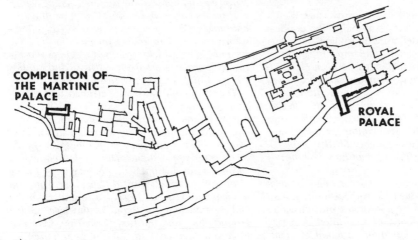

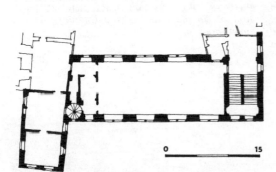

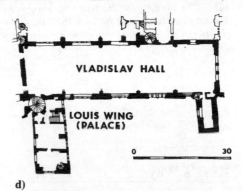

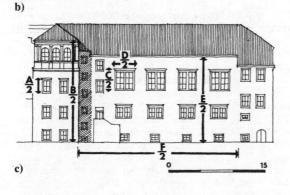

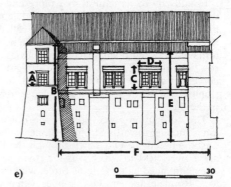

a) Baroque renovation of Martinic Palace—situation
b) ground plan of the renovated palace
c) north façade with dimensions
d) ground plan of Vladislav Hall with Louis Wing
e) south façade of Royal Palace

and function.

All the above observations prove that Rieth's Royal Palace was used—probably for political reasons—as a model of the Martinic Palace.

A general renovation and modernization of the Martinic Palace took place between 1966 and 1972. Until that time, the palace had been used for more than a century as a dwelling-house with some thirty flats for the poor after the re-building in the late 18th century. After the large-scale and difficult renovation, prepared and conducted by Zdeněk Hölzel of SURPMO, the palace became the office of the Chief Architect of Prague.

The palace was neglected for a long time, as it was believed that due to its radical conversion in the 18th century into a poor-house the house had lost its historic layout and decoration. A survey showed, however, that many original elements had only been covered over. All the newer partition walls and inserted elements were then removed. A major problem was the renovation of the original baqueting hall on the first floor of the north wing, between the main staircase and the palace chapel. The intermediate ceiling was removed and the shallow coffered ceiling, which had partly survived, was restored, as well as the paintings. Many Renaissance painted ceilings were discovered in rooms on the first and the second floors, which were then restored and the rooms were converted into offices and studios for the Chief Architect Office.

The main courtyard was cleaned and a new grille by Josef Vitvar was placed over the original well, the sgraffiti discovered on the east courtyard façade and dating from about 1580 were renovated, and arched openings were made in the staircase vestibule. During the renovation of the main façade with three gables facing Hradčany Square beautiful figural sgraffiti with biblical motifs from Joseph's life and from the Old Testament were found at the level of the ground floor and the first floor. They were restored and secured, and can now be admired.

The renovation and rebuilding of the Martinic Palace ranks among the best recent achievements and is an example of the social regeneration of an old building and its adaptation to meet modern needs.

King's Way

In addition to its natural axis represented by the Vltava, Prague has had since the Middle Ages a communication artery which is now called the King's Way. This busy street in the town now alternates between open spaces and masses, narrow streets and wide squares, straight and curved streets, in part on flat ground, in part sloping. The name King's Way is due to its role in the past.

The coronation processions of the Bohemian kings moving towards St. Vitus' Cathedral in the Castle entered the Old Town through the Powder Tower, next to which was the royal palace. They continued along Celetná Street with its historic Romanesque and Gothic houses that were later rebuilt in the Baroque style. The most important of them is the Hrzánský Palace (No. 12/558, Celetná Street), a high Baroque building with the remains of a Romanesque house, built after 1700 probably to a plan by Giovanni Alliprandi.

The old way passes the Old Town Square on its left side, past richly articulated patrician houses to Malý ryneček (Small Market), and along Karlova Street again through the Old Town towards a small square in front of the Clementinum Building (Křižovnické Square, see page 119). Karlova Street is closed by the Colloredo-Mansfeld Palace (No. 2/189, Karlova Street) built in 1735 by František I. Prée, a student of F. M. Kaňka. The sculptural decoration on its façade was made by Braun's workshop. The Old Town Bridge Tower opens the way to Charles Bridge. Mostecká (Bridge) Street was already in the Middle Ages the main artery of the once independent town now known as the Lesser Quarter (Malá Strana). Lined with sumptuous buildings from the medieval era, such as the Bishop's Palace from the 12th century (destroyed in 1419), or the beautiful palace of the Duke of Saxony from the mid-14th century, the street offers fine views of the greatest building of the Prague Ba-

King's Way

a)

POWDER TOWER

CELETNÁ

OLD TOWN SQUARE

SMALL SQUARE

KARLOVA

KŘIŽOVNICKÉ SQ.

CHARLES BRIDGE

MOSTECKÁ

LESSER TOWN SQ.

NERUDOVA

THE CASTLE

c)

d)

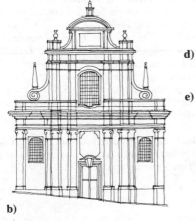

b)

e)

f)

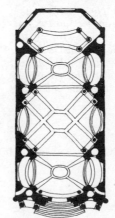

a) **King's Way**
b) **Church of Our Lady "U kajetánů"**
c) **Morzin Palace**
d) **Thun Palace**
e) f) **G. Guarini's plan** (not realized)

(131)

roque, the Church of St. Nicholas in the middle of Lesser Quarter Square (Malostranské náměstí; see page 133).

The west side of the square is occupied by the Liechtenstein Palace which has been rebuilt in the neo-Classical style, and in the western corner of the square the most beautiful street in Prague, Nerudova Street begins. The street is also the most beautiful part of the King's Way, climbing here towards the Castle. Its beauty was crowned with Baroque architecture which, however, only covers the original Renaissance and even Gothic houses with new façades. The narrow inclined street is lined mainly with middle-class houses and a few palaces, such as the Morzin Palace (now the Embassy of Romania) designed by the great Baroque architect Giovanni Santini-Aichel on the site of four earlier houses which the architect integrated in his palace in 1714. The façade of the palace is decorated with sculptures by Ferdinand M. Brokof and its centre is accented by figures of Moors supporting the balcony. Above the portal, there are allegorical busts of Day and Night and symbols of the four continents on the gable.

Another palace here is the Valkoun, or Thun Palace dating from 1725 (now the Embassy of Italy), with a beautiful portal and heraldic eagles by Matthias B. Braun. Giovanni Santini-Aichel had his house near the palace. The newest part of the Thun Palace, designed by Santini, adjoins the earlier core built after 1672 under Jan Jáchym Slavata, probably after a plan prepared by Francesco Caratti. The oldest part of the complex, the north section facing the Castle Steps, is the House of the Lords of Hradec from the mid-16th century whose magnificent Renaissance gables rank among the most impressive Renaissance motifs in Prague.

The first renovation of the King's Way, a popular tourist attraction, took place between the 1950s and 1970s, and then from 1985 to 1987. At the corner of Celetná Street and Ovocný trh (Fruit Market) a fine example of Cubist architecture can be seen, the house called "The Black Mother of God" by Josef Gočár, which was restored and has been used by the state enterprise Výstavnictví. Opposite it is a restored middle-class house, accommodating the management of SURPMO (State Institute for Renovation of Ancient Towns and Buildings), and the renovated Menhardt Palace (described in another chapter). On the other side of Celetná Street many houses can be admired that were renovated as part of the restoration of the Carolinum for Charles University, particularly the houses Nos. 560 and 562. On the right, there is another major building renovated in the 1960s, the Caretto-Millesimo Palace, No. 597, which now houses the Teacher's Institute of Charles University. There are a number of other historic buildings in the area, such as the Gothic house No. 478 with an original medieval roof truss. From here we enter Old Town Square where almost all houses have been renovated (see page 43).

Another interesting part of the King's Way is Karlova (Charles) Street where there are many shops and pubs at ground floor level and where some important buildings have been restored, such as the Central Bohemian Gallery, Nos. 156 and 220 (see page 119). Křižovnické (Knights of the Cross) Square in front of the Old Town Bridge Tower has also been renovated, as well as the bridge itself. Mostecká (Bridge) Street in the Lesser Quarter now has much charm with its renovated façades, interiors, shop fronts and modern signboards. There is also a modern house with the cinema "Na hradbách" built in the late 1950s. The houses on the south side of Lesser Quarter Square are still waiting for renovation, while the other façades have already been restored.

Houses in Nerudova Street were among the first to be renovated on the King's Way, such as, for instance, the middle-class houses called "U tří housliček" (At the Three Fiddles), "U zlatého lva" (At the Golden Lion), or the palaces of the Morzins and the Thuns. At the same time, houses in the immediate vicinity were restored, such as Na Úvozu, Na Radničních schodech, etc. A total renovation of Jánský vršek is now being prepared.

Another stage of the renovation of the King's Way has been taking place since 1988 and includes further areas towards Prague Castle.

Much attention was already paid to the Lesser Quarter in the reign of Emperor Rudolph II. The most important and busiest arteries connecting the Old Town with the Castle passed through the quarter, particularly Mostecká (Bridge) Street and the New Castle Steps, the main road leading to the Castle. Building activity in the town reached its peak in the Baroque epoch.

Some time after 1606 Zikmund Smiřický built his late Renaissance palace in the centre of the Lesser Quarter (No. 6, Lesser Quarter Square), a massive structure, square in plan with an inner courtyard. The original building had arcades, galleries and bartizans at the corners, and a beautiful arcaded courtyard. The house was later rebuilt in the late Baroque style and another storey was added. In 1763, Joser Jäger crowned the building with a segmental gable over the central projecting section. Of Renaissance origin also is the house No. 10/261, Lesser Quarter Square, with a beautiful volute gable. Dating from the same time are two houses with large halls with lunettes, namely the house No. 5/266, called "U Glaubiců", and the neighbouring house, No. 265, called "U černého jelena" (At the Black Stag), whose neo-Classical façade dating from 1780 is the work of the owner, Ignaz Palliardi.

The largest building on Lesser Quarter Square, of great architectural interest, was the new town-hall, No. 35, which was rebuilt from 1617 to 1622 when it acquired its present-day late Renaissance appearance. The two-storey block was built by Giovanni de Bossi and designed by Giovanni M. Filippi, replacing an earlier town-hall that had been severely damaged in 1611. The new building, particularly the part facing the square and the rear wing that was built at the same time, was nearly finished by 1619. The revolt of the Bohemian Estates affected the construction, so that the three towers of the town-hall shown in Hollar's vista from 1636 were not constructed until 1628. The Thirty Years' War slowed down the construction and affected the interior decoration. During the Swedish occupation the house was plundered and was not repaired until about 1690. In 1784, as the municipal administration concentrated on the town-hall of the Old Town, the town-hall of the Lesser Quarter ceased to serve the purpose of local administration. Its form changed in 1828, when due to its bad condition all three early Baroque towers were pulled down, and in 1883 even part of the east and north wing was also demolished and a two-storey annex built. The Lesser Quarter Town-Hall still displays late Renaissance, Manneristic features.

In the Baroque period the systematic series of architectural changes on the east side of the square was completed. In the middle of the square the architects Orsi and Lurago completed the block of a Jesuit college whose huge size brutally invaded the surrounding architecture and totally ignored the prevailing scale. Quite intentionally, the building had a plain, unarticulated façade which totally differed from the articulated mass of the Clementinum. The whole area of the Lesser Quarter, forming a large triangle, is on the slope from the Vltava up to the Castle and Petřín Hill, and Lesser Quarter Square with its uneven surface is no exception. The upper part of the square, west of the Jesuit complex which divides the square into two parts, features a harmony of forms, as all the houses along the western side belonged to the Liechtensteins who rebuilt them in the same style. This upper part of the square, which used to be called the Italian Market in the 16th century and the west side of which was entirely occupied by the new Liechtenstein Palace (No. 258) dating from the early 17th century, was separated from the lower part by the massive block of the Jesuit building and St. Nicholas' Church. The houses Nos. 3, 4, 5/26, 27, 28 in the middle of the square, which survived the expansion of the Jesuits and constituted a natural foreground of St. Nicholas' Church, were partly rebuilt in the Baroque time. Around 1791, the Liechtenstein Palace was rebuilt by Matthias Hummel who gave the west front of the square its present-day appearance and made the house one of the most typical neo-Classical buildings in Prague. Now it houses the Music Academy.

The houses on the lower east side, including the town-hall, were given Baroque façades and arcades. The Kaiserstein Palace, which was later called "U Pecoldů", No. 23/37, Lesser Quarter Square, was built after 1700 by Giovanni Alliprandi and replaced two older houses here. The palace has recently been renovated and its front wall faces the square, while its rear part facing Josefovská Street dates back to 1536.

The block of two houses on the north side of the square, namely the palace acquired in 1637 by the Sternbergs and the Fukovský House, were rebuilt in the early Baroque style. The latter was in 1684 purchased by Adolf of Sternberg and the façades of both houses were united. The house No. 20/518, Lesser Quarter Square, was acquired in 1680 by the Lord of Schönfeld and was largely rebuilt.

Another important event in the architectural history of Lesser Quarter Square was the rebuilding of the east part of the house No. 1. The

Lesser Quarter Square

a)

b)

c)

a) **Lesser Quarter (Malostranské) Square seen from St. Thomas'**
b) **Lesser Quarter Town-Hall, original appearance**
c) **plan of the square:** 1 St. Nicholas' Church, 2 former Jesuit College, 3 house U kamenného stolu (Malostranská Café), 4 Smiřický house No. 6, 5 Sternberg Palace No. 7, 6 former Lesser Quarter Town-Hall, No. 35, 7 Kaiserstein Palace, No. 37, 8 house U Petržilků, No. 272, 9 house U Glaubiců, No. 266, 10 Hartig Palace, No. 259, 11 Liechtenstein Palace, No. 258, 12 former Jesuit College, No. 1, 13 plague column with the Holy Trinity

Lesser Quarter Square

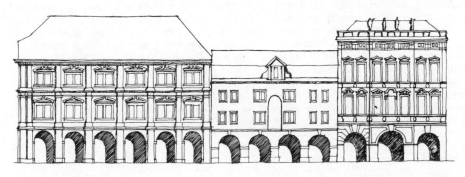

a) Upper part of square
b) North side of square
c) East side of square

house was rebuilt in the 17th century to meet the needs of a Jesuit College. The house No. 9/182, Thunovská Street, was rebuilt prior to 1725, probably by Kilian Ignaz Dientzenhofer, who created a fine building here. The Baroque era also had an impact on the architecture of the Hartig Palace, No. 12/259, in the southwest corner of the square. Two houses standing here were rebuilt after 1700 by the Count of Kolowrat and Countess Černín according to designs by Giovanni Alliprandi. His plan was realized in 1722 by František M. Kaňka.

In the Baroque period many sculptures were set in public places, such as the upper part of Lesser Quarter Square, where in 1715 a plague column to the Holy Trinity was placed. The column was designed by Alliprandi, the sculptural decoration was made by Johann O. Mayer. Of artistic interest also was a great public fountain that was placed in 1602 in the lower part of the square.

Due to the prevalence of the Baroque style, the appearance of the Lesser Quarter in the 18th century was no longer constituted by individual buildings, but by harmonious urban complexes. Thus, the process of conversion of the old Romanesque and Gothic buildings with Renaissance façades was completed by creating a townscape whose quality fully complied with the spirit of the prevailing Baroque style. Of all the towns of Prague this particularly applies to the Lesser Quarter.

This picturesque square which is dominated, as is the entire Lesser Quarter, by the monumental Church of St. Nicholas with the Profession House, is surrounded by a number of remarkable houses of different style and scale, and yet the general impression is of harmony. Being one of the most important points on the King's Way it has always been given great attention by conservationists. Early in this century, its protection was much discussed as a result, in particular, of the work of the Club for Old Prague. Particularly disputed was the house called "U klíčů" (At the Keys) which partly blocked the entrance into Karmelitská Street. There was only a narrow passageway, too small for the tram line which was planned here. A competition was therefore organized to solve the problem. Finally, Jan Kotěra's plan was accepted and realized according to which the south front of the square was interrupted by opening it into Karmelitská Street, and

a corner house with arcades featuring flattened Cubistic forms, designed by Ludvík Kysela, was built here. The project made it possible to lay tramlines in this part of the Lesser Quarter. Another major act of conservation was the protection of the Grömling Palace, now known as "U kamenného stolu" (At the Stone Table) or the Lesser Quarter Café. There were powerful lobbies interested in raising the height of the house by giving it two to three further storeys. The fight against the project proved victorious, the plan was rejected, and the fine architecture by Josef Jäger dating from 1778 was saved.

In the northeast corner of the square is No. 518, a Renaissance house with a Baroque gable and neo-Renaissance sgraffiti on the corner oriel. The decoration dates from 1899 when it was executed by Professor Celda Klouček during a renovation of the house. The house was rebuilt again after the war and the arcades were secured. Opposite it are the former Lesser Quarter town-hall, rebuilt in 1822 and again in the fifties to house the Malostranská beseda cultural centre, and the beautiful Kaiserstein Palace, No. 37, which was in 1896 converted into a tenement house. Its arcades were bricked in, which spoiled the original concept of the façade and the layout of the ground floor. The palace was renovated from 1979 to 1983 according to a plan prepared by a team of architects headed by Zdeněk Pokorný, and the interiors were restored and adapted to house the Czech Chamber of Commerce. A commemorative tablet was installed on the façade with a bust by Jan Simota of the Czech opera singer Ema Destinová who had lived on the first floor here.

SURPMO is now planning a renovation of the group of middle-class houses along the upper south front of the square: the houses No. 267 "U zlatého hroznu" (At the Golden Bunch of Grapes), No. 266 "U Glaubiců" with a well-known restaurant, and No. 265 "U černého jelena" (At the Black Stag) by Ignatius Palliardi from 1614 with a Renaissance layout.

Two more houses on the square are still awaiting renovation: the house called "U tří zlatých hvězd" (At the Three Gold Stars), No. 263, and the Trostovský House, also known as "Zlatý lev" (The Golden Lion), No. 261. With these, the current renovation of the square will be completed.

The central market-place, which has been known since 1869 as Lesser Quarter Square, was already in the Middle Ages a centre of the Lesser Quarter and contained a Romanesque church dedicated to St. Wenceslas. There was also a parish church to St. Nicholas, built in 1283. The centre of the square was then built-up, and a group of houses soon surrounded the church so that the large and sloping market-place was divided into two parts: the upper and the lower markets. The construction of a Baroque church here was part of a general plan covering the square.

After a great fire of 1541 which started here, in the heart of the Lesser Quarter, the square was surrounded with new houses and palaces. Step by step, architecturally interesting middle-class and noble houses were built here until the 18th century. The small houses in the middle of the square were converted by the Jesuits in the late 17th and the early 18th centuries into the massive block of the Profession House, which occupied a key position in the plan of the town.

The Jesuits, supported by the Emperor, struggled for a long time with the magistrate of the Lesser Quarter, and this hindered their building activity. Early in 1625 Emperor Ferdinand II consented to giving a church, a school, a parsonage and a parish house to the Jesuits. Having purchased several middle-class houses, they started building a profession house in 1668. In September 1673 Emperor Leopold himself came from Vienna to lay the foundation stone.

In 1672, the architect Giovanni Domenico Orsi (de Orsini) was for the first time mentioned in connection with the Lesser Quarter Jesuits. In 1673, plans of the profession house were prepared by Francesco Caratti. In 1676, however, Giovanni Domenico Orsi was invited to continue the construction of the profession house with a church according to the last plan that had been approved. Until his death in 1679, Orsi worked on the building, which developed into a massive closed four-wing block with two courtyards and with façades in a sober style. His successor was Francesco Lurago who between 1680 and 1688 constructed the Baroque church of St. Wenceslas as part of the complex, replacing the original Romanesque rotunda that had been pulled down in 1629. The last part of the profession house to be built was the west wing, completed in 1690. However, the construction of the church went far from smoothly. During its construction, St. Wenceslas' Church became a parish church for some time, and only in 1773 was the parish returned to St. Nicholas and the Baroque church of

St. Wenceslas was closed and converted into offices and storerooms.

Until 1773, there had been a corridor connecting the profession house with the Jesuit College in Sněmovní Street (No. 1), which is a large block-like builidng dating from the early 18th century whose west part from 1582 had originally belonged to the Lobkovics. The plans of the building that are still available are signed by Kilian I. Dientzenhofer and prove also the participation of his father Christoph (1711). The college was closed in 1773, at the same time as the Order. The house was rebuilt in the neo-Classical style by Anton Haffenecker and the interiors were adapted to house the Governor's Office and, as of 1850, the Vice-Regency. Of the original building only the rich portal (1727) facing Sněmovní Street still exists.

West of the old Gothic church of St. Nicholas, which had been used by the Jesuits during the construction of the new church until 1737, a new church slowly grew up that formed the south side of the profession house. Its origins lay in plans from the last third of the 17th century. The decisive period came after 1702 when a new, surprisingly bold design appeared after thirty years which was based on curved lines and which determined the character of both the main façade and the nave. The plans are certainly by Christoph Dientzenhofer, an outstanding architect and technician. The construction of the curved façade, forty metres long and featuring both convex and concave curves, and of the large nave was begun in 1703 and went on more or less without interruption. The plan was indeed a Baroque experiment in Europe. Christoph Dientzenhofer, an experienced vault-maker, built the dynamic façade and the large aisled nave, surmounted with intricate vaults over the intersection of three ovals; he was also mentioned as a technical advisor in pulling down the old Gothic tower. The main vault of the church is in harmony with the concave curves of the lateral chapels and the massive and oblique pilasters. The space is characterized by different curves, and the variety of forms is further increased by the contrast of light and shadow.

The construction of St. Nicholas' Church, a real symbol of Baroque art, took fifty years. Dientzenhofer the Elder had by 1715 built the major part of the nave, being followed by his son Kilian Ignaz who, as of 1737, continued the work done by his father by making the third vault bay, which shows the different technique of the young architect. He created the three-leaf chancel of the church with a 70 m high dome which

0   10

he finished shortly before his death (1751), when his art had fully matured. Dientzenhofer's dome was a totally new element in Prague; it had nothing in common with the small dome planned by his father that would have been quite inconspicuous on the skyline of Prague. In the construction of the dome Dientzenhofer applied Michelangelo's sickle-shaped construction, i.e., both jackets meet not at the lantern, but at the bottom of the dome. With the dome of St. Nicholas, Kilian I. Dientzenhofer carried out his finest work in his native town and also completed the process of creating a new townscape in Prague. At the same time, the slender belfry belonging to the town was constructed, being completed by Anselmo Lurago between 1752 and 1755. The dome of the Jesuit church and the top of the municipal belfry reach the same height of 74 metres. Their position, effect and harmony make them an inseparable part of the panorama of Hradčany.

The outstanding interiors of St. Nicholas, the chef d'oeuvre of Baroque illusionism, were decorated by the most important artists of the time. The huge fresco on the nave vault was painted by Johann L. Kracker (1761), those in the aisles and the chancel by František X. Balek, Josef Kramolín and Josef Hager. Of the other paintings the work of Karel Škréta must be stressed. The sculptures were made by Johann B. Kohl, Ignaz Platzer and members of the Prachner family.

Dientzenhofer's ability to harmonize the surrounding spaces and the mass of the adjacent structures with the main building reached its highest level of development here. The architect's concept was not confined to the church only, but he wished to incorporate the building into the architecture of the town and thereby contribute to the townscape. This aspect of his work is of utmost importance and that is why the church ranks among the best Baroque buildings in Europe.

This outstanding building was given much attention and care as early as the 1950s. In 1953, the church was measured and a technical survey was made. The most damaged part proved to be the important wall-painting in the dome surmounting the nave, the fresco by Johann Lukas Kracker dating from 1761—1770, which was due to the penetration of water from the dome cladding and to the condensation of humidity contained in the church. Some parts were so weathered and damaged that there were worries about the chances of restoring the whole painting, as some 60 per cent of its area was endangered. Through their responsible approach and hard work the restorers finally succeeded. The painting was carefully measured, documented and cleaned without causing any damage. More than 900 square metres of fresco were then restored, the loose plaster under the fresco was secured by means of grouts, the surface was then repainted and the damaged areas were toned so as not to spoil the general impression made by the painting. The interiors were stylistically integrated, the intrusive elements were removed, the stuccowork was renovated, the capitals of the columns and pilasters were gilded and the altar paintings and sculptures restored. The renovation of the fresco began in March 1954 and ended in September 1955, while the overall restoration and renovation of the interiors took two more years. The exterior underwent a renovation only of the surfaces. The nave cladding was replaced and the metal roofing of the dome and the tower was repaired. The repair and renovation of the façades did not include the modern procedures as we know them today, nor were the original colours applied. The colour was reduced to two tones of ochre. The church is an important religious monument and continues to serve its sacred purpose, but it is also used for concerts and is daily admired by thousands of visitors.

Clam-Gallas Palace

MARIÁNSKÉ SQUARE

KARLOVA

HUSOVA

0   50

Where Husova Street, one of the oldest roads in the Old Town, crosses Karlova Street a rare example of Viennese Baroque palace architecture can be seen, the Clam-Gallas Palace built by Johann Bernard Fischer of Erlach, an outstanding Imperial architect from Vienna.

The capital of the Empire, Vienna, and the Imperial Court were not far away and many Viennese architects worked also in Bohemia and Moravia around 1700. All this strongly influenced the work of architects in Prague. It was particularly Fischer's work that had repercussions in Bohemia and many architects here followed his example even before he himself had realized any buildings in Prague.

Johann Bernard Fischer built one of his major works in Prague, architecturally unique among Prague's Baroque buildings: a palace for one of the top Government officials, Johann Wenzel Gallas, Chief Marshall of the Kingdom of Bohemia, Imperial Ambassador to and also Vice-Regent of Naples. As of 1690, Gallas was systematically purchasing middle-class houses adjoining the old house of his family which no longer met the needs of an Imperial Ambassador, both in terms of size and architecture. In their place, he built a new large palace whose beauty was superior to all the neighbouring houses.

In the very heart of the Old Town, where centuries ago had been the residence of Jan Jindřich of Luxembourg, Governor of Moravia and a brother of Emperor Charles IV, replacing even older Romanesque houses, a brilliant work of Prague palace architecture was created.

Fischer's palace was built from 1713 to 1729 by G. A. Canevalle and Thomas Haffenecker. It was a corner building with several storeys on an irregular site, surrounding two courtyards and with a main façade with rich carved decoration. In the basement, remains of an old Romanesque house and of the later Gothic palace of the Emperor's brother Jan Jindřich can still be found.

All the sculptures that decorated the palace were made by Matthias Bernard Braun. His two giant figures standing on massive portals (1714) give monumentality to the façade which is articulated by three projecting parts and surmounted by an attic gable. Of the total of thirteen statues three are now replicas (Jupiter, Mercury and Venus). Their originals and five more statues were removed from the gable after 1900 and placed in the Museum of Decorative Arts, and in 1963 transferred to the National Gallery.

The rich interiors with a number of ceremonial and sumptuous rooms decorated in the course of the 18th century correspond to the rich exterior decoration in the spirit of Fischer. The sophisticated palace staircase is one of the most beautiful in Prague. The stuccowork in the remarkable staircase hall is partly due to Santin Bossi, the vases and lamp-posts were made by M. B. Braun and the ceiling fresco by Carlo Carlone.

The palace now houses the Archives of Prague which moved here in 1945 from the town-hall of the Old Town partly destroyed during the uprising in May 1945.

On the initiative of Jindřich Zdík, Bishop of Olomouc, King Vladislav I founded in 1140 a Premostratensian monastery on an important road leading to Prague Castle from the west. The monastery, which protected the Castle by controlling this road, was completed in 1182. Supported by Vladislav, the monastery flourished and soon became a major cultural centre in the country and a sign of the growing power of the Bohemian sovereign. From the very beginning, the monastery, which had a library of international renown, was of extreme cultural importance.

The large complex of buildings with its complicated ground plan, with several inner courtyards and a church to Our Lady, has long been considered to be from the 16th, and particularly from the 17th and 18th centuries. It was believed, due to an account by Vavřinec of Březová, a participant in the Hussite Wars, that the abbey had

Strahov Abbey

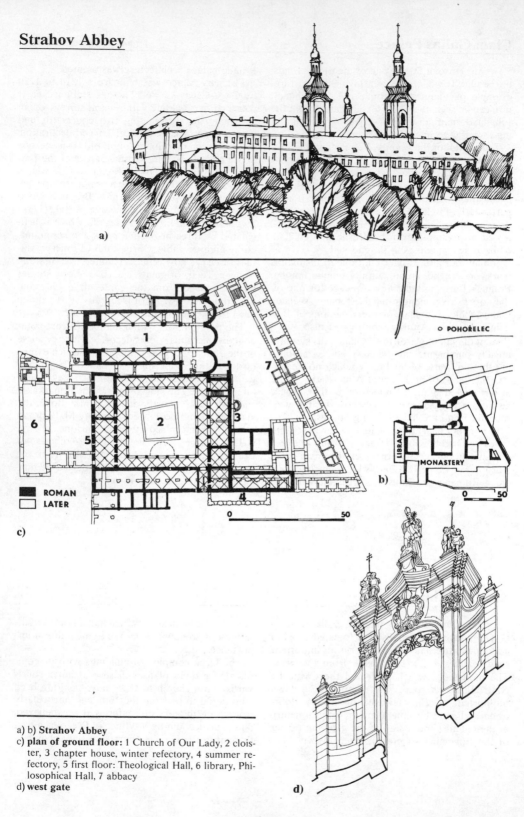

a) b) **Strahov Abbey**
c) **plan of ground floor:** 1 Church of Our Lady, 2 cloister, 3 chapter house, winter refectory, 4 summer refectory, 5 first floor: Theological Hall, 6 library, Philosophical Hall, 7 abbacy
d) **west gate**

been burned down in 1420 and totally destroyed. Archaeological research carried out here since 1950 has proved that this was false.

The tombs of the abbey founders, Bishop Zdík and King Vladislav I, have disappeared without any trace, however the original Romanesque masonry of white clay slate blocks has survived at its full height. After a fire in 1258 the masonry was plastered over, and in the Gothic period as well as in the late 16th century the complex was rebuilt so that it lost its medieval character. Under the renovations and later under the Baroque cladding the most important parts of the original Romanesque ground floor remained hidden, namely the chapter house, the refectory and the cellarium (service rooms).

The Premonstratensian Church of the Assumption of Our Lady, which was originally a typical Romanesque basilica with a nave and two aisles dating from the latter half of the 12th century, was rebuilt after 1250 and again after 1420. A large-scale Renaissance rebuilding took place in 1601, and then again in 1627 when Emperor Rudolph II also built an aisleless votive little church to St. Roche (1603—1612), a remarkable combination of the Gothic and the Renaissance styles, probably designed by Giovanni M. Filippi, which was once a parish church of Strahov. Now it is an exhibition hall called Musaion and is part of the Strahov Abbey complex. The Church of Our Lady was given its present appearance later, in the mid-18th century, when it was also enlarged and rebuilt. There are stucco cartouches and rich frescoes covering the Baroque vault. The Baroque façade and the towers date from 1743—1751 and were the work of Anselmo Lurago.

During the rebuilding of the abbey in the late 17th century the Theological Hall of the Strahov Library was built by G. D. Orsi from 1671 to 1679, richly decorated with stuccowork and painting by Siard Nosecký. Later, from 1682 to 1698, Silvestro Carloni and Marco Antonio Canevalle built a large annex designed by Jean B. Mathey and extended the abbey towards the southwest. The high Baroque entrance gate of the abbey dating from 1742 is decorated with a statue representing St. Norbert by Johann Anton Quitainer (1755). The very long and complicated architectural history of the abbey culminated in the Baroque epoch and ended in the years 1782—1784 with the construction of the library, an important neo-Classical work by Ignazio Palliardi. Soon after its completion, the abbey was temporarily closed by Emperor Joseph II.

After the Second World War, the Premonstratensians were expelled from the monastery, and in 1950, alongside archaeological research, a detailed historical and technical survey was carried out that had been prepared by Dobroslav Líbal and Alois Kubíček. The survey showed that under the Baroque surface, and particularly underground, much Romanesque architecture survived. Jan Sokol was invited to prepare a renovation plan of the abbey which was to acquire a new social function by being converted into a Museum of National Literature.

The exhibition plan, aimed at showing in an attractive and comprehensive way the history of Czech literature, was prepared by a special team appointed alongside the founding of the Museum. The renovation and rebuilding did not last long and was completed by 1953, but the work was very difficult as the buildings had to be made stable, some missing elements had to be restored (vaults, ceilings, pavements, carpentry, etc.), and all the available historical styles, from the Middle Ages to the Baroque, had to be harmonized to create a single architectural and artistic unit. During the renovation in the 1950s many surprising discoveries were made, as for instance the fact that original Romanesque ground floor, which had no cellars, gradually became a basement due to the raised level of the courtyards and the gardens, and thus the most valuable parts of the original abbey have survived. In the renovated Romanesque parts of the complex the early history of the Slavs is shown and objects related to that period are displayed. The restored old libraries in the Philosophical and the Theological Halls also form part of the exhibition and their collections and architectural beauty make them real pearls of the Museum.

The renovation of Strahov Abbey was one of the first examples after the Second World War of a new philosophy of renovation fully respecting the values of particular styles. The architect Sokol showed sobriety in his designs, without adding too many new elements. It is easy to see what is the original Romanesque part and what is Baroque. The new elements and the museum facilities act as links between the two architectural worlds.

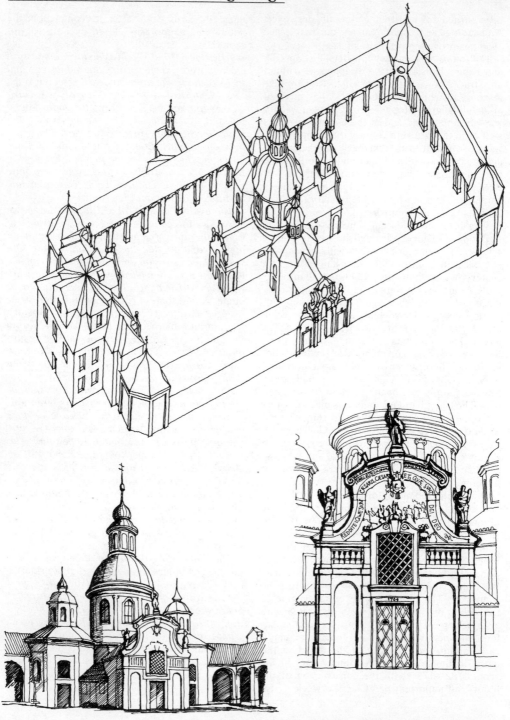

place of pilgrimage on White Mountain

Pilgrimage architecture is still prominent in Bohemia's landscape. Soon after the 1620 victory of the Habsburgs over the Bohemian Estates the places of pilgrimage were attributed a special and important role in the recatholization process. At the sites of old and new miracles that were believed to have occurred here, new and increasingly intricate religious buildings were constructed. At the same time, the cult of St. Mary was introduced and cultivated.

The places of pilgrimage were as a rule on hills, and although their architecture was different, they were always built to fit into the landscape. Some of them are architecturally complex, with a courtyard surrounded by arcades that were often built later to offer shelter and relaxation to pilgrims. Enriched with onion domes surmounting the corner chapels as well as the central chapel, they dominate the region through their siting and mass.

White Mountain (in Czech, Bílá Hora) is an example of one of the most common types of pilgrimage places with a cloister and corner chapels. Once outside the town, but now within the city there was originally a small chapel here consecrated to St. Wenceslas and built soon after the battle that had taken place here on 8th November 1620. A monastery with a chapel to Our Lady the Victorious was then founded here by Ferdinand II in 1628. However, only the chapel was built, and the unfinished monastery was converted into an inn still before the middle of the 17th century.

The main construction phase of the holy place started in 1704. Kristian Luna, a painter and a citizen of Hradčany worked here until his death in 1729. He worked untiringly on the construction site and invited outstanding painters and sculptors to contribute. He is believed to have prepared the construction plan, but other contemporary architects living in Prague certainly helped him with the design, possibly Giovanni B. Alliprandi, who is also known to have contributed financially, or Giovanni B. Santini-Aichel, who is now thought to have been responsible for rebuilding the church here.

Side chapels were attached to the church and in 1714 a new dome and chancel were added. Also the four corner chapels of the cloister were built and an enclosing wall was erected. Between 1717 and 1729, arcaded galleries for pilgrims and a house for the custodian were constructed. Václav Vavřinec Rainer, an important Prague painter, and Kosmas D. Asam of Bavaria decorated the dome and the vaults with frescoes. The main portal with its rich artistic decoration is slightly reminiscent of the work of Kilian Ignaz Dientzenhofer. The cloister was painted at the same time. The complex was finished in the mid-18th century. The Mountain, where many armies are reported to have camped since the Middle Ages, took its name from the white clay slate that was available here. In 1785, Joseph II closed the church, which was then reopened in the early 19th century.

Loretto of Prague

The Loretto of Prague is the oldest and the most exuberant of all the Loretto churches in Bohemia and is internationally renowned. The central building of each Loretto is the "Holy Stable", which is a small prismatoid structure representing the legendary stable in which Saint Mary was believed to have lived in Nazareth and which was then transported by angels to Loretto in Italy. After that model many shrines were built, from the 16th century onwards all over the Catholic Europe and they became very popular places of pilgrimage.

The Loretto of Prague was built in 1626—1627, replacing a group of houses that had been abandoned by their inhabitants who had emigrated after the 1620 Battle of White Mountain. The sloping site was gradually built up, the first building being the Capuchin monastery in the north, in the garden of Margaret of Lobkovic, which was the first monastery of this order in this country. It had a church to Our Lady, and was completed in 1602, in the plain style of the order. The Loretto then occupied the lower eastern part of the square, facing the massive Černín Palace and was later connected with the monastery by means of a covered bridge.

The construction of the Loretto took many years and started with the Holy Stable in

Loretto of Prague

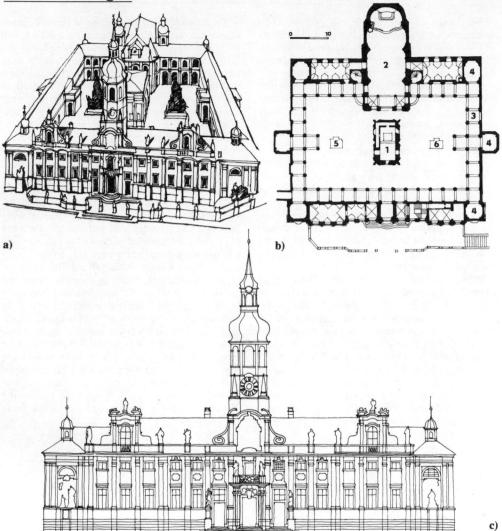

a)

b)

c)

a) b) c) **Prague's Loretto:** 1 Santa Casa, 2 Nativity
Church, 3 cloister, 4 chapel, 5 Resurrection: statue,
Our Lady's Ascension: statue
d) **Santa casa**

d)

1626—1631. The architect is said to have been Giovanni B. Orsi, being followed by Andrea Allio and Silvestro Carlone. The Holy Stable was initially only painted, and only after 1640 was it decorated with sculptures that still can be seen here. The Stable was gradually surrounded by a two-storey cloister with chapels in each corner and in the centre that were completed after 1740. In 1735, Kilian Ignaz Dientzenhofer replaced the central chapel of the east wing with a Church to the Nativity of the Lord, which is a rectangular building with a semicircular chancel and with rich architectural and artistic decoration. The fresco on the ceiling was painted in 1736 by Václav Vavřinec Rainer. The rich interiors made by leading Prague artists date from the same time.

The Holy Stable was consecrated in 1631, and more than a hundred years later the front wall and the upper storey of the cloister were built. The construction was completed by Kilian Ignaz Dientzenhofer who continued the work done by his father Christoph. The perpetual alterations to the plan and the involvement of different architects with different attitude gave a special character to different parts of the complex, particularly to the façades. The low front wall with three projecting sections and gables acquired its final appearance in the late 17th and the early 18th centuries. The entrance portal is on the axis of symmetry of the whole complex, passing through the central Santa Casa and continuing to the Church of the Nativity of the Lord at the rear. Two fountains decorated with rich sculptures stress the axis of symmetry, and consequently also the importance of the central structure.

An attractive part of the Loretto is the treasury where liturgical objects and jewels from the 17th and 18th centuries are preserved. The Loretto is also well-known for its beautiful carillon made by the clock-maker Peter Naumann and installed in 1694 in the main spire. The spire and the ground floor of the cloister date from 1661. The spire surmounting the main entrance portal and dominating the whole complex is eye-catching and still houses the carillon.

This unique Baroque complex, the Černín Palace and the Capuchin Monastery form what is now the unparalleled and beautiful Loretto (Loretánské) Square.

In the centre of the square in the 18th century there was also a chapel to St. Matthew whose origin goes back to the early Middle Ages and which was torn down in 1791. The site of the chapel was marked out in the paving of the square, and these marks can still be seen there. Its Baroque architecture was the work of František Maximilián Kaňka and his plan was realized between 1727 and 1732. The interiors were decorated by leading artists of that time, in particular the outstanding sculptor Matthias Bernard Braun. The appearance of the chapel is known to us from old drawings that still survive.

Břevnov Abbey

Břevnov, the oldest settlement known to us within today's Greater Prague, dates from almost a thousand years ago. Here, amidst forests, at the source of the Brusnice River and on a road leading from Prague westwards, Bishop Adalbert of the Slavník Dynasty and Prince Boleslav II of the Přemyslid Dynasty founded the very first monastery in Bohemia in 993. For centuries, Břevnov was only a small settlement which was later, particularly in the late 17th century, surrounded by farms.

The original Benedictine Monastery of Břevnov has been rebuilt many times. Its oldest parts dating from the late 10th century were discovered during an archaeological survey that started in 1964. A pre-Romanesque crypt was found under the choir of the church. The monastery was supported for a long time by princes and kings, which resulted in the high quality of its architecture. However, neither the Romanesque nor the later Gothic architecture of the monastery with its church (originally consecrated to St. Benedict and St. Adalbert) have survived. In the late 14th century, the church was reconsecrated to St. Margaret, a favourite patron-saint at that time. From the 15th century on, the monastery was in a state of poverty for three centuries, and it was not until the early 18th century, from 1708 to 1745, that the complex was largely rebuilt in the Baroque style and a new church was constructed.

The Baroque monastic buildings that can now be seen date from the early 18th century, and their architect was Christoph Dientzenhofer who

b)

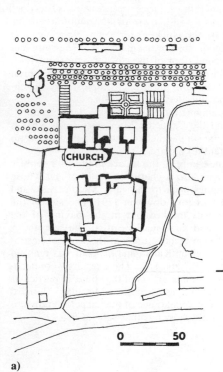

a)

0   50

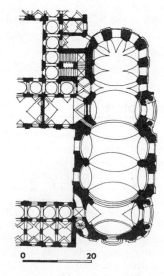

c)

d)

a) Břevnov Abbey—situation in 1811
b) c) St. Margaret's Church
d) entrance gate

also built here one of the most remarkable Baroque buildings in Bohemia: St. Margaret's Church.

Only few exclusively religious buildings, mostly outside Prague, are attributed to Christoph Dientzenhofer (1655–1722). They are the churches at Obořiště, Smiřice, Nová Paka, Cheb, and also St. Nicholas' Church in the Lesser Quarter. His authorship however, is still disputed.

The Church of St. Margaret at Břevnov from 1708–1714 is a typical example of a Baroque church conceived in the Roman illusive Baroque style whose aisleless plan makes an extremely large space possible. The beauty of the altar is stressed by a wall-painting. The ceiling frescoes representing motifs from the Legend of St. Adalbert were painted by Johann Jakob Steinfels before 1721. The south front features intricate architectural forms and in fact acts as the main façade. The presbytery and the belfry of the church were built by the younger Dientzenhofer.

Břevnov Abbey is a complex of outstanding architectural value and is also important from a town-planning point of view. The main building of the complex can be reached by entering through the ornamented main gate of 1740 by Kilian Ignaz Dientzenhofer, and crossing a large courtyard with a granary on the left-hand side and a service courtyard (1720–1721) on the opposite side adjoining the early Baroque monastic building from 1674. East of the church is the monastery with three courtyards in its centre. The complex was supposed to have been built by Paul Ignaz Bayer; however, in 1709 he was replaced by Christian Dientzenhofer, and later by Christoph's son.

The former ceremonial hall of the monastery, called the Theresian Hall, displays the most valuable and the best preserved painted ceiling by Kosmas Damian Asam of Bavaria, painted in 1727 and representing the Miracle of the Blessed Günther.

Behind the monastery, there is a large garden complying with the general Baroque layout. At its gate, opposite the church, is a pavilion called Vojtěška with a chapel above a well at which the monastery had been founded. It is, however, in a derelict condition and has been in need of overall renovation for a long time.

From 1980 to 1983, both the exterior and the interior of St. Margaret's Church were restored. In the interior, particularly in the presbytery which had been closed for ten years due to archaeological excavations in the Romanesque crypt, the frescoes on the vaulting and all the furniture were restored by Umělecká řemesla Praha and by ČFVU restorers. The building company Pražský stavební podnik renovated the sheathing and cladding. At the same time, a hot-water heating system was installed in the church.

An important archaeological finding, the pre-Romanesque crypt of the first monastic church at Břevnov under the presbytery of St. Margaret's, was renovated from 1978 to 1983 and made accessible to the public. The plan was prepared by Svatopluk Voděra and carried out by the Prague department of Pamiatkostav Žilina. There is a new entrance into the church at the point where the presbytery and the monastery meet.

Břevnov Abbey is now being returned to its original owners.

Today the abbey belongs again to the Benedictines. On 13 February, 1991 it was declared a national cultural monument. Pope John Paul is expected to attend the Millenium of the abbey in 1993.

Baroque Churches

Churches are the most numerous and remarkable Baroque buildings and show in their architecture the development of the style. There were many Gothic churches in Prague in the 17th and 18th centuries which were in a state of disrepair or were no longer suited to their needs and had therefore to be rebuilt.

The long series of Prague churches rebuilt in the Baroque style started with the former Lutheran Church of the Holy Trinity in the Lesser Quarter which was rebuilt from 1636 to 1644 and rededicated to Our Lady the Victorious. The architect coped with the task and with the new orientation of the rebuilding in a remarkable way, especially in the new façade which already had elements that were entirely Baroque. It is also here that for the first time in Prague the surrounding area was architecturally landscaped.

The first new religious building in Prague after the 1620 battle of White Mountain was the Loretto. Its construction began in 1626 and the first architect was Giovanni B. Orsi, who lived and worked in Prague in the 1660s. The chapel on the main cloister axis, built in 1661, was rebuilt in the 18th century by Christoph Dientzenhofer and converted into a Church of the Nativity of the Lord.

In 1635, a small round Chapel to St. Mary Magdalene was built under Letná Hill in a similar style to St. Roche's Church on Strahov Hill. The Capuchins in the New Town invited Melichar Mayer in 1636 to build a simple aisleless Church to St. Joseph, which was completed and consecrated in 1653, and later also a monastery in what is now Republic Square (náměstí Republiky). From 1638 to 1640, Carlo Lurago created the interior of the Church of the Holy Saviour in the Old Town, and Francesco Caratti crowned the church with a polygonal dome in 1648—1649. St. Francis' Church at the Hibernian Monastery built between 1652 and 1659 is a long building with inner lofts and its architect was probably Giovanni D. Orsi. The church was rebuilt by 1811 and has had an Empire façade since.

From 1665 to 1678, the Jesuits built the Church of St. Ignatius on Charles Square, the most valuable building in Prague of this kind prior to 1680. In 1673, the foundation stone was laid to St. Nicholas' Church in the Lesser Quarter whose plan was prepared by Giovanni D. Orsi. Later, in 1703, Christoph Dientzenhofer came and began working here. Francesco Caratti and Christoph Dientzenhofer joined in 1656—1673 to construct the Dominican Church of St. Mary Magdalene at Újezd where later the Dientzenhofers, both father and son, were buried. The basilica with a typical cruciform layout and a domical vault surmounting the crossing was closed in 1784 and in the 19th century rebuilt to serve civil purposes.

Impressed by Italian architecture, the Barnabites built an aisleless church to St. Benedict in 1655 at Hradčany. Two years later, another aisleless church consecrated to SS. Cosmas and Damian was built at Emmaus replacing the old Romanesque church here. Sobek of Bielenberg, the Archbishop of Prague, suggested in 1673 completing the nave of St. Vitus' Cathedral by building a Baroque addition, and Emperor Leopold II personally laid the foundation stone. In 1842 the unfinished Baroque masonry was removed.

Giovanni B. Mathey built the Church of St. Francis from 1679 to 1688 for the Knights of the Cross. With this building he introduced to our architects a new type of religious architecture where the weight of the central dome was counteracted by massive supports at the diagonals via triangular segments of spheres. With this church a new important period in the history of religious architecture in Baroque Prague began. Jean Baptiste Mathey, leading architect at that time, is believed also to have designed the oval church of St. Roche at Olšany, with chapels and a choir loft, which was built between 1680 and 1682. At the former seminary, which was later converted into a barracks, he built the Church of St. Adalbert at the Powder Tower (1694—1696) where the King's Court had once stood. The church was demolished in 1903 due to the construction of a Community House in the Art Nouveau style. Mathey, as well as Caratti before him, only designed his buildings and invited good builders in Prague to realize the plans (Marco A. Canevalle).

A unique building in Prague is the centralized Church of St. Joseph at the Carmelite Convent in the Lesser Quarter with a remarkable façade receding from the front of the neighbouring buildings. The church was built from 1683 to 1691 in the spirit of Belgian Baroque by the friar Donat Ignatius à Jesu of Louvain. Other architects to whom the church has sometimes been attributed are Abraham Paris and Giovanni B. Mathey.

Between 1699 and 1704 Marco Antonio Canevalle built an elongated Church to St. Ursula in Národní (National) Street with a dynamic inside space. The neighbouring monastery now houses a religious school. Particularly notable for its architecture is the side wall of the church which in fact plays the role of the main façade. A new type of space was created here of which many variations later appeared.

Baroque Churches

a)

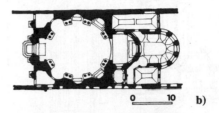

b)

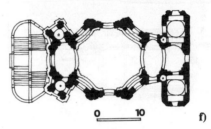

f)

c)

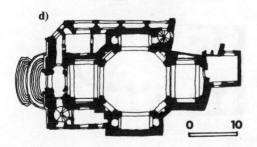

e)

d)

a) b) St. Joseph's, Lesser Quarter
c) d) Church of St. John of Nepomuk, Hradčany
e) f) Church of St. John "Na skalce"

(151)

Baroque Churches

a)

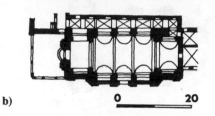

b)

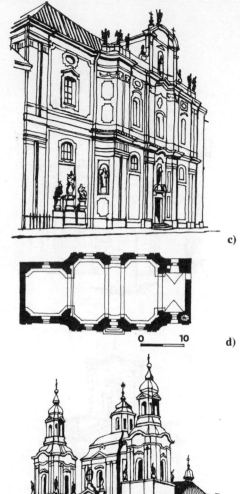

c)

d)

e)

f)

g)

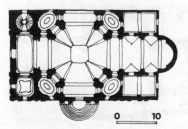

a) b) **Church of St. Charles Borromeo, now of SS. Cyril and Methodius**
c) d) **St. Ursula's Church**
e) **Holy Trinity Church**
f) g) **St. Nicholas' Church, Old Town**

(152)

Baroque Churches

The Czech architect František M. Kaňka designed many buildings in this country. St. Clement's Church at the Clementinum Building (1711—1715) was conceived by him as a hall-nave similar to that of St. Ursula's, with two bays of Bohemian sail vaulting, but without the central wide band.

One of the most important Baroque buildings in Prague is the aisleless Benedictine Church of St. Margaret at Břevnov (1708—1712). It has a very long chancel and very fine and technically difficult vaulting (see page 149). The Theatine Church of Our Lady in Nerudova Street from 1711—1717 has a ground plan resembling a Greek cross. The main façade was designed by Giovanni Santini-Aichel, the other parts being the work of several other architects. A plan of another Theatine church of the same type by Guarino Guarini, the leading Baroque architect in Italy, for Prague has survived. However, the plan was not realized.

The Holy Trinity Church in Spálená Street from 1713 was probably designed by Ottavio Broglio. Near here and not far from the Vltava is the two-aisle church of St. Adalbert dating from 1720 whose form is similar to that of Santini's buildings. The Chapel of the Annunciation of Our Lady in the Clementinum by František M. Kaňka, which is also called the Mirror Chapel, has a centrally-planned layout.

Another centralized church is that of St. John of Nepomuk at Hradčany which was built from 1720 to 1728 by K. I. Dientzenhofer, our leading Baroque architect, as his very first religious building in Prague. The so-called Baroque dualism is featured in St. Bartholomew's Church built between 1726 and 1731 at the Jesuit College in the Old Town by the same architect. Dientzenhofer applied the same layout to the Church of St. John of Nepomuk on the Rocks, built from 1730 to 1749. The latter, however, features a more intricate mass and space, the façade is curved and has the towers attached at oblique angles. Quite impressive also is the Church of St. Charles Borromeo in Resslova Street dating from 1730—1736, particularly due to its exterior with a central tower and a courtyard in front, which is very interestingly laid out. Kilian Ignaz at the same time built a church to St. Nicholas in the Old Town for the Benedictines of Emmaus with a cruciform ground plan. The two towers and the dome of the church are dominant elements of the Old Town. The main façade with rich architectural elements is on the south side which now faces Old Town Square (1732—1734). The chancel of St. Nicholas' Church in the Lesser Quarter

with its beautiful dome by Dientzenhofer was constructed from 1737 to 1752. In all the above cases Dientzenhofer used the experience gained from trips abroad and contacts with good foreign architects, including Lucas Hildebrandt of Vienna whose treatment of space was influential. As a result, a specifically Bohemian branch of Baroque crystallized by 1733, above all in Dientzenhofer's work.

Among the wide range of renovations that have been realized in Prague in the past decades, there is one which is of particular importance: the displacement and renovation of St. Mary Magdalene's Chapel. The reason for this unprecedented course of action to save the chapel was the construction of a new road on the left bank of the Vltava. However, there was an old raftsmen's and vintners' chapel, very derelict at that time, which blocked the new road. The chapel could be saved, but only by moving it elsewhere. Academician Stanislav Bechyně and a team of workers headed by Ladislav Pitín were charged with the task.

The chapel was braced inside with a timber structure and outside reinforced with adjustable steel segments. Under the masonry a concrete ring was made to support the structure and to carry it during the displacement. The new site was 31 metres away upstream; there was a service water reservoir for Letná Square in the form of a semicircular bastion, surmounted with a foundation to receive the centralized chapel. A concrete railway was built and then the building was displaced in two days, on 3rd and 4th February 1956, by means of a special pushing mechanism. After being reinstalled, the masonry was renovated and the interior restored, the chapel was surmounted with a new roof and a lantern. The cracks in the masonry were filled, the plaster was repaired both outside and inside, the stuccowork on the vault restored, the remaining wall paintings renovated as well as the six polychrome pilasters. The interior was renovated according to a plan prepared by Antonín Josef, and included also some new works of art, particularly the stained glass windows by Alena Nováková-Guttfreundová with motifs from the history of the chapel.

After the construction of the left-bank road and the access road to Čech Bridge the surroundings of the chapel were landscaped, and only a few older people still remember what happened to the chapel. However, being away from the road, the chapel ceased to be attractive to tourists and is now practically unused.

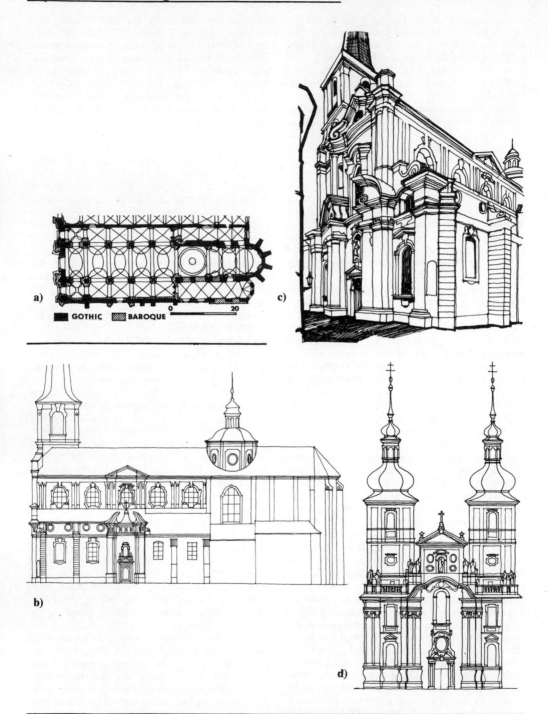

a) b) c) **Church of St. Thomas**
d) **Church of St. Gallus**

In addition to the construction of new churches in the 17th and 18th century older churches, Romanesque, Gothic and Renaissance were rebuilt in the Baroque style, often after damage caused by wars and fires, or because the pre-Baroque forms no longer met the new needs and had therefore to be adapted.

Baroque rebuilding, with much respect for the work done by previous generations, was a characteristic phenomenon in Prague. As of the mid-17th century, churches were being given new façades, for instance St. George's Church in the Castle and St. James' in the Old Town. Sometimes new curved front walls were built in front of the rebuilt exterior, as at St. Gallus' in the Old Town and at St. Thomas' in the Lesser Quarter. The entrance façade of the latter monastic church as well as the façade of the Church of St. John on the Rock (sv. Jan na Skalce) rank among the most progressive buildings by Kilian Ignaz Dientzenhofer in Prague.

Another stage of Baroque rebuilding of Prague's churches started in the second quarter of the 18th centruy when the interiors of many medieval churches were rebuilt, for instance that of Our Lady on Strahov Hill, or St. James', St. Thomas', and Our Lady at Karlov.

One of the major rebuilding works was the renovation of the interior of St. Thomas' Church in the Lesser Quarter. The last architectural changes to the old Gothic church at the Augustinian Monastery (founded by Wenceslas II

in 1285) took place here from 1723 to 1731 when the complex was rebuilt by Kilian Ignaz Dientzenhofer. Kilian Ignaz faced quite a difficult problem, as a technical examination requested by the Augustinians showed that the original vaulting of the nave had to be pulled down. The church was then rebuilt according to designs prepared by Dientzenhofer, who was already highly thought of and widely in demand.

The old Gothic layout of the church was respected. The building had developed in two stages: The chancel was completed in 1316, the nave in 1479. The medieval church is said to have been the most beautiful religious building of the high Gothic period. However, fifty years later it was badly damaged, and was not renovated until the 1480s. Further damage was caused by a fire in the mid-16th century, which was followed by another major renovation in the late 16th century. In the early 18th century, the church was in quite a derelict state and renovation was needed, which was then carried out by Dientzenhofer. Because of him, this important ancient building has survived.

Kilian Ignaz Dientzenhofer could always find excellent artists to join him in the construction and to meet his ambitious requirements. His favourite partners were Václav Vavřinec Reiner and Ferdinand Maxmilian Brokof. The extensive wall-paintings of St. Thomas were carried out by Reiner within an incredibly short span of two years.

Rebuilding of Karlov Church

Soon after the foundation of the New Town the construction of four important churches began. Of the churches, which were all closely linked with Emperor Charles IV, two were parish churches, St. Stephen's and St. Henry's, and two were monastic churches, namely that of the Benedictines at Emauzy (Emmaus) and that of the Augustinians at Karlov, each of them having a different layout. Quite unique is the layout of the centrally-planned church consecrated to Charles the Great, the Emperor's patron-saint, which imitated his octagonal funeral church in Aachen.

The importance of Karlov Church, one of the most remarkable buildings in Prague, lies in its

layout which was quite unusual at that time. Even though the original form of the interior remains unknown to us, as only the outer walls around the central octagonal nave and the chancel have survived, the present late Gothic architecture with a bold vaulting is very impressive and stylistically pure. The church was first rebuilt, and also re-dedicated to Our Lady, as early as the late 15th century. The structure was surmounted with a stellar vault of 24 m diameter dating from 1575, as proved by a beam bearing the data. The vault is believed to have been made by Bonifaz Wohlmut. The building was originally covered with a single high hipped roof, which later became a very popular type of

Rebuilding of Karlov Church

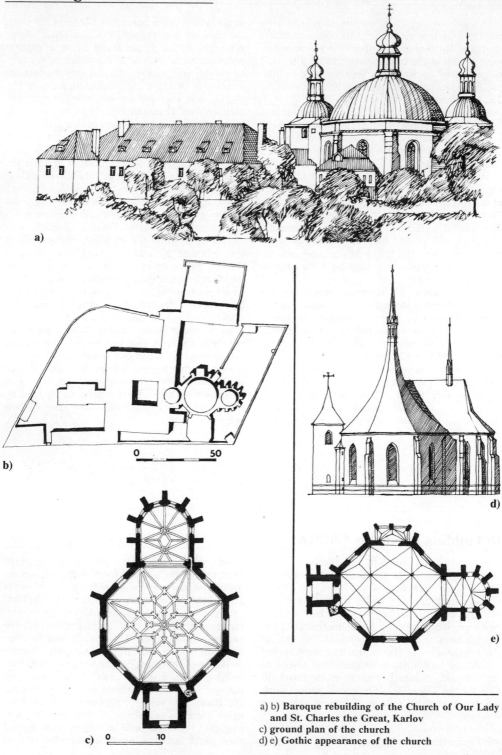

a)

b)

0   50

d)

c)   0   10

e)

a) b) **Baroque rebuilding of the Church of Our Lady
and St. Charles the Great, Karlov**
c) **ground plan of the church**
d) e) **Gothic appearance of the church**

late Gothic roof in Bohemia.

The symmetry of the central nave was respected also in the cloister of the monastery which was situated not to the south, but to the west. Only the southern Gothic wing of the lofty arcades has survived. The Gothic style of the church founded by Charles IV in 1350 can now be seen only in the chancel, while the nave is covered with Baroque decorations dating from 1733—1740. The exterior and the general outer appearance are also Baroque, as in the 18th century, in accordance with the general rebuilding of Gothic structures, the hipped roof was in 1756 replaced by a cupola.

West of the church are the former monastic buildings dating from the 14th century and rebuilt in their left part in the Baroque style probably by Giovanni Domenico Orsi (1660—1668); in the ground floor rooms beautiful stuccowork can be admired. Also still standing is the new prelature (1716—1719) by František Maxmilián Kaňka who also built the choir and the two side galleries from 1733 to 1738. In the 1750s, Orsi was apparently also responsible for much of the harmonious decoration in the interior.

Early in the 18th century, also due to its dominant position, Karlov became a place of pilgrimage. As a result, further buildings were needed. In 1708, an annex was built, probably by Giovanni B. Santini-Aichel, with the so-called "Holy Steps", and beneath them the Bethlehem Cave of the Nativity Chapel with trompe l'oeil stuccowork on the walls.

The general layout of the monastery corresponds to that of the Middle Ages. The Baroque rebuilding of Karlov, typical at that time, concealed the original Gothic sobriety under the abundant Baroque details of the interior. The outer appearance was enriched with Baroque cupolas which stressed the excellent position of the building in the landscape "crowning the Royal Mountain".

Today, the monastery houses the State Archives and the Police Museum.

In a quiet suburb of Prague, away from the traffic, Michna's Summer Palace was built in the New Town, in a small garden where the street Ke Karlovu now stands. This quite small but architecturally fine building was well planned for its site and resembles Hildebrandt's buildings in Vienna.

The Baroque summer palace called America (after an inn nearby), which was built around 1720 for Jan Michna of Vacínov by Kilian Ignaz Dientzenhofer, now houses the Antonín Dvořák Museum. The small two-storeyed building seems lost amidst the surrounding tall blocks of a teaching hospital, yet it still has much charm of the former summer palace.

The palace was the first building constructed by the young Kilian Ignaz Dientzenhofer in Prague after his return here from abroad, where he had studied modern European architecture for ten years. He was strongly impressed by Vienna, particularly by Lucas Hildebrandt in whose studio he learned about the inner relation between the modern Baroque and the lofty concept of neo-Classicism. Dientzenhofer's principles of a noble and clearly articulated palace architecture and fine decoration were fully applied to the small palace with its regular layout in an almost French taste. The small scale, elegance and intimacy of the building already anticipated the future ideas of the Rococo. The America Palace was the first building in Prague with flat ornamental shapes in the French strip style, which had been brought to Vienna from France by Dientzenhofer's teacher Lucas Hildebrandt.

The villa in the middle of the courtyard clearly displays the architectural forms applied to the Belvedere Palace in Vienna. The Michna Summer Palace, built from 1712 to 1720, is a charming building with a mansard roof and an articulated façade, symmetrically flanked by two single-storeyed pavilions. The building exhibits the typical Baroque principle of symmetry, both in the layout and the general concept, which is further stressed by the detailing, the sculpture, and the garden.

There are two sandstone sculptures, one representing Spring and Winter, and the other Summer and Autumn; they were both made around 1735 in Matthias B. Braun's workshop, which was already headed by his nephew Anton

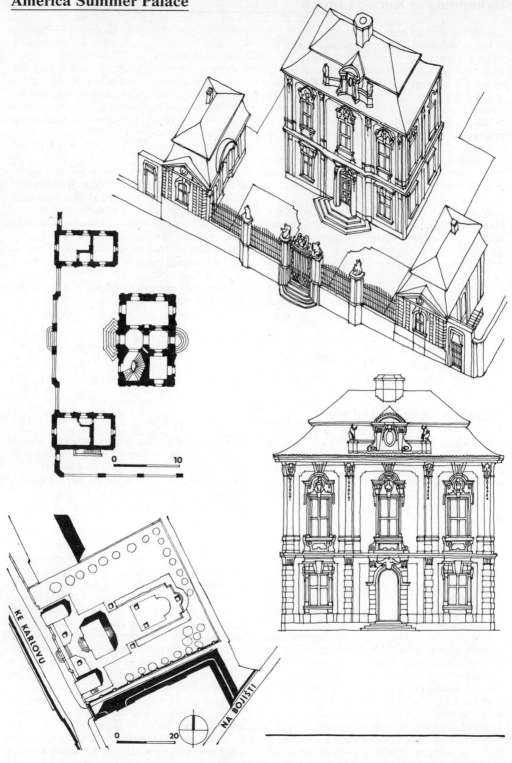

Braun. The sculptures replaced two earlier and anonymous Hercules figures that were then placed in front of the main façade. The villa was separated from its surroundings by beautiful Baroque railings (now a replica). The interiors were decorated by Johann Ferdinand Schor, professor at the then new Technical Institute of Prague.

Suburban villas were built at that time not only by aristocrats, but also by some other rich individuals, including Dientzenhofer himself, whose beautiful villa, later called "Portheimka", can still be seen in Smíchov District near St. Wenceslas' Church whose construction in 1884 spoiled the symmetrical plan of the villa, as its newer part had to be demolished. The "Portheimka" House certainly met all the needs of comfortable dwelling, and was decorated with paintings by the outstanding Baroque painter Václav Vavřinec Reiner. The small-scale summer palaces, their elegance and intimate character anticipated a new style in culture and the arts: the Rococo.

Even this exceptional example of Baroque architecture was forgotten in the 19th century. The derelict house and its large garden were purchased in 1843 by the Municipal Council of Prague, and were part of a large ground plot which was first used as a cattle market and then divided into a number of building plots for new houses. Only a small courtyard remained in front of the summer palace.

Only at the end of the 19th century, when conservation of ancient buildings began, was the Michna Palace rehabilitated. The house was repaired in 1884 by Antonín Baum, which was followed in 1911 by another renovation when the remaining courtyard in front of the palace was enclosed by cast-iron railings between four piers. They were a replica of the original Baroque railings which were taken to Dresden in 1884. Replicas of the damaged putti were also made and replaced the originals.

The palace was assigned a new function after the Second World War after being acquired by the Antonín Dvořák Society: it was intended to house the Dvořák Museum. For this purpose, to display the composer's manuscripts and photographs, the house was rebuilt between 1953 and 1955 by Ing. Feigl. At the same time, the remaining garden parterre surrounded by the tall hospital buildings was restored in front of both the entrance and the garden façades, with the rest of the original garden axis. Two big satyr figures and two stone urns made at A. Braun's workshop were also restored.

The paintings in the interior were restored by Bohumil Číla in 1956—1957. The original garden architecture lost much of its charm due to the loss of the large green parterre and due to the surrounding tall buildings, which the excellent renovation could not change.

Baroque Palaces

Just as churches were the highest expression of religious architecture, so it was also the ambition of nobles to live in the finest possible houses, and this impulse strongly influenced 17th century architecture. It was characteristic of the early stage of the Baroque style that the first major customers were the nouveaux riches from the war, for instance Pavel Michna of Vacínov who in the 1620s started rebuilding a summer palace in the Lesser Quarter and converting it into a late Renaissance palace (now the Tyrš House).

Michna's palace in Karmelitská Street was initially meant as an annex (probably designed by Francesco Caratti and built from 1640 to 1650)

to an older summer palace constructed by Ulrico Aostalli in 1580. The garden façade of the palace was conceived in the style of the north Italian late Renaissance. (For more information about the Michna Palace see page 164.) Another building contractor was Albrecht Wallenstein who also cleverly profited from the wars. His large palace in the Lesser Quarter was built soon after the Battle of White Mountain, from 1624 to 1630. (For more information about the Wallenstein Palace see page 109.)

Until the 1680s foreign artists had been coming here, mostly from northern Italy and bringing methods related to the older Italian architec-

Baroque Palaces

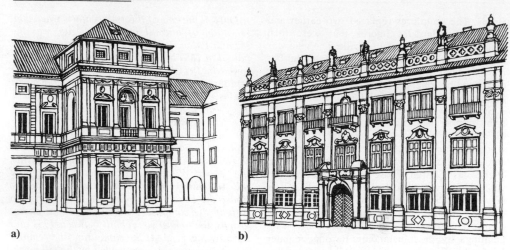

a)

b)

c) d)

e)

0   20

0   20

a) **Michna Palace** (Tyrš House)
b) **Nostic Palace**

c) d) **Lobkovic Palace**
e) **Sternberg Palace**

Baroque Palaces

tural styles. Some of them can be regarded as Renaissance or late Renaissance, others were based on the Manneristic morphology, and some already applied Baroque ideas.

One of the early Baroque palaces is the Schönborn Palace in the Lesser Quarter (the name dates from 1794), built from 1643 to 1656, which was owned by the Colloredos and was later, around 1715, rebuilt by Bartolomeo Scotti following plans by Giovanni B. Santini-Aichel or Giovanni B. Alliprandi. Adjoining the palace is a well-known garden.

Typical features of 17th century architecture are, in particular, simple and geometrically plain masses without major three-dimensional articulation. However, the palace walls were often enriched with impressive tall columns or pilasters whose vertical lines seemed to brace the storeys and stress the unity of the work. In addition to this basic artistic principle the walls between the windows were also geometrically articulated.

The character of new buildings reflected the social role and privileged position of the building contractors. The colossal Černín Palace (for more information see page 117) situated on the highest part of Hradčany Hill was a challenging counterpart of Prague Castle. Francesco Caratti probably also built the four-wing Nostic Palace (1658—1660) on Maltézské Square. The late Rococo alterations to the palace (the porch) were made in 1760 by Anton Haffenecker.

An important milestone in the history of architecture in Prague was the arrival of Jean B. Mathey by 1680, who brought to Prague a new, classically sober, well-balanced and technically bold architecture. Mathey was very good at siting his buildings in the surrounding landscape, which was a good lesson to local architects. With Mathey's work high Baroque principles came to Bohemia and on this basis the foundations of a new style adapted to the local conditions were laid.

Of course, other artists too, particularly those who were bringing the principles of Viennese architecture here, contributed to the development of the high Baroque in Prague. Particularly worth mention in this connection are Domenico Martinelli and Giovanni B. Alliprandi (1665—1720), who in their palace designs adopted the style of Fischer of Erlach. Alliprandi designed the Lobkovic Palace which was built from 1703 to 1707, while its second floor surmounted by a gable and an attic was added much later, in 1769 by Ignazio Palliardi. There is also a large terraced garden of Italian type dating from 1703 which was in the late 18th century converted into an English park. Domenico Martinelli (1655—1705) contributed to Prague's architecture with his design for the Sternberg Palace which was then realized by Giovanni B. Alliprandi. Another work by Alliprandi is the Hartig Palace in the Lesser Quarter dating from around 1722 and replacing two older houses.

The architecture of the Grand Prior's Palace built from 1726 to 1738 by Bartolomeo Scotti is stressed by the beauty of the sculptures by Matthias Braun. The walls of the palace still conceal the torso of the original Romanesque monastery of the Maltese Order.

An artistic revolution in Bohemia came with the general recognition of the principles of great Baroque masters—Boromini and Guarini. The most important element was the space, sculpturally conceived. Walls were no longer straight, but curved along both convex and concave lines. An outstanding Czech architect with much practical experience was František M. Kaňka (1674—1766) who futher developed Santini's monumental art. He did not invent any new principles, but rather contributed to the spreading and further development of the monumental and prospective trend of Baroque architecture in Prague. In his well-balanced layouts he sought inspiration in the art of both domestic and foreign masters and created works suiting the country's environment. Kaňka's sense of spatial composition can best be seen in his garden plans for the Vrtba Palace in the Lesser Quarter and for the Černín Palace at Hradčany.

Quite outstanding buildings in the dynamic Baroque style are the Morzin Palace and the Thun Palace in Nerudova Street (for detailed information see page 132) whose architect Giovanni Santini-Aichel collaborated with outstanding sculptors, such as Matthias B. Braun and Franz M. Brokof. Santini and Kaňka, together with the younger and artistically more vigorous Kilian I. Dientzenhofer contributed considerably to the constitution of a specific and typical Bohemian Baroque style.

In the second quarter of the 18th century, before the death of Kilian I. Dientzenhofer, another important change in the architectural atmosphere occurred. The Rococo with its ornamental motifs spread in the country after 1740, followed, around 1780, by the Louis XVI style. Ignazio Giovanni N. Palliardi (1737—1821), the most important representative of our architecture at that time, renovated in 1770 the façade of the Kolowrat (originally Černín) Palace in the Lesser Quarter still in the traditional Baroque style, while his small Fürstenberg Garden at the palace crowned the evolution of garden architecture in Prague. In 1787, Palliardi rebuilt the Ledeburg Palace

Baroque Palaces

a)

b)   d)

c)

a) Schönborn Palace
b) Sylva Taroucca Palace

c) Goltz-Kinsky Palace
d) Kaunic Palace

whose excellent terraced garden from the 1720s and sala terrena were the work of Giovanni Santini-Aichel.

A good example of the Rococo style with neo-Classical details is the Kaunic Palace in the Lesser Quarter by Anton K. Schmidt dating from 1773—1775. The sculptures were made in I. F. Platzer's workshop. The best known Rococo palace in Prague is the Archbishop's Palace by Wirch (for more information about the Archbishop's Palace see page 171).

Of the wide range of Baroque palaces in Prague one can hardly find any that have not been renovated and adapted to serve municipal and national administration or similar purposes. The renovations concentrated particularly in the Lesser Quarter whose palaces now house ministries, foreign embassies or cultural institutions. There are far fewer palaces in the Old Town and the New Town, however even here conversions are being carried out.

The palace of Johann Anton Los of Losinthal, No. 1033, Hybernská Street, is better known as the People's House and has been closely linked with the history of the country's labour movement. As of 1907, the building, including the adjoining wings, housed the printing office of the Právo lidu newspaper and the secretariat of the Social Democratic Workers' Party.

In 1951, it was decided to restore the People's House. Jan Feigl and Josef Halabala were charged with the respective plans. The first part to be renovated was the wing along the street, was the wing along the street, and thus the palace regained its 18th century appearance. The renovated interiors, used for exhibition purposes, are also very valuable, including the timber ceilings covered with paintings that were among the first to be discovered in Prague, being followed by dozens in the city. The house now belongs again to the Social Democratic Party.

In Celetná Street, to the right of the modern Baťa Shoe Shop by Josef Gočár, there is a large palace No. 595 with a beautiful courtyard and a small garden behind: the Manhart Palace, which was ignored for a long time and was used for housing only. In the 19th century, the palace was rebuilt and converted into a tenement house with a number of flats. It originated as two older palaces and still contains Gothic and Renaissance halls opening into Štupartská Street. The renovation brought excellent results in both architectural and artistic terms.

The last example to be mentioned in this brief survey is the renovation plan of one of the most important Baroque buildings in Prague, the Clam-Gallas Palace. The noble and beautiful building was used for many years to house the Archives of Prague, which was not a very suitable use. In spite of many studies and discussions the problem of its new use has not been solved yet.

Michna Palace (Tyrš House)

Between Karmelitská Street and Újezd, where in the Middle Ages there was a Dominican convent, a Renaissance summer palace was built in the late 16th century by Ottavio Aostalli for Count Jan Kinský. In the following four decades its owners changed many times and included, among others, Adam Slavata of Chlum, Adam of Sternberg and Heinrich Matthias of Thurn, who all enlarged the house and converted it into a comfortable Renaissance villa with sgraffiti on the façades, fine gables and a large garden.

In 1623, the house was purchased by Pavel Michna of Vacínov from Susanne, wife of Heinrich Matthias of Thurn. Michna, a nouveau riche and a supply officer of the Imperial Army, decided, following the example of Wallenstein's building activity, to convert the beautiful but old house into a monumental palace meeting the new, high social demands of the early Baroque style. He therefore invited Italian architects who extended and rebuilt the Renaissance house from 1631 to 1650, probably according to plans prepared by Francesco Caratti, and made it one of the most sumptuous Baroque palaces in Prague. As of 1632, the construction was financed by Pavel Michna's son, Václav Jan Michna. The original house was enlarged on both sides and heightened, the Renaissance arcades were bricked-in, and several excellent rooms with rich stuccowork were created in the interior. A very picturesque and attractive part is the section broken forward on the east side projecting into the garden, with the original sala terrena and with a sophisticated architectural layout and rich stuccowork.

Owing to the excellent artists who had contributed to the rebuilding, such as the plasterers Pietro Colombo, Zacharias Campione da Bossi and Domenico Galli, who made the intricate forms and decorations of the interiors and the façades, the Michna Palace became one of the most valuable architectural monuments in the town. Due to the lack of money the renovation had to be interrupted at the turn of the 1640s and 1650s, and the original plans were never realized. It was particularly the interior decoration that remained incomplete, and in the latter half of the 17th century the Michnas sold the palace to Johann Adolf of Schwarzenberg, who then adapted the garden and extended it as far as Kampa Island. He also built a large riding-school along Všehrdova Street.

In 1763, the Schwarzenbergs sold the palace to Johann Bornschein who bought the house for speculative reasons, and resold it four years later, in 1767, to the military administration.

As in many other cases, the military occupation of the palace brought about widespread devastation of both its interior and exterior. In 1772, the house was rebuilt and the west front heightened, an ammunition workshop was built in the most valuable part—the section projecting into the garden, and a large barracks constructed in the garden, with an inner courtyard called the Carré, known to us from city maps from as late as the 19th century.

The 150 years of military exploitation brought about such a degree of devastation that at the end of the First World War some parts of the palace were referred to as ruins.

In 1921, the derelict Michna Palace was purchased from the Municipal Council by the Czech sports association Sokol. There were no windows and no doors, the floors were destroyed, and the decayed ceilings were supported by timber. All the interiors and the wall-paintings were covered with many layers of lime, there were openings in the walls that destroyed the stuccowork, etc. Scaffolding was erected in 1922 and a survey was made. Professor Vojtěch Birnbaum examined the surface of the building and discovered some Renaissance remnants. A competition was organized and of the entries, the plan by František Krásný was selected. At the same time, additional buildings and rooms were constructed to serve the new function of the house, the major ones being the cloakrooms and dressing rooms and the gymansium facing the courtyard, perpendicular to the Čertovka (a branch of the Vltava). The former riding-school had a storey added and was used as a hostel for the Sokol House.

Through the renovation and reconstruction the Michna Palace was converted into a modern sports centre, being a totally new type of building which had no equivalent at that time. In addition to the exhibition rooms (seven halls), administrative rooms and offices, the kitchen, the dining-room and the various service rooms, completely new areas were built, such as the large gymnasium with a gallery, dressing rooms and washrooms. Beneath the gymnasium, there was a swimming pool, twenty metres long and ten metres wide. A large hostel was also built for the Sokol Sports Association. The former garden parterre, which was later converted into a drill square, became an open-air athletic ground separated from the building by a two-metre high terrace with a balustrade concealing some technical installations. In addition to the athletic and social facilities, there were a number of administrative and official rooms.

This example is an interesting symbiosis of two ways of approaching a renovation pro-

gramme. On the one hand, a fundamental reconstruction and modernization was carried out, but showing sensitivity to the historic character of the building and using traditional forms suited to the old architecture (arched windows in the gymnasium, the use of vaults, etc.). On the other hand, the "analytical conservation method" was applied, displaying as many as possible of the original architectural fragments discovered during the technical and historical survey. The latter can best be seen in the exhibition halls which feature a heterogeneous collection of architectural details.

The Tyrš House was in operation until the Second World War. Then, it housed the Institute of Physical Training and Sports. Now, the house is again in the hands of the Sokol Sports Association.

The Invalidovna House is the major secular work attributed to Kilian Ignaz Dientzenhofer and was inspired by the similar building in Paris sponsored by Louis XIV and constructed from 1671 to 1674. "Les Invalides" in Paris set an example that was often followed subsequently. At the same time as the Invalidovna House in Prague, hostels for disabled soldiers were also built in Vienna and Pest. The Prague hostel followed the Invalides of Paris by Mansart, including the general concept and architecture, however its inner layout was quite original and unique. The rigorous neo-Classical regularity of its façades confirms the participation of the Viennese architect Josef Emanuel Fischer of Erlach whose sketches were used by Dientzenhofer to complete the building. Dientzenhofer's plans made in 1729—1730 were approved in Vienna in 1731.

Many years of consideration preceded the decision of Emperor Charles VI in 1728 to build a central hostel for disabled soldiers near Prague. Ground plots were purchased outside the Poříčská Gate (now a busy intersection called Na poříčí) that had for centuries belonged to the Knights of the Cross. As early as the 13th century, the area was acquired by the nurses of St. Agnes Convent and known as "Špitálské pole" (Hospital Field). An old road leading from the Poříčská Gate along the Vltava to Boleslav and on to Lusatia passed through the Field. Much later, in the early 18th century, the Invalidovna House was built here, and still later, in 1817, the first suburb of Prague (Karlín) was founded outside the Poříčská Gate.

The original generous idea of building a hostel for four thousand disabled people, whose foundation stone was laid by the Emperor on 15th August 1732, required a no less generous architectural concept. The hostel was constructed at the time of the culmination of Dientzenhofer's technical skill and architectural sophistication. During this same period St. Nicholas' Church was built in the Lesser Quarter and the Profession House at the Church of St. Charles Borromeo was constructed near Charles Square.

The Invalidovna of Prague was intended as a social facility for disabled people and their families, with a special administration and service department, that is, a sort of military camp linked with the outside world by eight gates. Dientzenhofer's plan was quite modern and progressive, as it also included water mains and sewage drains. The layout was simple and functional, with two structural sections and a corridor. The ground plan of the large site was a square with each side 300 m long and with a big central courtyard dividing the complex into two parts, each of which had three smaller courtyards surrounded by dwelling buildings. All these plans have survived. However, the plan was too big and there was not enough money to realize it. In 1737, the construction had to be stopped with only one ninth of the total project having been completed. What remained was a fragment that the architect had to alter a little and adapt to the given situation. In spite of the fact that only a small part of the original generous plan could be realized the size of the complex is quite impressive. The four-wing two-stor-

Invalidovna

a)

b)   0   50

c)

d)

e)   0   10

a) b) **Invalidovna** (Disabled Soldiers' Hospital)
c) **original plan and realized part**
d) e) **dwelling unit**

eyed building with shallow projecting sections crowned with gables and attic roofs is of excellent proportions in its particular parts and in the rhythm of the outer walls, and has fine arcades in the inner courtyard.

Of the former military cemetery only a chapel dating from 1753 has survived, whose façade already displays some early neo-Classical features. In the surrounding park, a memorial statue was placed in 1898 to commemorate Count Peter Strozzi who had in 1664 organized a foundation for disabled soldiers. The Invalidovna House is now used as a museum and archives.

Middle-Class Houses

Building activity in Prague was restored soon after the Thirty Years' War. However, only aristocrats and the Church were building, not the middle-classes. They only got involved in the building activity much later, at the end of the 17th century when the Baroque style totally prevailed and the appearance of the town was undergoing the most dramatic transformation in its history.

Compared with the number of Baroque buildings constructed by nobles and the clergy, the contribution of the middle-class to the style was much smaller, and only at the end of the 17th century were the first new houses of middle-class people built in the town. It was at that time that an economic recovery started in Prague, the prices of houses went up, and the nobles and the clergy had to respect the medieval layout of the town again. Until that time, since the tragic defeat on White Mountain, many confiscated properties as well as many vacant houses had been abandoned by émigrés, and the time after the Thirty Years' War in general had not favoured any major building activity by the middle-class.

The 1705 census showed that there were less than 40 thousand inhabitants in Prague, and some years later, in 1713, their number was cut by one quarter due to a plague epidemic. Vienna, on the other hand, grew quite quickly, particularly after the elimination of the Turkish threat, and in 1754 its population amounted to 175 thousand.

In the 18th century, there were more old houses adapted and renovated than new houses built. Consequently, the Baroque façades mostly conceal old Gothic houses with Renaissance vaults. The external cladding of houses with stuccowork moulded in different shapes and patterns covered over the Renaissance sgraffiti, softened the street fronts and enriched them with the dynamics of light and shadow. The new Baroque houses (unless their ground plan was the result of an earlier narrow site) were quite wide and had a central wall parallel to the façade articulated by one or two sections broken forward, a carriage-way or two symmetrically situated entrances. The projecting sections usually had a triangular fronton, sometimes combined with an attic roof. The well articulated mansard roofs were adorned with dormer windows. As in palaces, the windows upstairs were taller and they often had richly moulded jambs. In the façades of some houses Baroque shop windows or window frames can still be seen, for instance in the house No. 38/222, Nerudova Street in the Lesser Quarter. As in other parts of Prague, in the Lesser Quarter the new style was rapidly spreading in the high Baroque period, particularly due to the Dientzenhofer family. In 1702, Christoph Dientzenhofer rebuilt—in addition to some other houses—his own house No. 2/465, Nosticova Street where his famous son Kilian Ignaz was born. Kilian Ignaz then built one of the most remarkable Baroque houses in the Lesser Quarter, "U zlatého jelena" (At the Golden Stag), No. 4/26, Tomášská Street whose central part is richly moulded and decorated with a sculpture by Ferdinand M. Brokof representing St. Hubert with a stag.

The Baroque rebuilding, over several decades and without being centrally organized, finally converted Prague into a homogeneous Baroque town with a great number of finely shaped details.

Most of the architectural monuments surviving in the historic centre of Prague are residential houses in streets and squares. As there had been many changes in the crafts, trades, and also in the way and standard of living, and as there had also been many changes in ownership and many fires, the structure of houses is mostly heterogeneous. It is quite typical that the layout

Middle-Class Houses

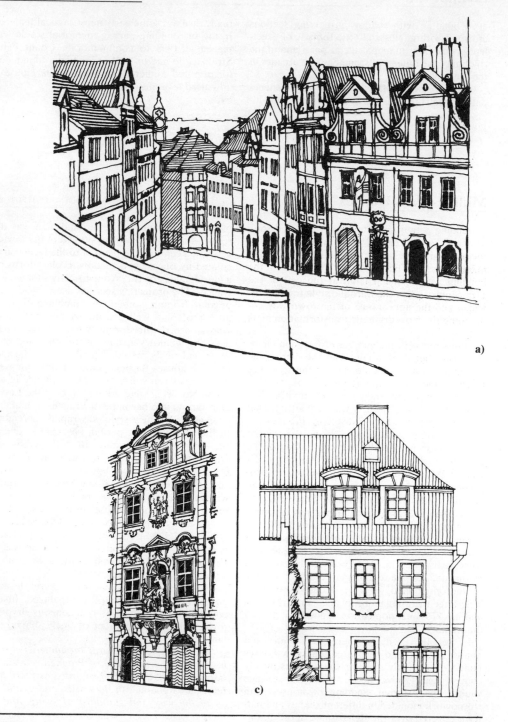

a)

b)

c)

a) **Nerudova Street**
b) **house U zlatého jelena, Tomášská Street**

c) **house No. 465, Nosticovská Street** (home of K. I. Dientzenhofer)

and the form of middle-class houses are a synthesis of different historic stages and architectural styles, which complicates the problem of finding the right form for their renovation.

Although a systematic general regeneration of the whole historic centre of Prague has not begun yet, there have been many partial individual renovations of particular houses since 1945, studies and surveys of whole areas and blocks are being prepared and some larger-scale renovations have already taken place in both the Old Town and the Lesser Quarter. One of the first renovations was that of the Gothic-Baroque house No. 798, "U obecního dvora"; the project was prepared by Rudolf Ječný of SURPMO and carried out from 1951 to 1953. The renovation of the Carolinum and of the whole block included the restoration of a number of middle-class houses of the palace type in Celetná Street whose rear parts are linked with the Carolinum complex and the new buildings of Charles University Rectorate. The plan was prepared by a team of SURPMO workers headed by Jaroslav Fragner and assisted by Marian Bělohradský. The

ground floors of the houses facing Celetná Street are used for municipal purposes, while the upper floors house various faculties and departments of Charles University.

Of the other major actions, the renovation of the houses within the town-hall of the Old Town that face Small Square (Malé náměstí; see the chapter Old Town Square) should be stressed as well as the recent restoration of middle-class houses in the street Na můstku which is the beginning of a renovation of houses along the pedestrian road from Wenceslas Square to Old Town Square, where the ground floor of houses had already been renovated and modernized previously. The remarkable renovation is the work of a team of SURPMO workers headed by Pavel Kupka.

Other individual renovations worth mention are the houses Nos. 156 and 229, Husova Street, called "U tří pštrosů" (At the Three Ostriches) which is now a hotel, or the complex restoration of Ungelt and of the house called "U zvonu" (At the Bell).

Baroque Rebuilding of the Town

The Baroque as a symbol of Catholicism and of imperial power, a style full of contradictions and excitement, suddenly invaded the town which in spite of its Renaissance appearance from the Rudolphinian era had conserved its old medieval character. In the course of the following two centuries the Baroque totally changed Prague's architecture by creating new dominant buildings, giving the streets and squares both a festive and an intimate atmosphere, and enriching them with a number of beautiful details.

Dramatic changes in the old layout of Prague took place in some places only. As the redevelopment went on, more and more attention and respect were paid to the surroundings of the new buildings. Streets and squares were enriched with new façades displaying the beautiful architecture of early, and particularly of high and late Baroque. These façades were full of both plain and refined, carefully calculated charms, taking advantage of curves, irregularities, sloping

streets, and sloping or terraced squares. The geographic situation of Prague offered many chances for creative architects to show their art.

A new principle of architectural design that the Baroque introduced in the town was the larger absolute scale, while respecting the network of old streets. However, some changes to the street plan did take place, for instance in the Castle ramp, the Town-Hall Steps and the Castle Steps. At the end of the 18th century there was already a new, quite modern street along the old moat between the Old Town and the New Town, from the Powder Tower to the Vltava River.

In spite of its great impact on Prague, the Baroque did not—with the exception of its early stage after the 1620 Battle of White Mountain——bring about any major changes in the medieval network of streets which remained, particularly in the Old Town. The Baroque redevelopment consisted mostly of minor changes of the building line, integrating building sites, removing

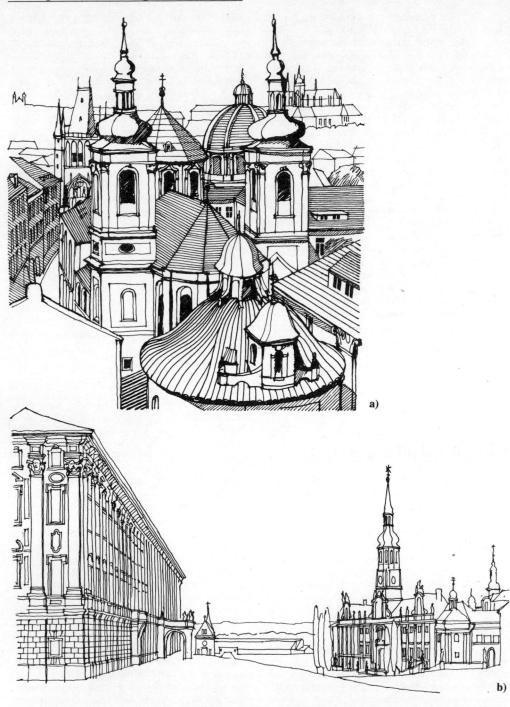

a)

b)

a) **view of Hradčany behind the churches of the Holy Saviour and St. Francis**   b) **Loretto Square** (by V. Morstadt, 1852)

the house arcades, and increasing the scale by adding superstructures integrating several buildings and rebuilding them.

Entirely new sites were exceptional in Prague, in spite of the amount of building activity in the 17th and 18th centuries. The one major exception was Valdštejn (Wallenstein) Square, which was to be extended as far as St. Thomas' Church so as to create a sufficiently large space to be dominated by the massive front wall of the Wallenstein Palace. This was a typical example of the grand type of square in the Baroque period. However, some changes in the building site were later introduced that made it impossible to realize the original plan. The architect Andrea Spezza had to shorten the façade by making a blind main porch so as to preserve the symmetry of the entrance façade. Unlike this monumental trend, the composition of Loretto Square at Hradčany is full of contrasts: there is the articulated Loretto complex, the plain structure of the Capuchin Monastery, and the huge monolithic Černín Palace. Křižovnické (Knights of the Cross) Square was completed with the new Church of the Knights of the Cross. There were already three earlier important structures on this very old square: the Old Town Bridge Tower, the Clementinum Building, and the Jesuit Church of the Holy Saviour whose old façade was given a three-part portico in 1651—1653 opening into the square with three arches surmounted by Bohemian vaults and bearing a balcony with a heavy balustrade and a gallery of figures of saints. Due to this, the scale increased, the space was three-dimensionally articulated, and an important initiative was undertaken to install statues on the Gothic bridge and thus create the impression of a procession coming from the Clementinum (see page 114) and proceeding towards the Castle.

The Baroque was the only style that was able to use the configuration of land in Prague to stress dramatically its architectural beauty and to harmonize its panorama. The central component part of the townscape of Prague was St. Nicholas' Church in the Lesser Quarter.

Archbishop's Palace

While Kilian Ignaz Dientzenhofer, the greatest Baroque architect in this country, was still alive, a change in the architectural mood occurred some time after 1740: the Rococo started to penetrate into the country. Although it did not feature such a clarity of forms here as in France, it strongly influenced the ornamentation. In the second quarter of the 18th century small architectural works appeared, Dientzenhofer's sophisticated centrally-planned buildings saw modest counterparts in the Rococo rotundas and simple centralized chapels, while the large Baroque residences had their counterparts in small palaces.

Both architecture and painting abandoned their traditional monumentality and tended towards decorativism. The architects continued applying the traditional Baroque tools which, however, were becoming refined and miniaturized. The light and graceful style of the French Rococo was just a short intermezzo here as at the same time as the Rococo, whose ornamental motifs prevailed in the country just before the middle of the 18th century, neo-Classicism penetrated into Bohemia and found favourable conditions here. Baroque neo-Classicism spread in Bohemia around 1770 and, unlike the playful Rococo, featured a sobriety of forms.

The leading Rococo architect in Prague was Johann Josef Wirch (1732—1782) who followed the example of Vienna architecture. In 1759, he prepared a project for the renovation of a mint, house No. 587, Celetná Street, and rebuilt the Bretsfeld Palace, No. 240, Nerudova Street (in 1765). One of his major works is the rebuilding of the Archbishop's Palace at Hradčany in 1764—1765.

The bishops of Prague had their original seat from the 10th to the late 12th century in the Castle, in the Old Provost's Lodgings at St. Vitus' Cathedral in the Third Courtyard. Then, still in the 12th century, they had a residence at Judith Bridge (Bishop's Court). The bishopric of Prague was promoted to an archbishopric in 1344; consequently, the Bishop's Court was rebuilt and used as the archbishop's residence. The Court, of which only the tower has survived that can be

Archbishop's Palace

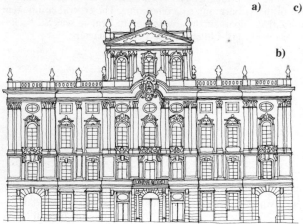

a)   c)

b)

d)

a) b) **Archbishop's Palace**
c) **portal of the palace**
d) **original form**

seen in the yard of the house No. 47, Mostecká Street, was destroyed in 1419. Much later, in the 16th century, the new Catholic archbishop felt the need for a new residence. Therefore, in 1562 Ferdinand I gave Antonín Brus of Mohelnice the Renaissance Gryspek House which was then rebuilt by Ulrico Aostalli to meet the needs of an archbishop's residence. In 1599, the interiors of the palace were renovated and a chapel was built with ceiling paintings and stucco portraits of Bohemian prelates which have all survived. In the latter half of the 17th century the palace was rebuilt in the Baroque style by Jean Mathey (1669—1679), paid for by Archbishop Johann Friedrich of Wallenstein. Mathey introduced in Prague a new type of palace façade. The Archishop's Palace was rebuilt again between 1722 and 1725, probably by Paul I. Bayer.

The present-day Rococo form of the palace is due to a third major rebuilding, which was made by the young architect Wirch. The impressive and lofty façade of the palace strongly contributes, together with the neighbouring Castle, to the panorama of the town. Influenced by neo-Classicism, Wirch managed to unite in his work large monumental masses with playful Rococo decoration. He also had much respect for the work done by his predecessor, Jean B. Mathey, whose entrance porch and attic were incorporated in the new plan. Thus, he managed to create a monumental façade corresponding to the new style.

The architect's Rococo taste can best be seen in the inner staircase of the palace which displays, unlike the monumental Baroque compositions, intimate forms with stuccowork and stone sculptures by Ignaz F. Platzer. Wirch's staircase has tranquility and height, the bright rooms of the palace display the white and gold colours of the refined rocaille ornamentation that was so typical of the Rococo style. The interiors were decorated with eight beautiful French tapestries representing New India motifs (1754—1765), and rank among the most valuable interiors in this country.

The Baroque saw its heyday in the reign of Charles VI (1711—1740) when the town lost its prevalent old Gothic character and acquired new forms that have been admired up to now. For several decades, the town was one large building site and underwent fundamental changes both in its general appearance and in its details as well. The transformation process was completed under Maria Theresa (1740—1780) by a large-scale redevelopment of the Castle between 1753 and 1774, which was the last phase of the Baroque development in this country.

The Castle was seriously damaged after the War of Austrian Succession as it was twice occupied by enemy armies and bombarded by the Prussians in 1757. The parts of the Castle destroyed by the war were reconstructed and the old parts facing the town were modernized. Niccolo F. L. Paccassi, the architect of Vienna's Schönbrunn and the Court architect in Vienna (1716—1790) was invited to deal with the renovation. He gave the Castle a new and impressive façade, already in the neo-Classical style, which concealed almost all the old buildings in the Castle. As a result, Prague Castle lost its medieval appearance and became a modern royal residence.

Just as in 1541, when a great fire destroyed many houses and left Gothic sites empty for the construction of large new palaces, so two hundred years later the Castle, damaged by wars, required a large-scale rebuilding. Most of the damage caused to the monumental parts of the Castle occurred in 1757 as Prague was besieged by the Prussian army. Of the 3,200 houses in Prague 900 were destroyed. In the Castle, the Riding-School and the Small Ball-Game Hall were destroyed, as well as the Opera House and the Powder Bridge. The Spanish Hall and the New Hall were damaged, and so were St. George's Convent, the tower and the interior of St. Vitus' Cathedral. The first part to be rebuilt was the Rožmberk Palace that was purchased for the Institute of Gentlewomen and in 1753—1755 its façade facing Prague was transformed. Its characteristic five Renaissance towers with onion-like roofs were demolished and replaced by a long monotonous façade with three big sections broken forward. These changes in the spirit of sober French neo-Classicism, which can still be seen

Theresian Redevelopment of the Castle

a) west façade of the renovated Castle
b) ground plan of the Castle after rebuilding

c) panorama of the Castle, early 17th century (van den Bosch)
d) panorama of the Castle after Theresian rebuilding

here, were prepared by Niccolo Paccassi and realized by Anselmo Lurago, director of the Castle Construction Office. He was followed in this work by Johann Kunz and Anton Haffenecker. After the renovation of the south façade the entrance façade in the west part of the Castle was built and a new (now the First) courtyard was created here by constructing two side wings and a west wing. Paccassi incorporated the old Matthias Gate as a main entrance to the Castle and at the same time as a monumental end to the King's Way. It was also at that time that the old moat separating the Castle from Hradčany was filled and an entrance (ceremonial) courtyard was created that was closed by a gate with statues by Platzer. Thus, a visual connection between the Castle and Hradčany was created.

The old medieval appearance remained almost unchanged in the northern front of the Castle and partly also on the south side of the complex, in the old Royal Palace, with the Vladislav Hall and the Louis Wing.

Unlike the redevelopment of the exterior in a plain, neo-Classical style, the interiors were adorned with rich Rococo decoration. The Theresian rebuilding, which constituted a dramatic change in the architecture of the historic complex, gave the Castle its present-day appearance dominating the panorama of the city.

This "new part" of the Castle now has its own history and has seen several renovations, such as the rebuilding of the Theresian Wing beneath the Vladislav Hall by Otakar Rothmayer as already mentioned (see the chapter Romanesque Castle of Prague, page 15).

The first modern redevelopment of the Castle was the Presidential Apartment that was realized in 1923–1924 by Josip Plečnik. The entrance is from the passageway between the First and the Second Courtyards, to the right of the Matthias Gate. The staircase hall has white mortar-pointed walls and several stone columns, and its plainness is surprisingly effective. As unobtrusive as the vestibule is also the Presidential Apartment on the second floor with a fine view of Prague. Only minumum changes were made in the layout here, as only the sanitary facilities were added. The living-room and the working-rooms were dealt with differently, but they are all quite plain and in good taste. There is, in particular, a great library, a Harp Room (also called the Golden Room), and a consulting room.

Plečnik also rebuilt the First Courtyard (in 1922–1923), paved it with granite slabs, and erected two flagpoles with gilded tops and bases.

The public had less understanding for Plečnik's high Column Hall in the north-west part in front of the Spanish Hall. It was meant as a gathering room before entering the ceremonial Rudolphinian rooms, particularly the Spanish Hall and the Rudolph Gallery. Its architecture is autonomous, formally well-conceived and quite impressive in its harmony of materials and colours. The old architecture of the palace, however, was just a formal background for this intervention. The work was completed by Plečnik's successor Otto Rothmayer from 1940 to 1954. As of 1954, Rothmayer continued redeveloping the anteroom of the Spanish Hall by following Plečnik's concept. He created a fine staircase from the carriageway to the left of the Matthias Gate, followed by a large hall covering three storeys of the west wing whose main characteristic feature is its white marble paving, the gilded coffered ceiling and the monumental staircase of black marble. He also created the so-called Wedge Corridor as an anteroom for the Spanish Hall.

Other changes in the Theresian part of the Castle were carried out by Pavel Janák, who until 1965 gave full freedom to O. Rothmayer in his work. From 1956 to 1958, Rothmayer rebuilt three sides of the First Courtyard according to Janák's plans; new windows made of oak, receding 15 cm into the brickwork were installed. However, this change of Paccassi's façade did not prove to be very good, and the replacement of the slate cladding by pantiles was not very successful, either.

The last building worth mention in this chapter is the Institute of Gentlewomen, No. 2, at the end of the Third Courtyard, built by Anselmo Lurago and Niccolo Paccassi in 1754–1755. Its façades were renovated in colours that are historically accurate. Another architectural work that took place here was the redevelopment of the gardens, which is the topic of the following chapter.

Baroque Gardens

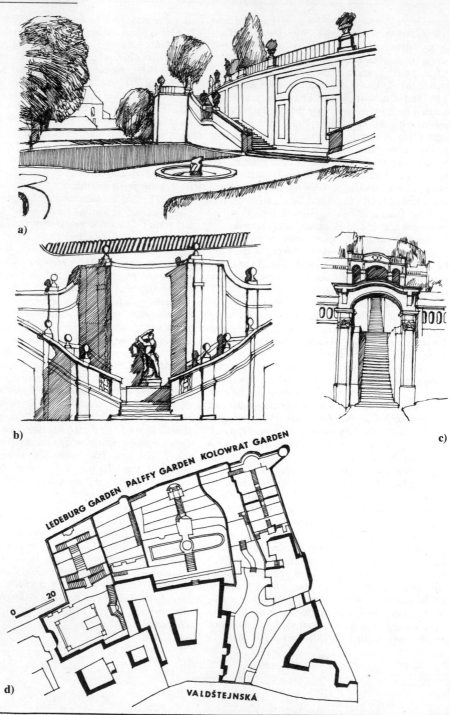

a) **Vrtba Garden**
b) **steps of Ledeburg Garden**

c) **steps of Kolowrat Garden**
d) **plan of gardens under the Castle**

(176)

Baroque Gardens

Most of the gardens in Prague were created on irregular vacant sites. This disadvantage, however, was well confronted by architects, and even used to increase the general effect.

The first major garden was Wallenstein Garden in the Lesser Quarter created between 1627 and 1630. Later, in the early 18th century, F. M. Kaňka made a garden at the Černín Palace. Colloredo (later Schönborn) Garden on the slopes of Petřín Hill had a clear axial layout. There were also other gardens, even outside the city walls, such as Slavata Garden in Smíchov and Martinic Garden at Bubny. The French pattern was applied to the large and intricate Troja Palace Garden.

Garden architecture culminated in the high Baroque period. At that time the main aim was not so much to increase the size of gardens as to improve their layout, better use the space and increase the originality of concept. In spite of their intimate character and small scale, the traditional Italian gardens in the Lesser Quarter made a monumental and quite individual impression.

Vrtba Garden, one of the most beautiful in Prague, was created around 1725 on three terraces of Petřín Hill by František M. Kaňka and its sculptures were made by Matthias B. Braun. The entrance to the garden, hidden behind an old palace No. 375, Karmelitská Street, is guarded by a figure of Atlas. Until the 1620 defeat on White Mountain, the Vrtba House, to which the garden belonged, was in the hands of Kryštof Harant of Polžice and Bezdružice who was executed in 1621 on Old Town Square together with other leaders of the Bohemian uprising. His house was confiscated and passed over to Sezima of Vrtba who rebuilt it in the late Renaissance style. This basic form has survived until now. Some hundred years later, around 1720, the palace was altered again and, at the same time, a garden was laid out here by the Chief Burgrave of Prague Castle Johann Joseph of Vrtba. The small and irregular garden is of great beauty, both architecturally and sculpturally.

In the lower part of the garden, there is a sala terrena with mythological paintings by Reiner and with statues of Bacchus and Ceres by Braun. The central part has a rich double staircase, and in its upper part there is a viewing terrace decorated with urns and figures of ancient gods.

Vrtba Garden was probably inspired by the earlier gardens at the Colloredo and Přehořovský palaces. The terraced garden at the Schönborn Palace (until 1795 Colloredo Palace) dates from 1715–1718 when the old palace was rebuilt and enlarged according to a plan prepared by G. Alliprandi. A beautiful garden of Italian type was created in 1703 at the Přehořovský Palace which ten years later, in 1713, came into the hands of the Lobkovics.

In the Baroque period, an almost uninterrupted band of gardens emerged on the north slope of Petřín Hill, the slope beneath Strahov Abbey and on the southern slope of the Hradčany headland. Terraces and steps climbed the hills along the axes of the rear palace façades, and in places even reached as far as the Castle. It was in this area, on the southern slope near the Wallenstein Palace that the most remarkable terrace gardens appeared, namely Ledeburg Garden, Pálffy Garden, Kolowrat Garden and Fürstenberg Garden, whose individual and refined architecture and valuable sculptures by the leading Baroque masters still attract our attention.

On this site, St. Wenceslas Vineyard had stood for a short period in the 10th century. For safety and strategic reasons the steep southern slopes beneath the Castle remained desolate and uncultivated for several centuries. An important milestone in the history of this region was the great fire of 1541 that destroyed the Lesser Quarter and the Castle, but which also cleared the space needed for new, mostly aristocratic palaces. In the place of the middle-class houses destroyed by the fire, particularly in the vicinity of the Royal Palace, comfortable palaces of aristocratic families appeared, conceived in the Renaissance style and later in the Baroque style. The garden was an inseparable part of their layout, except where the site did not allow it. The steep slopes beneath the Castle became a challenge to the architects inspiring them to create the most beautiful Italianate gardens in this country.

Ledeburg Garden, which had terraces with retaining walls, steps leading up to the high viewing terrace close to the wall of the Castle and a sala terrena, was designed in the late 17th century by Giovanni Santini-Aichel and Giovanni Alliprandi. Of the original garden, the Hercules figure on the front wall of the terrace has been preserved, as well as wall paintings by Václav V. Reiner from about 1730, which were later covered over by another fresco. In 1784, the garden was redeveloped by Ignazio Palliardi.

Another in the series of gardens, Pálffy Garden is of exceptional quality. Two gardens, the Smaller and the Greater, were united. Due to their layout and the architectural concept of the early 18th century they appear as a rather massive variant of the late Baroque and Rococo garden. There are also a number of retaining walls and wide terraces with steep axial and enclosed steps leading to the viewing terrace. The chronogram on a sundial informs us of the exact year of

Baroque Gardens

the renovation: 1751.

The adjoining garden called Small Fürstenberg (or Kolowrat) was built for Countess Černín and later, a hundred years ago, it was amalgamated with the narrow Kolowrat Garden containing fruit trees, whose name it now bears. It is much smaller than the other gardens here, but there are many terraces on the steep slope with light bowers and gloriettes along the steps that lead to a loggia. Ignazio Palliardi designed the garden around 1787 and applied a great many architectural forms here.

The last of the gardens beneath the Castle, called Great Fürstenberg Garden, dates from 1822 and adjoins a palace built in the mid-18th century probably by František M. Kaňka. Its beautiful landscaping with only few architectural details differs from the concept of the above gardens that are filled with architectural elements.

At the end of 1949 a plan for the renovation and rehabilitation of five palaces beneath the Castle and for the Wallenstein Palace was prepared. All the buildings came into the hands of the Ministry of Information. It was also decided to renovate their derelict gardens covering the entire area of the former royal vineyards.

A team of workers from Stavoprojekt Atelier (predecessor of the present-day SURPMO) headed by Josef Čihák was invited to prepare plans covering the following palaces and gardens: Small Fürstenberg, Kolowrat, Pálffy, Ledeburg, and Auersperg.

The general concept was to respect the characteristic and specific features of the gardens, but link them with each other so that they could be entered through one gate and opened to the public. The largest of them is Fürstenberg Garden which, however, is not accessible to the public as its palace houses the Polish Embassy. Unlike the

other gardens, its typical features are not architectural elements, but a beautiful, well-selected vegetation. The neighbouring Small Fürstenberg (Kolowrat) Garden, by contrast, is dominated by architectural features: the central steps and gates, and the small upper sala terrena. It is followed by Pálffy Garden which has high terraces, steps and a gate to the connecting steps. The best known is Ledeburg Garden behind the palace bearing the same name. It is renowned for excellent open-air concerts which take place in its courtyard and the sala terrena. The vaults of the sala terrena are decorated with frescoes on mythological themes; they have been restored, after many repaintings, by Bohumil Číla. Číla also restored the paintings in the other gardens mentioned. On the lower retaining wall in Ledeburg Garden, the original fresco by Václav V. Reiner, totally destroyed by the weather, was replaced by a work of sgraffito entitled "My Country" by Adolf Zábranský.

The gardens served the public for three decades and many cultural events took place here. In 1981, another general renovation was begun and, in particular, the retaining walls were repaired as well as other structural elements that were in bad condition.

Of the other Baroque gardens Vrtba Garden on the slope of Petřín Hill behind the Vrtba Palace also deserves mention as its architecture and sculptural decoration rank among the most important and best known in the city. After the Second World War, the garden was renovated by Hubert Ječný following a plan prepared by SURPMO. The garden is known for being an oasis of tranquility and calm. The palace houses offices of the Czechoslovak Foreign Office and in its garden wing there is a kindergarten which also occupies the lower part of the garden.

Suburban farmsteads were a typical element of the rural landscape around Prague, and also had a specific architectural character. There were hundreds of such buildings, but many have disappeared, and those that have survived are of great value. They now lie within the boundaries of the city, particularly in the districts Smíchov, Košíře, Dejvice, Šárka, Libeň and Vinohrady. In the last district, where once most of the farmsteads were, only very few can now be seen. Yet they have given their names to the streets that have emerged here. Most of these farmsteads, of various types and forms, developed from medieval vintners' houses lying amidst vineyards. Many of them were situated on elevated sites and are still at prominent points, such as the Sklenářka House in Troja District. Some vintners' houses that were built from the 16th to the 18th century and were originally seasonal workshops, later developed into farmsteads and summer houses. Dozens of such buildings, which now only survive in the names of streets, have been swallowed up by the rapidly expanding town.

The function of such farmsteads has changed since the last century. As of the mid-18th century, some were used for the new industrial production. Some were demolished to clear the site for workshops or factories, but in many cases they were just adapted to house them (Zvonařka, Stará Balabenka). Another example is Jenerálka which is still used for manufacturing.

Some of the farmsteads now belong to the State Farm of Prague, so that they continue serving their original purpose (e.g., Kotlářka in Smíchov District). Most of them are now dwelling-houses.

Kolčavka, one of the loveliest farmsteads in Libeň District, has been sacrificed to road construction, as well as many others, such as Malovanka in the 1950s or, ten years later, Folimanka.

Once important elements in the green belt around Prague, they became to some extent isolated during the expansion of the capital. The farmsteads are mostly not as elegant as the major buildings inside the town, yet they constitute an architectural entity. If the farmsteads continue vanishing it will deprive Prague of much of its beauty, as the remaining half of the original three hundred farmsteads rank among the characteristic elements of Prague's architecture. Of those that survive, several can be named here: Andělka, Cibulka, Malvazinka, Nikolajka, Pernikářka, Šmukýřka, Vondračka. The Bertramka in Smíchov District and the renowned Hanspaulka in Dejvice have particular charm.

Bertramka, whose surroundings have considerably changed, could be reached in the past by passing through the old Újezdská Gate and going along Kartouzská Road which crossed the Motolský Creek and climbed, between lines of chestnut trees, through a steep hollow up to its gate. Bertramka was, and still is, almost hidden at the northern end of the hollow, amidst vineyards covering Black Hill (Černý vrch). The configuration of the surrounding ground has protected and saved one of the most charming farmsteads whose history can be traced back in the vintner's books. They inform us that the house was built in the early 17th century. The original wooden vintner's house was rebuilt at the turn of the 17th and 18th century, the main building being made of quarried clay slate. Its name is due to one of the many subsequent owners, Franz of Bertram (1743—1764). In 1784, the house was purchased by the famous opera singer Josefina Dušková. W. A. Mozart lived here during his stays in Prague in 1787 and 1791 as a guest of the composer F. X. Dušek and his wife. He also stayed at their home at the Coal Market (Uhelný trh), but he spent much time in their suburban villa where he also composed the overture to his opera Don Giovanni.

The main part of the complex is a long two-storey house whose main façade, architecturally articulated, faces the courtyard. Opposite the house, there is a large barn and, next to it, a three-storey granary. There used to be a hayloft in the former press-shed; however, it burned down and a garden terrace was built here instead opposite the sala terrena of the south front of the house.

The cultural public in Prague wanted to restore Mozart's house as early as the 1870s. In 1873, the house was partly rebuilt after a fire. A guest book was available here until 1927 for visitors, among them many important figures.

In the same year, a Mozart Community was founded which tried to purchase Bertramka in order to renovate it. The house, however, was bought by the Community only much later, in the late 1930s, and during the war only the most urgent maintenance work could be done because the Community did not have enough money for a major renovation. Only later, in 1955, on the occasion of Mozart's 200th birthday was it decided to build a memorial here. By that time, Bertramka had already passed from the Mozart Community into the hands of the Ancient Building Preservation Office.

A survey showed that in spite of the 1871 fire there were many original elements. In addition, a detailed description of the farmstead was

Farmsteads around Prague

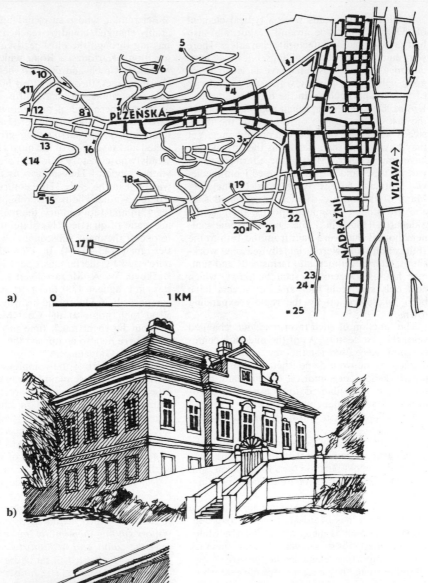

a) **plan of farmsteads and summer palaces in Smíchov, Košíře and Radlice:** 1 Kinský Villa, 2 Portheimka, 3 Betramka, 4 Hřebenka, 5 Horní Palata, 6 Perníkářka, 7 Klamovka, 8 Demartinka, 9 Klikovka, 10 Skalka, 11 Kotlářka, 12 Zámečnice, 13 Kavalírka, 14 Cibulka, 15 Šmukýřka, 16 Turbová, 17 Bulovka, 18 Šalamounka, 19 Nikolajka, 20 Malvazinka, 21 Santoška, 22 Doubková, 23 Voskářka, 24 Koulka, 25 Kesnerka
b) **Hanspaulka**
c) **Bertramka**

(180)

available in the contract of purchase between the Dušeks and the new owner, Alžběta Ballabenová, which made it possible to restore the 18th century appearance of the villa. Now it is a Museum to W. A. Mozart and the Dušeks. Of the seven rooms, two are devoted to Mozart and four other rooms contain rare documents and objects, such as pieces of music and even a hapsichord used by W. A. Mozart. The seventh room is devoted to the Dušeks, both important artists and Mozart's hosts. The furniture used here has come from the Museum of Decorative Arts. The Museum was opened to the public on 25th May 1956 and has been one of the most visited places in Prague since.

There are also other former farmsteads that have been successfully renovated, for instance in Dejvice District the farmstead called Beránka, which for the last fifteen years has housed the Design Section of the company Středočeský podnik pro obnovu památek (Central Bohemian Ancient Building Renovation Enterprise), or Fišerka (No. 19) and the Hendl Farm (Nos. 23 and 24) that were restored in the late 1970s.

The farmstead Ryšánka at Dolní Krč was rebuilt in 1860 and converted into a neo-Gothic manor house. In the early 1980s, another quite costly renovation took place; the house was modernized and architecturally completed according to a plan by Jan Štípek.

Other former farmsteads, too, have found a new place in the life of Prague.

Not only the large complexes and important buildings, but also small architectural details such as windows and portals make up the Baroque atmosphere of Prague.

A decade before the Baroque became prevalent in Prague, its principles were applied to portals in the town. The situation was similar to that at the early stage of the Renaissance in Prague. Portals entered the Baroque era as a mature architectural detail of the new style. Throughout the 17th century typical Renaissance portals were being reshaped in the Baroque spirit. A good example of this is the Matthias Gate from 1614, which is generally considered to have been the first Baroque structure in Prague. Another type of early Baroque portal is that of Our Lady the Victorious in the Lesser Quarter.

A new wave of north Italian architects continued designing portals according to traditional styles and types used by their predecessors. They mostly used the educula, column and pilaster type of portal, which appeared in a number of middle-class houses, palaces, and other secular buildings.

Baroque art reached its peak in Prague in the early 18th century. It was a time of strong artistic personalities who refused just to follow the traditional patterns, but wanted to develop their own creative art. And this had repercussions also in the variety of portal forms. On the other hand, however, the portals lost their homogeneous style, the Renaissance elements being—without any respect for their constructive role—reshaped absolutely freely according to the imagination of each architect. Prague architects in the 18th century showed inexhaustible inventiveness in shaping and combining the various elements. Nevertheless, portals continued to be framed with pillars and surmounted with a smooth archivolt, moulded in a variety of forms. This was a typical type applied to middle-class houses that were rebuilt in the 18th century.

Architectural Details

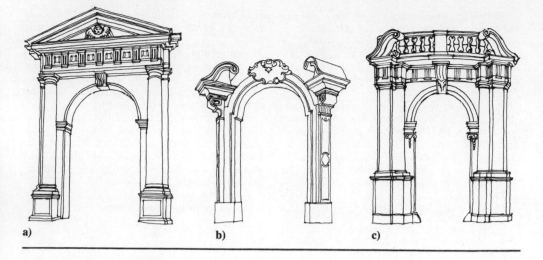

a) original portal of Our Lady the Victorious
b) portal of the Buquoy Palace
c) east portal of the Clementinum

d) portal of the former prelate's office at St. Nicholas', Lesser Quarter
e) portal of St. Nicholas' Church, Old Town
f) side portal of St. John's "Na skalce"

An excellent example of a portal with a rugged tympanum and an upper cornice scrolled into volutes can be seen in the Buquoy Palace, No. 486, Velkopřevorské (Grand Priory) Square, from the early 18th century, the Morzin Palace, No. 5/256, Nerudova Street (1714), and the Millesimo Palace, No. 13/597, Celetná Street, from 1750. An extremely noble form of Baroque portal with a balcony is that of the Clementinum Building by Kaňka from 1726. Here Kaňka further developed the Roman type of portal conceived by Jean B. Mathey.

A new and quickly spreading element of the Baroque portals in Prague was figural sculpture, under the particular influence of Vienna architecture. The sculptures on portals were not just decorative elements, but played the role of supporting parts, for instance in the portal of the Clam-Gallas Palace in the Old Town.

Of great importance were Dientzenhofer's works. The portals of his major buildings, such as St. John of Nepomuk at Hradčany, SS. Cyril and Methodius and St. John "Na Skalce" (On the Rock) in the New Town of Prague, as well as his portal of the former Jesuit College in Sněmovní Street in the Lesser Quarter were a source of inspiration for subsequent architects until the latter half of the 18th century.

The growing neo-Classical feeling in Prague's architecture at the end of the 18th century led to greater sobriety both in structures and details.

NEO-CLASSICAL AND ROMANTIC ARCHITECTURE

NEO-CLASSICAL ARCHITECTURE

Neo-Classical and Romantic Architecture

The evolution of architecture from the third quarter of the 18th century onwards was linked with the forthcoming Industrial Revolution and mass-production in factories. The motive force of this process was the new middle-class, the bourgeoisie, which started occupying the former positions of the clergy, the sovereigns and the nobility. Of growing importance was the philosophy based on scientific cognition: rationalism. As a result, Baroque illusion was replaced by the tectonics of neo-Classicism based on classical forms. Simultaneously, Romanticism, postulating individual creative fantasy, came into being.

The neo-Classicism of governmental buildings in the Austrian Empire was intended to express the rationality of Joseph's reforms. The construction activity controlled by the regional and provincial administration offices was of a very high standard, which was due to the good technical education of their workers, graduates from the Engineering Institute of Prague founded in 1707 by Christian Wilhelm Willenberg. Building structures were theoretically calculated, and iron structures appeared, initially of cast iron.

The construction of churches and palaces slowed down while other new tasks increased both in number and significance: municipal tenement houses, schools, hospitals, administrative buildings, barracks, etc. In 1780, important building regulations were introduced in this country which specified, for instance, the maximum height of buildings, roof construction, etc. New towns were built with much boldness of concept: Josefov, Terezín, west Bohemian spas, and the first suburb of Prague—Karlín. Green areas were introduced in the town and desolate hills were converted into gardens; embankments and new roads were constructed.

Romantic principles were often applied to the renovation of palaces and to the new parks imitating nature with artificial ruins, grottoes, and arbours. New churches, town-halls, administrative buildings, schools and tenement houses were built in the medieval style. In the latter half of the 19th century, with late Romanticism, a type of restoration developed which was based on the purity of medieval styles and their imitation.

Strahov Library

The Philosophical Hall Building, whose monumental façade faces the monastery forecourt, is the main part of the monastic library, the biggest in Bohemia and Moravia. Libraries prove the important role of monasteries and convents in the past, for instance those at Rajhrad, Teplá and in Prague's Clementinum.

Strahov Abbey belonged to St. Norbert's Order, the Premonstratensians, and was one of the richest Catholic institutions in the country. Damaged by several fires, it was rebuilt in the 17th century in the Baroque style, enlarged, and a new library hall was built, now known as the Theological Hall. A corridor connects it with the detached building of the Philosophical Hall (No. 132) dominating the forecourt of the monastery. It was built from 1782 to 1784 under Abbot Wenzel Mayer by Ignaz Johann Palliardi, a renowned Prague architect, and probably also designed by him, although some specialists believe that the plans were the work of Damian Kolba. The high façade of the building is a marked and valuable example of the dramatic contradiction between the dying spirit of feudalism and Catholicism and the ascending ideas of enlightened rationalism, the transition from Baroque to neo-Classicism. This stage of architectural evolution is sometimes called the "braid style", or is named after the then French king Louis XVI.

The façade, in accordance with the spirit of neo-Classicism, is calm in conception, with three flat zones separated from each other by tall pilasters with Tuscan capitals. Typical details are festoons, rosettes and triglyphs in the entablature frieze above the pilasters. The window jambs, the richly decorated pediments above the windows, and the entrance portal, connected with the large central window upstairs by means of

Strahov Library

a)

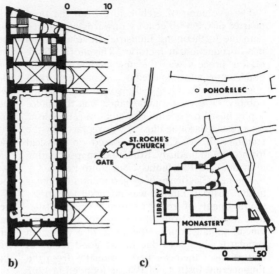

b)

c)

d)

e)

a) b) **Strahov Library**
c) **location**
d) **original appearance**
e) **Philosophical Hall, interior**

an elliptical window above the door, are elements continuing the previous Baroque tradition. Palliardi's authorship seems to be confirmed by the large segmental gable, pantiled and filled with a figural relief, and with a medallion of Emperor Joseph II in its centre made by Ignaz Platzer Junior. The gable has typical "braided" urns on its corners and sculptures in the middle with motifs from science and literature.

The large Philosophical Hall extends to both storeys of the building. Its tunnel vault has a ceiling fresco from 1794 with motifs from the History of Mankind by Anton Franz Maulbertsch, a Rococo painter of Vienna. The walls of the hall are covered with wooden bookcases, richly decorated, and at two thirds of its height, there is a gallery with a balustrade bearing decorative vases. The bookcases were brought here from

the closed monastery at Louka near Znojmo and were made by the cabinet-maker and artist Johann Lachhover. The hall therefore had to be made to fit their proportions. The bookcases contain valuable books, both old and new, that were in part donated to the monastery from abroad. In one of the departments, on a tall pedestal, there is a bust of Emperor Francis I by Franz X Lederer. Before entering the Philosophical Hall, the visitor passes through an inlaid door from 1749, brought here from the closed Cistercian Monastery in Prague, into the vestibule with a collection of Old Prague views and Baroque book bindings.

The interior of the Philosophical Hall integrates works of literature, sculpture, painting and architecture in a homogeneous entity and is still very impressive. The Hall was an apotheosis of science and the arts.

Theatre of the Estates

In the early 1780s, Prague joined other European cities in building a big new theatre, called the Nostic Theatre.

Some aristocrats in the Kingdom of Bohemia standing in opposition to the Imperial Court in Vienna were anxious at that time to enhance the level of culture in Prague. Count Nostic-Rieneck therefore decided to finance the construction of a building for this purpose. The detached house No. 540 on the Fruit Market (Ovocný trh) was built from 1781 to 1783, bearing an inscription "Patriae et Musis".

The first plans were made by Count Künigel who, however, conceived the building still in the Baroque style, particularly its flat façade that was vertically articulated by lesenes. The plans were reworked by the Prague architect Anton Haffenecker already in the spirit of the neo-Classical style. On a rectangular ground plan, he suggested building a theatre with boxes. All four front walls were symmetrical, each with a central section broken forward and crowned with a tympanum. The projecting section of the main façade, which previously had a tall window to the full height of the building, with four Corinthian columns and a carriage-way on the ground floor, however remained curved, an echo of Haffenecker's Baroque past. All the front walls were link-

ed by a rusticated ground floor and, above, by a horizontal entablature. The central band, now two storeys high, is articulated by tall, flat Corinthian pilasters. The tall windows were in the past crowned with pediments and brackets, and also with pairs of festoons in the Louis XVI style; now they are framed by Corinthian pilasters and a cornice above. The theatre has a simple hipped roof, clad with tiles.

On the first floor, in the projecting section of the main façade a social hall (later entrance foyer) was created. In the corners of the front façade were two staircases. The boxes could be entered from the corridor passing along their outer side. In this way a type of theatre was developed that remained popular for a very long time.

The original wooden structure of the auditorium was replaced by a steel structure in 1859. After the disastrous fire in Vienna's Rundtheater, the theatre here known since 1799 as the Theatre of the Estates was rebuilt in 1882 by Achille Wolf, a Prague architect who added new stairs, enlarged the old staircases and exits, and built iron balconies on the first floor of the side walls with access to the pavement, so that the building could be emptied in five minutes. A separate decorative staircase oriented towards the Kolowrat Palace was built that led to the Imperial Box.

Theatre of the Estates

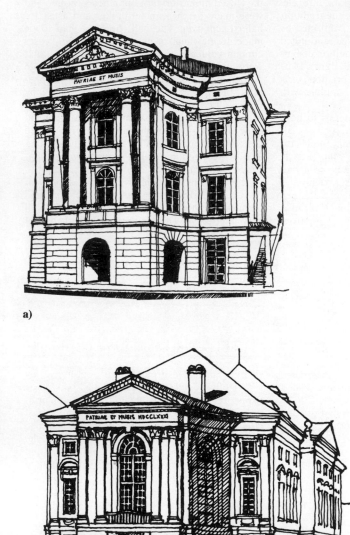

a)

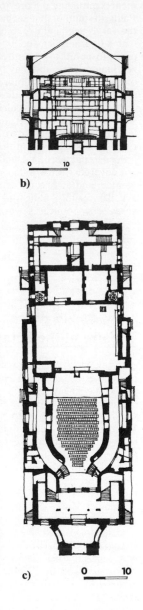

b)

c)

d)

a) b) c) **Theatre of the Estates** (Stavovské divadlo)
d) **original appearance** (by V. Morstadt, 1830)

The tall windows in the façade were replaced by two rows of smaller windows, in accordance with the internal organization of corridors. An annex with the stage and dressing-rooms was added towards the Fruit Market.

The theatre, which was also called the German Theatre, was rebuilt in 1920 and became another stage for the National Theatre. As a result, the stage was enlarged and an inserted steel structure made it possible to install a trapdoor mechanism and to increase the height of the entrance portico. The original high hallway on the first floor was divided by inserting an intermediate ceiling.

The neo-Classical Theatre of the Estates (now Tyl Theatre) is reputed for the fact that in January 1787 the Marriage of Figaro by Mozart was performed here with much success, and on 29th October of the same year the premiere of Don Giovanni took place here, conducted by the composer. To celebrate the crowning of Emperor Leopold II as King of Bohemia in 1791, the premiere of Mozart's opera La Clemenza di Tito was held in this theatre.

Thanks to Jan Nepomuk Štěpánek, as of the 1820s some performances in the theatre were in Czech. In 1827, the first Czech opera "Dráteník" (Tinker) by Chmelenský was performed here and several years later, in 1834, the comedy "Fidlovačka" (Spring Festival) by Tyl. The music for both pieces was composed by František Škroup, and in Tyl's comedy the song "Kde domov můj" (Where is My Home) was heard for the first time, which later became the Czech national anthem.

The last adaptation, or modernization of the technical installations took place in 1946. Then, the theatre was in full theatrical operation until 1983 when the renovated National Theatre was reopened and the current renovation and modernization of the Tyl Theatre started.

What was needed here in particular was a modernization of the technical installations, an improvement in the standard of the dressing-rooms and other facilities for actors, a modernization of the stage with an improvement of its mobility, and in particular, the construction of storerooms and the installation of equipment for shifting scenery, which until that time had to be done through a rear corridor from Fruit Market.

The surveys, analyses, feasibility studies and preliminary projects of the whole redevelopment were prepared by a team of SURPMO workers headed by František Soukup. The final scheme was prepared by a team of workers of the Krajský projektový ústav (Regional Planning Institute), particularly by Svatopluk Zeman and Ivan Skála, headed by Zdeněk Kuna.

The redevelopment includes the historic building and Fruit Market (Ovocný trh Square) and there will also be a scenery store under the square operated by means of a special elevator and linked to the space below the stage by an underground corridor, which will enable rapid scene changes. The scenes will be easily movable on pallets, as in the National Theatre.

Part of the redevelopment is also a renovation of the Kolowrat Palace, which will be connected with the theatre. It is a fine Baroque building with painted timbered ceilings. The palace will house the technical departments, the administration, and other departments of the National Theatre, as well as a dining-room, actors' club, and a number of other social institutions.

The renovation is an extremely difficult technical process, as the building is technically not as sound as the National Theatre. The Theatre of the Estates was reopened after renovation at the end of 1991 with Mozart's Don Giovanni.

House "U hybernů"

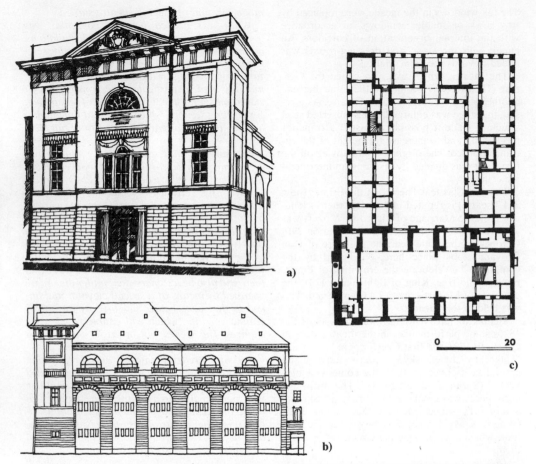

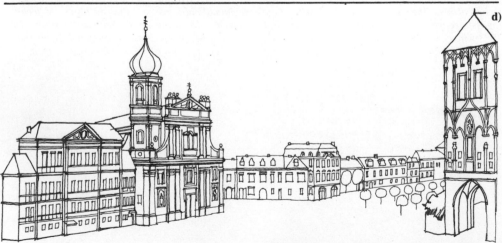

a) b) c) **house "U hybernů"**
d) **contemporary view** (by F. and F. Heger, 1792)

(192)

The house is a large building dominating two streets in the Old Town of Prague, whose architecture expresses some of the ideas of urban building of the Napoleonic period.

The massive prismatic front wall of the former Prague customs office, No. 3/1057, facing the square in front of the Powder Tower, is a high neo-Classical work, quite unique in Bohemia and Moravia. The house was built from 1808 to 1811 according to a plan prepared by Georg Fisher, a provincial construction director and a professor at the Bohemian Engineering Institute in Prague. The house replaced the early Baroque Church of Our Lady by Carlo Lurago, built between 1652 and 1659 together with the adjoining monastery of the Order of Irish Franciscans, known in Prague as the Hibernians. Its conversion into a customs office was made by Jan Zobel, a Prague architect, and the church lost its tower. The nave could hardly be used, and was therefore divided into two floors by inserting a massive tunnel vault. A model for Fischer's project, although much simpler, was the Old Mint in Berlin built in 1798—1800 and designed by Heinrich Gentz, which has since been demolished.

The bossed and cone-shaped ground floor of the Customs Office is broken in the middle by an entrance niche with a couple of robust early-Doric columns. The two-storey building with a central section broken forward is vertically articulated by wide lesenes, between which there are tall windows upstairs and, in the projecting section, a three-light window. On the second floor, there is a semicircular window in the projecting section while the side bays have shallow fillings. The façade is crowned with a massive Doric cornice supported by consoles, with triglyphs in the frieze and with a tympanum above the projecting section. Over the cornice, there is a low unarticulated attic, raised in the central part. The side front facing Hybernská Street is flat, articulated only by bossed lesenes that are connected at the top by archivolts. The sculptural decoration was made by F. X. Lederer and includes a high relief of the imperial two-headed eagle in the tympanum gable, and two festoons above the window in the central part on the first floor. A decorative frieze above the ground floor designed in 1811 was not realized.

In 1786, after the closing of the monastery and the deconsecration of the church, the house was purchased by Count Johann F. K. Sweerts-Sporck, and for several years Czech plays were performed here, after the "Bouda" Theatre on Wenceslas Square had been closed in 1789. The house then came into the hands of the Austrian Government, which made the above-mentioned alterations here. The former monastery housed finance offices and in the former church a customs office was established.

The specific general layout and the architectural and decorative motifs applied here made the customs office a high neo-Classical building, incorrectly called the Empire style (after Napoleon I), of which it was the most important example in Prague.

At the corner of Na příkopě and Panská Streets another work by Fischer, the Church of the Holy Cross, can be seen, which was originally a church for the Piarists and the students at their college. It is a late neo-Classical building constructed between 1816 and 1824, without aisles and with original interiors and fittings. The front wall is enriched with two tall Ionic columns.

The former Hibernian Monastery and its church had undergone many changes in their history before the monastery was converted into the customs office and the church became one of the largest and most popular exhibition halls in Prague.

A number of redevelopment plans and competitions have been prepared and organized since the turn of this century that have had a strong impact on Republic Square (náměstí Republiky) and the Hibernian complex. Jiří Kroha presented a competition plan in 1922 containing the idea of a great boulevard from Republic Square to Karlín that would allow a view of Vítkov Hill. Other plans were presented up to 1949, and some studies even after that date which did not hesitate to pull down some parts of the complex. Just before the outbreak of the Second World War it was decided that the former monastery and church would be preserved.

Czech fine artists suggested adapting the former church to an exhibition hall. This was accepted, and Josef Karel Říha was invited to prepare the respective project. Říha decided to remove several inserted timber ceilings and create instead an intermediate gallery-floor, which makes it possible to admire the whole interior and the main vaults of the former church. A new axial staircase was built to reach the gallery.

The adaptation began in 1941, but was interrupted during the war. The former church started serving its new purpose in 1949.

The radical adaptation of the building was well planned and well executed, and is a good example of the conversion of a religious building into a modern public building.

Governor's Summer Palace

The romantic rebuilding of the hunting-lodge in the Royal Deer Park (now Stromovka Park) was an example of the application of medieval architectural styles that had started in the 18th century in England. In this country, Giovanni Santini-Aichel rebuilt the churches at Žďár nad Sázavou, Kladruby and Sedlec near Kutná Hora in the Baroque-Gothic style.

A deer park was founded here by King John of Luxembourg in the early 14th century near the village called Ovenec. During the Hussite Wars the park was devastated by an army setting up camp here. The park was restored under Vladislav Jagiello in the late 15th century and, at the same time, a summer palace was built on a hill north of the park. From that period a Gothic window in the tower, "saddle" porches and, in particular, a figure of a lion holding a shield with Vladislav's monogram have survived. The lion is on the newel of the spiral staircase in the tower. A wood engraving from 1562 shows us the appearance of the building. The engraving shows a separate tower. This, however, is contradicted by the existence of a Gothic portal between the tower and a gallery upstairs. The view also shows another circular tower which is now much lower and is incorporated in the mass of the house. Ferdinand I enlarged the park from 1536 to 1548, and in 1569 a lake was created here which, as of 1584 in the reign of Rudolph II, was fed through a tunnel under Letná Square from the Vltava. Under Rudolph II the palace was surrounded with an open loggia, and the ground plan of the building has remained intact since. Surviving from that time are the vaults in the oriel (called the chapel) and above the spiral staircase. An imitation of this summer palace in Prague was the summer palace of Adam Trčka

in Opočno dating from 1602, which thus informs us about the original appearance of its model. The summer palace was linked with Prague Castle as of 1664 by an alley lined with chestnut trees. These were cut down by the French army during their occupation of Prague in 1742 and were later restored. In the latter half of the 18th century, large folk feasts with weddings were held in the Royal Deer Park, which were sponsored by the sovereign.

In 1804, the country's governor Count Jan Rudolf Chotek decided to open the park to the public. A renovation of the summer palace started in 1805 and its architect, Georg Fischer, took as his model the Franzenburg Palace in Luxembourg Park in Vienna built between 1801 and 1836. He was also inspired by the English neo-Gothic style. Fischer only changed the façade and did not make any major alterations to the Renaissance structure, as is seen in the coupled Renaissance windows that were originally in the façade and are now in the arcades around the building. The large arches of the arcades were pointed, sometimes doubled and filled with wooden glazed tracery. On the piers between the windows Fischer created striking Gothic-style verticals in the form of flying buttresses that made the building look slender. At the top, they bear a lunette cornice and, above, an attic with tracery which is particularly rich in the tower. The buttresses are crowned with stone pinnacles. With his neo-Gothic rebuilding of the summer palace Fischer anticipated the future development of architecture and his later Empire work.

At present, the former summer palace, No. 56, houses the Department of Periodicals of the National Museum. The building dominates Stromovka Park in the south.

Governor's Summer Palace

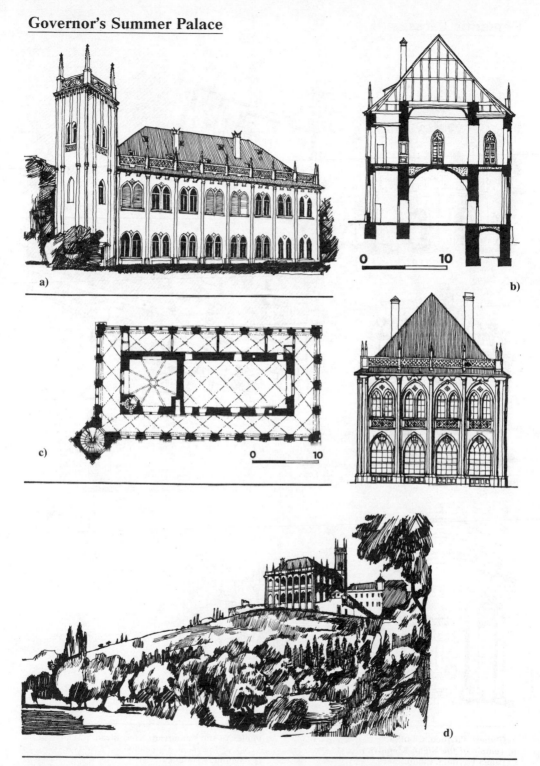

a) b) c) **Governor's summer palace**   d) **contemporary view** (by A. Pucherny, 1806)

Romantic Parks

a)

b)

c)

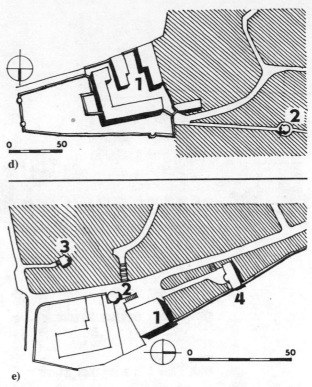

d)

e)

f)

a) **Chinese Pavilion, Cibulka**
b) **Temple of the Night, Klamovka**
c) **Diana Pavilion, Cibulka**
d) **plan of the Cibulka:** 1 farmstead, 2 Chinese Pavilion

e) **plan of the Klamovka:** 1 farmstead, 2 Temple of the Night, 3 pavilion, 4 greenhouse
f) **pavilion, Klamovka**

Romantic Parks

Until the early 19th century, Prague was surrounded by a ring of gardens outside the Baroque walls, around farms and aristocratic or bourgeois summer palaces. Most of these charming green islands fell victim to the spontaneous growth of the town in the 19th century. Only some of them survived and were converted into public parks (Kinský Park, Santoška, Jezerka, etc.). Two of them still have their original garden architecture.

On the southern slope of Strahov Hill, near the road leading to Beroun and Plzeň, there was a farmstead called Klamovka which, in 1757, was purchased by Count Clam-Gallas. Over eight years his family converted the garden into an English-type park. There were cages with bears, wolves, lynxes, and aviaries with birds of prey. Later on, small buildings and various memorials were scattered in the park. Walking through Klamovka Park now, one can see a neo-Gothic pavilion from 1820 made of bricks on a square ground plan, with pointed doors and windows, stone tracery, and rich battlements. Higher up, on the main park thoroughfare is a Temple of the Night from 1790, which is a centralized structure of circular ground plan, domed and crowned with a fully glazed lantern bearing an owl-shaped weather cock made of metal. The exterior of the temple is articulated by half columns with Ionic capitals and clad with pebbles. The copper cladding of the dome has irregular circular holes which create the illusion of stars in the sky in the interior. In the plinth of the temple, on the lower side of the park, there is a stone grotto called "The Inferno." The temple as a whole has harmonious proportions creating the illusion of a much bigger building. Unfortunately, the wall-paintings in the interior are in a very bad state. Still higher in the park, there is a greenhouse with a two-storey transverse wing and a domed roof. Of the original sculptures in the park only the bust of Charles IV from the mid-19th century has survived and is still in place.

Cibulka, which is a garden displaying different types of garden architecture, and a summer residence of the enlightened Count Leopold Thun-Hohenstein (No. 118), was created in 1817 on the southern slope of Košíře Valley. Proceeding from the entrance, near which there is a statue of St. John of Nepomuk by Václav Nedoma from 1818, we come to the Chinese Pavilion, a miniature pagoda of octagonal ground plan with a receding first floor and a curved pointed roof. The road leads beyond this to an Empire palace whose blind windows once contained busts of rustic figures by Josef Malínský. Behind the palace is the smaller part of the garden with arbours, once decorated inside with mirrors, and with a memorial to Bishop Thun by Václav Prachner from 1822. In the lower part of the garden, there is a terrace with four statues of Chinese figures. The park under the palace contained a pseudo-antique circular garden-house, crowned with a cupola, and there are still statues of Diana and Chronos by Václav Prachner from 1820. The highest point is an artificial ruin of a castle with a tower used as a look-out tower. It is a pity that the charming and artistically interesting natural enclave of Cibulka is not sufficiently maintained and better used.

Karlín-the First Suburb of Prague

Due to growing industry and to masses of country people flooding into Prague in the early 19th century the territory of the town enclosed by its walls became insufficient. New houses were built outside the walls, at first spontaneously, but soon the construction was planned. The first new settlements appeared east of Prague, on a plain between the Vltava and Vítkov Hill.

There had been a settlement here since the 10th century, called Poříčí, which belonged to Břevnov Abbey. In the 13th century, the Order of the Knights of the Cross with a Red Star built St. Francis' Hospital here and in 1504 the Church of St. Paul's Conversion; the area was therefore called "Špitálské pole" (Hospital Field). In its eastern part a Hostel for Disabled Soldiers was built between 1731 and 1737, and in the late 18th century a public garden and a tavern called Růžodol appeared in its western part. In the early 19th century, new mills, paper-mills, granaries, shipyards and a port were built along the river, as well as storehouses for goods coming from northern Bohemia and Germany. Tenement houses and inns were built between the gardens here.

Karlín-the First Suburb of Prague

a)

b)

c)

d)

a) **view of Karlín** (after J. Rybička, 1870)
b) **development plan of Karlín:** 1 Poříčská Gate, 2 Imperial Road, 3 Invalidovna

c) **house No. 81, Sokolovská Street** (former pub "U města Hamburku")
d) **house No. 128, Sokolovská Street** ("U dělokříže")

By a governmental decree of 1817 construction regulations were introduced in the country in the spirit of enlightened town-planning. Following the system that had proved successful at the fortified towns Terezín and Josefov a grid of streets perpendicular to each other was planned. Three main roads leading from the west to the east with a number of transverse streets were foreseen. In the middle, there was a square with a church, a town-hall and a school, covering the entire width of the area. In honour of Empress Carolina Augusta, wife of Francis I, the new suburb was called Karlín. The suburb was given the status of a borough rather late, in 1903.

The official plan did not take into consideration the interests of particular land owners and reckoned with broad avenues and streets that even now meet the needs of modern traffic. There are also large blocks of houses between streets, larger than in any later Prague suburb. In spite of many later renovations the original network of streets as well as many neo-Classical houses have survived, such as the houses No. 81 "U města Hamburku" (At the Town of Hamburg), No. 265 "U červené hvězdy" (At the Red Star), No. 91 "U větrostřelce" (At the Windshooter), etc. Notable buildings are the neo-Romanesque Church of SS. Cyril and Methodius from 1854—1863 by Karl Rösner and Ignác Ullmann, the late neo-Classical Žižka Barracks, No. 20, from 1844—1848, the stone railway viaduct from 1846—1850, the former Variété Theatre built by Friedrich Ohmann from 1896—1898, and the former National House by Josef Sakař from 1910—1911. This last building stands in the eastern part of Karlín District constructed after 1900 around Lyčka Square where there is also a large school building from 1906 by Josef Sakař conceived in the Bohemian neo-Renaissance style.

Many technical innovations were applied for the first time at Karlín: a textile factory (1818), a steam engine works (1833), a steamboat (1841), Prague gasworks (1847), a horse-drawn tram line (1875), electric street lighting and electric tram lines (1895).

The Karlín suburb has become, due to the rapid growth of Prague, an important part of its central region, which must be taken into consideration when deciding on particular restoration and regeneration projects. Karlín is preserved as an interesting urban complex, with its bold original plan, large blocks, broad streets, and a system of vacant areas. The buildings here have a distinct architectural quality, and the approach to their renovation must therefore be differentiated. The present-day high number of manufacturing works and factories is unacceptable for the future regeneration and a considerable degree of reconstruction will be needed. There are, on the other hand, many notable buildings, both from the neo-Classical period, and from the late 19th and the early 20th century, that will require a different approach to reconstruction than for instance in Žižkov. Therefore, two different proposals of reconstruction were prepared in 1971—1972 by Projektový ústav výstavby hlavního města Prahy (Prague Construction Design Institute) and SURPMO (architects Václav Tatíček, Milan Pavlík, Josef Lácha). The regeneration of the area should begin in the 1990s to return to Karlín some of its original residential character. For services and communal facilities, the large areas within blocks will be used, as well as for recreation.

Part of the Karlín regeneration plan is also the construction of an Olympic sports stadium whose design has been the subject of several competitions. Feasibility studies and preliminary plans have also been carried out for an International Trade Centre on an important site between the north-south axial road and the Negrelli Viaduct, a notable technical monument. There is also a large international hotel under construction designed by a team of architects headed by Stanislav Franc.

Kinský Villa

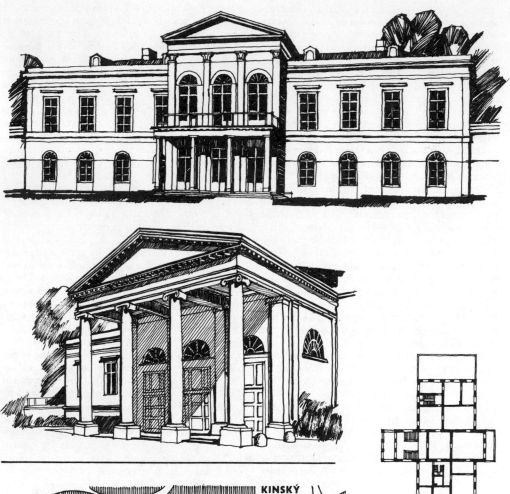

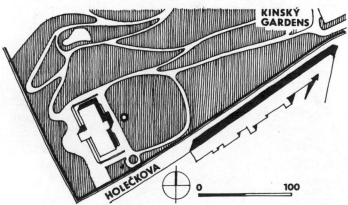

Kinský Villa

The neo-Classical epoch in the early 19th century resulted, particularly in this country, in the construction of palaces surrounded by English-type parks imitating nature. Typical examples are a park and a summer palace at the foot of Petřín Hill on its southern side, and Richter's summer palace above Klárov. The southern slope of Petřín Hill was covered with vineyards from the 14th century until the Thirty Years' War. They were destroyed during the war and the wasteland was called Brabcovna. Later on, vegetable gardens were established on the lower part of the slope, and above them greenhouses and factories for ceramic pots were built. On the top of the hill, there were only rocks.

Count Rudolf Kinský, a patriotic aristocrat and one of the sponsors of the Czech Cultural Foundation, established here in 1825 a park in the English style designed by Franz Höhnel. Later, from 1827 to 1831, he constructed a neo-Classical villa in the park (No. 98) that had been designed by the Viennese architect Heinrich Koch. The house was adorned with marble statues, of Psyche by the famous sculptor Antonio Canova, and of Vlasta (leader of Czech Amazons) by Emanuel Max. As of 1866 the house was used by the Kurfürst (Elector) of Hessen and Kassel, an ally of Austria dethroned by the victorious Prussians, and later also by the Austrian crown prince Rudolph and by Archduke Franz Ferdinand. Now it houses the Ethnographic Department of the National Museum with a notable collection of historical rustic furniture, furnishings of middle-class houses from the Baroque period and the 19th century, a collection of folk paintings, woodcuts, ceramics, costumes and embroideries.

The villa stands on uneven ground that is levelled by a terrace, so that the east part facing the large park parterre has two storeys. It is here that pedestrians can enter the house through a portico with Doric columns in front of a lofty section broken forward in the middle of the house. The gallery over the entrance lined with ornamental railings can be entered through a French window in the main hall upstairs. At the south end of the ground floor, there is a former winter garden with five large windows allowing a lot of light to enter. On the west side, there is a tall portico for coaches, crowned with a tympanum supported by four Ionic columns. From here, one comes to a three-flight staircase, at the top of which is the domed, columned central hall of the building, lit from above.

The garden was extended in 1848 and again in 1860 by Franz Wünsch. It was purchased in 1901 by the Municipal Council of Prague and, in 1908, enriched with lakes, a waterfall and rare plants, and connected through passages in the Hunger Wall with Petřín Gardens. As of 1902, the Kinský Villa was used to display collections of exhibits from the Ethnographic Exhibition held in Prague in 1895. The house has also been used by the Ethnographic Department of the National Museum which organizes various ad hoc exhibitions here.

On a lower part of the site there is also a service building called Švýcárna, built by Heinrich Koch in 1829—1830, to which in 1923 a glazed hall designed by Jan Víšek was attached. From 1918 to 1946, the building was used as an exhibition hall of the Agricultural Museum. Higher on the slope, there is a greenhouse built by Koch between 1829 and 1831.

The building, which now houses the Ethnographic Museum, is a type of neo-Classical villa that can be found in many other places throughout the country, including Slovakia.

By the road leading from the entrance of the park, which is called Kinský Garden, there now stands a bronze sculpture "Fourteen-year-old Girl" by Karel Dvořák (1928), and higher up, there is a memorial to the actress Hana Kvapilová made in 1913 by Jan Štursa from white marble. By the lake above the villa, there is a bronze sculpture of a fur seal by Jan Lauda (1953), and at the top the visitor can see the 18th century Orthodox church of St. Michael which was brought here from a Ruthenian village called Medvedovce near Mukachevo.

In a garden, which is sometimes called St. Wenceslas' Vineyards and which is situated on a hill between the Old Castle Steps and the old lane called Na Opyši, is the neo-Classical Richter Villa, No. 148, constructed by Josef Peschka in 1832, with a portico in its north side, with Tuscan columns and a tympanum. The villa is a dominant building in the area under the Castle if viewed from Chotek Garden. Adjoining the garden and the villa is a tall house No. 147 in the north part of Klárov where the actor Eduard Vojan, the writers Růžena Svobodová, František X. Svoboda and, at an advanced age, also Václav Vilém Štech lived.

Tenement House "Platýz"

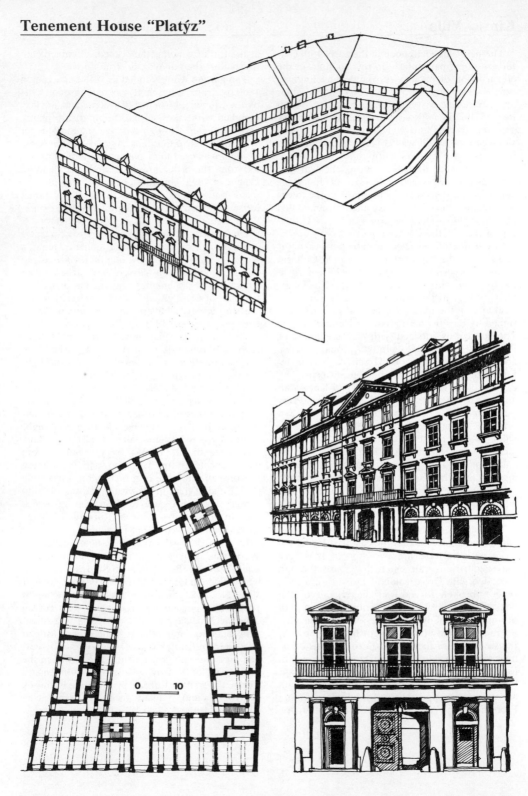

Tenement House "Platýz"

With the building boom in Prague in the 19th century new houses were built and, in particular, old middle-class houses were rebuilt which either no longer met modern needs or stood in places that promised better profits. One such street was called Nové aleje (New Alleys) and was part of Prague's circular avenue that had been created here in 1781 by filling the moat separating the Old Town and the New Town. Here, in the early 1820s, the house No. 416, which was called "Platýz", was rebuilt.

The house consists of several parts surrounding a large yard with passageways. The oldest part faces Uhelný trh (Coal Market) and dates from the reign of Charles IV. At the outbreak of the Hussite Wars, the house belonged to Jan Bradatý, the burgrave of the Old Town, and in 1585 was sold to Jan Plateys of Plattenstein. The house was later purchased by the Sternbergs who extended the garden into the New Town. Another owner, František Daubek, invited the architect Heinrich Hausknecht to build a three-storey house on Nové aleje in the high neo-Classical style. Hausknecht built the house from 1817 to 1825 and, at the same time, rebuilt and architecturally harmonized the whole complex of buildings with five staircases, creating here large apartments and rooms for social purposes, entertainment and trade.

The façade of the newer part is articulated with three shallow projecting sections. The central projecting section contains a stone portico with four Doric columns and a balcony with ornamental wrought-iron railings. Comparatively plain is the façade on Uhelný trh with a stone balcony over the passageway bearing a decorative balustrade. Unifying elements of all three street façades are classical male and female masks on the window pediments of the ground floor, partly original and partly new. The building, rebuilt by Plateys, contains a room with a timbered ceiling on the first floor, with original Renaissance ornamental and figural painting, and other rooms with 17th century wall-paintings. The basement conceals remains of the Gothic Old Town walls.

The house "Platýz" was rebuilt in 1938—1939 by František Krásný. The shops on Národní třída (National Avenue) and Uhelný trh (Coal Market) were modernized, the pavement around the yard was covered with a projecting glass roof, and an attic storey was added with Empire-style dormers in the roof.

First Blocks of Flats in Prague

With the first Industrial Revolution resulting from the introduction of steam engines in new factories in the early 1770s, and with the abolition of serfdom in 1781, a new type of urban growth began.

The newcomers did not require comfortable dwellings; they just had one or two rooms for one family. In addition to these wage labourers, better-off social classes came to the city, from small shopkeepers and artisans through to wealthy citizens and to nobles, many of whom became businessmen.

This social structure was reflected in the structure of dwellings. Nobles and rich burghers lived in the historic towns within the town-walls, and some of them built summer palaces and villas with gardens. To provide housing for the newcomers to the city, side and transverse wings were attached to houses in their courtyards, which brought more profits from the rent. The new flats could be entered from galleries.

At the turn of the 1830s and 1840s, new municipal houses were built along the main streets or in the new side streets outside the town-walls, in suburbs, or, more rarely, they replaced derelict and unprofitable houses in the town centre or former gardens. The landlord's flat was the largest, facing the street, on the first floor, with several rooms, a kitchen, and a storage-room. The balcony above the passageway could be entered from the largest room in the centre of the façade. The other flats had just two rooms or even one room only and a kitchen, mostly without a hallway, and were entered from a gallery, in some cases from the stairs. The flats in typical gallery houses have a kitchen with a door and a window opening onto the gallery, and a room entered from the kitchen facing the street.

The flats included a storage-room or pantry, or only a cellar in the basement to store wood

First Blocks of Flats in Prague

a)

c)

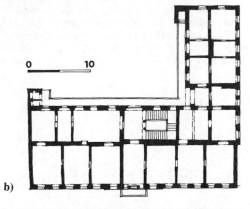

b)

d)

e)

a) b) **house No. 59, Štefánikova Street**
c) **house No. 59, view of the staircase**
d) e) **house in the workers' housing estate Mrázovka,
     Smíchov** (demolished)

and coal. There was a common water main or a well with a pump in the yard; water mains were later available on the galleries. There were dry toilets with a cesspit at the end of the gallery, sometimes by the staircase. Sewage and waste-water were poured into a drain in the yard. A progressive element was the cooking stove in the kitchen and the tiled stove—called "plzeň-ky"—in the room. The neo-Classical architecture of these houses was quite attractive.

There were many houses of the above type in Smíchov District, such as the house "U vévody Přemysla", No. 59. The house was built around 1840 and its architect is not known; it may have been Heinrich Koch, who built the villa in Kins-

ký Garden nearby. The house is decorated with ornamental reliefs below the window sills, in the frieze above the second floor, and on the sides of the stone consoles supporting a balcony over the entrance from the street, which still has attractive cast-iron railings. The three-flight staircase inside is of the palace type, carried by pairs of slender stone columns with Doric capitals. The general condition of the house is comparatively good, only the interiors and the yard are in disrepair. The relatively good appearance is spoiled by the lower part of the street front which has suffered from many alterations and now badly needs renovation.

Smetana Embankment

Until the end of the 18th century European cities had turned away from the rivers passing through them. New town-planning ideas came to Prague in the 1840s, according to which the river should be used to adorn the city. What were the riverside parts of Prague like before? When Prague was enclosed with walls in 1253 under King Wenceslas I, there was only a simple wall along the river bank, and the Old Town mills were already standing outside the wall. Charles IV had the wall pulled down in 1367, and only one part remained at the Church of St. John "Na zábradlí" in Anenská Street, which was consecrated in 1130 and demolished in 1896. There was a gate in the wall leading to the river, and all the waste was thrown out on the bank; that is why the church was in the 16th century referred to as St. John "Na smetišti" (On a Rubbish Heap). Next to the church was a cemetery which was closed, together with the church, under Emperor Joseph II. The authorities decided to rebuild the church and convert it into a dwelling-house.

For centuries, the river banks sloping down to the river were lined with timber yards for rafting, fishermen's huts, small gardens, fishing nets and boats on the bank. There was a ferry called "Hořejší" (Upper Ferry) connecting the two banks, and later there were wash-houses, public baths in a painted house known as "Písaná",

a lime kiln and a brick-yard (Ellenberger's). With high water the river flooded the flat riverside, and even the town itself, as for instance in February 1784, when "as water splashing with waves and ice-floes was doing its evils in streets and squares, peoples had to leave their homes and look for refuge".

These were the reasons why in 1841—1845 the Provincial Diet of the Kingdom of Bohemia, on the initiative of the Chief Burgrave Count Karel Chotek decided to purchase all the yards, houses, baths and mills on the river bank between the end of Nové aleje Street and the Old Town mills, and to construct here a high embankment of hewn granite ashlar blocks. The embankment was lined with solid cast iron railings between granite posts, acacias were planted here and a wide road with a pavement was built. Thus, the first embankment of Prague appeared, and was named "Františkovo nábřeží" (Francis Embankment) after the ruling Austrian emperor. It was designed by Bernard Grueber, the plans were prepared by the director of the Construction Office Strobach in 1836 and carried out by Vojtěch Lanna's building firm.

In the northern and the southern parts of the embankment two groups of tenement houses were built (Nos. 324, 331, 334, 995) to plans by the architects Josef Tredrovský, Bernard Grueb-

Smetana Embankment

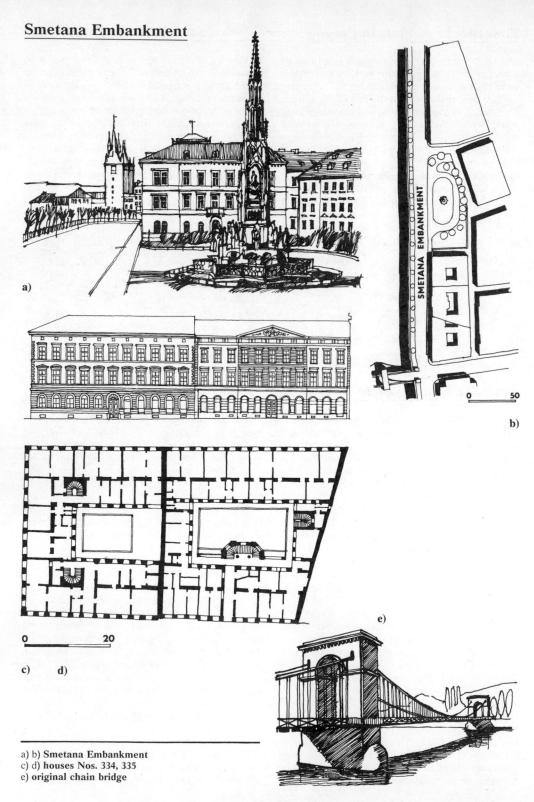

a)

b)

c) d)

e)

a) b) **Smetana Embankment**
c) d) **houses Nos. 334, 335**
e) **original chain bridge**

er, Franz Wolf and Josef Kaura (1845—1848), mostly with inner yards surrounded by galleries. At the rear, the houses had entrances from Poštovská Street (now Karoliny Světlé Street). The consistency of the level of the storeys and of the façades conceived in the late neo-Classical style gave the embankment a tranquil unity. In the middle, a little park was laid out with a memorial to Emperor Francis I and with a fountain, 29 m high and resembling a Gothic tower; the memorial and the fountain were designed by Josef C. Kranner and made in 1844—1846 by the stonemason Karel Svoboda. The memorial is decorated with statues by Josef Max and Josef Kamil Böhm representing the particular trades and crafts, as well as Prague and Bohemia's regions. In the middle of the tower there was a bronze equestrian statue of the Emperor. František Palacký, the political leader of the Czech nation, suggested building at the end of the square a palace of Czech science, arts and history. A plan was prepared by Jan Schöbl, but it could not be realized. In 1870, Antonín Barvitius designed a Gallery of Patriotic Friends of the Arts to be constructed on the same site. The unity of style of the embankment was spoiled in 1861 by the construction of the Lažanský Palace in the southern part, and even more in 1895 by a tall house conceived in the style of Dutch Renaissance, with a tower and a mansard roof, built by Konstantin Mráček in the north part of the embankment. It has a glazed hall (former café) and a terrace on the ground floor. In 1848, Jan Bělský built the Romantic tall building of Charles Baths at the north end of the embankment. Karel Havlíček Borovský lived here and edited his newspaper Národní noviny.

At the same time as the embankment, from 1839 to 1841, a suspension bridge was built linking the avenue "Nové aleje" with Újezd in the Lesser Quarter. The two strong chains made of wrought iron were suspended from four granite gates, of which two were embedded in the river and two on Střelecký Island. The bridge structure was designed by Bedřich Schnirch, the Classical gates by Jan Straka, and the bridge was constructed by Vojtěch Lanna, a building contractor from České Budějovice in southern Bohemia. The roadway was made of wood boards supported by transverse beams suspended from the chains by means of tie bars. The railing was also made of wood. After half a century of op-

eration, the bridge no longer met the needs of modern traffic, particularly trams and cars, and had to be replaced in 1898 by a new stone bridge, now called Bridge of the Legions.

Smetana Embankment with its beautiful view of the panorama of Hradčany has often been the subject of discussions and studies aimed at making it more accessible to the public and more tranquil. The last occasion for this was the recent collapse of the embankment wall in spring 1983. One part of the wall had to be rebuilt and the rest, as far as Novotného lávka, was grouted and secured against further destruction. Simultaneously, the pavement was widened and a tranquil promenade along the Vltava was created. The successful renovation was completed in 1986.

Together with the embankment, the Old Town mills on Novotného lávka were rebuilt (see the chapter Working Structures, page 95).

The Smetana Museum ranks among the monuments in Prague where the early stages and forms of conservation and rebuilding can be well demonstrated. Originally a waterworks, designed by Antonín Wiehl, the building was completed in 1887 in the Czech neo-Classical style. Notable artists contributed to its beautiful sgraffiti, such as František Ženíšek and Mikoláš Aleš, who made the cartoons, and Janez Šubič, who made the sgraffiti. The building contained an engine room for the waterworks on the ground floor, and flats on the two higher floors. The flats were used between 1886 and 1895 as a girls' secondary school. The waterworks was closed here in 1913, and in 1935 the building was purchased to house the Smetana Museum. For this purpose, it was adapted by Rudolf Stockar who fully respected Wiehl's architecture. The walls of the main rooms were decorated by František Kysela. The Museum was solemnly opened in 1936. Stockar made some alterations to the layout, inserted an intermediate ceiling in the engine room and adapted the former flats to display the Museum's collections and to house a reading-room, studies, and archives. The most recent changes to the building were made in 1964 and a large new exhibition room was created on the first floor. Quite recently, an extended viewing platform was made at the end of Novotného lávka, in front of the façade of the Museum, and in 1984 a statue of Bedřich Smetana by Josef Malejovský was placed here.

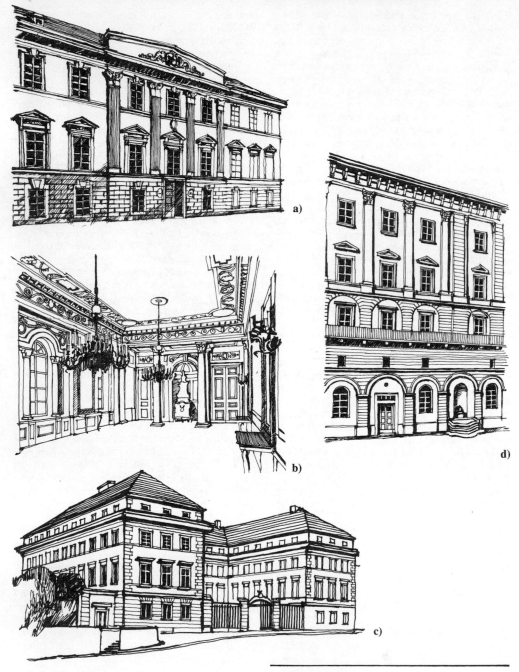

a) Rohan Palace
b) dancing-hall, Rohan Palace
c) Schwarzenberg (Salm) Palace, No. 186, Hradčany Square
d) Thun Palace, courtyard façade, No. 193, Nerudova Street

Prague's Palaces from the First Half of the 19th Century

The centralization of state administration in the Austrian Empire by Maria Theresa and Joseph II and its concentration in Vienna was another blow to the position of Prague as capital of the Kingdom of Bohemia which had existed until then. The role of aristocrats in the city was diminishing while the middle-class was becoming wealthier. As a result, palaces in the town ceased to be the seats of feudal lords. The coronation of Austrian Emperors in 1791, 1792 and 1836 as kings of Bohemia brought temporarily some splendour and glory to Prague as a capital, and the participation of nobles in industrial activity stressed its economic position.

Only a few aristocratic palaces were built in Prague in the early 19th century whereas before, palaces had been main centres of music, social life, theatre, art collections and scientific discussion. František Pavíček, the archiepiscopal construction director, rebuilt from 1800 to 1810 the Sternberg Palace and the Bretfeld House for Archbishop Wilhelm F. Salm and thus created a new palace (No. 186) on Hradčany Square. It has two two-storey wings articulated by windows and surmounted with an attic storey separated by a massive cornice around a "court of honour". The courtyard was separated from the square by massive railings. In the mid-19th century, the house passed into the hands of the Schwarzenbergs and thus became their second palace on Hradčany Square. The palace imitates on a smaller scale the layout of the Theresian Palace in Prague Castle.

In 1796 Josef Zobel built the Rohan Palace, No. 8/386, Karmelitská Street, in the Lesser Quarter (now the Czech Ministry of Education), which was rebuilt in 1807 for Duchess Paula Kuronsky. A neo-Classical dancing-hall from that time still exists, which was designed by Louis Montoyer imitating the hall of the Hofburg in Vienna, with columns, rich decoration, chandeliers and tiled stoves, in the Second Rococo style of the 1860s. The front wall of the palace was rebuilt in 1838 by Vincenc Kulhánek in the spirit of late neo-Classicism. The triangular gable made by him was given its present pentagonal form in the 1950s.

In 1847, a courtyard façade of the Thun Palace in the Lesser Quarter, No. 214, Nerudova Street was built. The palace is now the Italian Embassy. The monumental front, articulated horizontally by cornices and a gallery and vertically by Corinthian pilasters in the two top storeys, was created by Jan Bělský. The staircase was rebuilt by Josef Zítek in 1871.

The Baroque Kinský Palace on Old Town Square, No. 606 (now National Gallery), was enlarged in its courtyard part in 1834 by Prince Rudolf Kinský following designs by Josef O. Kranner, and a new lofty staircase was built in the front part of the building.

Classicizing forms are featured in the former Chotek Palace in Hellichova Street, No. 458, Lesser Quarter, built to plans by Johann Philipp Jöndl who also designed the carriage-way of the Colloredo-Mansfeld Palace, No. 189, Karlova Street, Old Town. The Generalate Building of the Knights of the Cross with Red Star, No. 191 at Charles Bridge, was rebuilt in 1846 by Johann Brunn who added a third storey and a plain neo-Classical façade. The large chapter house was decorated with ceiling frescoes by Josef Navrátil. The Šlik Palace at the corner of Spálená Street and Národní (National) Avenue, pulled down after World War II, was reconstructed in the late 1840s by Josef O. Kranner with a front wall in the early Florentine Renaissance style.

To complete the list we should also mention here the later Stallburg Palace, No. 895, Panská Street, Prague 1, built by Josef Maličký in 1861—1862 in the romantic Second Rococo style.

Masaryk Station

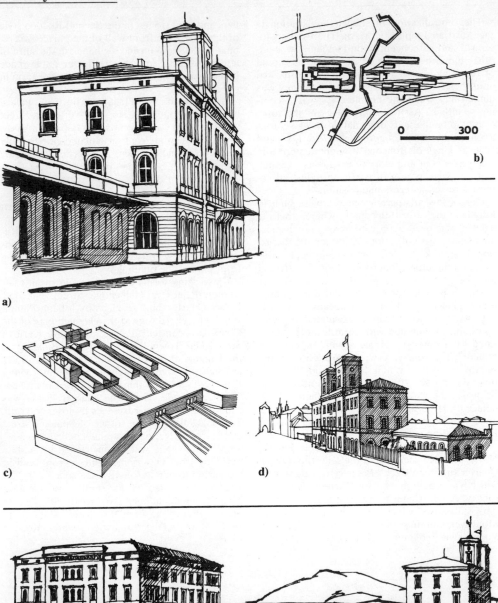

a) **departure building**
b) c) **location in 1845**

d) **departure building** (drawing from 1850)
e) **arrival building** (drawing)

(210)

The development of industrial production, trade and social life in the first third of the 19th century also affected the Austrian Empire. An example is the first steam-driven railway (invented previously in England). In 1839, railway transport in the Empire started with the line from Vienna to Brno. In 1841, another railway from Vienna to Olomouc was put into operation and a line between Prague and Olomouc was planned. On 20th August 1845, just before 5 p.m., the first train arrived at the railway station of Prague, now Masaryk Station.

After complex feasibility studies made in 1842 and 1843 it was decided to build a railway station at the border between the New Town and Karlín District, on both sides of the still existing Baroque walls, in the place of gardens and small houses. In October 1843 the Chief Engineer Anton Jüngling finished the general plan for the railway station which was adopted in summer 1844 and the construction began in November of the same year. By February 1845, the area had been levelled and the old walls demolished. A new wall was built with six gates for the arriving and departing trains, which were closed every night. Four thousand workers took part in the construction. The station was expected to be one of the greatest in Europe in both its size and capacity, as well as in the scale and beauty of the building.

In the New Town part of the station the facilities for both passenger and freight transport were constructed. The departure building in Hybernská Street is still standing, and has two clock towers and a large station-hall inside with booking-offices, a post office and waiting-rooms. The railway offices were situated both downstairs and upstairs. On the other side, in Jezdecká Street (now Havlíčkova) an arrival building was constructed with a hall covered by a glass roof.

There were customs and police stations, and flats for railway workers upstairs. There were five lines and four platforms, of which the first and the fourth were protected by projecting roofs. There was also a connecting platform at the end of the lines, roofed, with a colonnade for coaches. Later, in 1866, a two-storey building with a large restaurant was constructed at the corner of Hybernská and Havlíčkova Streets and the roofing of the platforms was extended as far as the façade in Havlíčkova Street by means of cast iron elements.

Across the street Na Florenci two large storehouses were built for goods. The outer part of the station outside the town-walls was three times as large as the enclosed part and, in addition to the rails interconnected by turntables, it contained workshops, locomotive sheds, wagon sheds, lumber yards, coal and rail stores.

The original front walls of the main railway building have survived. They have calm late neo-Classical forms with some elements anticipating the later Romanticism, particularly in the semi-circular window arches. There is controversy as to who was the author of the architectural plan, whether it was Antonín Jüngling, who signed the plan, but was more a technical engineer than an architect, or the Viennese architects Paul Sprenger and Pietro Nobile who at that time were participating in the renovation of the town-hall of the Old Town. This last possibility is supported by the fact that there are striking similarities between the architecture of the station and that of the renovated Metternich Palace at Kynžvart. The last adaptation of the interiors was made in the early 1950s after plans by Hanuš Parkman, and then in 1985 when all the inserted elements were removed and the original neo-Classical architecture was restored.

Church of SS. Cyril and Methodius in Karlín

Church of SS. Cyril and Methodius in Karlín

The military defeat of the radical democratic revolution of 1848 and the subsequent return to imperial absolutism in the Austrian Empire brought about a wave of romantic patriotism, idealizing the beginnings of Christianity in Bohemia and Moravia.

In the early 1850s, Archbishop Prince Friedrich of Schwarzenberg and Václav Štulc, provost of the Vyšehrad Chapter, initiated the construction of the Church of SS. Cyril and Methodius on the main square of the Prague suburb Karlín. The church was designed in 1851 by the Viennese architect Karl Rösner in the late Romanesque style, and modified by the Prague architect Ignác Ullmann who also directed the construction carried out by Jan Bělský and master mason Karel Svoboda. The foundation stone was laid on 10th June, 1854. The costly structure, which was partly made of hewn ashlar and paid for from collections organized by Count Johann Harrach, was completed and consecrated on 10th October 1863, on the occasion of the millenium of the arrival in the Great Moravian Empire of SS. Cyril and Methodius who, at the invitation of Prince Rastislav, brought the Christian religion here from Salonia in the Eastern Roman Empire, using the Slavic language and alphabet.

This typical basilica is unusually large (length 75 m, width 31 m, height 27.5 m) and ranks among the greatest churches in Prague. On each side of the chancel there is a steeple, each 75 m tall. The entrance façade has three portals with richly moulded jambs and semicircular arches with reliefs by Václav Levý. The bronze gate bears reliefs with motifs from the lives of the Czech patron saints, made by Ludvík Šimek and Karel Dvořák after sketches supplied by Josef Mánes. On the Romanesque "dwarfish gallery" above the central entrance there are statues of Jesus Christ and the apostles by Čeněk Vosmík from 1913.

The interior is decorated with ceiling frescoes in the main apse by Josef Trenkwald from 1867—1873, over the aisle arcades by František Sequens and Zikmund Rudl, on the vaults and between windows by the brothers Jan and Karel Jobst, in the aisles by Petr Maixner, and in the baptism chapel by Bedřich Wachsmann. The side altars contain paintings of four Czech patron saints by Josef Mánes and Antonín Lhota. The main baldachin altar was designed by Bedřich Wachsmann, the statues of Jesus Christ and St. Mary were made by Josef Klíma in 1916. The stained glass windows were made after models by Josef Mocker and František Ženíšek. The wall decoration was designed by the Jobst brothers.

The rear façade with an organ loft is the most picturesque part of the church, the three semicircular apses remind us of the 12th century chancel at Tismice near Český Brod.

Social Institutes in the First Half of the 19th Century

Not only the efforts of some philanthropists, but also, and chiefly, the need to secure the labour capacity of people and to prevent disastrous epidemics killing both the poor and the rich, medical care, which in the past had been an ad hoc matter of charity in some monastic hospitals, started extending and improving in the late 18th century.

The Baroque palace of the Institute of Poor Gentlewomen by Marco Antonio Canevalle from 1700, No. 499, in the south end of Dobytčí trh (Cattle Market, now Charles Square), was in 1787 on the decision of Emperor Joseph II converted into a general hospital and rebuilt for this purpose by František Antonín Herget. Then, between 1820 and 1848, the building was extended and new structures appeared in the yard. Herget's plain renovation of the street front in the spirit of governmental buildings looks unattractive, yet the building, continuously modernized, still suits its purpose and has helped to return health to thousands of sick people. Next to it new neo-Classical and neo-Renaissance buildings of anatomical institutes were constructed, and also the larger building opposite the former Jesuit monastery adjoining St. Ignatius' Church was used as a hospital.

At the lower end of Chotek Road, which is now called Klárov, the two-storey neo-Classical house of the Klár Institute of the Blind, No. 131, was built from 1836 to 1844 after a plan by Vincenc Kulhánek, and the perpendicular Chapel of

a)

b)

c)

a) **Klár Institute**
b) **Klár Institute, chapel**
c) **department of physiology, Charles University** (former hospital of Prague's tradesmen)

Social Institutes in the First Half of the 19th Century

St. Raphael was attached to it, designed by Josef O. Kranner. The Institute was founded in 1832 by Professor Alois Klár, who himself later became blind, and the house was built by his son Paul Alois Klár. The centre of the building, stressed by a section broken forward, is crowned by a triangular pediment containing a relief by Josef Max which represents the biblical motif of Tobiah's son restoring his father's sight. The roof is surmounted in the middle by a turret with a clock. The paintings in the chapel and the arched windows in the façade are already features of Romanticism. The interior of the chapel is decorated with frescoes representing God the Father on the apse vault and Blessing Jesus beneath by Vilém Kandler, and with wall paintings of the four Evangelists by Antonín Lhota made after cartoons by Josef Führich. The altar bears a statue representing the Archangel Raphael by Emanuel Max (Josef's brother), and the pilaster recesses between the windows contain busts of Klár's family.

The Prague Association of the Blind constructed a neo-Gothic hospital in 1861 in a garden near the New Town walls (No. 458), designed by Bernard Grueber and Josef Niklas. The appearance of the house corresponded to the romantic movement imitating medieval styles, which prevailed in European architecture in the mid-19th century. The building had a central corridor flanked by two rows of rooms, with light coming through the end windows of the side façades. This layout was the first application of the three-aisle type of building in this country. The small two-storeyed building in the street Ke Karlovu, with many decorative stone elements in its front wall, is now part of the Teaching Hospital.

Completion of St. Vitus' Cathedral

Some one hundred years after its foundation by King Charles IV in 1344, the construction of St. Vitus' Cathedral was interrupted after the completion of the eastern choir, the window arch in the south transept, and the lower part of the tower. In the reign of Vladislav Jagiello the Royal Oratory was built and, in 1509—1511, the foundations of the north tower and of the columns of the nave were laid. With this, the Gothic phase of the building ended, and it was only later, under Leopold I, in 1673, that the foundation stone of a Baroque church was laid, designed by J. D. Orsini. However, only some columns were constructed, and the next project of 1729, made by Johann Ferdinand Schor, professor at the Engineering Institute of Prague (who painted the fresco "Czech patron saints in the Celestial Empire" on the outer side of the provisional wall of the Cathedral choir), in the Baroque-Gothic style was not realized, either. Only the Renaissance triple cupola surmounting the tower was replaced by a taller Baroque one after the 1770 fire. The first systematic idea as to how the construction could be completed, still respecting its original style appeared in the drawings made by 1810—1816 by Ludwig Kohl, a Prague painter and architect. He envisaged a twelve-sided Gothic dome over the church crossing.

New ideas appeared in the 1830s, as for example that of K. Řivnáč who suggested completing the west end with two towers. The already existing tower would be matched by another identical one to the north, both with a stone cladding imitating Parler's metal reliquary in St. Wenceslas' Chapel. Metropolitan Canon Václav Pešina of Čechorod set up the Association for the Completion of St. Vitus' Cathedral in 1843, and a collection of money for this purpose was organized. The construction work was directed by Josef O. Kranner. Kranner prepared a plan in 1867 which foresaw only one tower crowned with an octagonal spire, 160 m high, and elongation of the nave and aisles westwards. Foundations of columns in the church crossing and in the nave were laid.

After Kranner's death in 1871, the work was continued by Josef Mocker (1835—1899) who prepared a new plan in the spirit of Purism, respecting Parler's elements both in its details and its spaces. Mocker planned a west façade with two steeples, each 83 m tall. The foundation stone was laid on 1st October 1872, and the main structure was built by Mocker at the end of the century, in 1899, and roofed in 1900. Mocker's successor Kamil Hilbert (1869—1933), who already followed new principles of architectural

Completion of St. Vitus' Cathedral

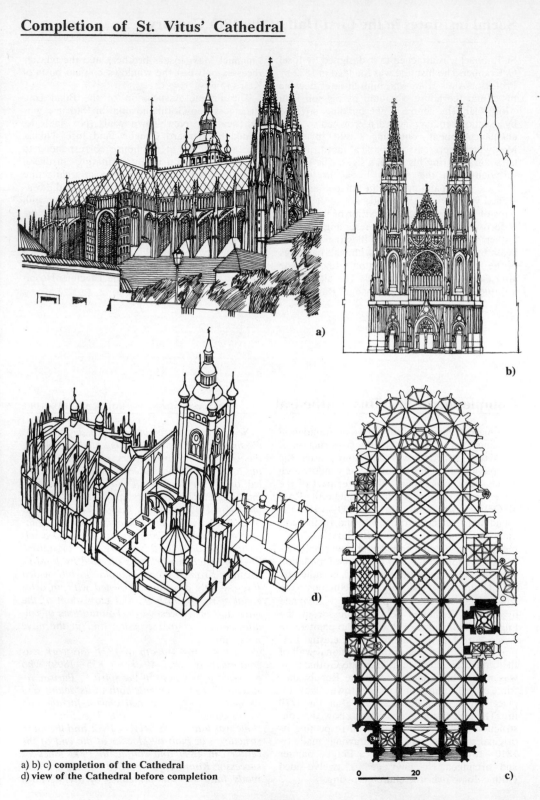

a) b) c) **completion of the Cathedral**
d) **view of the Cathedral before completion**

0   20

conservation, made the vaulting in the nave (1903) and the tracery in the large transept windows. Inside, he created a new sacristy and treasury with a spiral staircase. He also replaced the pointed window in the western façade with an ambitious rose window, left the Baroque cupola over the main tower, stopped the planned demolition of the Old Provost's Lodge, which gives the right proportion to the Cathedral, and saved Wohlmut's Renaissance loft closing the original choir by displacing it to the northern part of the transept. Thus, in 1925 the old and the new parts of the Cathedral could be combined into one organic building which was consecrated on 12th May 1929, on the occasion of the millenium of Prince Wenceslas' assassination.

Sculptural decoration of the new part of the Cathedral started in 1903 with the installation of figures of saints on the western twin-steeple (František Hegesel, Josef Kalvoda, Čeněk Vosmík, Jan Kastner, Štěpán Zálešák, Emanuel Halman). The tympanums of the portals in the west façade are adorned with reliefs by Karel Dvořák and Ladislav Pícha dating from 1948—1952. The bronze gate reliefs were made by Otakar Španiel to sketches by V. H. Brunner from 1927—1929. Busts of the architects and sponsors of the construction are on the west façade (by Vojtěch Sucharda, 1929), and on the triforium (by Jan Štur-

sa, Bohumil Kafka and Václav Žalud). The wooden crucifix in the northern side wall was made in 1899 by František Bílek. Inside the south transept is a memorial to soldiers killed in the First World War (by Karel Pokorný, 1921).

In the Royal Crypt new sarcophagi of Bohemian kings designed by Kamil Roškot were placed in 1933—1934. The railings of St. Ludmila's Chapel and those of the Golden Gate opening into the southern transept were decorated with bronze figures of the Months by Jaroslav Horejc and Karel Štipl in 1938 and 1954, respectively, the Golden Gate was made by the sculptor Josef Wagner and the architect Jan Sokol, and was installed in 1961. The Gate portico contains mosaics made in 1939 by Marie Forsterová to cartoons by Karel Svolinský. The mosaics on the chapel walls were made in the 1930s to cartoons by Max Švabinský and František Kysela. The stained glass in the rose window by František Kysela from 1921 represents the Creation, the side chapels have windows with glazing designed by Max Švabinský, František Kysela, Karel Svolinský, Cyril Bouda and Alfons Mucha, while the glazing of the windows of St. Wenceslas' Chapel was made by Stanislav Libenský and Josef Soukup, and that in the window of the south transept, representing the Last Judgment, by Max Švabinský between 1937 and 1939.

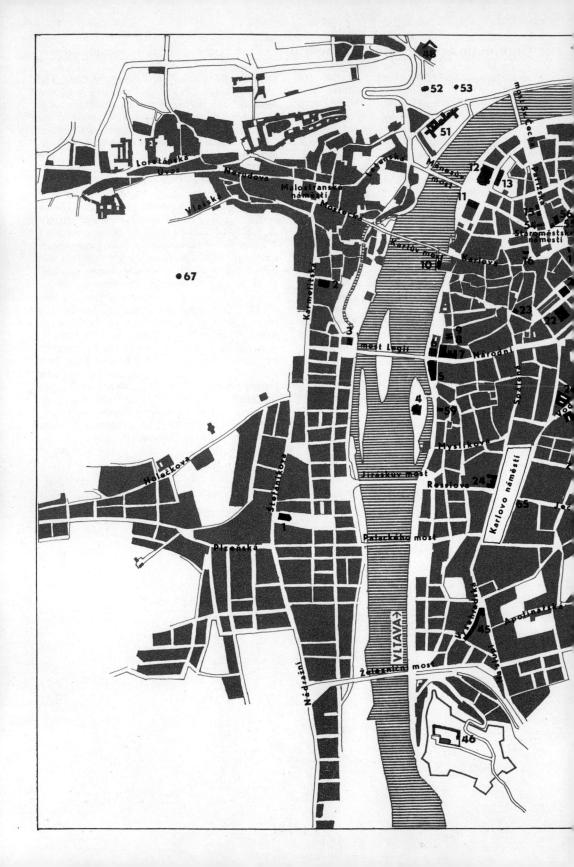

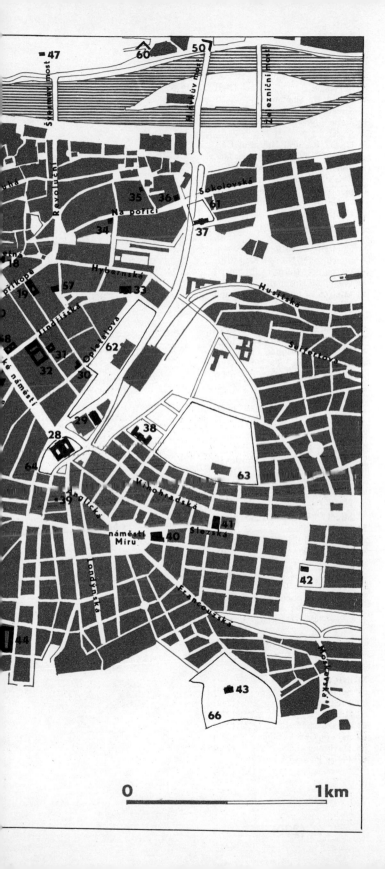

NEO-RENAISSANCE
AND NEO-BAROQUE
ARCHITECTURE

Architecture of the Last Third of the 19th Century

With the decline of the feudal system and with political power coming into the hands of the middle-class in the 1860s new ideas and views of the role of architecture emerged from these social changes. The Italian Renaissance became a source of inspiration for architects. As compared with the simple plan and form of neo-Classicism, architecture now featured greater articulation, ornamentation, and was combined with painting and sculpture.

The neo-Renaissance was an international style of the middle-class and was typically applied to banks, parliaments, theatres, concert halls, railway stations, museums, schools, and administrative buildings. World exhibition pavilions displayed the technical opportunities offered by steel structures. The concept behind buildings lost its former simplicity and became specialized according to the particular purpose. Dwelling houses reflected the deepening social differences, as can be seen in villas in the garden districts on the one hand and in tenement blocks in the industrial suburbs on the other.

The main contribution made at that time was Gottfried Semper's idea of a new form of architecture, developing and resulting from many factors, such as the purpose of the building, the construction material used, the type of structure, the ideas deriving from the function of the work, the influence of the environment, and the individuality of the architect.

In Bohemia and Moravia, the neo-Renaissance became a typical style of the National Theatre Generation artists, supporting economic and political independence for the nation. The style was modified by the attention paid to traditional domestic forms, which resulted in a special Czech type of neo-Renaissance and in a growing interest in our folk rustic architecture. Both these aspects prepared the ground for new ideas that appeared in the beginning of the 20th century.

At the end of the 19th century efforts were made to find new forms of architecture. However, these concepts were still based on historicism and eclectically combined in one building the plan and form of different styles. This contributed to the loosening of the then strict respect for the principles of the past styles, and anticipated a new type of architecture, oriented towards the future.

National Theatre

After the demolition of the "Bouda" provisional theatre in 1789 there was no central place for Czech theatrical performances, and various temporary rooms were therefore used for this purpose until 1844 when a movement emerged, instigated by František Palacký, František Ladislav Rieger and Alois Pravoslav Trojan, striving for a permanent Czech theatre. In 1850, the Municipal Council of Prague put a plot of ground at the lower end of Wenceslas Square at their disposal and a plan was prepared by the Prague architect Johann Heinrich Frenzel. Money was collected, and then in 1852 a piece of land was purchased at the corner of Vltava Embankment and Ferdinand (now Národní) Avenue, where once a salthouse had stood. A National Theatre competition was organized, and in 1862 a provisional theatre for 900 spectators was built in the rear part of the plot, designed by Ignác Ullmann, where performances took place every day.

A new competition was organized with entries presented by Ullmann and Niklas, countered by Josef Zítek, professor at the Polytechnical Institute of Prague, whose plan was conceived in the style of the north Italian late Renaissance.

In an enthusiastic atmosphere further collections were organized under the motto "People to Themselves", and in 1868 the foundation stone was solemnly laid of a structure that was expected to be a symbol of the nation's rebirth. This was expressed by Zítek's architecture based on a harmonized prism crowned with a domed roof. To better express the idea of national victory the building abandoned the then progressive idea, probably originating from Semper, that the exterior of building should reflect its interior — in this case the distinction between the stage and the auditorium. The reduction in size of the site, due to the construction of the Provisional Theatre, was compensated by moving the entrance part, i.e., the portico supporting a lofty column loggia, into Národní (National) Avenue. By doing so, Zítek also stressed the building in a vista of the chain bridge and Petřín Hill. The wall facing the Vltava has five arcaded window arches between two sections broken forward, the last one with a covered carriage-way. The wall along Divadelní Street is rather plain, articulated only with pilasters and decorated in its lower part with an arcaded gallery projecting over the street and supported by big stone cantilevers. Zítek's ground plan and layout of the interior with a semicircular auditorium with four balconies for 1700 spectators on a confined and irregular site are really remarkable.

The building was completed in 1881, but soon afterwards neglectful metalworkers finishing the roof caused a fire that destroyed the stage and the auditorium. As there were arguments with Zítek about the realization of his restoration plan, Josef Schulz, Zítek's student, assistant and collaborator was assigned the task of carrying out the plan. The interior layout underwent some changes that improved the view from galleries and the situation in the auditorium by moving the proscenium wall back to the stage. The Provisional Theatre and the neighbouring tenement block were pulled down and in their place a building called the Schulz House was built which contained the actors' dressing rooms and the technical facilities of the theatre. Its façade is in the same style as Zítek's building, however it is not of stone, but plastered brickwork.

The decoration of the theatre is the work of members of the National Theatre generation: the painters Mikoláš Aleš, František Ženíšek (foyer, ceiling of the auditorium), Josef Tulka (loggias), Vojtěch Hynais (curtain), Julius Mařák, Václav Brožík, Adolf Liebscher (VIP rooms), the sculptors Bohuslav Schnirch (statues on the attic), Antonín Wagner, Josef Václav Myslbek (statues on the embankment wall). The Roman chariots on a pedestal on the main façade were cast in 1910—1911 by Ladislav Šaloun, František Rous and Emanuel Halman after models by Bohuslav Schnirch. The busts in the foyer were made by Josef Myslbek, Jan Štursa, Bohumil Kafka, Ladislav Kofránek, Otakar Španiel, Ladislav Šaloun, Josef Mařatka and others.

In 1952 and 1953, two painting and architectural competitions were organized for the small foyer of the first gallery. The winners, whose designs and models were realized, were the architects Viktor Formáček and Rudolf Ječný, and the painter Vincenc Beneš. Their works enriched the National Theatre in the spirit of its original artistic concept.

For a long time the unsatisfactory state of the National Theatre, and particularly the critical situation of the electrical mains, the problems with scene handling, the lamentable state of the actors' facilities and the obsolete technical equipment were the subject of much criticism. At the same time, it was necessary to solve the problem of the administrative and social facilities of the National Theatre. It was therefore decided in 1956 to demolish the Kaura Houses in Národní (National) Avenue so as to make room for a new construction. The renovation of the historic building of the theatre began after the modernization of the Smetana Theatre so that cultural life in Prague was not significantly reduced. The renovation plan was prepared by SURPMO, namely its atelier headed by Zdeněk Vávra and František Flašar, in cooperation with Vladimír Gleich. A very radical form was adopted which made it possible to install in the building, particularly in the stage part, all the theatrical technical facilities. The stage space was therefore deepened and enlarged, including the backstage, and changes were made in the layout, particularly in the Schulz House, whose exterior forms a unity with the National Theatre, to modernize the dressing and rehearsal rooms. In spite of these losses a work of renovation unique in this country has been carried out. The social area was heavily modernized, yet it remained visually almost intact. New central dressing rooms were built under the entrance vestibule. To make them accessible, the staircases in the corners had to be deepened. There was also a new snack bar and a smoking-room, and the rear "pocket" under the balcony was used to house a technical block. All the interiors were restored including the floor cladding, and new seats were installed in the auditorium, made by the firm Ton Bystřice pod Hostýnem according to the original draft by Schulz. The biggest changes occurred in the stage, the ropes, the orchestra space, and particularly in the scene handling system. Scenes are moved via a tunnel under Divadelní Street connecting the historic building with the annex underground, where there are depositories with scenes for dozens of stagings. The scenes and the palettes for their transportation are standardized and can be used on all the National Theatre stages. The final form of the building also owes a great deal to Pozemní stavby České Budějovice as the chief supplier, as well as to dozens of lesser suppliers, such as ČFVU (Czech Fine Arts Fund), Štuko Cooperative, Umělecká řemesla Cooperative, among others.

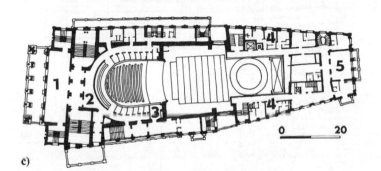

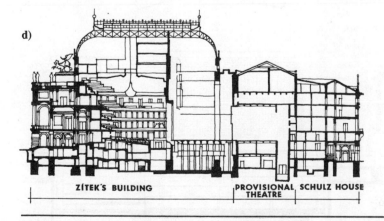

a)

b)

c)

d)

ZÍTEK'S BUILDING   PROVISIONAL SCHULZ HOUSE
THEATRE

a) b) **National Theatre**
c) **plan at the level of the first gallery:** 1 main foyer, 2 corridor, 3 presidential box and rooms,

4 dressing-rooms for actors, 5 original director's office
d) **section**

National Theatre

a)

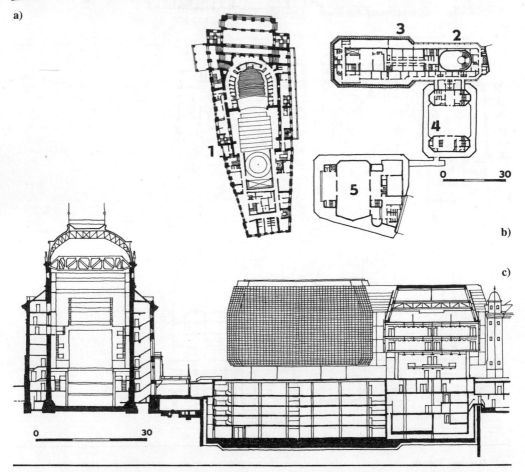

b)

c)

a) b) c) **National Theatre—New Stage:** 1 National Theatre, 2 entrance hall, 3 New Stage, 4 café and restaurant, 5 National Theatre Administration

Growing demands placed on the work of the National Theatre led to discussion in the 1950s as to how the technical situation of the theatre could be improved. A competition was organized in 1962 to solve the problem of building up the area beltween Národní (National) Avenue, Divadelní Street and Ostrovní Street, vacated after the demolition of the Kaura Houses from the mid-19th century and of the Theatre Administration Building of 1928. The site was to be filled with a three-wing building for the administrative, technical and social parts of the National Theatre.

The winning project was presented by Bohuslav Fuchs of Brno. However, Fuchs died in 1972, and Pavel Kupka from SURPMO (State Institute for Renovation of Historic Towns and Buildings) was invited to prepare the final plan. To his design the south and the east wings of the complex were built between 1977 and 1981 in Ostrovní Street and at St. Ursula's Convent. The plan of the north wing in Národní Avenue was changed, as it was decided to build a second theatre here called "Nová scéna" (New Stage). This necessitated changes in the steel construction that had already been built, and the project had to be totally rethought.

Karel Prager from the Construction Institute of the City of Prague was charged with the new project. Prager decided, due to the proximity of the historic building of the National Theatre, to divide the façade of the new building into two parts. He also reduced the length of the building and set it further back from Divadelní Street, which improved the view of the east façade of the National Theatre that had been underestimated until that time. Národní Avenue gained more light by opening the ground floor of the new building between the street and the new courtyard, by cladding the part of the façade next to St. Ursula's Convent with large panels of dethermal glass, and by using massive sheets of glass to cover the projecting part of the façade, closest to the National Theatre, to reflect the façades of the buildings opposite and neutralize the otherwise unpleasant impression of the north-facing front.

The entrance hall of the New Stage has walls covered with plates of Cuban serpentine, and there is a sculpture "Song of My Country" by Miloš Axman. In the foyer, there is a painting "Bohemian Landscape" by František Jiroudek and a relief "Art" by Jan Simota. The circular auditorium is surrounded by metal latticed walls absorbing the noise. The wing facing the convent garden has a café and a restaurant on the ground floor, and in the garden, which was laid out by Pavel Kupka and Otakar Kuča, is a marble statue "Dialogue" by Stanislav Hanzík and Milan Vácha. The interiors were designed by Karel Prager in cooperation with a group of artists, namely Martin Sladký, Zorka Smetanová, Pavel Hlava, Jaroslav Štursa and František Vízner. In the courtyard in front of the National Theatre, a bronze statue "Undine" by Josef Malejovský is displayed on a pedestal designed by Vratislav Růžička.

The renovation of the National Theatre took six years and the buildings were opened on 18th November 1983.

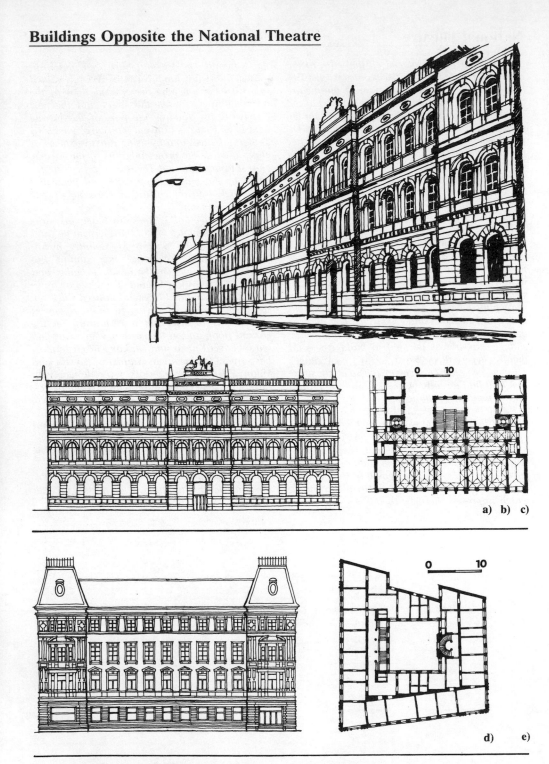

a) b) c)

d) e)

a) b) c) **Presidium of the Czechoslovak Academy of**
Sciences (former Czech Savings Bank)

d) e) **Lažanský Palace**

(226)

Buildings Opposite the National Theatre

After the construction of a chain bridge and an embankment between 1841 and 1845, the end of Národní (National) Avenue (as of 1781 called "Nové aleje", then "U řetězového mostu", and then Ferdinand Avenue) assumed a greater role in the life of the town. However, until the late 1850s there had been banks for waste along either side of the road leading to the bridge, with just a wooden fence. On the southern side, where the National Theatre now stands, stood a single-storey state salt-house and, on the other side of the road, a brickworks and a lime kiln in the place where the Academy of Sciences now stands.

This situation changed between 1858 and 1862 when a building for the Czech Savings Bank, No. 1009, in the Italian high Renaissance style was built to designs by Ignác Ullmann, a leading Prague architect, on an empty site between four-storey tenement houses that had been built here shortly before. The main façade is reminiscent of St. Mark's Library in Venice built by Jacopo Sansovino in the 1530s. The Czech Savings Bank (since 1952 the centre of the Czechoslovak Academy of Sciences) was the first mature work of the neo-Renaissance in Bohemia, a style that consequently applied Renaissance morphology to modern planning, and that restored the co-operation of architects with sculptors, painters and other artists.

The sumptuous stone façade with three high storeys is crowned above the central projecting section with an allegorical sculpture representing "Čechie" receiving the savings of the people, carved in stone by Antonín Wildt after a drawing by Josef Mánes. The neighbouring house was demolished and from 1894 to 1896 the building was extended westwards. The annex, designed by Franz Schachner, continued Ullmann's façade. The sculpture above the cornice is by Otto Mentzel. The interiors also have sculptural decoration: figures of lions in the entrance hall and female figures representing Economy and Thrift made by J. V. Myslbek in 1895.

In the layout, Ullmann avoided a central corridor without light and used a covered corridor along the courtyard wall with windows allowing light to enter. For the first time in this country, concrete was used (by the master-builder Quido Bělský, in the foundations).

Soon afterwards, in 1862, a luxurious four-storey house with town apartments for nobles and the rich was built on the embankment as far as Divadelní Street. The house, which replaced the Lažanský Palace (No. 1012), was also designed by Ignác Ullmann, although this time in the style of the French Renaissance, with roof turrets at the corners in the form of truncated pyramids. There are large rooms in the deep bays along the three street fronts. The hallways, kitchens, pantries, maids' rooms and lavatories are located in shallow bays surrounding the square inner courtyard. On each floor, there are two five- to six-room apartments accessible from the palace staircase, and two smaller apartments reached by a spiral staircase, facing Divadelní Street. All the apartment rooms are directly lit. The basement under the courtyard with stables and carriage sheds can be entered through a carriage-way from Divadelní Street. On the ground floor of the house is the famed theatre café Slavia and a wine bar Parnas that were rebuilt in the 1930s by Oldřich Stefan and renovated in the 1980s. Bedřich Smetana lived in one of the apartments from 1868 to 1869 when he directed the Provisional Theatre Opera, and this is commemorated by a marble memorial tablet over the gateway to the courtyard, designed in 1924 by the painter František Kysela. The building now houses the Cinematography and Television Faculty of the Academy of Arts.

Both Ullmann's buildings have enriched Prague with a street front comparable with the finest in Europe.

Prague Parks

a) **view of Prague from Chotek Garden** (by V. Morstadt, 1836)
b) **look-out tower, Petřín Hill**
c) **layout of Chotek Garden, 1839:** 1 Royal Summer
   Palace, 2 Klárov
d) **plan of Charles Square**
e) **Charles Square** (situation in 1876)

With the changing position of the social classes in the late 18th century a new urban element appeared in Prague: the public park, accessible—unlike the gardens of noble palaces and monasteries—to all the people of the town.

Johann Ferdinand Schönfeld, a rich printer and a great art lover, built in the 1780s on Špitálské pole (Hospital Field, now Karlín District) a pleasure palace called Růžodol. It featured a tavern, a dancing-hall, and a park with pavilions and castle ruins in miniature in a flower garden shaped like the map of Bohemia. At the same time, Count Josef Emanuel Canal created a public park "Kanálka" with orchards, artificial brooks, greenhouses and memorials. South of here, towards Karlov, Jakob Wimmer, a Prague entrepreneur, created a garden with alleys and vineyards that remained a favourite promenade of the Praguers until the 1820s. However, all the above parks had to give way to the spreading suburbs of Prague.

Stromovka Park (earlier Royal Game Park) was a place of relaxation and entertainment for Prague's inhabitants. The park was opened to the public in 1804, and in 1845 a garden called Štěpnice, laid out by the burgrave, Count Rottenhahn, was added. Stromovka Park, initially covering an area of 115 ha, was reduced by the construction of the Jubilee Exhibition Grounds in 1891, and still further in 1948 due to the Slav Agricultural Exhibition. The former Baroque hunting-lodge near the southwestern park gate was rebuilt in 1855 by Bernard Grueber in the neo-Gothic style and converted into a restaurant which is now closed.

New parks also appeared on the hill above Klárov. A road was built here and a park established in 1833 on the initiative of the then burgrave, Count Karel Chotek. The lawn in the centre of Chotek Gardens offers a beautiful view of the Belvedere Palace. In 1913, a memorial to the poet Julius Zeyer was placed by the lake here, resembling a rock with a grotto and with a marble statue by Josef Mauder.

Thanks to Chotek, the slopes of Petřín Hill became a green belt from the street Újezd upward and a network of paths was created here. In 1891, a funicular was built here to connect the town with a steel look-out tower, 60 m high, on the top of the hill (designed by František Prášil). Petřín Park was connected in 1901 with Kinský Garden through a passage in the Hunger Wall, which was followed in 1920 by the former Seminary Garden in the north and, after 1950, also by the garden of Strahov Abbey. Memorials were scattered among the trees: in 1911 to Karel Hynek Mácha by Josef Václav Myslbek, in 1912 to

Hana Kvapilová by Jan Štursa, in 1950 to Vítězslav Novák by Jan Kodet and Jiří Gočár, and in 1960 to Jaroslav Vrchlický by Josef and Marie Wagner.

From 1850 to 1860, the slope between the Vltava and Letná Plain was planted with trees and shrubs, as was the adjoining part of the plain. Letná Park was laid out after a plan by the supervisor of Kinský Garden, František Wünsch, and carried out by Josef Braul, a gardener of Bubeneč. The park was reshaped in 1877—1879, and several sculptures have been placed here since, such as a sandstone sculpture "The Kiss" by Bohumil Kafka from 1907, "Woman" by Jan Kodet from 1978, and a bronze figure of a girl by Marta Jirásková from 1950. In the east part of the park, extended between 1893 and 1911, there is a bronze sculptural group "Diana with Red-Deer Hinds" by František Rous. From 1950 to 1953, a double flight of granite steps with many branches was built from Čech Bridge up to Letná Park after a plan prepared by Jiří Štursa and Vlasta Štursová. The steps lead to a viewing platform and a massive base which once supported a monument to J. V. Stalin by Otakar Švec, which was taken down in 1962. The northern part of Letná Park can also be reached by following one of four radial paths with steps.

Large flat parks were established between 1843 and 1863 on waste areas in Karlín and on Charles Square in the New Town. František J. Thomayer, Municipal Garden Architect, created here on an area of 80 ha an excellent combination of lawns lined with groups of trees, flower beds and water pools with fountains. Several monuments can be seen here: to Vítězslav Hálek (1881) by Bohuslav Schnirch, to the botanist Benedikt Roezl (1898) by Čeněk Vosmík and Gustav Zoula, to Eliška Krásnohorská (1931) by Karla Vobišová, to Karolina Světlá (1910) by Gustav Zoula, and to J. E. Purkyně (1861) by Otakar Kozák and Vladimír Štrunc.

In the early 1870s, the Baroque walls between the Horse Gate and Špitálská Gate were pulled down and the area was used for gardens. In 1875, the garden at Těšnov (now Šverma Garden) was laid out by the municipal gardener Ferdinand Malý, and in 1878 a neo-Renaissance pavilion was built here, including a café (by František Saller and Jan Beninger), but was demolished in 1971 to make way for the construction of the north-south axis road. In front of the then new railway station (now Main Station) of Prague a park was laid out by Ferdinand Malý and František J. Thomayer (now Vrchlický Park). A water pool with a fountain recently had to give way to the north-south axis road and the new station hall. Around the National Museum, constructed in 1885, a park was established which is now much smaller and is called Čelakovský Park. A marble statue of the actress Otylie Sklenářová-Malá by Ladislav Šaloun was placed here in 1933.

All the above parks were of the English type, imitating nature. No public parks of the French type, with geometrical forms, as known to us from Wallenstein (Valdštejn) Garden or from Dobříš Palace Garden, were established in Prague at that time.

School Buildings

The social class controlling trade and industry and, consequently, also the government of the Austro-Hungarian Empire, including Bohemia and Moravia, soon understood the importance of education for the productivity of people at all levels of qualification. With the end of Bach's absolutism in the early 1860s the country started developing rapidly, including national education.

The Municipal Council of Prague also fully recognized the need for the higher education of girls. Its representatives visited girls' schools abroad, after which the Council built in 1866—1867 a girls' college (now elementary school), No. 22/683, Vodičkova Street. The college was designed by Ignác Ullmann, and its architecture, unlike the flat front walls of Bohemian Renaissance buildings which had sgraffiti imitating faceted walls, reminds us of the Dutch Renaissance. In particular, it stresses the light colour of both horizontal and vertical elements, such as the projecting voussoirs above the ground floor windows. However, the walls did not expose the then usual pale coloured brickwork, but were decorated with red and white ornamental sgraffiti designed by Jan Scheiwl.

The Polytechnical Institute of the Kingdom of Bohemia in Prague, which was in 1864 divided into Czech and German branches, built in 1872—1874 a massive neo-Renaissance building, No. 293, at the corner of Charles Square and Resslova Street. The building was also designed by Ignác Ullmann who won the competition for its design. The façade is markedly articulated with all the typical elements of the high Italian Renaissance. The niches between the three entrance portals contain statues representing "Labour" and "Science" on pedestals, by Antonín Popp. Over the second floor windows, there are figures of genii by Josef Václav Myslbek. The curving stairs inside the building, supported by Tuscan columns, are reminiscent of similar stairs in north Italian palaces. The building was intended to be the first part of a large school complex in the place of an old clergymen's house. In the end, the house was left and was just adapted to serve the Polytechnical Institute. Ullmann's building was renovated in the 1920s and an atelier attic storey was added.

From 1847 to 1876, the Municipal Council of Prague built a large Municipal Secondary School (later a technical college) in the Lesser Quarter, No. 457, Hellichova Street, which replaced the former Mirbach Palace. The neo-Renaissance building was designed by the municipal architect Josef Srdínek who had worked in Ullmann's studio before. The school had two parts: the street wing and the courtyard wing, connected by a staircase with several flights. The sumptuous front façade has a gallery above the entrance, supported by eight Tuscan columns, and its central section broken forward is crowned with an assembly-hall above the cornice.

On the territory of Smetanka farmstead in Vinohrady District the District Council built between 1886 and 1888 a large technical college, No. 505, in the neo-Renaissance style, designed by Antonín Turek and Josef Frankl. The façade has three sections broken forward and is articulated with Corinthian half-columns and pilasters, three storeys high; the central projecting section is crowned with a segmental roof dome and closes the vista of Balbínova Street from Vinohradská Avenue.

In addition to many other notable buildings, the architects Srdínko and Turek had by 1890 designed ten large schools in Prague, all of which still serve their educational purpose. At that time, about eighty schools were built in Prague and its suburbs.

School Buildings

a)

b)

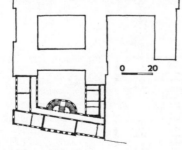

c) d)

e)

a) school, Vodičkova Street
b) school, Hellichova Street
c) Czech Technical University, Charles Square
d) Czech Technical University, original plan and realized part
e) school, Na Smetance Street

0   20

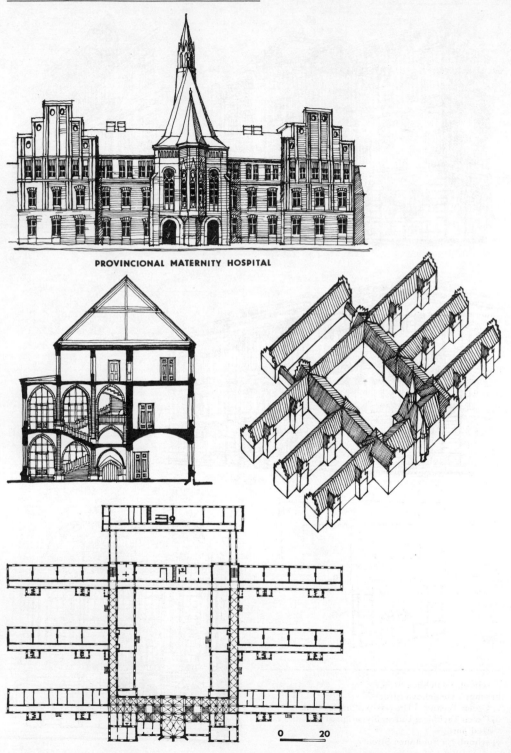

PROVINCIONAL MATERNITY HOSPITAL

0   20

Old People's and Children's Homes

The economic boom in Bohemia and Moravia in the 1860s brought about a rising standard of living, which also had repercussions in better care for new-born children and old people. The first maternity hospital, which saved the lives of many children, particularly those of unmarried mothers, was sponsored by Empress Maria Theresa and built in 1762. In 1787, the hospital moved to the former canonry at St. Apollinaire's. An old people's home was built as early as 1505 in the southern corner of the New Town.

The construction of a Provincial Maternity Hospital began in 1862 on the initiative of Count Franz Thun-Hohenstein with the choice of a site in Herz Garden in Apolinářská Street, New Town. The Provincial Committee of the Kingdom of Bohemia invited a young architect Josef Hlávka (1831—1908) to carry out the project. Hlávka, who was already well thought of for his design and construction of the Bishop's Residence at Černovice, Bukovina, and for his contribution to the Hofoper of Vienna, dealt with the plan of the Maternity Hospital in an original way: six parallel pavilions were interconnected by two corridors with obstetric theatres. Two such groups are linked together in the north side by an administrative building and a chapel, and in the south by a single-storey building containing the kitchen, the laundry and the boiler house of the central heating. All wards were oriented towards the south. The building No. 441 was constructed from 1867 to 1875 and its concept was very progressive, anticipating trends that prevailed decades later. The striking neo-Gothic exterior of the building is characterized by exposed brickwork; the cornices and some details are black- and green-glazed, the plinth and the window tracery of the chapel are of stone. The oriel chapel at the front of the building has four bays of "diamond" vaulting supported by a central pillar, and wall paintings by Adolf Hörber and Adolf Liebscher.

Near here, a large orphanage was built from 1896 to 1901 in the street Ke Karlovu. The Provincial Orphanage replaced the earlier foundling hospital, established as early as the 17th century, which in 1789 housed over 900 foundlings. The new complex of buildings, No. 5/455, was designed in the neo-Renaissance style and consisted of a domed administration building, two side buildings with wards, dining-rooms and bedrooms, and of a hospital behind. All these buildings are now part of the Children's Teaching Hospital of Charles University.

Dating from the same time is the modernization of the Rococo pleasure palace from the latter half of the 18th century near the farmstead Rokoska in Prague's Libeň District, which was used as of 1903 as a reformatory. Now it houses the department of internal diseases of Bulovka Hospital.

On the site of St. Bartholomew's Almshouse, a low single-storey building terminating in a Baroque church, a new Municipal Poorhouse, No. 4/427, designed by the municipal construction surveyor Josef Srdínek in the neo-Renaissance style, was built in 1884—1885 and offered shelter to some 400 old men and women. It consisted of three buildings along Vyšehradská Street, with a large garden behind. The façade of the central building is adorned with an allegorical sculpture "Prague Protects the Poor" by Josef Václav Myslbek, who also made four figures representing good deeds on columns in the façade. The corner building contained a chapel, the sculptures here and on the opposite building were made by František Hergessel and Josef Strachovský. The buildings are now used by the Czech Ministry of Justice.

Jan Palach Square

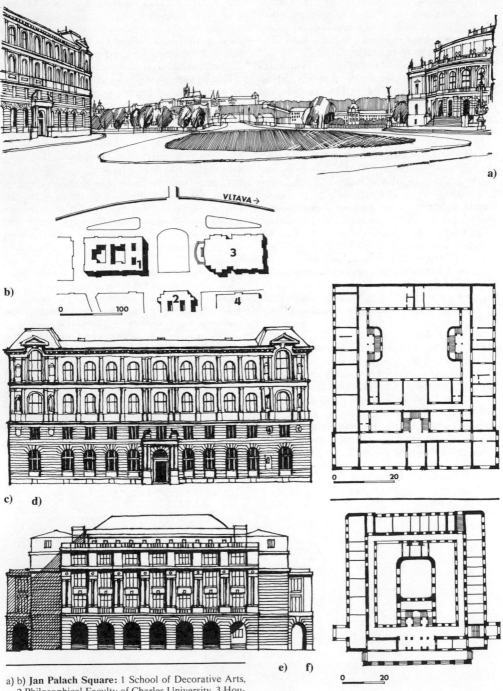

a) b) **Jan Palach Square:** 1 School of Decorative Arts,
2 Philosophical Faculty of Charles University, 3 House of Artists, 4 Museum of Decorative Arts
c) d) **School of Decorative Arts**
e) f) **Philosophical Faculty, Charles University**

The riverside band between the Old Town walls and the river, which had for centuries been filled with heaps of municipal waste, wood stores and riding-grounds, began to change in the late 1860s. In 1868, a suspension footbridge from Kaprova Street to the Lesser Quarter was built, and in 1875 the construction of an embankment began, starting from the Monastery of the Knights of the Cross. The old "sweat house" and prison were demolished, a wide grass band with trees and shrubs was created here and a large area was marked out opposite the footbridge as a yet unnamed square. Then, monumental buildings were constructed on either side of the area, proceeding downstream.

On the south side of the square a four-storey building was constructed from 1881 to 1884 which is now the School of Decorative Arts (No. 80), in the neo-Renaissance style, designed by František Schmoranz Jun. and Jan Machytka. The horizontally articulated north façade facing the square is rusticated on the ground and mezzanine floors. The tall windows oriented so as to suit atelier work are separated from each other by Ionic half-columns on the third floor and by Corinthian pilasters on the fourth floor. The centre and the ends of the building are stressed by larger windows and by truncated pyramids at the corners. The entrance porch is flanked by pairs of Tuscan columns surmounted with replicas of Michelangelo's statues "Day" and "Night". The niches on the third storey near the corners contain replicas of ancient statues by Antonín Popp and Bohuslav Schnirch. The three-flight staircase is supported by Tuscan columns. At the embankment corner, there is a marble bust of Jan Kotěra by Bohumil Kafka in a niche designed by Pavel Janák. Kotěra headed the School of Architecture here from 1898 to 1910. As of 1885, the building housed the School of Decorative Arts and, as of 1902, the Academy of Fine Arts (professors J. V. Myslbek, Julius Mařák, etc.).

From 1911 to 1916, the iron Rudolph Footbridge was replaced by a reinforced concrete bridge named after Josef Mánes and designed by František Mendl and Alois Nový, in coooperation with Mečislav Petrů. The piers are decorated with figural friezes by Jan Štursa and Josef Mařatka, with motifs from the lives of Vltava raftsmen. The east side of the square was unbuilt for a long time, and not until 1928—1929 was a building of the Philosophical Faculty of Charles University constructed here, designed by Josef Sakař who tried to adapt the style to the surrounding architecture. His efforts resulted in a pseudohistorical layout and concept, both in the whole and in details, very much against the trend in the development of Prague architecture.

The northern side of the square is occupied by the neo-Renaissance House of Artists (Rudolfinum, see page 237). There are two areas of lawn separated by the bridge; on the northern lawn, there is a bronze memorial to Josef Mánes from 1951 by Bohumil Kafka, on a pedestal designed by Josef Havlíček. The lawn in the middle of the square has still to be properly set out.

The fourth side of the square is open, offering a view of Prague Castle above the roofs and gardens of the Lesser Quarter. The panoramic view and the harmony of the site make the square one of the best urban spaces in Prague from the 19th century, and one of the most beautiful points in the city.

Rudolfinum

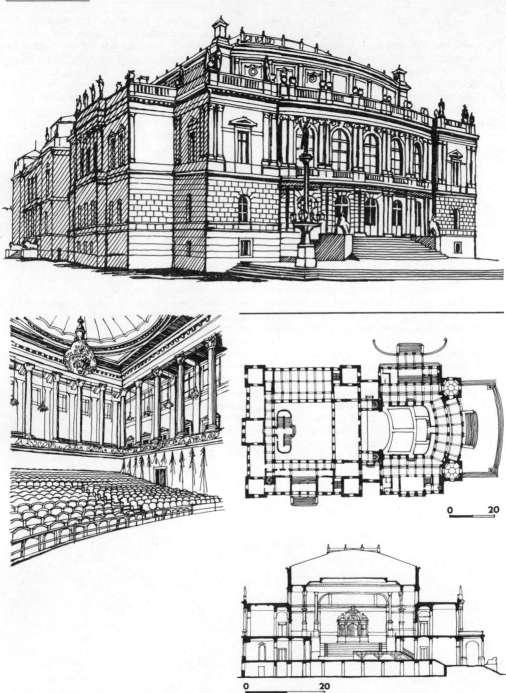

a) b) c) d) **House of Artists** (Rudolfinum)

The booming cultural life in Prague in the 1860s failed to produce a concert hall and a centre for the fine arts, the Provisional Theatre, the future National Theatre or any other facility being unable to serve this purpose. The Czech and German management of the Bohemian Savings Bank, wishing to express their "provincial patriotic feelings" and their rivalry with Vienna, decided in 1872 to build such a cultural centre to mark the fiftieth anniversary of the bank's existence.

A competition was organized in 1874 with eight architects from Prague and Vienna taking part. Two separate buildings were required: one for exhibitions and the other with a concert hall. Two architects, however, Josef Zítek and Josef Schulz, both professors at the Polytechnical Institute of Prague, planned one building only, the interior of which would be divided in two parts. Their concept was adopted and both architects were invited to prepare a final plan. The plan was carried out by Václav Vejrych and the construction, the cost of which amounted to 2 million guilders, was completed in 1884. The palace was named the Rudolfinum after the then Austrian Crown Prince; the general public, however, links the name with the art-loving Emperor Rudolph II who had his residence in Prague Castle.

The front part of the neo-Renaissance House of Artists, No. 79, faces Jan Palach Square and contains a 1200-seat concert hall with excellent acoustics. There are eighteen Corinthian columns on the edge of its gallery that support the conical ceiling. The hall is surrounded both on the ground floor and the upper floor by promenoirs divided by columns. There is a richly illuminated foyer facing the square, flanked by two meeting-rooms in the corners of the building. The rear part of the building has a top-lit exhibition hall in its centre where the Art-lovers' Association once organized exhibitions. Facing the street and the embankment are a number of rooms and exhibition halls both downstairs and upstairs where, in the past, collections of the Society of Patriotic Friends of the Arts were displayed; the collections now form the nucleus of the National Gallery.

The main southern façade of the Rudolfinum facing the square is convex, following the curve of the auditorium. The two parts of the buildings are separated from each other by deep recesses in the side façades. The side and rear façades are shaped according to the interiors. The roof balustrade bears statues of composers made by Ludvík Šimek, Tomáš Seidan, Bohuslav Schnirch, Jindřich Čapek and other sculptors.

The same sculptors also made the statues of two sitting muses on either side of the external stairs facing the square, the pairs of lions by the carriage-way on the east front and the sphinxes at the entrance to the exhibition hall on the west side of the building.

The general architectural concept of the Rudolfinum could be fully applied on the large vacant site and the most progressive ideas of the time could be put into practice in accordance with the motto "putting old clothes on a young body" (G. Semper). The building became "a point of intersection of ideas, some of which met here for the first and some for the last time" (Pavel Janák).

After the creation of the Czechoslovak Republic a suitable place had to be found for the Parliament until a new building could be erected. It was decided to use the Rudolfinum due to its architectural quality, its situation, and the large auditorium. Antonín Engel was invited in the early 1920s to reorganize the layout of the building and make the necessary adaptations of Zítek's and Schulz' architecture to the new function. Most of the adaptations were made in the rear, administrative part where meeting-rooms and clubs for members of Parliament were created. Engel did his job with much understanding of and respect for the architecture of his predecessors. The house remained the seat of Parliament until the German occupation of the country in 1939. After twenty years of daily use many elements, such as paving, stuccowork, mouldings and woodwork had worn.

In 1943, the Germans themselves wanted to have a concert hall in Prague and decided to restore the Rudolfinum for this purpose. Their interest was used to renovate the building and Antonín Engel was charged with the task. He restored the original layout and renovated the damaged or worn elements in cooperation with many artists and craftsmen.

After the liberation of the country the seat of the Parliament moved to the former Stock Exchange at the end of Vinohradská Avenue that had been built by Jaroslav Rössler between 1936 and 1938 (see page 324), and the Rudolfinum was converted into the House of Artists. In its front and rear parts (the former Academic Grammar School) the building housed several institutions, such as the Conservatory of Prague, the Academy of Music, and the Czech Philharmony. At present, a general renovation of the building is taking place, under Karel Prager. The whole building will then be used exclusively for concerts and exhibitions.

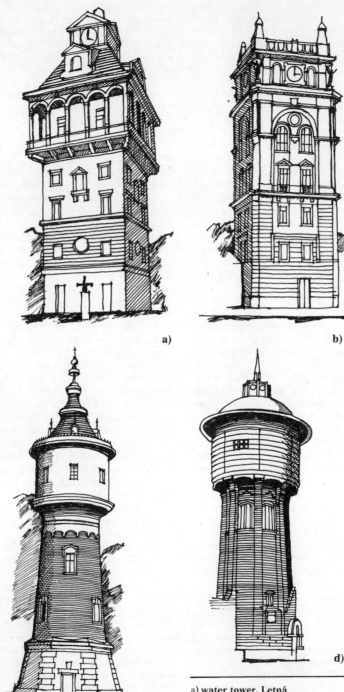

a) water tower, Letná
b) water tower, Vinohrady
c) water tower, Libeň
d) water tower, Vršovice

New Waterworks

Water towers have always been characteristic landmarks in the town, some from the 15th to the 17th centuries at weirs on the Vltava and some from the 19th century and the early 20th century, erected on elevated sites. The most recent tower of this type was erected in the 1980s on a hill above Zlíchov.

The 19th century waterworks carried on the old tradition of pumping water from the Vltava into tower tanks, which had started here as early as 1489, for the first time in Europe. In 1854, the first steam-driven waterworks was put into operation on Žofín Island. One innovation was the use of sand-filtration of river water in the new steam-driven waterworks at Podolí that started working in 1885. Water was pumped from here to the supply reservoir on Karlov Hill from where it was fed by gravity to the water mains reaching even the top floors of houses in the New Town. The public fountains on squares could therefore be gradually closed as of 1888. Královské Vinohrady, a suburb which was raised to the status of a town in 1879, erected in 1882 its own stream-driven waterworks in Podolí from where water was pumped up to a water tower on a hill above Vršovice. As of the 1860s, waterworks using river water or wells were also built in Karlín, Smíchov, Vršovice and Bubeneč. In 1899, the municipal councils of Prague, Karlín, Smíchov, Vinohrady and Žižkov worked together to build a common water mains system using underground water from the sandy subsoil of the Elbe and Jizera at Káraně. The project was carried out between 1909 and 1914.

The water tower of Vinohrady was erected in 1882 to plans by Antonín Turek in the neo-Renaissance style. It has seven storeys surmounted with a terrace which was once used as a look-out tower. Adjoining the tower is a water reservoir and a boiler house with an engine pumping water into the tank on the top floor of the tower. The chimney of the boiler house passes through the centre of the tower. The massive structure, crowned with pylons in each corner, bearing clocks and figures of angels blowing bugles, is still a major landmark in Vinohrady. It ceased to serve its original purpose in 1962, and now houses the waterworks administration offices and workshops.

The neo-Renaissance water tower on Letná Square was designed by the municipal architect Jindřich Fialka and erected in 1885 by Karel Hübschmann and František Schlaffer. The tower has a tent roof with large dormer windows at the sides and is crowned with a superstructure with clocks and triangular gables. The fifth storey of the tower contains a water tank and is surrounded by an arcaded gallery resting on stone cantilevers. Adjoining the tower is a boiler house with an engine room, and a water reservoir linked with the Karlov water tank. The tower stopped working in 1913, and since 1976 it has been used as a centre for the youth and children of the district. The new owners installed a social hall, meeting-rooms and a cinema inside. The tower dominates Letná Square and has been designated, along with the water tower of Vinohrady, a technical monument.

The smallest water tower in Prague was built in 1903—1904 above the Mazanka farmstead in Libeň in a romantic style reminiscent of a lighthouse. Since 1970, the cylindrical water tank has been used for training divers.

When the Old Town waterworks at Charles Bridge were modernized and steam power was installed here in 1883, the group of former water-mills above the level of the Vltava River was rebuilt in the Bohemian Renaissance style to plans by Antonín Wiehl (see page 207), and adapted to house the administration of Prague's waterworks.

To complete the list, we should also mention here the later water tower "Na zelené lišce" (No. 365) in Michle from 1907, designed by Jan Kotěra in the Art Nouveau style, the water tower at Krč from 1913, the structure of which is made of reinforced concrete, and the newest water reservoir on Dívčí hrady from 1980 which consists of three steel tubes, 49 m high, and was designed by Karel Hubáček.

a)

b)

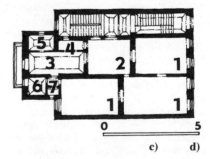

0   5

c)   d)

e)

a) **houses Nos. 558, 563, Janáček Embankment** (former Jechental Houses)
b) **part of façade**
c) d) **plans of flats, late 19th century:** 1 room, 2 hallway, 3 kitchen, 4 pantry, 5 maid's room, 6 bathroom, 7 WC
e) **Hlávka Houses, No. 736**

Tenement Houses from the Late 19th Century

Tenement houses appeared in Prague in the 1860s, and later also in other towns in this country, with apartments containing all amenities, each with one main door from the staircase.

The first apartment houses were built for the rich, both nobles and businessmen, and later also for tradesmen, craftsmen and members of liberal professions, who were moving from the old houses in Central Prague to new blocks in the upper New Town, Vinohrady, on the embankments of the Vltava, and elsewhere. Due to competition between building contractors, the quality of tenement houses was increasing, as the contractors wanted their houses to meet future needs and thus bring also prospective profits. In the late 1880s, the traditional houses with yards surrounded by galleries started giving way in the suburbs mostly to three-floor houses with one- to two-room flats, including a hallway, a kitchen, a toilet and a pantry, for clerks, employees and better-paid workers. Bathrooms appeared in such flats in the 20th century, and in luxury apartments even before, in the late 1880s.

A direct water supply (at the early stage water from the Vltava) to some flats after the construction of a steam power plant at Podolí in 1885 made it possible to meet modern hygienic needs, with water mains and drains, and to install flushing toilets and bathrooms. In the 1860s, a type of coal-fired bath stove was developed, and later gas from the town mains was used to heat water in bathrooms and in kitchen stoves. As of the 1890s, electricity was introduced to flats for lighting and later for cooking and heating. The first lifts were introduced in blocks with five or more storeys. Double windows were generally installed, opening inside, with roll-up shutters, and in luxury houses wooden louvres providing shade from the sun and protection against burglars were introduced.

The most advanced blocks of flats had in the centre a band of hallways, 1.5 to 2 m wide, sometimes even 3 to 4m. The toilet, the pantry and the bathroom were ventilated through a light well, which was a new innovation. In some cases there was also a maid's room. Balconies and oriels appeared that projected from the street façade and rested on steel beams fixed in the wall. The roofs were gently sloping and the roofing material was slate. As of the 1870s, the street façades were neo-Renaissance, their horizontal articulation being stressed by conical fillings under the windows, and were surmounted by a massive cornice. In the late 1880s, façades in the style of the Bohemian Renaissance appeared, which were later superceded by neo-Baroque, neo-Gothic, and eventually Art Nouvau façades.

Examples of larger uniform complexes are a row of neo-Renaissance buildings called the Jechenthal Houses, No. 558, in the Lesser Quarter by Leopold Řechka from 1887, and the Hlávka Houses in the Bohemian neo-Renaissance style between Vodičkova and Jungmannova Streets, Nos. 735—736, designed by Bedřich Tesař and completed after Tesař's death by Josef Fanta in 1889 (who worked particularly on the façade).

Bohemian Neo-Renaissance

a)

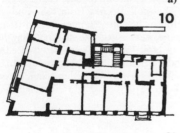

b)

0 10

c)

e)

d)

a) b) **Wiehl House**
c) **gables of the house No. 729, Smíchov**
d) **parsonage at St. Peter's**
e) **house No. 527, Skořepka**

As in other European countries, there were efforts in Bohemia aimed at developing a typical national style to replace the prevailing international neo-Renaissance. These efforts culminated in the 1880s in a style imitating 16th century architecture, the period when the local Gothic tradition amalgamated with the north Italian Renaissance. An excellent example of this is the former Schwarzenberg Palace on Hradčany Square (now Military Museum), No. 185.

The Bohemian neo-Renaissance, based on the ideas and work of Antonín Wiehl (1846—1910), over several years brought new motifs into the streets of Prague and of other towns in the country. Its main contribution, however, was that it eroded the dogma of traditional historic styles and thus opened the door for a future more free evolution of architecture. Façades lost their excess decoration and false monumentality, the cornices crowning buildings and the free parts of façades were decorated with sgraffito, or with ornamental and figural paintings, the doors and windows had plain frames, and the architects sometimes also applied medallions and reliefs. The attic was articulated and crowned with gables and turrets.

The first house conceived in this spirit was the tenement block No. 1035 in Karoliny Světlé Street, Old Town, which was built in 1876 and designed by Antonín Wiehl and Jan Zeyer. The typical lunette cornice displays sgraffiti designed by František Ženíšek, and four medallions with allegories of the Arts by Josef Václav Myslbek. The Old Town Waterworks Administration on Novotného lávka above the Vltava replaced the old Mysliveček Mill here and was built in 1884 also to plans by A. Wiehl.

The Hlávka Houses in the New Town, between Vodičkova and Jungmannova Streets, Nos. 735—736, were built in 1889 by Bedřich Tesař and Josef Fanta, and included a group of seven five-storey houses facing the streets and surrounding two courtyards, each 12 m wide. The houses have two 6 m aisles, there are rooms with two windows and an area of 30 m² each, the kitchens in the flats facing the street are separated by a verandah in the courtyard wing, and all rooms, except the toilets and bathrooms facing onto the light well, have direct lighting. Restaurants and shops on the ground floor have a continuous decorated portal while the upper floors, the attic and the gables are adorned with rich sgraffiti.

Three corner houses are also similar in concept: the first at the corner of the streets Skořepka and Jilská, No. 527, in the Old Town, on the site of an earlier house called "U Bechyňů" (by Antonín Wiehl and Karel Gemperle, 1886), the second and the third at the corners of Pavla Švandy ze Semčic Street, No. 729, and Malátova Street, No. 91, in Smíchov on Janáček Embankment, both from 1890—1891. The ground floor with bossed plaster is surmounted by three upper storeys with exposed brickwork and decorative oriels in the corners, the fifth storey is decorated with sgraffiti and in places with paintings representing historical or ethnographic motifs after cartoons by Mikoláš Aleš.

Decorated apartment houses in the Bohemian Renaissance style appeared in the 1890s also outside the centre of Prague. In the former Bělského Street (now Dukelských hrdinů) leading to the then new Exhibition Grounds three corner houses were built in 1894: Nos. 693, 694 and 696 at corners of Heřmanova and Veletržní Streets. They were designed by Jan Zeyer and featured a figural frieze with paintings made by means of the chiaroscuro technique or colour ceramics. At the same time, a house was built in Křesomyslova Street, No. 293, Nusle District, with a decorative oriel and paintings of Czech patron saints made by Láďa Novák after cartoons by Celda Klouček.

In 1896, Antonín Wiehl built at the corner of Wenceslas Square and Vodičkova Street a large five-storey corner house No. 792 which is now used by the Academia Publishing House, with rich ornamental and figural sgraffiti on historical and ethnographic motifs, made by Luděk Novák and František Urban after cartoons by Mikoláš Aleš and Josef Fanta.

Towards the end of this architectural phase, in 1902, the Municipal Council of Prague built the best equipped complex of schools from that time on Letná Square in the street U studánky near Stromovka Park, with central heating and with cloakrooms in the corridors. The complex included large grammar school and elementary school buildings designed by Josef Zlatník, with two wings perpendicular to the main block, and a small kindergarten. The cornice lunettes by Vojtěch Bartoněk represent Czech patron saints. Bartoněk also made a portrait of St. Wenceslas in the former chapel.

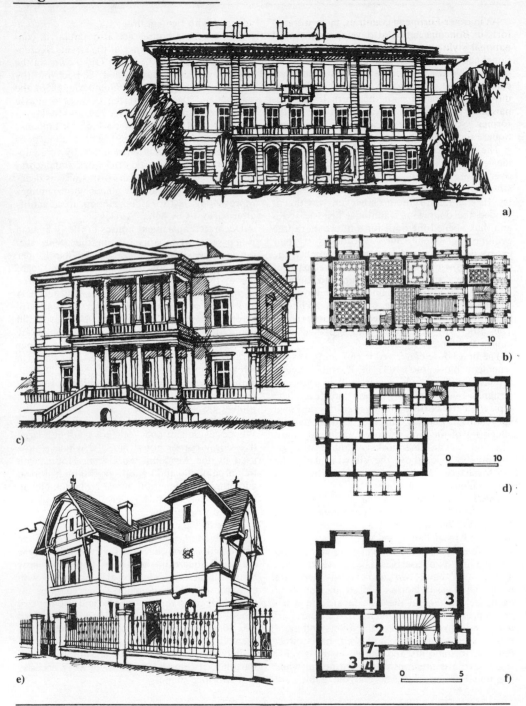

a) b) **former Gröbe Villa**
c) d) **former Lanna Villa**

e) f) **architect Koula's own house:** 1 room, 2 hallway, 3 kitchen, 4 pantry, 7 WC

In the latter half of the 19th century the first private detached houses appeared in Prague: villas, which were initially more for recreation and entertainment than for living in. Such houses were built in beautiful, well-kept gardens to the north of Hradčany: in Bubeneč, Liboc, and further out, in Roztoky, as well as to the south of Prague in Krč, Hodkovičky, Chuchle and Zbraslav.

North of the Bruska Gate at the edge of Bubeneč, in Majakovského Street, Ignác Ullmann and Antonín Barvitius designed and built several luxury villas in the neo-Renaissance style, in parks of Italian or French ornamental layout with terraces, pergolas and a decorative pool and fountain. One was the villa of the banker Lippmann of 1869, which has been recently demolished. Another was built in 1870 for a rich building contractor and patron of the arts, Vojtěch Lanna (No. 1, now belonging to the Czechoslovak Academy of Sciences). The architects followed here the example of the Italian Renaissance villa. However, they did not just imitate this example, but adapted it to the local climatic conditions. In both villas the rooms were situated around a staircase of palace type and with a hall. The stylistic harmony of the buildings was stressed by the interior painting in the Pompeian style; the Lanna House also has in the upper rooms wall paintings by Viktor Barvitius with motifs from the Italian Alps, and in the loggia copies (larger than the originals) also by Barvitius of the children's cycle "Entertainment in a noble house" by Josef Mánes.

Near the deer park Hvězda in Liboc Street, a villa was built in 1888 in the Italian neo-Renaissance style, No. 276, designed by Zdeněk Schubert of Soldern. As in the above cases, the layout, symmetrical both inside and outside and dominated by an asymmetrically situated tower, did not allow a suitable solution to the interior, which probably was not required at that time.

This architecture culminated in a large summer house conceived in the spirit of the Italian Renaissance and built between 1871 and 1888 on the slopes of the eastern side of Vinohrady, above Vršovice, for a mill owner Moritz Groebe. The three-storey villa No. 58, designed by Antonín Barvitius and with interiors of very high quality by Josef Schulz, was built in a terraced garden with scattered artificial grottoes, a pool with a statue of Neptune by Bohuslav Schnirch, with cascades, fountains and a wooden arbour in the north Italian style above the vineyard. The villa was destroyed by fire during the Second World War in February 1945, and restored by Pavel Smetana in 1953. It has been the Centre of Youth since.

From the late 1880s on groups of villas for the wealthy, the middle and professional classes and artists were being already built as permanent residences. They were often conceived in the style of the Bohemian Renaissance with a tower to express the idea: "My house is my castle". The detached house of the architect Jan Koula at Bubeneč from 1896, No. 153, had an exterior which, inspired by ethnographic motifs, was already quite simple and functional as well.

National Museum ARCHITECTURE OF THE LAST THIRD OF THE 19th CENTURY

The idea of establishing a Museum of Bohemia emerged as early as the end of the 18th century. It was also at that time that the Royal Society of Science of Bohemia and the Society of Patriotic Friends of the Arts were founded, being a manifestation of enlightened patriotism opposing the centralization policy of Maria Theresa and Joseph II. The museum was established in 1818; its main sponsors were the Czech patriotic nobles Kašpar of Šternberk, František Antonín Kolow-rat-Libštejnský and František Klebelsberk. The driving spirit behind it all was the historiographer František Palacký, along with Josef Jungmann, Jan Svatopluk Presl, Pavel Josef Šafařík, and others. The museum had its seat in the Schwarzenberg Palace at Hradčany, and in 1846 moved to the Nostic Palace in the avenue Na příkopě, which had been purchased for this purpose and which was later demolished.

In 1864, the Provincial Diet of the Kingdom of

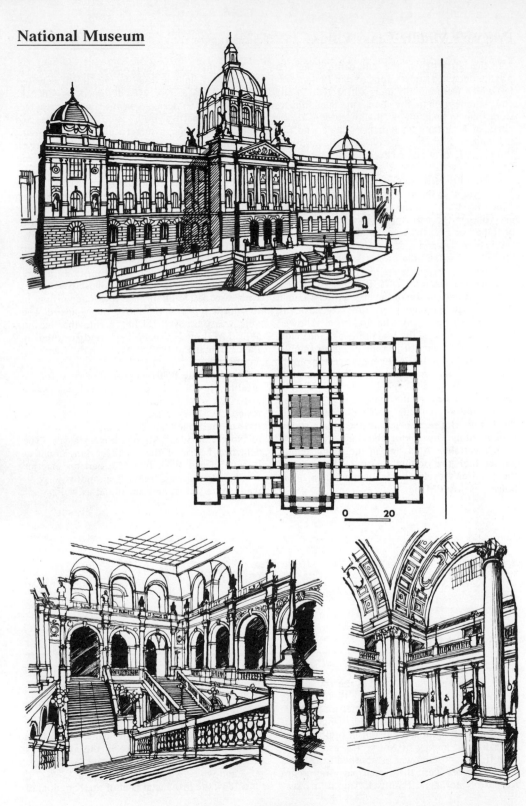

National Museum

Bohemia decided to construct a new building for the museum. Count Jan Harrach and František Ladislav Rieger, who were responsible for the construction, organized a competition which, however, took place much later, in 1883. The building was to replace the neo-Classical Horse Gate at the upper end of Wenceslas Square. Of the presented entries that of Josef Schulz was awarded the first prize and the construction to this plan started in 1885. The building was completed in 1890 and the costs amounted to two million guilders.

The monumental neo-Renaissance palace of the National Museum, No. 1700, has a rectangular ground plan of 104 by 75 m and rises above two access ramps and a three-flight staircase with a fountain. Above the plinth is the rusticated band of the basement and the ground floor, surmounted by two upper floors that are articulated with Corinthian columns and pilasters. The central projecting section with the main entrance in its lower part has a tympanum above the main cornice and is crowned with a tower covered by a dome on a square base, and with a lantern reaching a height of 70 m. The parts broken forward at the four corners are stressed by smaller octagonal domes. The exhibition halls on the upper floors are single-aisled, with windows on either side. In the middle of the building, between two courtyards is a monumental six-flight staircase, top-lit and with arcaded galleries around. In the front part of the building, facing Wenceslas Square, is a Pantheon, as well as a ceremony hall, two storeys high, where major scientific and cultural events used to take place, including funeral ceremonies.

Of the sculptural works here the group "Čechie" above the fountain by Antonín Wagner should be particularly stressed. Many others are worth mention: the statues "History" and "Art" flanking the entrance by Josef Mauder, the reliefs in the façade and the statues in the tympanum by Antonín Wagner, the statues that crown the side walls by Josef Strachovský, Tomáš Seidan, and others; the statues of the Přemyslids in the colonnaded vestibule by Ludvík Schwanthaler; the busts of scientists lining the staircase by Antonín Popp and Bohuslav Schnirch, the statues and busts of prominent figures in the Pantheon by Josef Václav Myslbek, Jan Štursa, Ladislav Šaloun, Karel Dvořák, and others. Notable works in the Pantheon are four historical wall-paintings by František Ženíšek and Václav Brožík, and allegories of Science, Art, Inspiration and Power by Vojtěch Hynais in the segments under the cupola.

In the past, the National Museum building also housed Matice česká (Czech Cultural Society), the Czech Academy of Science and Arts, and the Museum Archives.

There has been a shift in the interest of Czechoslovak conservationists towards more recent stages of development in architecture and the arts. Many late 19th century monuments have been renovated, including the façades, the cladding and the artistic decoration of the National Museum, which on 30th March 1962 was put on the list of National Cultural Monuments of the Czech Republic.

The key position of the Museum in Prague's traffic network has had very negative consequences. The fact that the New Town was incorporated in the Prague Conservation Area as late as mid-1971 made it possible to plan and realize in its immediate vicinity major unsuitable projects, such as the north-south axis road and the crossing of the Underground lines A and C. All these developments have strongly affected both the building and the work of the National Museum. Both the north-south axis road and, in particular, the Underground station brought about temporary disruption to the area immediately in front of the museum: the fountain and the ramp had to be taken to pieces and the foundations of the main façade secured.

The National Museum was damaged during the anti-German uprising in May 1945, and soon after the war the building was repaired and restored. Another restoration of the façades took place in 1956, and the most recent renovation was carried out as a result of various surveys after the completion of the axis road and the Underground station, and also due to the 1968 invasion when the main façade was damaged. The renovation was directed by the State Institute of Monument Preservation and Environment Protection, and carried out by Pražský stavební podnik, Štuko Cooperative and the restoration section of ČFVU (Czech Fine Arts Fund). The restoration work was supervised by specialists from the above Institute and the Ministry of Culture, namely by the historians Jakub Pavel and Ludvík Losos, the architect Jaroslav Blažek from the Ministry, as well as by Jiří Aron and Vratislav Černý from the National Museum.

The work began in March 1971 and was finished in December 1972. It included resurfacing the exterior, renovation and conservation of the sculpture, renovation of the sgraffiti in the courtyards and of the gilding on the façades, the repair of the roof cladding, large-scale regilding of the domes, and water-proofing of the entire surface of the building.

Museum Buildings

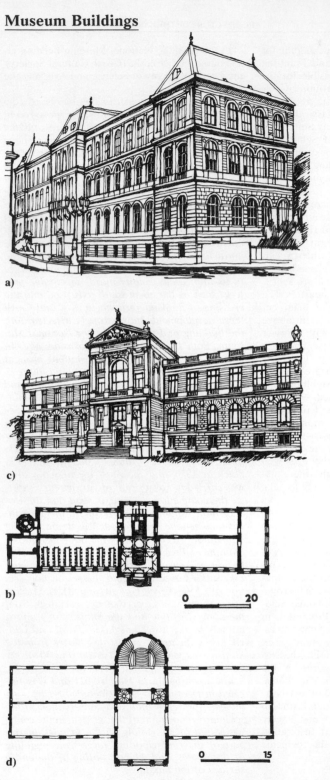

a)

c)

b)

0   20

d)

0   15

a) b) **Museum of Decorative Arts**
c) d) **Museum of the City of Prague**

The boom of cultural life in the country in the late 19th century made it necessary to have museums of different specialization. Their collections were not only documents of the past, but also objects of scientific study aimed at a better understanding of the country's history.

The first of the new museums was the Museum of the City of Prague, No. 1554, which was established in 1874 on the initiative of Antonín Otakar Zeithammer and Tomáš Černý. In 1883, the Museum was situated in the former café pavilion in Šverma Park at Těšnov. As the collections increased, a new museum building was constructed nearby from 1896 to 1898, designed by Antonín Balšánek from a sketch made by Antonín Wiehl, and conceived in a modern neo-Renaissance style with decorative details showing the first signs of naturalism.

The two-storey, two-aisled building with a raised basement has a high and markedly projecting section in its centre, crowned with a tympanum containing an allegorical sculpture of Christianity and Hospitality by František Stránský and bearing a statue representing Prague by Ladislav Šaloun. The side and rear walls are decorated with reliefs by Vojtěch Šafr, František Hergesel and O. Šmejkal. The stuccowork inside was made by Vilém Amort, Ladislav Wurzel, František Hergesel and František Procházka. The three-flight circular stairway lit from above is adorned with a wall-painting of Prague by Antonín Saccheti and with seven views of the town by Karel Liebscher and Václav Jansa. The collections are now too large to be displayed in the nine exhibition halls on the upper floor, and even the lapidary is too small to house them.

The Museum of Decorative Arts was founded in 1885 together with the School of Decorative Arts. The Chamber of Commerce and Trade, the Provincial Diet of the Kingdom of Bohemia, the Austrian Government and the Municipal Council of Prague donated large sums of money for a new building for the museum. The construction began in 1897 on a site that had been part of the old Jewish cemetery opposite the Rudolfinum. The museum building, No. 2, has three storeys with a central and two side sections broken forward, and was designed by Josef Schulz in the neo-Renaissance style. The arches of the windows in the front wall of the building contain emblems representing different crafts by Bohuslav Schnirch and Antonín Popp. The situation of the building, which was completed in 1901, between the street and the historic cemetery made it impossible to develop a more articulated layout and to leave enough space for satisfactory vistas. On the other hand, the design of its north end introduced a romanticizing motif in the staircase tower. On the entrance staircase, there are wall-paintings representing allegories of crafts by František Herčík and Karel Vítězslav Mašek.

The exhibition halls in two aisles, decorated with Pompeian wall and ceiling paintings, contain valuable collections related to the history of the arts and crafts, particularly of glass, ceramics and cabinet-making, from ancient times to the present day, of which, however, only one part can be displayed. The Museum also has a large library and a reading-room.

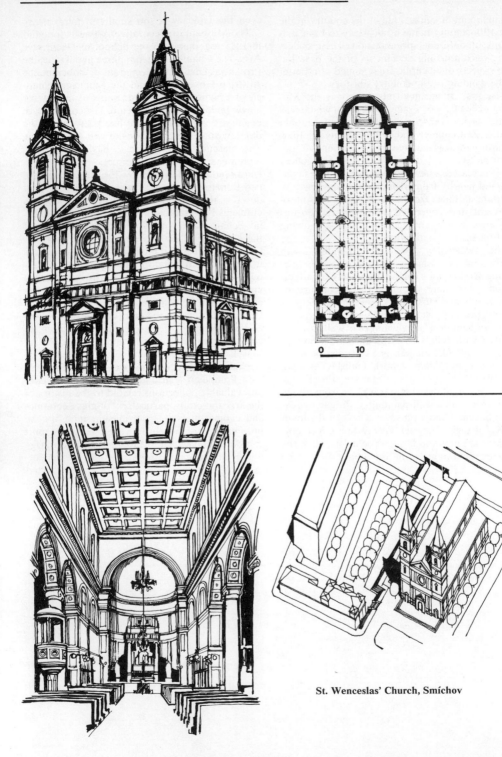

St. Wenceslas' Church, Smíchov

St. Wenceslas' Church in Smíchov District

Smíchov, the second suburb of Prague after Karlín, developed in the 19th century on the left bank of the river where many gardens and villages had existed since the 14th century. In 1785, the village had only 60 houses, but their number had already reached 200 by 1836, with 3,500 inhabitants. In 1836, the village was granted the status of a suburb, and in 1850 the status of a town with a coat-of-arms. The textile industry developed here (Porges, Przibram) as well as metallurgy (Ringhoffer) in the latter half of the 19th century. This brought about a rapid increase in the number of inhabitants, which in 1880 reached 25,000, mostly factory workers.

Smíchov was the scene of the first workers' riots in Bohemia in 1844, and the workers' movement got a firm political base here in 1878 as the Czechoslovak Social Democratic Workers' Party was founded.

In 1881, the foundation stone was laid in the main street of the town of a new monumental Church to St. Wenceslas to replace the former small Church of SS. Philip and James on what is now Arbes Square. The construction was generously subsidized by members of the Imperial Habsburg family. It was necessary to demolish the left wing of the Baroque Portheimka Villa, once a summer palace by Kilian Ignaz Dientzenhofer.

The neo-Renaissance basilica with a nave and two aisles and with two steeples 50 m tall flanking the west façade and crowned with spires is a masterpiece by Antonín Barvitius; it was executed by Jan Linhart and Václav Milde from 1881 to 1885. Petr Fischer, the mayor of Smíchov and a great art-lover, contributed a great deal to the construction. The interior of the church is characterized by the difference between the stone plinth, the entrance gates, the pilasters, the cornices and the window jambs on the one hand and the exposed brickwork on the other. Above the entrances in the west façade, there are coloured ceramic medallions of SS. Wenceslas, Agnes and Hroznata by Ludvík Šimek.

The nave, separated on either side from the aisles by four columns made of Swedish granite, with Ionic capitals of white marble, is surmounted with a wooden coffered ceiling. On the vault of the apse is a mosaic of Christ and the Czech patron saints by Josef Trenkwald, who also made the angels above the triumphal arch. Beneath, there are wall-paintings with motifs from the Legend of St. Wenceslas by František Sequens. The ciborium over the high altar is supported by four Ionic columns. In the aisle apses, in the frieze between the arcade arches, on the altars and on the walls there are paintings by Zikmund Rudl, Max Pirner and František Sequens. The aisles terminate behind the apses in a baptistery and sacristy. The marble statues in the niches of the towers, on either side of the high altar, and the various statues on the high altar and the auxiliary altar were made by Čeněk Vosmík.

The Church of St. Wenceslas ranks among the most important late 19th century buildings in Prague, particularly due to its artistic significance.

Another religious building at Smíchov was the Monastery and Church of St. Gabriel, No. 105, belonging to the parish of St. Wenceslas, which was built in the garden under the south slope of Strahov Hill in Holečkova Street by the Order of Beuron Benedictines from 1888 to 1891 in the neo-Renaissance style with a façade of white brick. The Romanesque basilica was designed by Gislin Bethune and Hildebrandt Hebtirne, members of the order, and its interior was decorated with paintings of the Beuron religious painting school. The same applies to the nearby monastery and church of Sacré-Coeur built in the neo-Gothic style between 1882 and 1884.

Prague's Market-Halls

a)

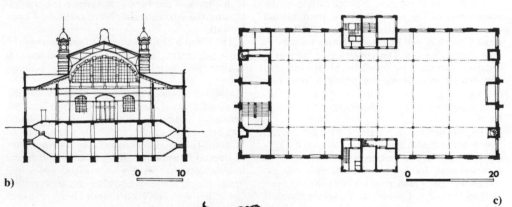

b)

0   10

c)

0   20

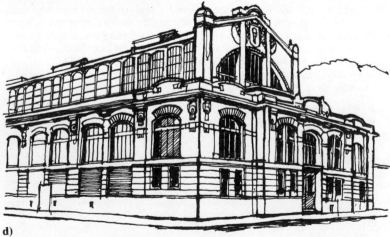

d)

a) b) c) **Vinohrady market-hall**   d) **Smíchov market-hall**

By the end of the 1880s technical progress (water mains, electricity, refrigeration) and hygienic standards had developed so much in Prague that it was possible to concentrate the sale of foodstuffs, which until that time had been taking place in the open air, in covered markets, and for this purpose covered halls were constructed with all amenities, such as storerooms, cold storage rooms, cleaning and heating.

In the place of several medieval houses rebuilt in the Renaissance and Baroque style, No. 14/8, Rytířská Street in the Old Town, a large Old Town market-hall No. 406 was built between 1893 and 1896 to designs by the municipal architect Jindřich Fialka. The construction costs amounted to 500,000 guilders, and the five-storey building in the style of the Italian neo-Renaissance had on the ground floor two carriageways, a café, an alehouse, shops, an office of the municipal gas company, and on the upper floor further municipal offices. The entrances have stone portals with columns and caryatids, the façade bears the coats-of-arms of the towns of Prague, and the lunettes of the main entrance inside the building contain motifs of Prague's markets by Vojtěch Bartoněk.

The market-hall covers a site reaching the Street of 28th October and contained 360 private stands with 2 m wide counters for market stallholders coming from around Prague. The free stands, of which there were seventy, were just enclosed spaces with numbers. The market-hall was accessible from both streets and was divided by a network of lanes paved with granite slabs. Along the lanes and around the market-hall there were cast-iron pillars supporting a steel structure with side glazed walls and roofs with a light well in the middle. There was electric lighting by means of arc lamps. In the basement, there were storerooms, cold stores with an engine room, and even a steam power plant. Two decades ago, sales were limited here. In the late 1970s, the market-hall was converted into a grocery supermarket.

The market-hall of Královské Vinohrady, No. 1200, was built in 1902 to a neo-Renaissance design by Antonín Turek on the slope along Budečská Street, and the costs amounted to 670,000 crowns. The building has three storeys and can be entered from Vinohradská Avenue at the level of the first basement, another entrance being from Slezská Street directly into the hall. The hall is side-lit in the way of a basilica, and has a roof supported by steel arched girders. At the entrance from Vinohradská Avenue, there was an alehouse and a porter's lodge, and there were also flats for the pub's keeper and the porter. In the middle of the side walls sections were broken forward that contained offices, stairs and elevators. The basement contained storerooms and cold stores for foodstuffs. The general layout of the building was very practical and until recently the building fulfilled its function. It is expected now to be rebuilt for modern forms of food sales.

The town of Smíchov also built a market-hall for groceries, fruit and vegetables from 1907 to 1908 next to the new National House on the square (now Square of 14th October). Both buildings were designed by Alois Čenský in a local version of the Art Nouveau style. The market-hall, No. 83, has a steel structure inside, arched girders for the roof, and tall windows of the basilican type. There were 125 stalls and technically well equipped storerooms and cold stores in the basement. In the late 1970s, the market-hall was rebuilt and converted into a supermarket. The original high basilican interior was divided in two parts by inserting a ceiling, and there were new stairs to the upper floor. The large hall was divided into areas for selling and storage, with a network of communications and a space behind for personnel with changing rooms and toilet facilities.

Vyšehrad in the 19th Century

The Vyšehrad Citadel was closed after the 1866 defeat of Austria by the Prussian army, and in 1883 Vyšehrad became part of Prague, a memorial to Bohemia's great past.

There is, first of all, a National Cemetery which developed in the 1870s from an old graveyard dating from 1660. The reconstruction was initiated by the provost, Václav Štulc, and the architectural work was by Antonín Barvitius, who made the marble tombs in the south and east, and by Antonín Wiehl, who designed the arcades along the northern edge as well as part of the southern and eastern sides that were completed in 1902. The Tuscan sandstone columns support groin vaults decorated with Pompeian paintings.

The part which is called Slavín is a place where prominent national figures are buried. It was constructed from 1889 to 1893 to a design by Antonín Wiehl, on the initiative of Mikuláš Karlach, the Dean of Vyšehrad, and of Petr

Vyšehrad in the 19th Century

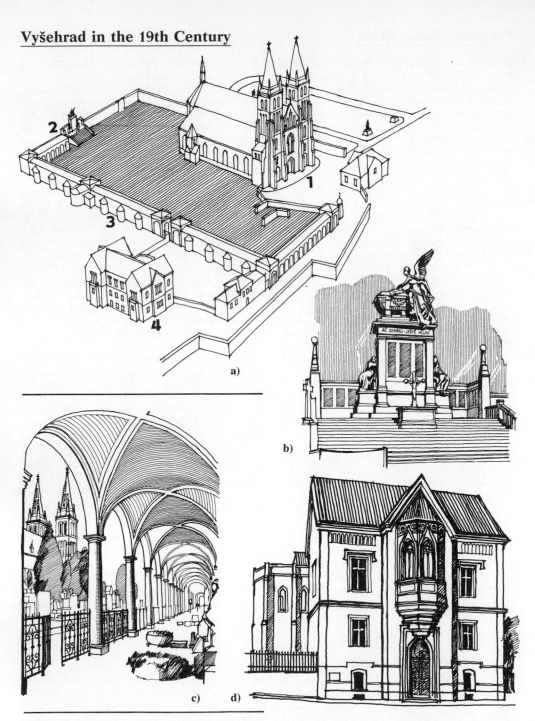

a) **National Cemetery:** 1 Church of SS. Peter and Paul,
2 cemetery and Slavín, 3 arcades, 4 New Provost's
Lodgings
b) **Slavín**
c) **arcades**
d) **New Provost's Lodgings**

Fischer, a representative of the patriotic movement. The sculpture including a winged genius over a coffin and a weeping woman on each side was made by Josef Mauder in 1892—1893. Beneath, there is a large crypt with 44 coffin recesses. The general arrangement of the cemetery with an area of 0.81 ha and with a main path in the centre leading to Slavín is quite modest, although there are many tombstones of great artistic value marking the graves of prominent representatives of the arts and science.

To the north of the church is the single-storey building of the New Provost's Lodging (No. 89) from 1872—1874 designed by Josef Niklas in the neo-Gothic style. Notable parts in the interior are the stairs and the former chapel, which is now a wedding-hall of the District Council, with paintings representing the Czech patron saints by Josef Hellich. Niklas also designed the former canon's houses No. 90, 91 and 100 in the neo-Gothic style in the street K rotundě that were constructed from 1874 to 1877. They are now used by the administration of the Vyšehrad National Memorial. The Vyšehrad Chapter also owned the semi-detached house No. 81—82 built in 1848—1849 to a design by Jan Ripota.

Vyšehrad, the first royal seat in the territory of Prague and now a national cultural monument, was always a place of inspiration for Czech culture throughout the period of the rebirth of national consiousness, even in this century. Therefore, as concern about the protection of historic monuments increased, a great deal of attention was paid to protecting Vyšehrad against further devastation, as many parts had been seriously damaged or even destroyed after its conversion into a Baroque citadel. The first historic monument at Vyšehrad whose preservation was strongly argued is the Romanesque rotunda of St. Martin which was saved thanks to Count Karel Chotek's intervention in 1841. A new road was constructed at that time that linked the New Town with Pankrác (at the same time the northern brick gateway in the old Baroque fortification was built), and the Rotunda was to have been demolished (see the description of the chapel, page 24).

The second oldest religious building here is St. Lawrence's Basilica, the archaeological remains of which were discovered in 1903 and conserved as ruins. The only addition is a neo-Romanesque entrance portal and a reinforced concrete slab that covers the site.

The most beautiful building in the Vyšehrad acropolis is the chapter church of SS. Peter and Paul, which has undergone many rebuildings of which the last took place in 1885—1887, when Josef Mocker totally remodelled its layout and form, removed the Renaissance and Baroque parts and covered the nave and the aisles with rich polychrome decoration. However, the greatest changes took place here at the turn of the century when even the Baroque façade that had been respected by Mocker was removed and in 1902—1903 replaced by a neo-Gothic façade by František Mikš, exaggerated in size and out of tune with its time, with two towers crowned with spires. The main portal is surmounted by a tympanum containing a relief "The Last Judgment" by Štěpán Zálešák from 1901, the wall-paintings in the interior were painted by František and Marie Urban. The neo-Gothic altar in the nave is decorated with a woodcut by Josef Hrubeš, and that in the right aisle by Jan Kastner.

Of the Gothic treasures only some fragments have remained above the Cliff of Vyšehrad: the remains of a bridge, the outer masonry of a guard bastion (called Libuše's Bath), and another building, which since the renovation in the 1960s has been used to display documents related to Vyšehrad. At the exit towards Pankrác there is a relic of the Špička Gate from the reign of Charles IV, which several architects have already tried to incorporate in the redevelopment studies of the south-east front park. At present, Zdenka Nováková is preparing an extension of the cemetery eastwards.

In the park that has replaced a former armoury south of the church, destroyed by a fire in 1927, three monumental sculptures were erected between 1948 and 1970 representing figures from Czech mythology, made by Josef Václav Myslbek between 1889 and 1897: Lumír and the Song, Záboj and Slavoj, Ctirad and Šárka. The sculptures were originally placed on the piers of the Palacký Bridge which, however, had to give way in the late 1960s to new access roads. The sculptures were damaged in February 1945 by air raids, and later renovated. The fourth sculpture represents Přemysl and Libuše. The chapel here was built in 1978.

At present, the Great Bastion and its casemates in the north-east corner of the former citadel are being redeveloped.

The Czech national renaissance reached its peak in the last decade of the 19th century. The sciences and arts reached a high level; Czech industry, trade and banks were successfully competing with their German and Austrian rivals in spite of the disapproval of Vienna. As a result, Bohemia and Moravia became the economic powerhouse of the Habsburg Empire. It was decided to display the progress achieved over the previous one hundred years in a unique exhibition.

The idea in 1888 of organizing a Provincial Jubilee Exhibition matured at a session of the Provincial Diet of the Bohemian Kingdom in 1889 where a Preparatory Committee was set up. Both the province and the City of Prague heavily subsidized the event. Antonín Wiehl and Bedřich Münzberger prepared several general projects for the Exhibition Grounds. The construction began in summer 1890 and the exhibition was officially opened on 14th May 1891.

The main entrance to the Grounds was bridged by the 20 m arch of the wooden entrance gate (pulled down in 1948). Behind the gate, there were (and still are) administration buildings and a post-office designed by A. Wiehl in the Bohemian neo-Renaissance style. The main courtyard, 200 m long and 70 m wide, was designed by the landscape architect František Thomayer and was lined with neo-Renaissance pavilions for the Arts and History, also designed by A. Wiehl. In the foreground, there was an equestrian statue of King George of Poděbrady by Bohumil Schnirch, which was later removed and installed on George Square in Poděbrady. The courtyard was closed by a transverse promenade, 250 m long and 60 m wide, behind which the main exhibition building, the Industrial Palace, was built following the third version of a project by Bedřich Münzberger. The steel structure was designed by František Prášil and erected by Českomoravská strojírna. On the axis of the façade there is a decorative tower, 51 m high. The statues of genii above the entrance and the busts of Czech technicians on the side wings were made by František Hergesel, Antonín Procházka and Ludvík Wurzel.

Behind the palace, under a look-out terrace with steps was a large light fountain designed by František Křižík, the main spirit behind the Exhibition. The event lasted five months and ranked among the major exhibitions held in European capitals throughout the 19th century: there were 146 exhibition buildings, the construction costs amounted to 1.5 million guilders, and over two million people visited the Exhibition. Some minor pavilions, particularly those that were made of wood, were later pulled down, including unfortunately the Mechanical Engineering Hall behind the Industrial Palace, which was 17.5 m high, 135 m long and 30 m wide. Its steel structure, designed by Albert Vojtěch Velflík, was made by Ruston Company.

Along with the Exhibition Grounds a 60 m tall look-out tower designed by František Prášil was built on Petřín Hill, and could be reached by a new funicular from Újezd. Another funicular led from the Vltava embankment to Letná Park, from where an electric tram line ran to the Exhibition Grounds at the south end of Stromovka Park.

Much attention was paid to the Bohemian Cottage designed by Antonín Wiehl, and due to this success it was decided to organize an Ethnographic Exhibition here, which took place in 1895 and gathered large quantities of objects related to the life of the Czech people in the past. In 1898, an Exhibition of Architects and Engineers was held here, and in 1908 an exhibition of the Chamber of Commerce and Trade, which enriched the Grounds with a large Engine Hall designed by Rudolf Kříženecký, the structure of which was the work of the engineer Rautenkranz.

Jan Koula built a new pavilion for the large panoramic view of the Battle of Lipany painted in 1898 by Luděk Marold and other painters and collaborators. Antonín Hrubý remodelled in the Baroque style Wiehl's old pavilion for the lapidary of the City of Prague, with reliefs by Gustav Zoula in the friezes and with sculptures at the entrance by František Hergesel (now in the lapidary of the National Museum). The Pavilion of Commerce designed by Jan Kotěra (together with Pavel Janák and Otakar Novotný), with sculptures and reliefs at the entrances by Jan Štursa, was unfortunately later demolished.

Other changes occurred here in connection with the 1948 Slav Agricultural Exhibition, and then in 1952 and 1953 when it was converted into a Park of Culture and Relaxation. The Industrial Palace was rebuilt to a design by Pavel Smetana to accommodate congresses and large social events. A small and a great stage, a summer theatre, and a panoramic cinema were built in the north part of the area, and in 1959 the Czechoslovak Pavilion from the 1958 World Exhibition in Brussels was reinstalled here (designed by František Cubr, Josef Hrubý, Zdeněk Pokorný). The Engine Hall was rebuilt from 1960 to 1962 at great cost as a Sports Hall designed by Jiří Krásný.

Exhibition Grounds of Prague

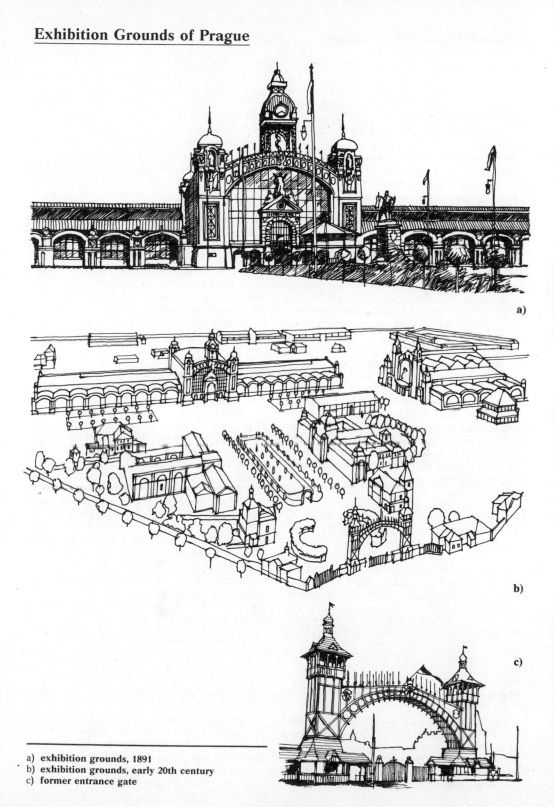

a) exhibition grounds, 1891
b) exhibition grounds, early 20th century
c) former entrance gate

As another suburb of Prague, Královské Vinohrady was constructed in the latter half of the 19th century, the problem of its central square emerged in the late 1860s. An excellent place was chosen at the crossing of two alleys in Wimmer Garden, which are now the streets Anglická and Jugoslávská.

In the 1890s, the square was surrounded by houses on all sides except the north. On the axes of the streets Žitná and Jugoslávská, in the centre of the square, the neo-Gothic church of St. Ludmila was built from 1883 to 1893 to a design by and under the direction of Josef Mocker, the architect who designed the final part of St. Vitus' Cathedral. The two-aisled church has an exterior of exposed red brickwork and is conceived in the early Gothic style, with transepts and a second crossing created by the sacristy and the baptism chapel in the chancel. Its west façade is flanked by two towers, 60 m tall and surmounted with full octaganal spires. Although the church is not very big, its harmony, simplicity, dignity of form and, in particular, its position on top of the sloping square make it very impressive and comparable even with more splendid neo-Gothic buildings in Europe, such as the votive house in Vienna or St. Clothilde's Church in Paris. The façade of the nave above a flight of steps has a portal with a relief in the tympanum by Josef Václav Myslbek, and with symbols of the Evangelists by Jan Čapek. The statues of Czech patron saints in the gables of the nave and of the transepts are by Ludvík Šimek and Bernard Seeling, those in niches flanking the portal by František Hergesel and Antonín Procházka. The rich polychrome decoration of the walls and vaults inside the church was designed by Josef Jobst, the figurative stained glass in the windows was the work of František Sequens, František Ženíšek, Adolf Liebscher and František Urban. The Gothic pulpit was designed by Jiljí Zika, the wooden altars were made later after models by Jan Kastner and Štěpán Zálešák.

The organ in the loft has three thousand pipes, the belfries contain four large bells with well-harmonized tones.

Behind the church, between Slezská and Korunní Streets the former National House, now the House of Culture of the Transport and Communication Workers, No. 280, was built in the neo-Renaissance style to a design by Antonín Turek. The statues and busts on the façade are by Antonín Popp. The large Mayakovsky Hall is decorated with paintings by Adolf Liebscher and with busts of prominent Czech personalities by Josef Strachovský. The layout is quite sophisticated and the building contains a number of rooms of different size for cultural, sports and social events. On the ground floor, at the street corner, there is a large café, a wine bar and a restaurant.

On the north side of the square a theatre called Divadlo na Vinohradech, No. 1450, was built from 1905 to 1907 in the Art Nouveau style and designed by Alois Černý, whose winning entry presented at the 1903 competition was still conceived in the neo-Renaissance style. The façade is crowned with a couple of pylons bearing symbolic sculptures representing "Opera" and "Drama" by Milan Havlíček, the cornice is decorated with terms by Bohumil Kafka. The auditorium ceiling has frescoes by František Urban representing a "Tribute to the Arts". The sculptural decoration of the proscenium and the boxes were made by Antonín Mára, and that in the foyer is by Antonín Popp the Younger; the curtain was made between 1906 and 1909 by Vladimír Županský, a very promising painter who unfortunately died young. The neighbouring block of neo-Baroque tenement houses with luxury apartments was built in 1903 to designs by Josef Pospíšil.

In the early 1930s, the traffic was diverted from the centre to the sides of the square, which made it possible to introduce green lawns with promenade paths. The well-solved spaces of the square and the height of the surrounding buildings make the square one of the best enclosed spaces in the town.

On and Under Letná Park

The large level area, which was later called Letná Plain, extended from the top of the Vltava bank northwards as far as the road leading from the village called Bubny to the Strahov Gate (now Avenue of Dr. Marie Horákové). Until the end of the 1880s, it had been a military exercise ground. Later, there were sports and children's playing-fields here. At the turn of the century, as the old Jewish Town between the Old Town and the Vltava was demolished and a new residential district was constructed here, it was suggested to link Letná with Prague by means of a cutting

Náměstí Míru (Peace Square)

a) náměstí Míru
b) Vinohrady Theatre

c) St. Ludmila's Church
d) Central House of Culture of Railwaymen (former National House)

(Jan Koula) or a tunnel (Richard Klenka z Vlastimilu).

On top of the sloping park above the Vltava and in the axis of the former chain bridge and what is now Revoluční Street, a restaurant in the neo-Renaissance style was built in 1863 by Ignác Ullmann (No. 341). In 1898, the exhibition pavilion of Komárov Ironworks, No. 143, from the 1891 Jubilee Exhibition was reconstructed at the west end of Letná Park. The pavilion was donated to Prague by the owner of the ironworks, the Duke of Hanau, and has since also been known as Hanau Pavilion. It was made of cast-iron to designs by the architect Heiser, the sculptural decoration was made by Zdeněk Fiala after drawings by Josef Hercík. Built on a high base, it can be seen from the Vltava embankment. The pavilion was rebuilt from 1966 to 1968 at high cost and converted into a café and a restaurant.

The last building to be constructed in the eastern part of Letná Park was a café and restaurant, No. 1500, with extensive terraces. Parts of the building, which was designed by František Cubr, Josef Hrubý and Zdeněk Pokorný, came here from the 1958 World Exhibition in Brussels.

The area of the Bastion XIX above Klárov, which was the most important part of the Baroque fortifications, was donated at the beginning of this century by the Municipal Council of Prague to Karel Kramář, a Czech political representative, who then built here from 1908 to 1911 a villa designed for him by Bedřich Ohmann. The design of this villa, No. 212, which is symmetrical and crowned with a mansard roof, including the garden gate and two service buildings, reminds us of Prague Baroque mansions, although it has some modern details in its surface decoration. An important part of the interior is the large study facing south over Prague, as well as the social hall with mosaics on the walls with Orthodox decoration. The villa is now used as a residence for important visitors to the country.

Under Letná Square, east of Klárov up to the Vltava, there had been since the 15th century a large garden which in 1600 came into the hands of Jesuits. They established here a botanical garden with a chapel and, in the 18th century, a "summer house", which after the dissolution of the order in 1773 became a dance-hall for some time. The garden became derelict, and in the 1890s a street called Pod Letnou was constructed here, which is now Captain Jaroš Embankment. In 1896, a school and boarding house for children of the aristocracy was built here by the Foundation of Count J. P. Straka of Nedabylice. The neo-Baroque building, No. 128, was designed by Václav Roštlapil and constructed by Quido Bělský. The costs amounted to more than one million guilders. Its wings at right angles to one another form a "courtyard of honour" towards the river and the street. The central projecting section facing the river is crowned with an unusual cupola and decorated with allegorical sculptures by Josef Mauder, the former chapel was adorned with a painting representing St. Wenceslas by Emanuel Dítě, and with interior stuccowork by Celda Klouček. The layout with many halls and with directly lit corridors is very practical. The architect distributed the masses of the monumental building in a way that fitted perfectly with the Hradčany panorama. Between the First and the Second World Wars the building was an Academic House for University Students. It was later rebuilt by Ladislav Machoň and is now the Czechoslovak Prime Minister's Office.

The economy of the country was booming at the end of the 19th century and, as a result, the Czech banks, savings banks and insurance companies represented 37 per cent of the total financial funds available in Bohemia. Zemská banka (the Provincial Bank) was of particular importance and was a safe source of credits for the entire Czech banking system.

The power of Czech capital had repercussions also in the appearance of Prague. Between 1894 and 1896 the bank built its "palace", No. 20/858, on the busiest avenue of Prague, Na příkopě, on the site of the former Nostic Palace, which had housed the collections of the National Museum from 1845 to 1890.

The tall three-storey façade, crowned with

On and Under Letná Park

a)

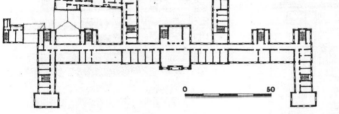

b)

c)

d)

a) b) **Czechoslovak Prime Minister's Office** (former
   Straka Academy)
c) **public swimming-pool** (contemporary drawing)
d) **Hanau Pavilion**

Banks

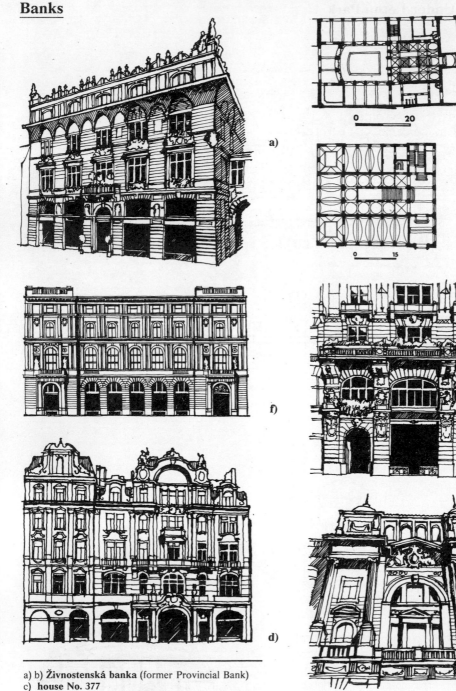

a) b) **Živnostenská banka** (former Provincial Bank)
c) **house No. 377**
d) **Czech Ministry of Trade** (former Municipal Insurance Company)
e) **post office, Senovážné Square** (former Hypoteční banka)
f—g) **Czech State Savings Bank** (former Municipal Savings Bank)

a lunette cornice supporting an attic storey, is made of sandstone blocks and conceived in the neo-Renaissance style. Its decoration already features naturalistic motifs characteristic of Art Nouveau. The lunettes of the cornice contain allegorical mosaics after cartoons by Mikoláš Aleš, the mezzanine piers are embellished with reliefs representing Technology, Agriculture, Industry and Trade by Celda Klouček and Stanislav Sucharda, who also made the corner statues above the attic storey. In the vestibule, there are bronze statues of torch-bearers by Bohuslav Schnirch and figural paintings representing St. Wenceslas and Labour by Max Švabinský. The staircase, made of marble and granite, is adorned on the walls with paintings by Karel V. Mašek and Karel Klusáček. On the first floor, in the bank hall, twelve statues can be seen in niches representing various regions of Bohemia that were made by František Hergesel, Antonín Procházka, Stanislav Sucharda and Bohuslav Schnirch, and there is also a fountain with figural decoration by Ladislav Šaloun. The session hall contains paintings by Emil Holárek. Today, the building is a branch of Živnostenská banka.

Zemská banka expanded in 1911—1912 to the corner across Nekázanka Street and built the corner house, No. 857, designed by Osvald Polívka in a style still based on the main principles of the Bohemian neo-Renaissance, but already in the spirit of Art Nouveau. There are large mosaics on the façade after cartoons by Jan Preisler, the sculptural decoration was made by Celda Klouček and Ladislav Šaloun. The hall of the building, which is now used by Čedok Travel Agency, was remodelled in 1940 by Karel Stráník, the mosaics were made by Josef Novák to drawings by Jan Bauch, the ceramic frieze is by Jan Lauda and František Tichý, the symbolic marble female figure by Bedřich Stefan.

In the Street of 28th October, earlier Ovocná Street, a palatial building for Pražská úvěrní banka, No. 377, was built in 1902 in the place of the very old houses "U zlatého jablka" (At the Golden Apple) and "Větrník". The building was designed by Matěj Blecha, the rich Art Nouveau decoration of the sandstone façade was by Celda Klouček, a professor at the School of Decorative Arts, and the sculptural decoration inside by Karel Novák.

On the north side of Senovážné Square, on the site of the former "New Barracks" demolished in 1874—1875, the former Hypoteční banka was built in 1889—1890, a palace-type building in the neo-Renaissance style (No. 991) which was designed by Achille Wolf and is now used by the Post Office. Its sculptural decoration was by Antonín Popp, professor at the Czech Polytechnical Institute, while the interiors were decorated by Celda Klouček.

On the site of three Baroque houses renovated after the great fire of Prague in 1689, a neo-Baroque building of Pražská městská pojišťovna (Municipal Insurance Company of Prague), No. 931, designed by Osvald Polívka, was built in 1900 on the north side of Old Town Square and is now used by the Czech Ministry of Trade. By articulating the mansard roof and using decorative chimneys the architect made this side of the square quite picturesque. Outside, the house is divided in two parts corresponding to the previous buildings: the right-hand part, which is wider and decorated with sculptures by František Procházka, Ladislav Šaloun and Hanuš Folkmann, and the left-hand side, which is narrower and has a marble portal with allegorical figures by Ladislav Šaloun. The gable of the building contains a mosaic expressing the values of the insurance company, made after a cartoon by František Urban, and at the highest point is a sandstone statue of St. Wenceslas from the façade of the demolished house. Quite remarkable is the former bank hall with a structure of reinforced concrete vaults and with frescowork on the front wall. Stone portals from the demolished houses were installed in the courtyard.

The Czech National Savings Bank, No. 536, has its seat in the noble neo-Renaissance building of the former Municipal Savings Bank of Prague that was designed by Antonín Wiehl and Osvald Polívka and built by Quido Bělský from 1892 to 1894 in place of former market stalls between Havelské Square and Rytířská Street. The building originally had three storeys on a rectangular ground plan, a hall with stairs, and was lit from above; another storey was added in the 1930s and was placed in the frieze of the top cornice.

The façade is decorated with statues by Stanislav Sucharda, František Hergesel, Ladislav Wurzel and other artists, and with reliefs by Bohuslav Schnirch. The interior is embellished with stuccowork by Celda Klouček and paintings by František Ženíšek, Karel Mašek and Jaroslav Věšín. The sculptural decoration of the hall is by František Hergesel, Antonín Popp and Antonín Procházka.

19th Century Bridges

a) **former Francis I Bridge**
b) **former Francis Joseph I Bridge**
c) **Karlín viaduct** (drawing by K. Brantl, 1857)
d) **Palacký Bridge**
e) **Legion Bridge**

The beauty of towns that are situated on big rivers is enhanced not only by the reflection of houses in the water, but also by the bridges connecting the river banks. As early as the 12th century, Prague was a European city famed for bridges. Prague's millers were wise enough to build weirs across the narrow river and thus made it in some places as wide as the major European rivers.

The two medieval stone bridges, namely Judith Bridge from the period 1158–1172 that collapsed in 1342 and Charles Bridge from 1357–1383 which is still a major landmark in Prague, were followed by two chain bridges, neither of which survives: Francis I Bridge from 1840–1841, removed in 1897, and Francis Joseph I Bridge (later called Štefánik Bridge) from 1865–1868, which was dismantled in 1941 and later replaced by Šverma Bridge.

From 1846 to 1850, a stone viaduct was built between Karlín and Holešovice for a railway from Prague to Děčín and further to Dresden that was under construction. The two arms of the Vltava are bridged by eight segmental arches with a total length of 200 m, and there are in addition 77 semicircular arches above Štvanice Island and the territory of Karlín. The total length of the viaduct is 1100 m. In the river bed, the bridge piers had foundations built on an oak framework. The viaduct was designed by Alois Negrelli, an outstanding civil engineer of that time, in collaboration with Jan Perner, J. Köpp and J. Kada. Zdeněk Wirth characterized the structure as "a document of the monumentality of the Empire era in the field of technical structures".

The railway from the main station and from Tábor to Smíchov Station and on to Plzeň crossed the Vltava at Vyšehrad on a steel truss-bridge built in 1871 with five spans of a total length of 296.3 m. The traffic was quite busy here, and the line had to be doubled, which led to a fundamental change in the structural concept of the bridge in 1900–1901: new piers were built and the bridge was given three steel trusses with a parabolic upper section.

The industrial boom at Smíchov also had repercussions in the traffic system, and in 1876 another bridge, named after Palacký was built as continuation of Plzeňská Street. The bridge is 228 m long, and the piers and seven segmental vaults are made of granite blocks of different colours. The bridge was designed by Josef Reiter and Bedřich Münzberger in the neo-Renaissance style, and built by Klein Bros. However, it was quite narrow, only 11.4 m wide, and had to be widened in 1950–1951 by means of consoles. At the same time, the stone pylons at both ends bearing sandstone sculptures by Josef Václav Myslbek with motifs from Czech mythology were removed. They had been damaged by bombs during World War II, but were restored and reinstalled in Vyšehrad Garden (see page 255).

The granite bridge called "most Legií" (Legion Bridge) between the National Theatre and Újezd replaced in 1899–1901 the earlier Francis I Chain Bridge, and was built to designs by Antonín Balšánek who had been awarded the first prize in a competition in 1889, vhere entries with stone, iron, and already concrete bridges had been presented. The bridge is 16 m wide and 343.5 m long, and is divided into nine elliptical arches. The structure was made lighter by cutting out the so-called "cow horns" at the piers. The architectural details were conceived in a style that is a combination of neo-Baroque and Art Nouveau. Střelecký Island can be reached from the bridge by climbing down a wide staircase. The bridge was constructed by Gregersen of Budapest. Along with the renovation of the National Theatre, the bridge was restored from 1881 to 1983, particularly the decoration, including the balustrade and the bronze, partly gilded lamp posts.

ART NOUVEAU, MODERNISM,
CUBISM

0   1km

32
V

Early 20th Century Architecture

20th century architecture reflects the progress of science and technology, as well as of social ideas, political progress and new forms of government. At the end of the 19th century the first efforts appeared at abandoning historicism in architecture and introducing a new form meeting the practical needs and responding to the technical achievements of the time. A general feature of the new trend was the harmony of all the arts in their philosophy and style. Thus, specific styles developed, for instance the Arts and Crafts, and later the Modern Style in Great Britain, l'Art Nouveau in France, the Jugendstil in Germany, the Vienna Sezession in the Austro-Hungarian Empire, and the Chicago School in the USA which anticipated the future development.

Typical features of this style in Prague were the application of decorative vegetable and figural motifs in sculpture and painting, of stained glass, ceramics, exposed brickwork and masonry, concrete, moulded plaster, large windows, façades with unarticulated surfaces, and an end to symmetry of plan.

A subsequent stage of architectural development which began at the end of the first decade of the 20th century postulated matter-of-factness and functional logic in construction. Typical features of this "individualistic modern style" were an almost total lack of ornament on the façade, application of new structural materials, particularly concrete, a free layout, and a primarily functional ground plan.

In the second decade, however, ideas and forms appeared that were directly contrary to the principles of Modernism, resulting in a formal abstraction, as in Italian Futurism, Czech Cubism, German Expressionism, Dutch Neoplasticism and Russian Suprematism. A specific trend after the war was Czech national decorativism reflecting the nationalism provoked by the restoration of national sovereignty.

Rebuilding in the Old Town

The Municipal Council of Prague decided in 1885 to demolish Josefov, the former Jewish Ghetto and later a refuge for the poor, which had become part of Prague in 1850. The main reasons for the rebuilding was the high death rate, contagious diseases, sanitation problems (particularly due to "dead" sewers), dense development of land, overpopulation, too much bad and crowded housing (78.4 per cent, twice the mean level in Prague), lack of ventilation and drinking water, and the danger of floods.

A competition was organized in 1886 which was won by Alfred Hurtig whose rehabilitation plan, prepared together with A. Štrunc and F. Hejda, was confirmed in 1889. In February 1893 a Sanitation Law was enacted and, as a result, 600 houses were demolished and a new residential district was built instead.

Hurtig's plan made the network of streets at Josefov simpler, the main axis of the district being Pařížská Street (then Mikulášská), 24 m wide, leading from Old Town Square to the north and intended as a centre of Prague's social life. The streets Kaprova, Maislova, Josefovská (now Široká) and Dušní retained their lines, but were now to be widened. Of the old buildings, only the old Jewish Town Hall, six synagogues and the old Jewish Cemetery remained. However, there was a drawback: Hurtig planned quite small blocks of flats, which with the deep modern tenement blocks left too little space for yards. Green plots were therefore reduced to one small park near the Old-New Synagogue only.

The redevelopment began at the beginning of this century at the corner of Old Town Square where a tenement block designed by Professor Rudolf Kříženecký was built, and across the street, next to the church, a house designed by Jan Koula. Both houses were conceived in the neo-Baroque style. Other neo-Baroque houses were built in Mikulášská Street by Alois Dlabač, as well as houses in the Art Nouveau style by Rudolf Koukola, František Buldra, and others. At the intersection of Jáchymova Street and Salvátorská Street large corner houses (Nos. 66, 68, 1068 and 1076) appeared that had been designed by Jan Vejrych in the Bohemian neo-Renaissance style with Art Nouveau ornament. Some time later the neo-Romantic houses (Nos. 97 and 98) between Široká Street and the Old-New Synagogue designed by Richard Klenka of Vlastimil were built. Antonín Engel, František Weyr and Bohumil Hypšman later designed the houses Nos. 36, 37 and 40 in the nearby streets conceived in the style of individualistic Modernism.

The wide street Mikulášská, which was the axis of the new district, brought about the idea of building a general axis road of Prague passing through Old Town Square to Můstek (lower part of Wenceslas Square), along Wenceslas Square and, on the other side, to the north on a bridge across the Vltava, through a cutting in Letná Park up to the north side of Letná Square. This is what Jan Koula planned in 1897 to express symbolically the nation's history from the National Museum in the south to a future palace of the Czech Diet and Government (there was no doubt about the country's acquiring independence very soon) in the northern part of Letná Square. In accordance with Koula's plan a steel bridge named after Svatopluk Čech was built from 1906 to 1908 which was a continuation of Mikulášská Street and which was to be followed on the other side of the river by a sunken road up to Letná Park.

The Old Town rehabilitation was the largest town-development scheme of the late 19th century in Prague. As a result, a part of the centre of the town was rebuilt, although to a smaller extent than the redevelopment of the centre of Paris by Prefect Haussmann, or that in Vienna, Berlin, and other large European cities where the old medieval and Renaissance parts practically disappeared. Vilém Mrštík in his article "Bestia triumphans" condemned the thoughtless destruction of ancient buildings and thus initiated a movement that hindered a general demolition and reconstruction of the Old Town and the Lesser Quarter.

Rebuilding in the Old Town

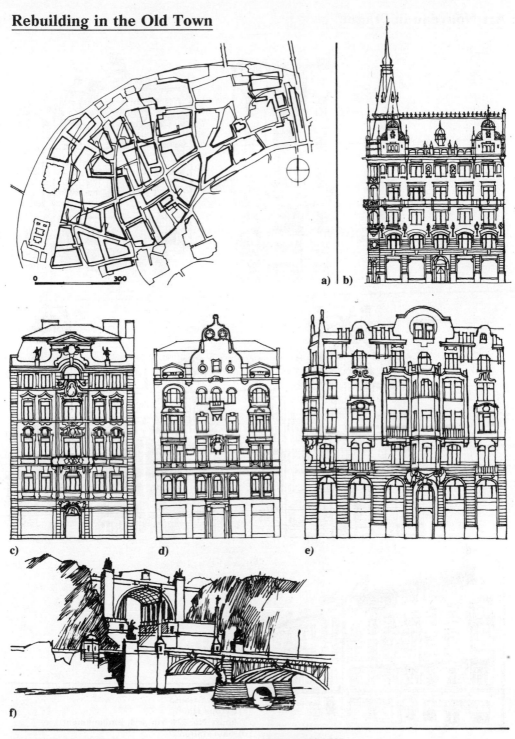

a) **redevelopment plan**
b) **house No. 68** (former trade association Merkur)
c) **house No. 1073**
d) **house No. 205**
e) **house No. 131**
f) **plan of Letná cutting** (J. Koula, 1907)

Art Nouveau in Prague

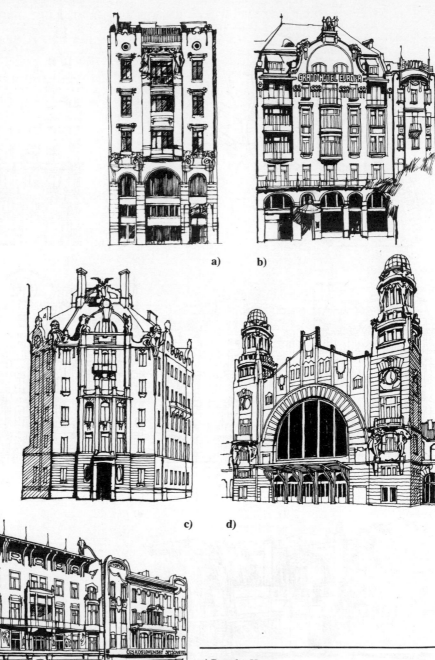

a) **Peterka House**
b) **Evropa Hotel**
c) **house No. 224, Masaryk Embankment**
d) **main station**
e) **house No. 1011** (former Prague Insurance Company)
and house No. 1010 (Czechoslovak Writers' House, former Topič Publishing House)

The era of historicism, i.e., imitation of historic architecture came to an end in the late 1890s, and soon the stage of eclecticism ended as well. Naturalistic motifs, mostly vegetable were increasingly applied and finally prevailed. At the same time, some elements were changing and gradually disappearing, such as columns and pilasters, consoles and cornices, the façades became coherent, with some isolated ornamentation, such as leaves and flowers, faces and figures of young women. Natural stone was used, as well as glass and coloured ceramics, and buildings were crowned with curved gables. A quite new architectural style developed which has been called in this country "secese" (German "Sezession" or "Jugendstil", French "Art Nouveau"), the late 19th century decorative style.

An important representative of the transition from historicism to the Art Nouveau was Bedřich Ohmann, professor at the School of Decorative Arts in Prague, native of Lvov in the Ukraine, who until 1889 had studied and worked in Vienna. He began by designing neo-Baroque buildings: the former Walter Palace in Voršilská Street (No. 12/140) from 1891 and what is now the Patent and Invention Office, No. 823, at the corner of Wenceslas Square and Jindřišská Street, from 1895. His work continued with a neo-Baroque rebuilding of the Music Theatre at Karlín, No. 283, from 1896, as well as with the house "U české orlice" (At the Bohemian Eagle), No. 15/356, Celetná Street, and the former Štorch House, No. 16/552, Old Town Square, conceived in a specific Bohemian neo-Renaissance style and built in 1897. He was the first in this country to create Art Nouveau façades, in the café Corso of 1898 in the street Na příkopě (later demolished), and from 1899 to 1901 in the Central Hotel, No. 10/1001, Hybernská Street (built by Quido Bělský). Unfortunately, the portals of the hotel and the theatre hall (now Komorní Theatre) were rebuilt and modernized in 1923 by Petr Kropáček.

Soon afterwards, in 1899 Jan Kotěra, Ohmann's successor at UMPRUM (School of Decorative Arts), built the house No. 12/72, Wenceslas Square (originally called Peterka House), whose sober and unusual Art Nouveau decoration was the work of Josef Pekárek and Stanislav Sucharda. The striking plain façade and the unusual internal layout expressed the hierarchy of particular features of architectural work postulated by Kotěra, namely purpose, structure, and then form.

The façade of the two buildings of the Evropa Hotel, Nos. 825 and 826, is very sumptuous. It was designed by Alois Dryák and Bedřich Bendelmayer in 1906, and the arcades of the café mezzanine were obviously inspired by Kotěra's building. The Art Nouveau also influenced older architects who until that time had imitated historic styles. Osvald Polívka designed in 1902—1903 the great building of a department store called "U Nováků", No. 30/699, Vodičkova Street, with a sales hall two storeys high and reminiscent, on a smaller scale, of halls in the department stores of Paris. In the centre of its façade there was a figural mosaic, an allegory of Trade and Industry after a cartoon by Jan Preisler. The same architect made renovation plans for the former insurance company and Topič's Publishing House, No. 79/1011—1010, Národní Avenue, conceived in a richly decorated Art Nouveau style. The ceramic reliefs and statues on the gable were made by Ladislav Šaloun.

Among the many eclectic tenement houses on Masaryk Embankment some important examples of Art Nouveau architecture can be found. Jiří Stibral built the corner house No. 32/224 with sculptural decoration by Ladislav Šaloun, Kamil Hilbert designed the house No. 26/234 in a combination of the Romantic style and Art Nouveau, Matěj Blech made the luxury apartment block, No. 28/235, and the vocal ensemble Hlahol had their house No. 248 built here, designed by Josef Fanta, with sculptural decoration on the façade by Josef Pekárek, a mosaic in the gable representing "Music", and ornamental decoration by Karel Mottl.

Art Nouveau is also the style of Prague's main station, No. 300, designed by Josef Fanta and built from 1901 to 1909. Fanta's concept was originally a modernized version of the Renaissance style and won the first prize in the competition for the railway station, but was then gradually altered. The central hall for passengers, flanked by two towers terminating in crystal glass cupolas, has a large semicircular window above the wide entrance which is covered with a projecting roof supported by an iron structure with Art Nouveau forms. The sculptural decoration in the hall was made by František Kraumann, J. Pikart, J. Šimanovský, the statues on the façade and the towers were by Stanislav Sucharda and Hanuš Folkmann. The symmetrical lower wings with service rooms for passengers are closed with office buildings and their towers; the towers bear clocks and are decorated with sculptures by Čeněk Vosmík. A new architectural element in Prague was the large two-aisled steel hall disigned by the engineers Marjanek and Kornfeld.

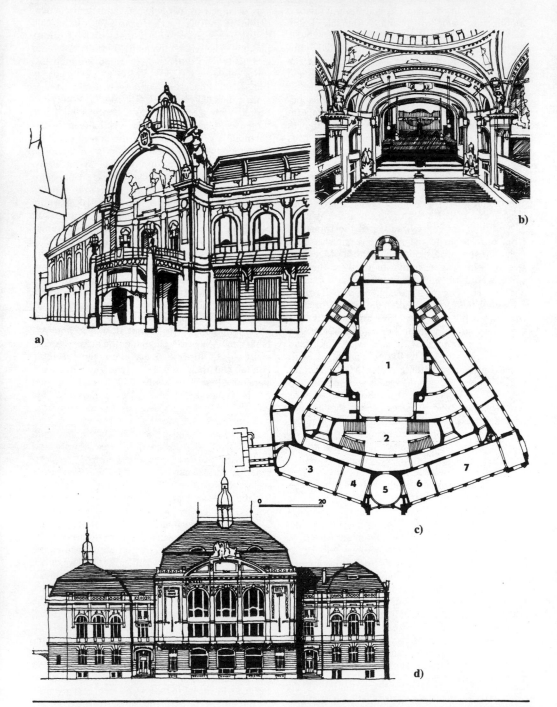

a) b) **Community House**
d) **House of Culture of Metalworkers** (former National House)

c) **plan of first floor:** 1 Smetana Hall, 2 foyer, 3 "Besední" Hall, 4 Palacký Hall, 5 Mayor's Hall, 6 Rieger Hall, 7 Lecture Hall

Due to the boom in industrial production our towns grew considerably in the last decade of the 19th century, particularly Prague where the number of inhabitants exceeded half a million, which corresponds to an increase of more than 25 per cent. The standard of living and the needs of people increased, too. Profiting from the economic development of industry and trade were also the municipal councils, which made it possible to construct technical and social facilities in towns, such as the buildings called community or national houses intended for theatre performances, dancing, balls, concerts, ceremonies, feasts, and other forms of social life. There were also, of course, cafés and restaurants.

Next to the Powder Tower, on the site of the former King's Court, where in the Middle Ages Bohemian kings, from Wenceslas IV to Vladislav Jagiello had lived and which was converted into a barracks in the 18th century, a Community House for the City of Prague was built from 1905 to 1911 (No. 1090) by the Municipal Council of the City. The house was conceived in the Art Nouveau Style by Antonín Balšánek and Osvald Polívka who had won an open competition organized in 1903. Their winning idea was based on a symmetrical design along the diagonal of a rhombic site covering an area of 4,200 m². The Smetana Hall, which is the central room of the building, is situated in the middle of the first floor on this axis, and can accommodate 1,500 seated visitors. Under the hall, on the ground floor, there is a large central cloakroom, and around the edges of the first floor there are various social rooms, meeting rooms and gambling areas, while on the ground floor beneath them are a large café and a restaurant, and in the basement a beer lounge and a wine bar. The attic storey contains top-lit exhibition halls.

The house is crowned with a dome, and the arched gable of the main façade, flanked with statues by Ladislav Šaloun, contains a mosaic "Homage to Prague" by Karel Špillar. The sculptural decoration of the façade and the statues of torch-bearers in the corners of the projecting roof above the entrance are by Karel Novák, the statues on the side walls are by Antonín Mára, Josef Mařatka and František Uprka. The figure of Matěj Rejsek at the corner near the Powder Tower was made by Čeněk Vosmík. The stage in the Smetana Hall is flanked by sculptures "Bohemian Dances" and "Vyšehrad" by Šaloun, the balcony walls are embellished with pictures "Music", "Dance", "Poetry" and "Drama" by Karel Špillar, the dome of the hall has figural paintings by František Ženíšek and reliefs by Václav Novák. The rooms on the first floor are decorated with paintings by Alfons Mucha, Max Švabinský, Josef Ullmann, František Ženíšek and Jan Preisler, and with statues by Josef Václav Myslbek and Emanuel Hallmann. The statue of Josef Hlávka on the gallery of the second floor was made by Josef Mařatka. The café on the ground floor is enlivened by a fountain by Josef Pekárek, the beer lounge and the wine bar in the basement are adorned with paintings by Mikoláš Aleš and with ceramics by Jakub Obrovský, Jaroslav Panuška, Václav Jansa and Roman Havelka. The interiors have a stylistic harmony, including the inlaid floors, stained glass windows, staircase railings, window and door fittings, elevator grilles, marble and wooden polished wall-lining.

The Smetana Hall witnessed a number of important events. In January 1918 Czech and Moravian MPs adopted the so-called Epiphany Declaration here demanding an independent Czechoslovak state.

In 1907—1908, the National House of Smíchov was built on the Square of 14th October, No. 82, which is now the Metal Workers' House of Culture. The house, conceived in the Art Nouveau style and designed by Alois Čenský, together with the parallel market-hall, encloses a restaurant garden with a music pavillon and covered side sections. The clear and quite simple layout of the house starts with the staircase hall surrounded by an arcaded gallery on the first floor. The ground floor contains a restaurant and a café, the first floor has a small and a great hall with a stage, and there are also several meeting-rooms. The sculpture on the exterior, a group of statues in the gable of the main façade facing Zborovská Street, was made by Josef Pekárek, the terms on the main staircase by Antonín Mára.

The National House of Karlín, No. 10, Hybešova Street was built by Josef Sakař in 1910—1911. The house is now a music studio of the Czechoslovak Radio. The flat ornamental detail on the façade is a sort of post-Art-Nouveau neo-Classicism. The building, standing in a garden, has large projecting sections; it is articulated in steps and has a mansard roof with gables and dormer-windows. Inside, behind the entrance is a three-flight staircase, and on the ground floor there used to be a restaurant, a café and a gambling-room, as well as a bowling alley and two verandahs surmounted with terraces. The basement contained a popular restaurant and a wine bar. On the first floor, there is a great hall with a stage, and a small hall, and on the second a gallery for the great hall and various meeting-rooms. There was a garden restaurant for 2,000 visitors, and a theatre was to have been built in the garden. The conversion to a studio of the Czechoslovak Radio has necessitated considerable rebuilding inside.

By the mid-1960s most of the technical infrastructure of the Community House was very outmoded and worn out. The State Institute for Renovation of Historic Towns and Buildings, namely its Centre 08 headed by František Soukup was charged with the task of a study and a project of general renovation and modernization of this important cultural building. In 1969, it was decided to divide the renovation into three stages, as it was impossible to put this cultural centre out of operation for five years. For this reason the axial character of the layout with two side stairs was used; incidentally, both the right and the left sides of the building have catering facilities. The axis includes the entrance, the hall, and the Smetana Hall.

The first stage of renovation included the left-hand side next to the Powder Tower, as this part was more dilapidated and had better access from the street U Prašné brány. The second stage envisaged the construction of a gas-fired boiler house in the basement and in the central part of the roof, and a renovation of the Smetana Hall. The third stage included the right-hand part along the street U Obecního domu.

The renovation plan did not foresee any major changes in the layout of the social part. In the exterior, the original windows, shop-windows and entrances were to be respected. A new boiler house and engine room for the heating and ventilation system was built on the roof, wirings and fittings were replaced and modernized, and this was done so that they did not spoil the interior decoration. New service entrances were made and some new facilities added, a snack-bar was built in the street U Prašné brány, lifts were installed, etc. Some alterations were also made in the Smetana Hall where the lighting and the acoustics were improved, the stage was rebuilt and the boxes remodelled. The meeting-rooms on the main social axis were modernized, and all the rich artistic decoration in the house was renovated.

The National House in Smíchov has not so far undergone any major renovation or alteration, and is therefore still an intact example of the Art Nouveau style applied to a social building.

The National House in Karlín, on the other hand, underwent a large-scale adaptation in the 1960s when, in particular, the original social halls were converted into studios for the Czechoslovak Radio, lost their original form and ceased to be accessible to the public.

New Villas

The detached family house is an architectural type that directly reflects the way of life and the philosophy of the customer. In the mid-19th century, a class of people emerged in Britain, the most highly developed country of that time, who had a new concept of the dwelling-house and its interior furnishings, seeing their ideal in plainness, solidity and comfort. The movement postulated a return to natural materials, sought inspiration and models in folk architecture, required shapes dictated by the purpose, material and structure, and rejected any useless decoration. This meant a departure from the then prevailing ideal of the Italian Renaissance villa as it had developed in the 19th century neo-Renaissance period.

The new concepts and trends came to this country via western countries with some modifications. The 1895 Ethnographic Exhibition in Prague contributed considerably to the general interest in folk architecture. The first architectural work conceived in the spirit of the new philosophy was the afore-mentioned villa in Bubeneč by Koula from 1896. Another step in this direction was made by Jan Kotěra in his Trmal House in Prague, No. 11/91, Vilová Street, Strašnice District. The villa was built in 1902—1903, and consequently followed the principles of folk architecture. More freedom in meeting modern needs and artistic requirements was applied by Kotěra in his next work, a villa and atelier for the sculptor Stanislav Sucharda in Bubeneč District, No. 1/248, 628, Slavíčkova Street, from 1904. Quite unusual in concept is the large detached house in Bubeneč District, No. 4/284, Suchardova Street, designed by Dušan Jurkovič and built in 1907, which is a typical Nordic type of structure with compact mass and a steep roof.

The transition to individualistic Modernism,

New Villas

a)

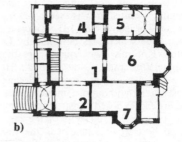

b)

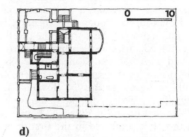

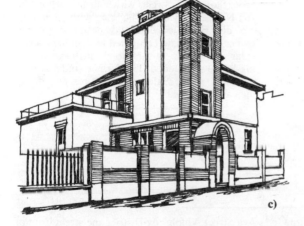

c)

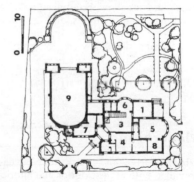

d)

e)   f)

a) b) **No. 4/284, Suchardova Street** (by Jurkovič)
c) d) **Jan Kotěra's own villa, No. 6/1542, Hradešínská Street**

e) f) **sculptor Sucharda's villa, No. 6/248, Slavíčkova Street** (by Jan Kotěra): 1 room, 2 hallway, 3 hall, 4 kitchen, 5 dining-room, 6 living-room, 7 library, 8 music room, 9 studio

which was the next stage in the evolution of Prague architecture, is seen in the villa in Prague-Zbraslav, No. 135, Žitavského Street, from 1908 which was designed by Otakar Novotný. Kotěra's own house from that time, in Prague-Vinohrady, No. 6/1542, Hradešínská Street, is already in a mature Modern style, almost totally without ornamentation and displaying instead exposed construction materials.

A typical new element in the interior introduced here at that time was the staircase hall linking the ground floor with the bedrooms upstairs; there were also a bathroom, a cloakroom and built-in wardrobes. This meant a functional differentiation of the layout. The dwelling-house was linked to the garden by means of a terrace paved with quarried stone, with grass between the stones. In the garden was a pergola, a lawn with scattered groups of flowers, shrubs and trees, and a water-pool situated off the axis.

The first groups of detached houses conceived in this style appeared in the first decade of the present century on the slopes above Smíchov, Na Hřebenkách and Na Václavce. The sloping ground did not allow the application of the traditional grid plan of streets, and the streets were therefore oblique, some being linked by steps, others rising diagonally or going up and then down. Between 1910 and 1912, Viktor Beneš built a residence on a headland above Košíře which included his own house, No. 1258, a villa for his brother, No. 1285, a house for the gardener, and some outbuildings. The complex recalls former aristocratic palaces and was a dominant point that could be clearly seen from the right bank of the river.

František Bílek, a sculptor, designed a house with an atelier for himself (No. 1/233, Mickiewiczova Street) which was built in 1911 and was an unusual work, something like a symbolic sculpture, with a segmental mass of exposed brickwork, moulded concrete columns and a massive flat roof. Today, there is an exhibition of Bílek's sculptures as part of the Gallery of the City of Prague.

The studio of Ladislav Šaloun, a sculptor and a National Artist, in Vinohrady District, No. 1566, Slovenská Street, was built in 1910 in the Art Nouveau style. The building with an adjoining decorative garden was designed by the owner himself, and contained two ateliers, a circular study and a "rustic room"; in 1934, a dwelling-house was added. The former studio is now a gallery where Šaloun's sculptures and drawings are exhibited.

Modernism

In the early 20th century Art Nouveau totally prevailed both in the exterior and interior design of houses, including the furniture, wall-paintings, etc., and developed into a unified general style. Its characteristic vegetable and flower motifs, were later replaced by geometrical shapes: spiral, elliptical, rectangular lines, etc. This "geometrical" Art Nouveau then developed at the end of the first decade into the "individualist Modern Style", losing its ornamentation and displaying structural materials, such as exposed brickwork, concrete, plaster and structural steel. In architectural discourse the free layout of mass as a result of a free and functional organization of the interior became more and more apparent.

Owners of publishing houses and other institutions of art in Prague gave much freedom to the architects building houses for them and allowed them to apply the most progressive trends in architecture. Jan Kotěra designed in 1908 a house for the publisher Jan Laichter, No. 1543, Chopinova Street, Vinohrady District, the street front of which was shaped according to the purpose of the particular rooms. There was no longer any sculptural decoration, and the wall featured different bonds of brickwork instead. In 1909—1910, Kotěra's student and collaborator, Otakar Novotný, designed a house for the photographer Jan Štenc, No. 8/931, Salvátorská Street, in the Old Town of Prague, with a flat and plain façade displaying exposed brickwork and crowned with the arched windows of the photographic studio. Mojmír Urbánek, a music publisher, invited Kotěra in 1911 to build a house with concert hall, called the Mozarteum. The house No. 30/745, Jungmannova Street has a façade of exposed brickwork, displaying the supporting verticals meeting horizontal beams. There was only one elongated office window on the first floor while the ground floor was adorned with two female figures made of stone by Jan Štursa.

Modernism

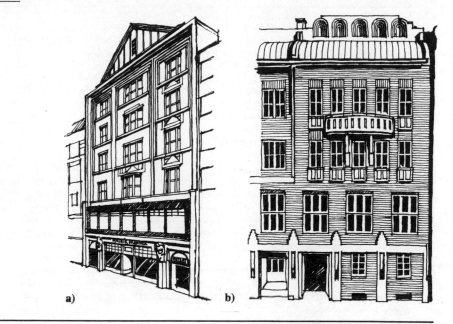

a) **Urbánek House** (Mozarteum)
b) **Štenc House**
c) **Koruna House**
d) **house No. 795**

Modernism

Kotěra also designed the big building No. 42/390 on Rašínovo Embankment built in 1912—1913, which now houses the State Pension Office. The furnishings were designed by Kotěra's friend Josef Zasche. The façade of the building, displaying the granite ground floor while the two upper floors are plastered and painted in colours of different tone, proved that Modernism was able to create monumental architecture.

North of Hradčany, on a site where there had previously been Baroque fortifications, an orphanage was built in 1913 by the Municipal Council. The house No. 220 was designed by Josef Rosipal, who was later killed in the First World War. The white prism of the house, with a flat roof and featuring on all sides a regular network of large windows, anticipated the future evolution of modern architecture.

The boom in Prague in those years necessitated the construction of a series of multipurpose buildings in the centre of the town. In 1911, the Koruna Building was constructed at the corner of Wenceslas Square and Na příkopě Street (No. 846). The house, designed by Antonín Pfeiffer, has three lower storeys almost without any massive construction between the large windows. The basement contains baths with a swimming pool, and the neighbouring streets are connected at ground floor level by a spacious passageway. It became a model of other buildings in the neighbourhood.

The largest of this group of buildings were the Rokoko House (Nos. 794, 795) and the Lucerna House (No. 704) at the corner of Wenceslas Square and Štěpánská Street, with one wing reaching Vodičkova Street. The complex was built from 1912 to 1916 by the building contractors Matěj Blecha and Václav Havel. There are seven storeys above the ground and four basements, with a passageway on the ground floor, lit through the ceiling and lined with shops and a snack bar; a large cinema, a dancing-hall, offices, clubrooms and flats on the upper floors, and studios at the top which gave the house its characteristic external motif. The basements contain a restaurant, a bar, and what was then the largest social hall in Prague with two galleries. The reinforced concrete structure with suspended ceilings as a new element was designed by Stanislav Bechyně. The appearance of the two buildings is different, and both also depart considerably from the general spirit of Prague architecture, recalling rather buildings in western Europe or overseas. The architectural authorship of the complex is not quite clear. The scale of the buildings was very large at that time, they were quite new elements in the townscape and have remained dominant buildings in the centre of Prague until now.

Cubism

At the end of the first decade of the 20th century new trends in the arts, particularly painting, came into this country, mostly from France: Expressionism, Fauvism, and then Cubism. Remembering the integration of the fine arts and architecture in the Art Nouveau period, our architects wanted to carry this integration over to the new situation. Cubist painting was characterized by a pattern of oblique lines and by dramatic contrasts of light and shadow. Tired of what they saw as the monotony of Modernist rationalism in design, Czech architects confronted the challenge of Cubist painting by creating unusual façades with a system of broken surfaces, on many planes, articulated by diagonal and radiating lines, creating striking boundaries between areas of light and shadow. As a result, a specific Czech branch of Cubist architecture developed.

At the corner of Celetná Street and Ovocný trh (Fruit Market), in place of an old house of the Granovský Knights that had been called The House of the Black Mother of the Lord, No. 19/569, a four-storey house crowned with two receding mansard storeys was built in 1911—1912 after a plan by Josef Gočár. There was a café on the first floor which was frequented by artists, particularly painters and sculptors, and the upper floors contained offices with free and arbitrarily divisible spaces. The reinforced concrete structure made it possible to open up the façade fully by means of large windows. This work by Gočár, with fine Cubist details as well as a general Cubist concept, well suited its historic surroundings and inspired much sympathy among Prague's citizens for the new style. The house "Diamant" at the corner of Spálená and Lazarská Streets, No. 82, designed by Emil Králíček and built by Matěj Blecha in 1912, has small-scale Cubist details that were more or less used only for surface decoration.

Cubism

a)

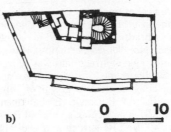

b)

0   10

d)

c)

e)

a) b) **House U černé matky Boží** (Black Mother of the
Lord)
c) **house No. 98, Neklanova Street**
d) **villa No. 49, Libušina Street**
e) **house No. 124, E. Krásnohorské Street**

The most radical examples of Cubist architecture were made in 1911—1913 by Josef Chochol under the Vyšehrad. They included a corner dwelling-house, No. 30/98, Neklanova Street, where the acute angle of street lines was reflected by plain wedge-shaped front surfaces and a boldly projecting cornice, a group of three connected houses on Rašínovo Embankment, Nos. 42, 47, 71, and in particular, a villa in Libušina Street, No. 49, with its garden and wall also conceived in the Cubist style. In these buildings the breaking down of the surface and the dynamic game of light and shadow on the façade have increased still further. Chochol's buildings were major works of art of international importance. Realized in brickwork, they intuitively anticipated the fractured surfaces of reinforced concrete shell systems fifty years after.

Despite the great variety and intellectual sophistication of his sketches Vlastimil Hofman was unfortunately only able to realize the entrance pavilions and walls of the cemetery at Ďáblice in 1912 and a Cubist column with a lantern on Jungmann Square in 1913. His authorship of the latter has not been confirmed and it may have been made by Emil Králíček, who also designed the neighbouring house and Adam's Pharmacy on Wenceslas Square.

A rather late, but formally sophisticated type of Cubist architecture is that of a number of cooperative blocks of houses, Nos. 10—14, Elišky Krásnohorské Street, realized from 1919 to 1921 and designed by Otakar Novotný. Anticipating a new post-war movement in our architecture the houses featured, unlike the deliberately colourless Cubist architecture, a harmony of bright colours on plastered façades and painted wooden and metal fittings.

Architecture between the Two World Wars

This era in the history of architecture was inspired by the avant-garde movement in several European countries at the end of the First World War. They all showed a common aim: a rational programme of new free forms, a rethinking of layout and plan, a new role and social function for architecture, and the application of modern construction materials and structures. In France it was the purism of the architect Le Corbusier and the painter Amédé Ozenfant, in Germany the Bauhaus School in Weimar, in the Netherlands the De Stijl movement, in the Soviet Union the programme of Constructivism, and in Czechoslovakia the group of people around the review Stavba. In the early 1930s, they all amalgamated by creating a common programme of functionalism which added to the formal and technical aspects of architecture the questions of its spacial and functional economy, and made all aspects of architectural production subject to scientific research. Architectural work was proclaimed to be an organization of life processes in the biological, social, technical, economic and psychological senses, and its progress was seen as inseparable from social conditions.

The principles of functional architecture were declared at the 1928 International Congress of Modern Architecture (CIAM) which postulated a universal form of dwelling for all and defined the main functions of the town: dwelling, work, recreation. The same was incorporated in the Athens Charter of 1933.

Modern architecture in Czechoslovakia was initially, in the early 1920s, linked with the avant-garde group Devětsil and, in the mid-1920s, with progressive groups of architects, among whom two general trends could be observed: the first based on rational cognition of purpose and function, and the second starting from the artistic concept of space and form. A Union of Socialist Architects was founded in 1932 whose activity focused on the scientific methods of preparing architectural concepts, the collectivization of design work and the industrialization of building technology.

The one-sided rational conception of Functionalism between the two world wars brought about in the late 1930s critical theories of psychoplasticity (i.e., design based on spiritual creativity), trends of traditionalism and continuity with folk and national art-history. Also, interest in architectural monuments and their preservation increased.

The first trends to appear after the First World War were based on traditional concepts of architecture, and flourished in the 1920s.

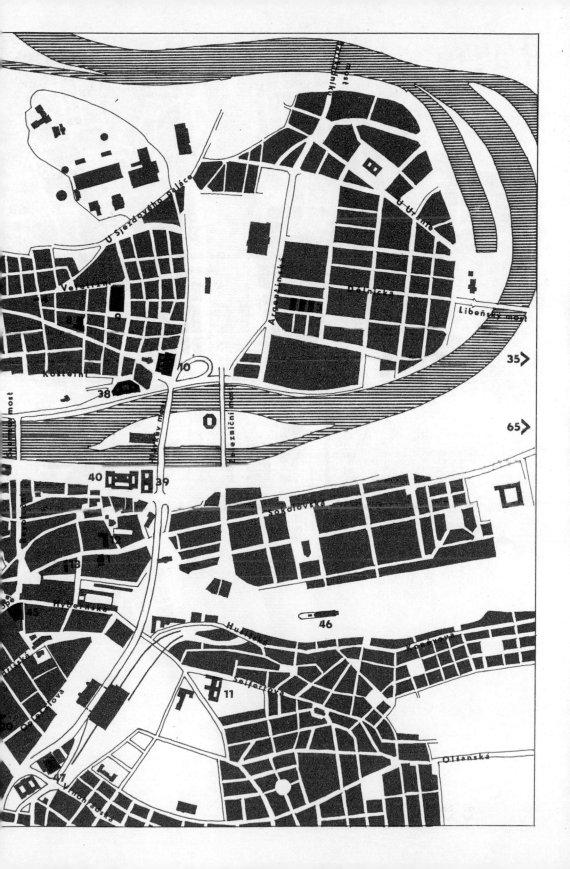

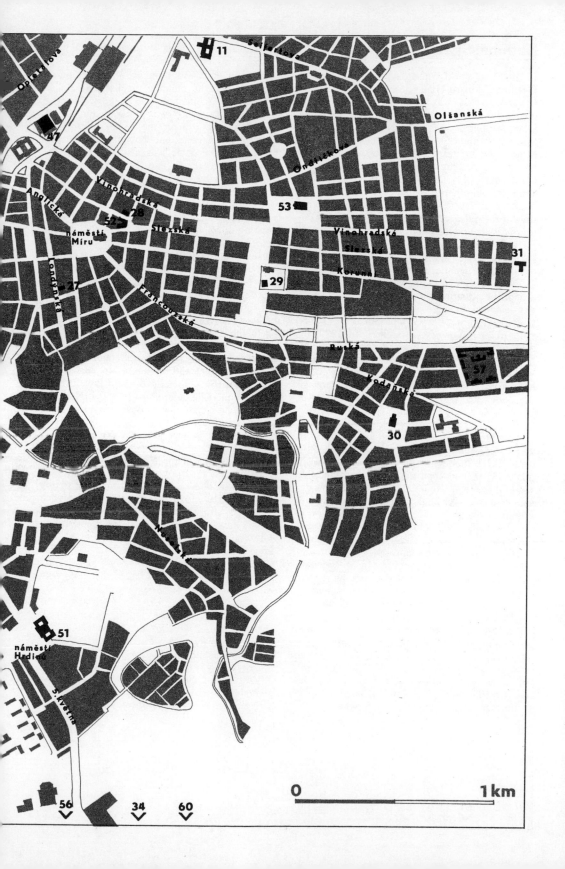

Opatovova

11

Seifertova

Olšanská

47

Vinohradská

Anglická

28

52

náměstí
Míru

Slezská

53

Vinohradská

Slezská

31

Londýnská

27

29

Korunní

Francouzská

Ruská

Kodaňská

57

Nuselská

30

51

náměstí
Hrdinů

5.května

0   1 km

56   34   60

National Style

The First World War ended with the defeat of Germany, Austro-Hungary and their allies, and Czechoslovakia was given its national sovereignty. Folklore became very popular, including folk costumes, painted Easter eggs, painted Moravian and Slovakian portals, decorated Moravian cottages, etc. This also strongly influenced the fine arts, such as the paintings and decorations by František Kysela, Vratislav Hugo Brunner, and others. In architecture, sharp edges, points and grey render were proclaimed as symbols of the defeated Germanism while bright colours and roundness were attributed to the victorious Slavs. Cubism was over, and a colourful "National Style" appeared that was later sometimes called "Rondocubism".

The first sign of the new style in Prague was a department store, No. 8, Street of 28th October, designed in 1920 by Rudolf Stockar, but which was in fact the work of Gočár and Janák, who frequently worked together. In 1921, Josef Gočár realized a temporary exhibition pavilion for the artists' group Mánes in a courtyard in Vodičkova Street, and two decorative wooden houses at the national airport of Kbely (now in the Zoological Garden at Troja, No. 120). Pavel Janák designed in the same year a detached house at Hodkovičky. A common feature of their architecture were semicircles and dentils, in white, red, and blue. As Gočár's fantastic "ancient Slavic" plan for bridging over the street Na můstku (1922) was not realized, a representative work of the then "National Style" became his design of the former Banka čs. legií (Czechoslovak Legion Bank, now Czech Ministry of Industry) in the street Na poříčí, No. 24/1046, built between 1921 and 1923. The red and white façade, robustly articulated, and the semicircular profiled window arches recall ancient Russian architecture. The sculptural decoration of the building is quite unique, with sculptures between the windows by Jan Štursa and with a frieze with figures of soldiers by Otto Gutfreund. In the former bank hall the architect succeeded in combining folk ornamentation with the bold modern layout.

The Adria Palace, No. 36, at the corner of Národní (National) Avenue and Jungmannova Street, designed from 1923 to 1925 by Pavel Janák (together with Josef Zasche), has a colourful stone façade typical of that time, while on the other hand, the layout of mass and the sculptural decoration of the building recalls early Italian Renaissance architecture. The allegorical bronze sculpture "Sea faring" was made by Jan Štursa, the other sculptures are the work of Otto Gutfreund, Karel Dvořák and Bohumil Kafka.

The National Style was also applied in the early 1920s to the façades of dwelling-houses. Otakar Novotný gave the house No. 811, Kamenická Street, Prague-Letná a conspicuous façade; Rudolf Hrabě designed in 1921 a group of free-standing municipal blocks of flats with interesting forms and colours in Jateční Street, Holešovice District, as well as a number of houses with small flats conceived in the same style and surrounding a garden courtyard, Nos. 611—610, Rooseveltova Street, Dejvice District.

Older façades in the centre of Prague were at that time reworked "in the latest style", such as the house No. 782, on Wenceslas Square, belonging to the confectioner Juliš (designed by Pavel Janák and later pulled down), the house No. 710, Vodičkova Street, for the confectioner Myšák (by Josef Čapek), and the house No. 33/99, Spálená Street (by Tomáš Pražák and Pavel Moravec). Manneristic adaptations in the National Style can be seen in many houses from that time, particularly those built by housing cooperatives in the districts Dejvice, Bubeneč, Vinohrady and Žižkov.

Repercussions of the National Style can also be seen in the then popular garden suburbs also built on a cooperative basis. Their construction began in 1919—1920 with a group of detached houses in Strašnice District designed by Josef Gočár, Pavel Janák and František Zavadil who had won the competition for the area. The "Clerks' Housing Estate" built in 1920 in Dejvice by Rudolf Hrabě and František Novák (recently demolished) had rows of detached houses with colourful plastered façades and framed construction, and there were also architecturally interesting kindergarten and central laundry pavilions. The houses with wooden façades and plastered gable brickwork were designed by Václav Ložek. The estate was followed by the construction of real garden estates in the early 1920s: Ořechovka in Střešovice (Jaroslav Vondrák, Pavel Janák, etc.), Pernikářka, Šumava, Cibulka, Na Václavce above Košíře, among others.

National Style

a)

c)

b)

d)

---

a) b) **Czech Ministry of Industry** (former Banka čs. legií)
c) **house in Tusarova Street**
d) **Adria Palace, detail**

With the creation of the Czechoslovak Republic a new need emerged in its capital Prague: to create new government buildings. This provided a new challenge for Czechoslovak architects, and the problem required the architect to take on great responsibility. This was probably the reason why those who were invited to deal with the task, once representatives of pre-war Modernism in architecture, were now seeking models for their work within historical tradition without trying to develop new forms, as occurred later, at the end of the 1920s.

The first steps towards the solution of the problem were competitions in 1920, with the aim of finding the best projects for ministerial buildings in Petrská District, Letná Park and Dejvice Valley. After the winning projects of the first competition two large "palaces" were built from 1927 to 1931: the Ministry of Railways, No. 1222, designed by Antonín Engel and with sculptural decoration by Josef Pekárek and Josef Mařatka, and the Ministry of Agriculture, Forestry and Water by František Roith with sculptures by Jaroslav Brůha and Karel Štipl. A third building, the Ministry of Public Works by Bohumil Hypšman, was not realized.

None of the projects from the second competition concerned with the development of Letná Square were carried out. On the other hand, Dejvice Valley was developed as of 1921 according to a scheme by Antonín Engel. Three wide radial avenues were planned, meeting at Vítězné (Victory) Square, a large circus surrounded by blocks of flats with façades conceived in a similar style. An exception to this was the building of Military Administration designed by Antonín Pfeiffer, with a façade by A. Engel. Adjoining the circus is also the complex of buildings of the Czech Technical University whose general plan, including the façades was by A. Engel. Of the six street blocks, however, only one third was realized by 1936 (Nos. 1903, 1905). Engel's verticalizing architecture, which also includes the waterworks in Podolí, No. 15, from 1929—1939 and further developed from 1959 to 1962, was characterized by a simplified transformation of neo-Classical vocabulary.

The Ministry of Agriculture, No. 65, and the Municipal Library, No. 98, Mariánské Square in the Old Town, built from 1926 to 1930 by František Roith are less historicizing and make a greater attempt to fit in among the 17th century palaces in Prague, displaying the mass of the walls and the horizontal cornices in their façades.

Even greater efforts in this direction were applied by Bohumil Hypšman in his large complex of ministerial buildings, Nos. 375—376, built from 1924 to 1929 on Palacký Square, New Town, under Emmaus Abbey. The façades, mostly flat and with pantile roofs tend programmatically to express a sense of old Prague. This traditional form is also featured in the building of the Faculty of Law, Charles University, No. 901, originally designed by Jan Kotěra in 1914, but realized much later, in 1928—1929. Kotěra's plan was modernized and simplified by Ladislav Machoň.

In the garden of George of Poděbrady Square (náměstí Jiřího z Poděbrad) the Catholic Church of the Holy Heart of the Lord was built from 1929 to 1932 by Josip Plečnik who was inspired by ancient Christian architecture. The church is not only a dominant building on the square, but one of the major landmarks in the townscape as well. The interior hall space, 26 by 38 m and 13 m high, appears as a prism if seen from the outside with its lower two thirds lined with vitrified bricks, the top third being a white-plastered band with a rhythmical sequence of windows. On the east side, another prism rises, namely that of the tower, which is similarly shaped, 42 m tall, and has a clock in a circular window of 7.6 m diameter. The sculptural decoration in the interior was made by Damián Pešan.

Rather archaic buildings, departing from the character of Prague's architecture, are the Ministry of Mechanical Engineering, No. 1039, on the embankment Na Františku, made by Josef Fanta in 1932—1933 and conceived in a compilation of styles based on the Art Nouveau, with decorative details and with perhaps too many statues by Čeněk Vosmík and Josef Paukert, and the Philosophical Faculty of Charles University, No. 1, Jan Palach Square, by Josef Sakař from 1928—1929 with a robust façade articulated by pairs of travertine Tuscan semi-columns. Ladislav Kofránek incorporated various motifs on the voussoirs of the first floor windows.

Traditionalism

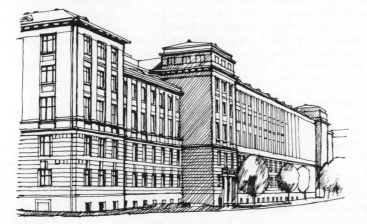

a)

b)   c)

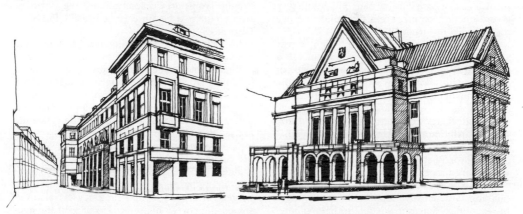

d)

a) **Ministry of Transport**
b) **Municipal Library**

c) **Faculty of Law, Charles University**
d) **municipal waterworks, Podolí**

Constructivism

The villas designed in Vienna in the early 20th century by Adolf Loos, a native of Brno, and Josef Chochol's sketches of Prague from 1914—1919 anticipated the postwar ideas of Soviet Constructivism and French Purism that penetrated into this country in the early 1920s. The common motto of all these efforts was as follows: "Decoration is no longer possible, the form of building is to be determined by its structure." In this country at that time, this meant reinforced concrete.

In 1924, the Prague Fair Company organized a competition for selected participants for exhibition buildings in Holešovice District, near the Exhibition Grounds. Oldřich Tyl was awarded the first prize for his entry which strictly respected the unity of layout, structure and form. The discipline of his design was highly thought of, and the architect was then invited, together with Josef Fuchs, whose interior plan best fulfilled the given function, to prepare a final plan that was then carried out from 1925 to 1928.

The huge building, No. 530, with eight storeys and two basements, occupying an area of 110 by 60 m and a volume of 250,000 m^3, contained corridors lined on both sides with exhibition rooms for permanent exhibitions, an entrance hall covering all the storeys and surrounded by galleries, and a large courtyard on the ground floor with an exhibition hall. Under the entrance hall, there was a cinema covering two storeys. On the eighth floor, there was a café and a restaurant with a large look-out terrace.

The reinforced concrete ceilings around the building are mostly supported by cantilever beams, which makes it possible to have uninterrupted, 110 m long continuous windows. The façades are absolutely plain, without any sculptural decoration. Four figural reliefs were planned above the main entrance, but not realized. The realization of the project was a significant event in European architecture and was the envy of exponents of Constructivism abroad. As of 1948, when major industrial exhibitions moved to Brno, the house lost its function. Since a fire in 1974 it has been adapted to house collections of modern art from the National Gallery.

The Electric Power Works Building of Prague, No. 1477, which houses the Electric Power Administration, was built north of Hlávka Bridge in 1926—1927 following a competition of invited architects. The winning entry by Adolf Beneš and Josef Kříž, unlike the other plans, did not foresee a block-like structure, but planned a seven-storey cube with a central top-lit hall, covering the full height of the building and with galleries around, adjoined by a couple of five-storey wings. In the corners of the plot and in its rear part there are two-storey buildings with halls and counters for contact with the public. The basement contains baths and a lecture hall with a gallery. The building was clad with white ceramic tiles. Now it houses the administration of Prague Transport Company, and in the rear two-storey part is a health care centre for Prague 7 District.

In 1926—1927, Constructivism became the prevailing style in the centre of Prague. In Spálená Street, on the site of a house called "U bílého beránka" (At the White Lamb) an eight-storey office building, No. 75, designed by Jaromír Krejcar was built, with a cinema and a dancing-hall in the basement. Ludvík Kysela designed the house No. 773, the former Lindt House, with a passage and a glass front wall facing Wenceslas Square. He also made the adjacent Alfa Building (earlier "U Stýblů" house), No. 785, with a shopping passageway, a café and a cinema, the biggest in Prague at that time. Kysela also designed the corner house No. 15/583 on the avenue Na příkopě, with offices, shops and a café, which is now known as the Children's House. Josef Havlíček designed at the same time the Chicago Building, No. 58, on Národní (National) Avenue with shops and offices, and the house No. 645 on Štěpánská Street, the former Habich House, with continuous windows, offices, and with loggia apartments on the top two floors.

Constructivism

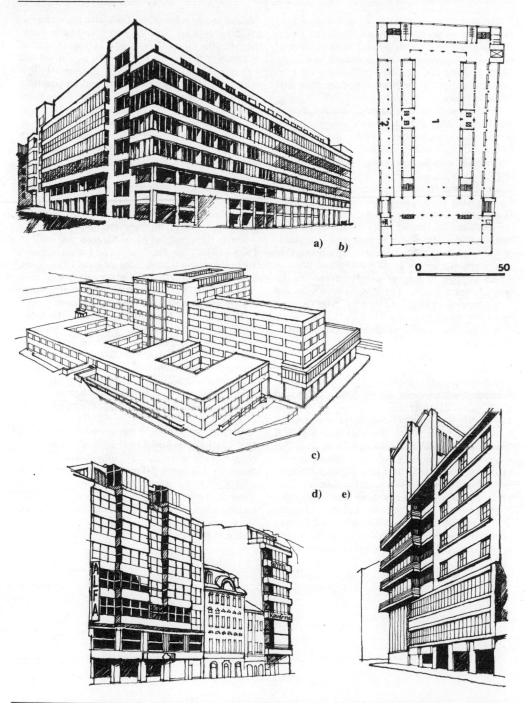

a) b) **Fair Palace:** 1 exhibition hall, 2 shops
c) **Municipal Transport Company Prague**

d) **ALFA** (former Stýblo House) **and Tatran Hotel** (former Juliš Hotel)
e) **House of the Czechoslovak Firemen's Association**

Monumentalism

The word is not intended to define an era in the history of art or any particular trend of architecture, but is meant to characterize several major buildings constructed in Prague in the late 1920s and the early 1930s. The buildings are no longer traditionally decorative nor are they particularly plain.

A forerunner of this concept of architecture was the building of the Military Cartographic Institute in Bubeneč, No. 23/620, Rooseveltova Street, built in 1925 and designed by Bedřich Feuerstein, with an interesting façade, horizontally articulated and repeated around the three-sided building. In corner recesses allegorical female statues representing the rivers Vltava and Danube by Břetislav Benda can be seen. A similar solution was applied to the façade of the Personal Accident Insurance Company (now Ministry of Economy) from 1926 to 1929 on the Embankment of Captain Jaroš by Jaroslav Rössler, which is however more articulated both vertically and horizontally. The figures representing four industries were made by Josef Mařatka, the reliefs by Karel Pokorný.

A very remarkable building with a conspicuous silhouette is that which now houses the State Committee for Development and Coordination of Science and Technology on a headland between the streets Slezská and Vinohradská, Vinohrady District, designed by Josef Gočár and built from 1924 to 1926, with walls of exposed brickwork. Živnostenská banka, the economically strongest bank in Czechoslovakia between the two world wars, built between 1936 and 1938 a massive, technically well-equipped building clad in granite (now the State Bank of Czechoslovakia) at a cross-roads near the Powder Tower. It was designed by František Roith following a competition. The new bank replaced a historicist building from 1898—1901 by Osvald Polívka with a statue by Popp representing the genius with a lion; the statue was used to crown the fa-

çade of the new building. Roith also designed the building of State Savings and Investment Bank, No. 42/796, from 1926—1931 at the corner of Wenceslas Square and Štěpánská Street, on the site of a former renowned beer brewery "U Primasů". Its façade, granite-faced and horizontally articulated, culminates in the middle of the front facing the square. The Stock Exchange Building, which is now part of the Federal Assembly of Czechoslovakia (i.e., Parliament), was built from 1936 to 1938 to a design by Jaroslav Rössler. The granite façade articulated with massive-pillars had an entrance flanked by two allegorical male bronze figures representing "Industry" and "Trade" by Vincenc Makovský.

A relatively modest building is the Crematorium of Prague at the east end of Vinohradská Avenue, designed by Alois Mezera and built in 1929—1930. The courtyard lined with arcades and columbaria is closed by the cube of the main funeral ceremony hall with a niche which contains a catafalque and a stone relief representing the course of man's life by Josef Palouš.

The National Memorial on Žižkov Hill, No. 1900, was built from 1927 to 1932 after the winning project of a 1925 competition by Jan Zázvorka and Jan Gillar. The structure dominates the surroundings and is also a major landmark in the general townscape. The tall, granite-faced cube of the main hall is where the remains of an unknown soldier are preserved. The main sarcophagus was made in 1953 by Karel Pokorný, the sculptural decoration is the work of Jan Kavan, Ladislav Kofránek and Otakar Švec, the mosaics on the walls were created by Vladimír Sychra, Stanislav Ullmann, Jakub Obrovský, and other artists. The equestrian statue on a tall pylon in front of the Memorial to Jan Žižka of Trocnov, commander of the Hussite army that defeated the German crusaders here in 1420, was cast by Bohumil Kafka.

Monumentalism

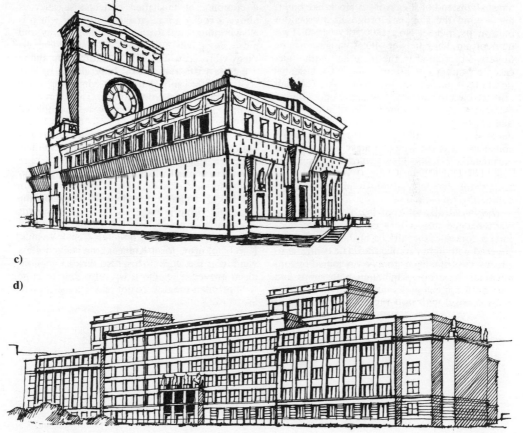

a) b)

c)

d)

a) **National Memorial, Žižkov Hill**
b) **Czechoslovak State Bank** (former Živnostenská banka)
c) **Church of the Holy Heart**
d) **Ministry of Economy**

There was a reason for the change in the name of the modern architectural movement at the end of the 1920s from "Constructivism" to "Functionalism". The essence of the architect's work came to be seen less in the structure and more in the purpose and function of the building. This can be demonstrated by looking at three buildings in Prague with different social functions.

The Direction of the General Pension Institute organized in 1928 a competition for a new administration building on the site of a former gasworks in the west part of Žižkov District. Although the competition was organized for selected architects only, two young architects, less than thirty years old, Josef Havlíček and Karel Honzík managed to be additionally included among the participants. Their entry was quite unusual: instead of suggesting a block-like building around the site they proposed a crucifom plan in its middle, Nos. 1800, 1839, 1840. Two pairs of parallel bands of offices with a corridor in-between crossed in the main hall with staircases, elevators, cloakrooms, and WCs. Orientation in the building was thus quite easy. The plan also enabled the architects to apply fully typified elements to the supporting structure of the building and to all other structural parts, which made it possible to reduce to a minimum the construction costs, with the mass production of particular elements. These were the main reasons why Havlíček and Honzík were chosen to realize the building, although many obstacles still had to be overcome.

The initial idea of applying a steel structure was changed and it was decided to use reinforced concrete; the surface of the building was covered with light ceramic tiles. The central cruciform mass of eleven storeys was joined by longitudinal three-storey buildings with shops and flats on the north and south sides. The building was equipped with the most advanced technical installations. Due to the layout, a great part of the site could be linked with the nearby public spaces. The building, which is now the seat of the Trade Unions, was completed in 1934.

Czechoslovak cinematography was looking at that time for large out-of-town sites for film studios making filming possible in the open air. Attention was drawn to an area south of Prague, between the valleys of the Vltava and the Hlubočepský Creek. In 1927, Max Urban was invited by a group of entrepreneurs to prepare a development plan for the area with film studios (No. 322), luxury villas and a look-out restaurant. The complex was named Barrandov to commemorate the French geologist Barrand who in the 19th century had studied the local limestone rocks and spread their renown. Urban proposed a complex of U-shaped coffeehouse terraces above a rocky gorge, at the bottom of which is a swimming pool with sun-bathing lawns and a dressing pavilion (by Václav Kolátor). The terraces were crowned with a building containing a café, a restaurant, and a fully glazed hall, as well as with a look-out tower containing some clubrooms and meeting-rooms. The recreation complex, unique in this country, was completed in 1929.

St. Wenceslas' Church in Vršovice District was built by Josef Gočár from 1928 to 1933. The structure, opening into Svatopluk Čech Square with wide lower halls of a single span, interrupted in the middle by two pillars carrying an 80 m tall tower, contains a main hall, lower on the sides and rising in steps in the middle towards a semicircular presbytery. The sculptural decoration was made by Bedřich Stefan, Čeněk Vosmík, Karel Pokorný, Josef Kubíček, the stained glass window is the work of Josef Kaplický. Functionalism proved here that it was also able to cope with problems that were not purely a question of use.

Functionalism

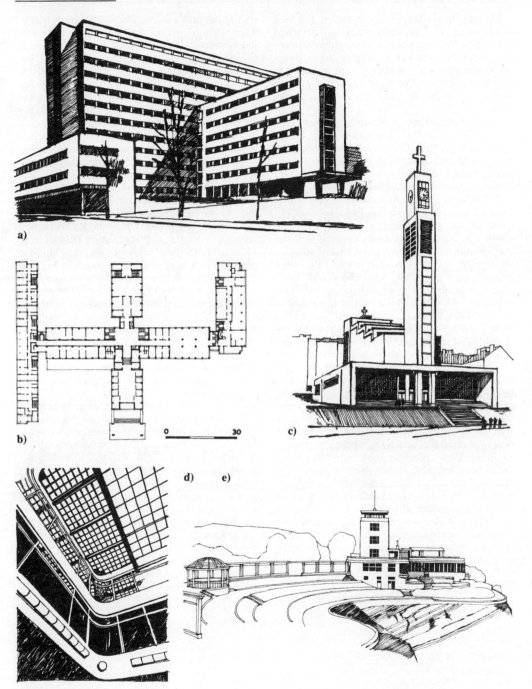

a) b) **Trade Unions House** (former General Pension Institute)
c) **St. Wenceslas' Church**

d) **House of Decorative Arts, hall**
e) **look-out restaurant, Barrandov**

Detached Houses in the 1920s and 1930s

During the twenty years between the two world wars in Czechoslovakia, the detached house type for individual families within residential garden districts was developing in two directions: towards rather modest groups of cooperative houses on the one hand and, on the other, towards comfortable villas amidst costly gardens.

The Savings Bank of Vinohrady constructed between 1925 and 1929 a small garden town Spořilov away from Prague, on a northern slope between Michle and Chodov. About 1,000 two-storey detached houses, terraced houses, semi-detached houses and larger free-standing villas were built on an area of some 80 hectares. The houses had a staircase in the living-room, a kitchen on the ground floor, and bedrooms upstairs. The development plan prepared by Josef Bertl and Josef Barek conceived a focal point for the estate, which was the central Roztylské Square, with a church, restaurants and shops, with four transverse and longitudinal wide avenues lined with trees and a central lawn strip in the middle, with main access streets as well as with back lanes between the gardens. All the buildings were designed by Jaroslav Polívka and Vlastimil Brožek. Prefabricated elements were already used here that were made on the spot: clinker concrete blocks for the foundations, building blocks variously shaped, lintels, staircase elements, concrete plates for ceilings and fences. Both tiled and flat roofs were used as well as terraces, balconies, wide-format windows, tube railings and plain, smooth façades.

Unlike this "consumer-type" of construction individual detached houses with studios were built in 1923–1924 for the fine artists Bohumil Kafka, Emil Filla and Vincenc Beneš by Pavel Janák in the garden district Ořechovka, Nos. 10, 12, 14, 16, Lomená Street. Made of exposed brickwork, with steep pantile roofs and amply articulated façades, they reflect the talent of the architect.

Typical functional detached houses in Prague were two villas made from 1926 to 1928 by Evžen Linhart and Jan Rosůlek in the garden district Hanspaulka on Na viničných horách Street. Their form is striking, and the windows are variously shaped. The large villa of the entrepreneur Gibian in Dejvice, No. 20, Sverdlova Street, designed by Jaromír Krejcar at the same time, displays a purposeful concept without any superfluous external effects. Differing from this is a remarkable work by Adolf Loos from 1930, the former Müller Villa in Střešovice, No. 14, Nad hradním vodojemem Street, which is a luxury residence with a plain exterior.

The attempt to find a functional type of detached house suiting the economic situation of the members of liberal arts and freelancers during the economic boom in this country between the two world wars resulted in an exhibition estate organized by the Czechoslovak Werkbund on a hill called Baba above Dejvice District from 1928 to 1933. According to the development plan by Pavel Janák with three streets parallel to the contour-lines, thirty-three two- to three-storey houses were built here with a reinforced concrete skeleton and modern structural materials and fittings after plans by leading architects of that time, such as Josef Gočár, Pavel Janák, Oldřich Starý, Ladislav Machoň, and others.

However, the initial idea of finding an economical type of house could not be fulfilled. The works that were closest to that goal were probably those of Ladislav Žák, the youngest architect taking part in the development, namely his villas Nos. 30 and 31 in the street Na ostrohu and No. 36 in the street Na Babě. They display a simplicity of mass and form, and a rational layout of their interior. The architect further developed this concept from 1933 to 1937 in the detached houses in Vysočany District, No. 20, U vysočanského cukrovaru Street, in Hodkovičky, No. 9, Na lysinách Street, and in Dejvice, No. 6/677, Neherovská Street. A totally different, rather romantic and even exotic form can be observed in the Barrandov villas by Vladimír Grégr from 1932–1935, Nos. 20 and 25, Barrandovská Street, which reflected the spirit of cinematographic production in this area.

Detached Houses in the 1920s and 1930s

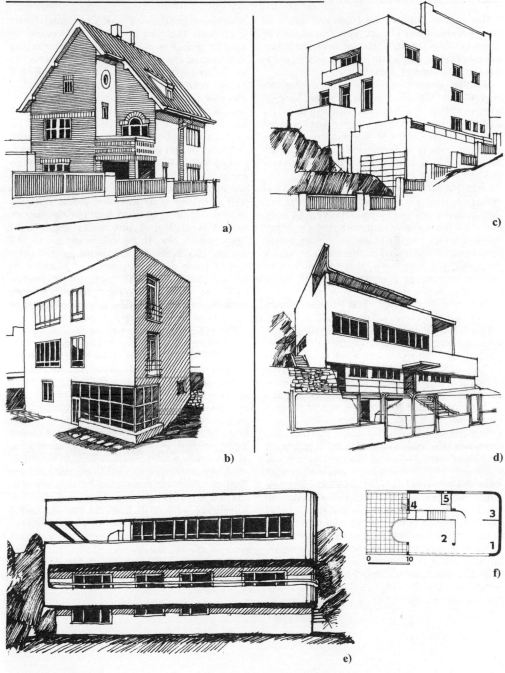

a)

b)

c)

d)

e)

f)

a) **painter V. Beneš's house, Ořechovka, No. 24/492, Cukrovarnická Street** (by P. Janák)
b) **villa No. 11/1777, Na Babě** (by Machoň)
c) **Müller Villa, No. 14/642, Nad hradním vodojemem, Střešovice** (by Loos)

d) **villa No. 24, Nad Paťankou, Na Babě** (by Kerhart)
e) **Frič Villa, No. 9/208, Na lysinách, Hodkovičky** (by Žák)
f) **Frič Villa, plan of the first floor:** 1 living-room, 2 dining room, 3 study, 4 kitchen, 5 pantry

Tenement Houses in the 1920s and 1930s

Most houses built in the 1920s and 1930s in Prague were blocks of flats. There were several different types of such blocks with flats and amenities of varying quality, which reflected the class stratification of society.

Building activity was interrupted during the First World War, resulting in a critical lack of housing after the war. Construction costs doubled and the rent in tenement houses rose by more than half. The new housing construction therefore mostly concentrated on very small flats, with just one room and a kitchen, or even one room only.

In 1921 a construction act was adopted to stimulate construction activity, both by central and local government and by cooperatives. As a result, more houses were built, with better sanitary conditions and a better functional layout, better lighting and ventilation. The first block of houses conceived in a homogeneous style was built in 1925 in Vršovice by František Libra. The block included eighteen four-storey houses surrounding a park with a children's playground, a roofed terrace and shops.

The Great Depression, which started in 1929, made the housing conditions extremely difficult, particularly of workers and employees. 24.2 to 34.5 per cent of the salary of these classes went in the rent. To improve the situation, the Municipal Council and the Social Insurance Company decided to sponsor the construction of "houses for the poor".

The first such houses had access galleries; later, houses with staircases and with four flats on each floor were built. The blocks were already free-standing, in rows on large green plots with children's playgrounds. They also had laundries, shops and schools. The first complex planned in this spirit by Pavel Janák was "U zelené lišky" (At the Green Fox), built in 1927 and with houses designed by František A. Libr, Antonín Černý, Bohumír Kozák, Ivan Šula, and Jarmila Lisková. In 1937, similar blocks were built in Vysočany by Josef Chochol and Richard Podzemný, and in Holešovice by František M. Černý and Kamil Ossendorf. The housing estate in Břevnov on a linear plan was planned in 1934 by Ladislav Machoň and the individual blocks were designed by Václav Hilský, Rudolf Jasenský, Karel Koželka and Antonín Černý.

A new building boom started in 1936. The investors wanted the capital they invested in buildings to be as competitive as possible, and required high quality flats and houses with perfect technical facilities. As a result, excellent apartment houses with the layout functionally differentiated and with well-designed façades appeared. Ceramic and glass facing was used, as well as oak or metal windows, sliding vertically or horizontally, or pivoted, with folding shutters, or with curtains protecting against the sunlight. They had all modern amenities, such as central heating, lifts, hot water, electric or gas refrigerators, faience kitchen sinks, etc. Metal door frames and plywood doors were widely used. The rent of a two-room flat of this type, with some 45 m² of living space, amounted to some 1,000 Kč (Czechoslovak crowns).

Direct lighting and ventilation became less important; they were last exclusively applied in 1937 by R. F. Podzemný in the house No. 728 built for the Provincial Bank in Dejvice, and were superceded by a three-aisle layout with the rooms on either side of a central hallway. The central aisle contained a bathroom and a cloakroom with built-in wardrobes. Such apartment houses were often built on the site of old demolished houses in the centre of Prague and in the adjacent areas of Vinohrady, Karlín, Smíchov and Letná, and also in new districts, such as Dejvice, Bubeneč and Pankrác. They were designed by Bohumír Kozák, Václav Kopecký, Jan Gillar, Josef Havlíček, Karel Janů, Jiří Štursa, Emanuel Hruška, Rudolf Stockar, Josef Šolc, and others. In some cases the staircase, the kitchen and some other spaces were lit and ventilated from internal yards lined with white ceramic tiles (Karel Hannauer, Jan Gillar).

Tenement Houses in the 1920s and 1930s

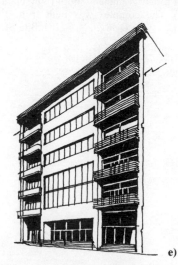

a) b) **house No. 596, Londýnská Street:** 1 room, 2 hall,
3 hallway, 4 kitchen, 5 maid's room, 6 cloakroom,
7 bathroom, 8 WC
c) **house No. 728, náměstí Svobody** (Freedom Square)
d) **house Nos. 460—461, F. Křížka Street**
e) **house No. 563, Žitná Street** (former YWCA House)

a)   b)

c)

d)

e)

Due to the growth of the population and to the construction of new housing districts from the 1920s onwards, it was felt necessary to construct new elementary, secondary and vocational schools.

The main idea of their architects was to rid such building types of the cold forms and traditional palace-like plans inherited from the 19th century, to improve their interiors by enlarging the windows, and to equip them with cloakrooms, dining-rooms, gymnasiums and playgrounds. In Dejvice, a new district of state officials and army officers, a block of elementary schools designed by Jan Pacl was built in 1928 on Svobody Square with a playground in the middle. Workers of the Building Office of the City of Prague, particularly Mečislav Petrů and Jiří Kodl, designed large and quite unusual school buildings in the districts Břevnov, Vršovice, Žižkov, Nusle, Holešovice and Podskalí that were built from 1925 to 1932. They all displayed an articulated layout, sloping roofs and red-plastered cornices as repercussions of the recent wave of the National Style.

In 1929, the first Functional school in Prague was built: the five-storey elementary school in Vysočany District, No. 2, Špitálská Street, designed by Vladimír Frýda, which already had a reinforced concrete structure. Instead of the then usual corridors the school had a central hall with stairs. Another work manifesting the functionalist principles of layout, such as the division of the building into particular functional elements and their independent external expression, was a complex of several educational facilities, including a kindergarten, an elementary school and a French grammar school (now elementary school). The complex was built from 1930 to 1933 in Dejvice District, No. 1784, Bílá Street, to a design by Jan Gillar that had been awarded the first prize in a competition for the project. The classrooms of the elementary school had large windows for daylight on the non-insulated side while those on the insulated side were smaller, of radiating type, and their size was determined by carefully calculated day light factors. The school included terraces for work in the open air and playgrounds in a garden. This functional work enjoyed a high reputation throughout Europe and became a model for many other schools in Prague.

The first to follow was a grammar school (now Teachers' College) in Dejvice District, No. 33, Evropská Avenue, designed by Evžen Linhart and built in 1937. Both the layout and the form follow the example of Gillar's school, but it was situated too close to the neighbouring streets, as a result of the district development plan current at that time. The architect dared to give the school seven storeys, which was quite unusual. Less purity of style can be observed in the five-storey grammar school (now elementary school) designed by Bohumil Kněžek and Josef Václavík and constructed in 1937 in Vinohrady District on Jiří z Lobkovic Square, No. 121, as well as in the elementary and grammar school (with education in Russian, now a Nurses' School) from 1936 in Nusle District, No. 51/200, designed by Ferdinand Fencl.

In all the above schools the particular functional parts are separated from each other, such as the classrooms, the administration offices, the technical classrooms and the gymnasium with dressing-rooms and showers. Classrooms had niches for coats in the corridor. Maximum light was achieved through large windows, which were made possible by the supporting structure of reinforced concrete.

School Buildings

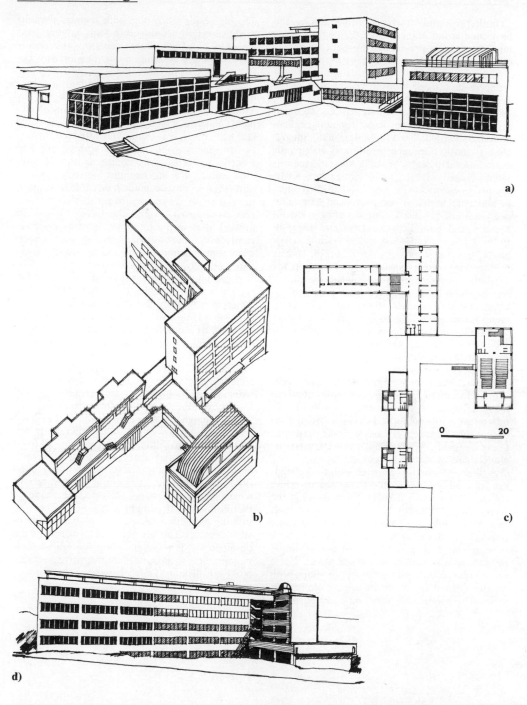

a)

b)

c)

d)

a) b) c) **elementary school, No. 1784, Bílá Street** (former French school)

d) **grammar school, No. 330, Evropská avenue**nue

With the fight for the consumer during the economic boom in the late 1920s, the first buildings appeared in Prague that were totally devoted to retail sales, from the basement to the roof.

Until that time there had only been a series of different specialized shops in Prague, such as the adapted old house No. 15/596, Celetná Street, called "U města Paříže" where various industrial products were sold, the Rott Ironmongery (rebuilt and adapted), No. 142, Malé (Small) Square, with a neo-Renaissance façade and wall-paintings after cartoons by Mikoláš Aleš, and the relatively small Haas' Carpet Shop, No. 4/847, Na příkopě Street, with a neo-Renaissance façade and a hall with cast-iron pillars and stairs, allegedly designed by the Viennese architect Theofil Hansen and built between 1869 and 1871. In 1927–1929, the old house called "U bílého kohouta" (At the White Cock), No. 6/774, and its passageway were replaced by a shoe shop for the Baťa Company of Zlín, designed by Ludvík Kysela, who also designed the neighbouring Lindt House. The eight storeys and two basements contained selling-halls, a rapid shoe repair shop (in the basement), a pedicure and orthopedic consultation centre and a snack bar (top floor). The standard system of Zlín's factory buildings was applied: reinforced concrete cast in removable metal sheet shuttering, coffered square ceilings of 6.15 by 6.15 m on circular pillars of 50 cm diameter, made of concrete and cast iron. The interior layout of the house is quite loose, the façade is made entirely of glass with the particular floors distinguished from each other by narrow white strips of matted Opaxit glass.

A different goal was pursued with the rebuilding of the romantic neo-Renaissance house called "U černé růže" (At the Black Rose) in the street Na příkopě, No. 12, which had been built in 1847 by Johann D. Frenzel. In 1935, a large passageway designed by Oldřich Tyl was built here. It was L-shaped, turning at a right angle towards a new building in Panská Street. There are two large halls with a number of shops both on the ground floor and in large galleries upstairs. The rooms now serve different purposes.

The high halls are roofed with segmental vaults made of reinforced concrete, with circular glass lenses. A spiral two-flight staircase with a decorative railing was built in the passageway between the halls in 1960.

The textile dealer Amschelberg built a corner department store in 1930–1931, designed by Milan Babuška and redesigned by František Řehák. The store, which was later called ARA and still later Perla, was exclusively intended for textile and fancy goods in seven storeys, and had a corner tower with two additional floors for administration. The steel supporting structure, one of the first in Prague, made it possible to suspend the corner of the house from the higher floors and, as a result, extend the pavement on the ground level in the future (which was done recently within the construction of the local pedestrian zone when a subway and an Underground entrance were constructed here).

A genuine department store of the highest European standard called "Bílá labuť" (The White Swan) was built by Brouk and Babka Company in 1938–1939 in the street Na poříčí (No. 23/1068) to a design by Josef Kittrich and Josef Hrubý. Built on an irregular plot, the house has two basements with storerooms, changing-rooms for the staff, distribution department, technical facilities, and six floors above the ground level with sales halls of a total area of 9,600 m², and four more storeys with a dining-room for the staff, a kitchen and an administration area. Three floors are in a tower-like superstructure. In the first years of operation there were some 20 to 30 thousand customers a day with some 500 members of staff. The entrance subway on the ground floor contains five exhibition stands, above which there is a huge glass façade made of thermolux, a sort of light-breaking and heat-insulating glass in a square grid of bars made of stainless steel. The interiors and furnishings were designed by Jan Gillar. After the war, a new building for social and administrative services, No. 1347, Biskupská Street, was attached, including a new approach to the service yard.

Department Stores

a)

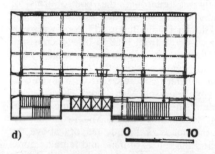

b)

d)

0   10

e)

c)

a) b) **Bílá labuť** (White Swan)
c) d) **Shoe House**
e) **passageway, Černá růže** (Black Rose)

Bridges of the First Third of the 20th Century

The structural material used for the construction of new bridges was no longer stone, but iron and, in particular, concrete and reinforced concrete.

The shortest bridge in Prague is the Svatopluk Čech Bridge, 170 m long and 16 m wide, built in 1905—1908 in connection with the demolition of the former Jewish Ghetto of Prague and as part of the Prague inner ringroad. The bridge has three steel arches the span of which increases as the bridge rises towards Letná Park. The bridge was designed by Jan Koula, Jiří Soukup and František Mencl, and built by Kapsa-Müller Company, ČKD Works, Ruston Company and Prášil Bros. The architecture of the bridge was conceived in the classicizing Art Nouveau style. The two pairs of columns on pylons at the end of the bridge bear figures of genii by Antonín Popp, the upstream side of the piers is decorated with bronze torch-bearers by Ludvík Herzl and Karel Opatrný, the down-stream side with six-headed hydra figures guarding the coat-of-arms of Prague by Karel Ladislav Wurzel.

The Hlávka Bridge linking Florenc with Holešovice was built from 1908 to 1912. It consisted of an elliptical steel arch between the New Town and Štvanice Island (by Mečislav Petrů), and of a northern concrete part with seven oval arches (by František Mencl and Pavel Janák). The style of the bridge with a well-finished concrete surface is neo-Classical. The medallions depicting the heads of Prague mayors above the arches and the reliefs of male and female figures on the piers on Štvanice Island were made by Josef Mařatka.

Between 1958 and 1962, the bridge was extended on the down-stream side to a width of 28 m. At the same time, the former steel structure was replaced by a concrete one and the elements designed by Janák were removed: the steps to Štvanice Island, the stand and the Cubist pylons bearing stone statues representing "Labour" and "Humanity" by Štursa on the Holešovice side. These have been lately reinstalled at the bridgehead with a two-level intersection of the Bubeneč Embankment and the north-south axis road, of which the bridge now forms part.

A concrete bridge connecting Alšovo nábřeží (Aleš Embankment) and the Rudolfinum with Klárov, named after the painter Mánes, was built from 1911 to 1914 and, as a result, the districts Bubeneč, Dejvice, Břevnov and Střešovice were linked with the centre of Prague. The bridge, conceived in the spirit of Modernism, was designed by František Mencl, Alois Nový and Mečislav Petrů. It is 186.4 m long, has four segmental arches, and is 16 m wide. The arch faces and the piers are clad in granite, the piers of the bridge support groups of reliefs by Jan Štursa and Josef Mařatka. After the completion of the bridge, the nearby suspended footbridge, called Rudolf Bridge from 1866—1868, was removed. It had only one pier in the middle of the river bed and was designed by František Schön and Karel Veselý.

Connecting Dělnická (Workers') Street in Holešovice with Libeň District is the concrete Libeňský (Libeň) Bridge built between 1924 and 1928, with a total length of 400 m and a width of 21 m, which is part of the future east-west axis road through the northern part of Prague. The bridge has six segmental arches and three beam spans on Libeňský (Libeň) Island. It was designed by František Mencl and Pavel Janák in a functional style, quite unusual and robust, without ornament.

One more bridge was built before the Second World War, which was made of reinforced concrete and connected Jirásek Square with Dientzenhofer Garden along the east-west axis road in the southern part of Prague between Košíře and Vinohrady. The bridge, named after the writer Jirásek and designed by František Mencl and Vlastimil Hofman, is 310 m long and 21 to 26 m wide. Its seven parabolic arches are composed of several separate ribs fixed in the piers, with wide access roads from the embankment. Prefabricated terrazzo elements were applied to some details, such as parapets and lamp posts.

Bridges of the First Third of the 20th Century

a)

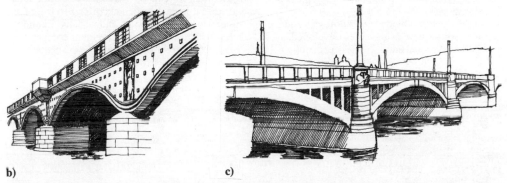

b)

c)

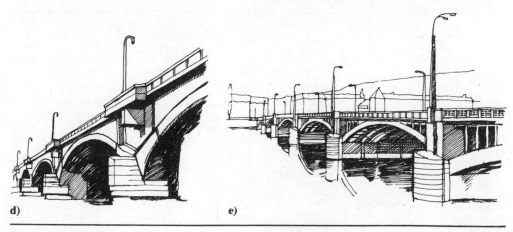

d)

e)

a) Svatopluk Čech Bridge
b) Hlávka Bridge
c) Mánes Bridge

d) Libeň Bridge
e) Jirásek Bridge

Architecture after World War II

The socio-political changes taking place in the East European countries liberated from the German occupation at the end of the Second World War brought about new ideas and problems in architectural work and building activity. In particular, a uniform standard in the function and size of flats was sought, as well as functional, spatial and structural typification of buildings, which was due to the development of a totalitarian society.

Czechoslovak architecture was in the early 1950s strongly influenced by the principles of the "socialist realism" which had been defined in the Soviet Union in the early 1930s as "an art socialist in its content and national in its form". These principles were applied to the construction of many new housing districts (Poruba, Havířov), villages (Zvírotice, Dubnica), and particular buildings.

In the late 1950s modern technologies and elements were applied and further developed, such as building engineering, series production of reinforced concrete panels and blocks, new construction materials, steel structures of both frame and suspended types, slab vaulting, suspended front walls, panel structures for dwelling-houses, etc. New concepts of "innovatory function", layout and construction appeared, particularly in education, culture, health care, administration, railway and air transport, hotels, telecommunications, exhibitions, memorials, funeral architecture, and in the renovation of ancient towns and buildings.

In the last decade, after a long period of rigid typification hindering architectural work, past trends of neo-Classicism, neo-Expressionism, Brutalism and other forms of Postmodernism have been applied again in individual architectural works. Only a very broad approach to architecture can be realistic, with functional and special forms applied according to their particular purpose, such as industrially manufactured structural elements. The main composition principles of architecture must be respected.

Not only the stagnation of building activity during the Second World War, but also the development of new social programmes brought about an unprecedented boom in housing construction in Prague from the mid-1950s onwards.

The first housing estate was built in 1946—1947 still on a cooperative basis. It was called "Solidarita" and was built in Strašnice District along Černokostelecká Street. Designed by František Jech, Karel Storch and Hanuš Majer, some 600 detached two-storey houses were built here as well as a number of mainly three-room flats in four-storey blocks, all in parallel lines perpendicular to the central garden band. The transverse supporting walls were made of brick, the infill was of insulation concrete slabs, the pitched roofs were pantiled.

Another housing estate, Petřiny, was built from 1956 to 1959, already by the state, east of the Hvězda (Star) hunting-lodge. The experimental estate designed by Evžen Benda and Vojtěch Mixa was initially conceived as a system of open blocks with sloping roofs. Three districts were constructed along the main road and another street perpendicular to it. At their intersection a department store, a 14-storey hostel and a noiseless manufacturing centre were built. The blocks of flats are panel buildings of G 57 type, with five to seven storeys; there are also twelve-storey point blocks made of brick at the entrance to the estate. There is a total of 4,000 flats for 13,000 inhabitants.

The experimental housing estate Invalidovna was designed by a team of workers of the Prague Design Institute headed by Josef Polák and constructed in 1959. A complex housing estate was built here on a site of 13 ha between Libeň and Karlín, with blocks of flats and all the necessary social facilities. The buildings are all made of panels of 6 m span, and there is a total of 1,260 flats for 4,000 inhabitants.

The largest housing estate in Prague until 1963 was that in Pankrác. A competition was organized and the entry by Jindřich Krise and Luděk Todl was awarded the first prize. The work was directed by Jiří Lasovský and in fact two housing estates were built here: Pankrác I (26 ha, 2,000 flats, 7,300 inhabitants) and Pankrác II (17 ha, 1,400 flats, 5,000 inhabitants) with 4, 8, and even 12 storeys. There are altogether three housing areas in each housing estate, surrounding a centre with schools, nurseries and playgrounds, and with shops and services on the main roads.

On a plain above the Vltava Valley in the north of Prague, the suburban North Town was constructed instead of garden districts with detached houses that had been initially planned here. The North Town extends along the main east-west road leading to the industrial district of Vysočany. Its western part, called Prosek, was built from 1961 on, according to a plan prepared by a team headed by Jiří Novotný. The estate has a central park 100 m wide and lined with longitudinal rows of twelve-storey blocks. Behind them there are seven housing districts with eight-storey blocks on the edge and groups of four-storey point blocks inside. The estate covers

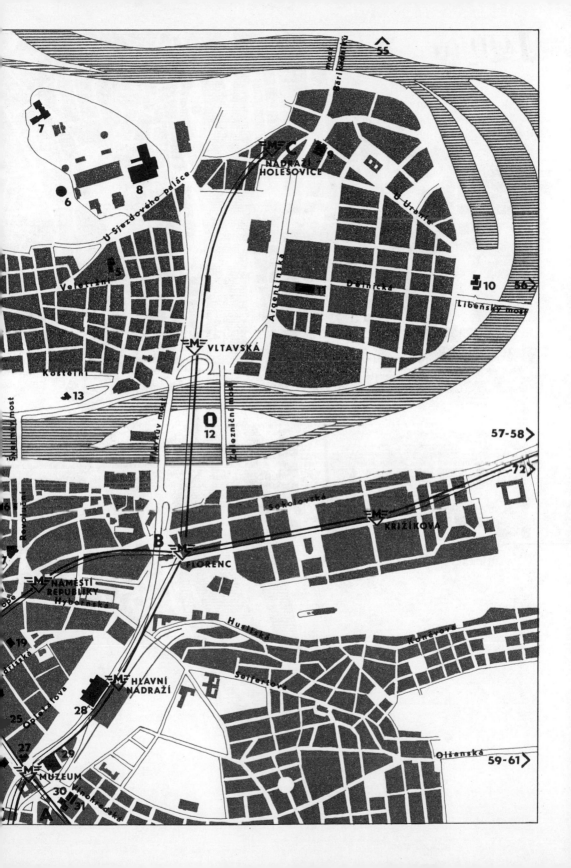

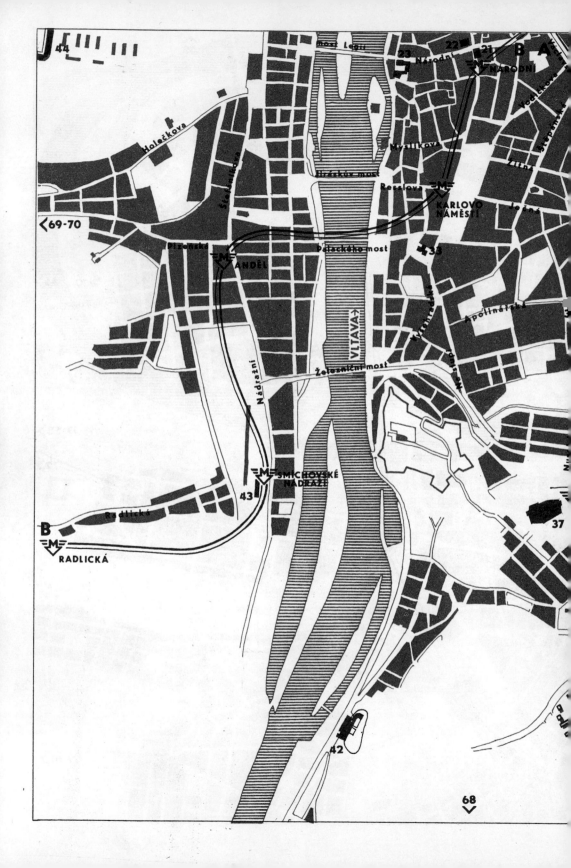

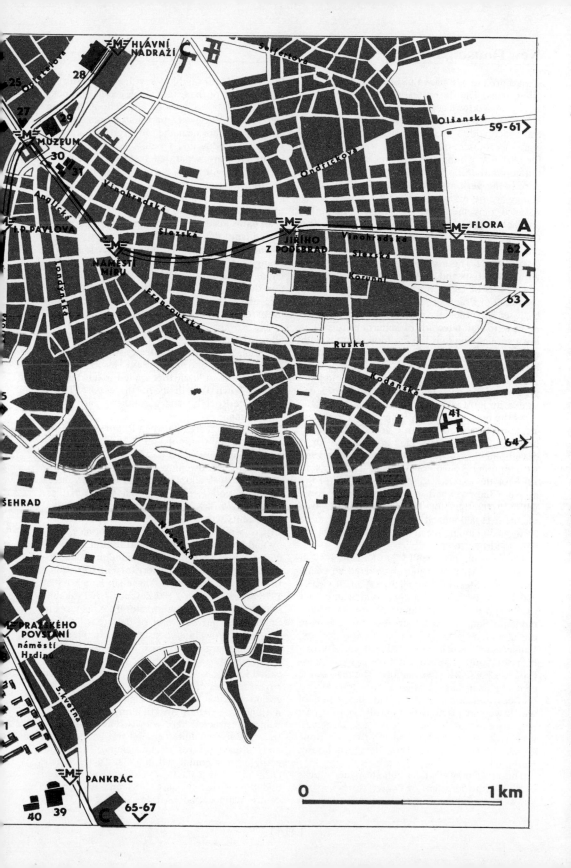

a total area of 178 ha with 8,600 flats and 29,300 inhabitants. The district called Ďáblice was designed by Viktor Tuček and built between Střelničná Avenue and Ďáblický Wood. It has a central space with a social centre, and a number of eight- to fourteen-storey blocks with 9,000 flats for 28,000 inhabitants. The architecture is unfortunately rather monotonous. An important place here is the park around the Kobylisy Shooting-Range where many heroes of the anti-Nazi resistance movement were executed. Sokolníky, another housing estate at Kobylisy adjoining the Čimický Wood, has houses distributed like an amphitheatre around the central space with social facilities. The northernmost estate, Bohnice, with 11,000 flats and 35,000 inhabitants, was constructed as of 1964 on a very significant site in the north of Prague. Designed by a team headed by Josef Havránek, the estate is another example of how the architecture of suburban areas has been spoiled and fails to enrich these areas with new architectural high-quality elements both in form and content.

On the northern edge of the estate an old people's home was built between 1973 and 1975, designed by Jan Línek and Vlado Milunič.

As the housing needs in Prague were growing, attention turned to the large areas in the south between the villages Chodov and Háje. A large development competition was organized in 1966 with another round for selected architects in 1967 for the area covering 1,200 ha south of the above villages, where a large suburban town with 20,000 flats for 100,000 inhabitants was planned; 15,000 inhabitants were expected to be employed in an industrial zone to the west of the new suburban town.

The final plan of 1968 by Jan Krásný, Jiří Lasovský and Miroslav Řihošek covered an estate called Jižní Město I (South Town I) on an area of 290 ha for 64,000 inhabitants divided into four residential districts. The main centre, with Kosmonautů Square and Litochlebské Square, is in Gustav Kliment Avenue leading to Spořilov and Pankrác, and touches the 2nd, 3rd and 4th districts of South Town. Near here is the Underground Line C with five stations. The plan of the central part included a hotel, a department store, services and administration buildings, some of which were realized. Adjoining the central part is a new town park, and there is also a large natural park above the Lake of Hostivař on Botič Creek. At Chodov and Háje detached houses were built.

The residential districts contain panel blocks of flats with four, eight or twelve storeys, as we know them from the other housing estates in Prague, and four tall blocks with 20 to 24 storeys in the centre of the estate. Each group of blocks has 1,200 flats, with shops and schools serving a couple of districts. Department stores and cultural centres are near the Underground stations Roztyly, Chodov and Opatov. Buildings of different type are separated from each other by green areas with trees, the motorway in the west part of the estate is lined by non-dwelling buildings (noiseless production facilities, administrative buildings, research institutes), and the pedestrian paths inside the residential districts are separated from the road traffic.

Due to the growing housing needs and to changes in the location of industrial plants the initial idea from the early 1970s of having only non-dwelling buildings west of the motorway was abandoned. In 1977, a development plan prepared by Jan Zelený, Vladimír Ježek, Vítězslava Rothbauerová and Jitka Thomasová was adopted, according to which housing, services, research, education and industry were divided into three types and four areas. This is how the construction of a district called Jižní Město I (South Town I) with its northern part (Horní Kunratice-Roztyly) and a southern part (Šeberov) began.

The elevated area between Řeporyje and Prokopské Valley south of Vidoul Hill in the southwestern part of Prague has excellent bioclimatic conditions for dwelling. Therefore, a development plan was adopted in 1970 for the villages Stodůlky and Řeporyje, which were then attached to Prague in 1974. 22,000 flats for 80,000 inhabitants were constructed here, and the construction is to extend further to Třebonice, Chaby and Horka as Jižní Město II (South Town II) with 13,000 flats for 50,000 inhabitants, and prospectively further to the territory of Chrášťany, Jinočany and Rudná (20,000 inhabitants). As of 1978 an estate with 2,100 flats for 7,300 inhabitants was constructed on a site of 29 hectares at Stodůlky in the west part of the area. The first complex of dwelling houses was completed in 1983. The largest complex in the South-West Town was started in 1980. The complex, which is called Lužiny, is situated further to the south and covers an area of 84 hectares with 7,550 flats for 25,500 inhabitants. It was designed by Milan Klíma and P. Sklenář. An Underground station is being constructed here with two shopping centres, service facilities, administrative buildings and cultural centres in its vicinity. The whole complex was completed in 1988. To the northeast, an estate called Nové Butovice has been under construction since 1984 and will be the centre of Jihozápadní Město (South west Town).

New Housing Estates

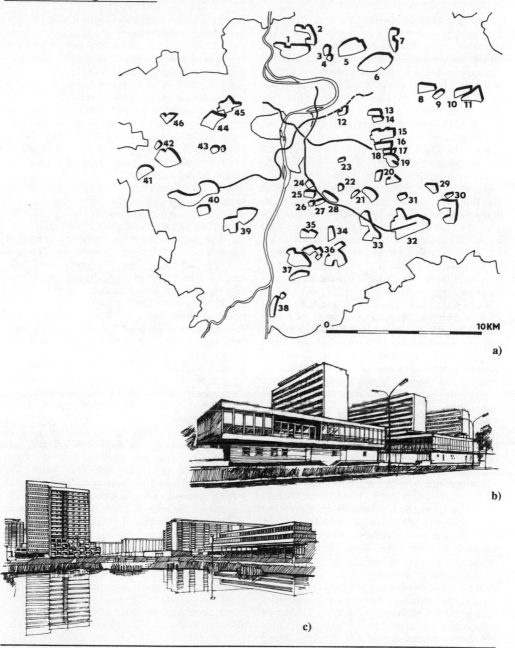

a)

b)

c)

a) **plan of housing estates:** 1 Bohnice, 2 Čimice, 3 Kobylisy, 4 Horňátecká, 5 Ďáblice, 6 Prosek, 7 Letňany, 8 Hloubětín, 9 Kyje-Lehovec, 10 Černý most I, 11 Černý most II, 12 Invalidovna, 13 Chmelnice, 14 Jarov, 15 Malešice, 16 Solidarita, 17 Úvalská, 18 Rybníčky, 19 Skalka, 20 Zahradní Město, 21 Spořilov, 22 Na Úlehli, 23 Vršovice, 24 Pankrác II, 25 Pankrác I, 26 Pankrác III, 27 Antala Staška, 28 Michelská, 29 Hornoměcholupská, 30 Petrovice-Horní Měcholupy, 31 Na Košíku, 32 Jižní Město I, 33 Jižní Město-West, 34 Krč, 35 Novodvorská, 36 Lhotka-Libuš, 37 Modřany, 38 Komořany, 39 Barrandov, 40 Jihozápadní Město, 41 Zličín, 42 Řepy, 43 Homolka, 44 Petřiny, 45 Červený vrch, 46 Na dědině

b) **housing estate Pankrác II**

c) **housing estate Ďáblice with water pool**

Hospitals

Only a few buildings were constructed in the 19th century with the aim of improving the level of health care in Prague. As the town was developing and medical science progressed, older medical facilities were modernized and rebuilt and new hospitals constructed, particularly between the two world wars. New municipal hospitals were built in Libeň (Na Bulovce) and Vinohrady. These efforts were interrupted by the war. After the war, health care needs considerably increased after the introduction of a general free health care service.

The first modern hospital building in Prague was the Pavilion of Dermatology of the hospital Na Bulovce, No. 67, built in 1937—1938 on a steep site to a design by Jan Rosůlek. The pavilion has 120 beds in several departments located in an elongated four-storey building and a central seven-storey building, the front walls of which differ in colour. The reinforced concrete structure made it possible to make large windows in the plain façades.

The Thomayer Hospital in Prague 4, Krč District on Vídeňská Street is a complex of buildings (Nos. 800—815) designed by Bohumír Kozák and built between 1926 and 1934. The complex was initially intended to be a social care institute in free-standing multi-storeyed pavilions forming two parallel blocks lining the central garden. The garden is closed by an administration building.

Soon after the war the most important health centres were built, starting with that in Sokolovská Street, Vysočany District (by Antonín Tenzer, built in 1950—1952). The only larger health centre is that in Prague 6, Břevnov District (by Richard Podzemný, built from 1959 to 1963), between the streets Pionýrů and Bělohorská, which is used by some 60,000 inhabitants living in that part of the town. The two-aisled six-storey building has a reinforced concrete structure with waiting-rooms facing the south while the examination rooms face the north. No wards for in-patients are available. The façade is articulated by vertical concrete piers between the windows at an interval of 180 cm and by moulded parts under the windows by Bohumír Těhlík; the gable walls are decorated with mosaics. Quite different is the health centre in Prague 4, Nový Spořilov District designed by Zdeněk Přáda and Pavel Bečvář and built from 1966 to 1970, which is a three-storey two-aisled building of rectangular plan with an atrium inside, and with the exterior articulated by horizontal cornices. There are 35 medical departments serving some 28,000 people living in the district. The biggest is the main health centre in Prague 4, Krč District, on Antala Staška Street, which grants general medical services to some 60,000 people and has specialized departments serving 200,000 people. The thirteen-storey three-aisled building with basic medical services is connected to several three-storey buildings with special services and technical facilities around the courtyard. The structure has a built-up reinforced concrete skeleton and the lower part of the outer wall is covered with mosaic while the rest is plastered in white. The centre was designed by Jiří Kubišta and Bohuslav Zaplatílek.

The first teaching hospital to be built in the capital was the department of internal diseases in Prague 10, designed by Karel Vlček and built from 1965 to 1970 within the Vinohrady Hospital. The department is a five-storey five-aisled building with 180 beds on three floors. The central aisle contains vertical communications, sanitary facilities and storerooms. It has a steel supporting structure with dark suspended walls, vertically divided at 120 cm intervals. The neighbouring Department of Plastic Surgery and Burns, designed by Ivan Šuhajík and built from 1972 to 1978, has 178 beds for in-patients and is supported by a structure of steel tubes and reinforced slab ceilings of suspended type. Its two structures of multi-aisled plan with seven and three storeys are enclosed within light horizontal galleries; the gable walls and plinths are faced with sandstone.

The Urology Teaching Hospital of Charles University in Prague 2, Ke Karlovu Street, was designed by Vratislav Růžička and built from 1971 to 1976 as a singly six-storey block. The Clinic of Orthopedics, built in 1975—1977, also has six storeys and was designed by Vladimír Černický. They both have multi-aisled plans, a reinforced concrete structure cast on site on a 7.2 m grid, and the exterior is designed in the spirit of "Brutalism" with walls made of exposed concrete and with the intermediate front surfaces covered with a ceramic cladding.

The largest hospital built after the war is the teaching hospital in Prague 5, Motol District, constructed between 1964 and 1977 to plans by Richard Podzemný and Antonín Tenzer who won a competition for the design in 1958. The building has a three-aisled cruciform plan, with fifteen storeys. The structure is made of reinforced concrete cast on site and filled with blocks of insulation concrete. The articulation is via balconies around all the in-patients' floors which also provide shading.

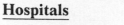

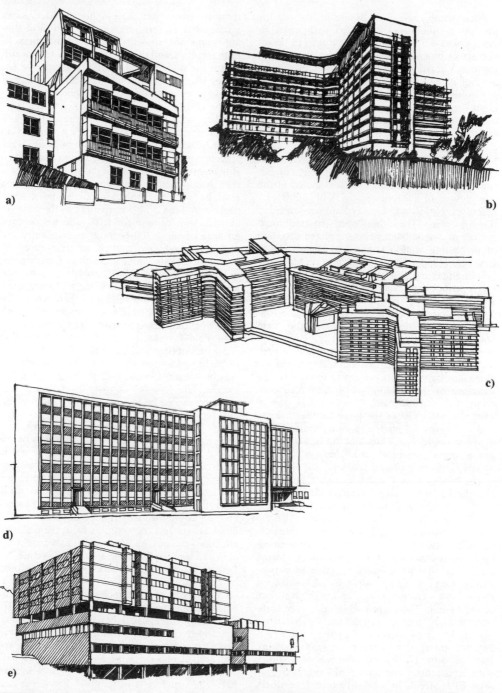

a) **pavilion of dermatology and venerology, hospital Na Bulovce**

b) **teaching hospital, Motol**

c) **teaching hospital, Motol, completion plan**

d) **health centre, Břevnov**

e) **pavilion of orthopedics, Na Bulovce**

After some 25 years of discussion the site for the future buildings of the Czech Technical University was determined in 1926. It was to be seven street blocks in Prague, Dejvice District adjoining Vítězné (Victory) Square, with a total area of 22 hectares, as required by Antonín Engel in his scheme. Between the two world wars, however, only two structures were built here according to Engel's scheme, with a total area of 400,000 square metres: that of the Faculty of Architecture and that of the Faculty of Civil Engineering, which were later joined by the Faculty of Chemical Technology. A public competition took place in 1957 that was aimed at the completion of the complex, and the entry by František Novák and Gustav Paul was awarded the first prize. They abandoned the traditional system of closed blocks and suggested a system of projecting wings. At the first stage of construction (1958—1960) the Faculty of Mechanical Engineering and the Faculty of Electrical Engineering were built on Suchbátárova Street with a total floor-area of 350,000 square metres for some five thousand students. From the longitudinal two-aisled building where the main corridor and classrooms are located, wings with drafting-rooms and large lecture-theatres project at right angles to the south, and wings for particular departments project to the north. The structure of the buildings is of reinforced concrete with curtain-walls of aluminium panels. The external walls of the large lecture-theatres and staircases are clad with violet mosaics. Behind is a single-storey block of top-lit workshops and a four-storey block of kitchens and dining-rooms for both staff and students.

The block of the Faculty of Civil Engineering and the Faculty of Architecture built from 1964 to 1970 was designed by František Čermák, Gustav Paul and Jaroslav Paroubek with a different concept: instead of the above system of projecting wings, two five-aisled buildings perpendicular to each other with seven to fourteen storeys were used that were linked together by a two-storey wing containing entrances, administration rooms and lecture-theatres, and with an atrium in the middle. There are two large lecture theatres whose masses project into Thákurova Street. The total floor-area of the buildings is 285,000 square metres for some 4,000 students. Parallel to the faculty buildings is another block with laboratories and workshops oriented towards Bílá Street. In 1984—1986, a four-storey Students' House designed by Oldřich Dudek and Jan Plessinger was constructed nearby. The ground floor on a site of 63 by 48 m contains exhibition rooms and a shop with professional literature, two other storeys house cloakrooms, a snack-bar, storerooms, kitchens and three dining-rooms for students and staff members of both faculties, and the top floor contains a health centre for students and staff with a separate entrance from external stairs. The colour facing of the walls enlivens the group of buildings.

The University of Agriculture separated from the Technical University of Prague in 1957 and began immediately to construct a campus in Prague, Suchdol District. The first buildings were students' hostels and dining-rooms conceived still according to the traditional symmetrical system. A competition was then organized in 1958 and the winning project prepared by a team headed by Jan Čejka was realized in the next years. The new campus for 1,700 students covered an area of some 100 hectares and included the well-conceived buildings of the rectorate, the ceremonial hall, three faculties, laboratories, greenhouses, workshops, social rooms and a sports centre, all of which are well integrated. The buildings have a reinforced concrete structure, clearly identifiable from outsise, filled with brickwork and covered with ceramic tiles.

In Pelc-Tyrolka, north of the bridge called Barikádníků (Barricade Fighters Bridge) a group of buildings of the Faculty of Nuclear Physics was built from 1965 to 1970 to designs by Karel Prager. The complex consists of a thirteen-storey three-aisled building containing the particular departments, three two- and three-storey square buildings with lecture rooms, laboratories and central workshops, and the buildings of the power generation block. The structure is made of circular steel vertical members and has suspended flat ceilings made of reinforced concrete. The curtain walls are unified suspended walls consisting of a network of metal window squares and of colour glass strips. Trees around the buildings protect the complex from the negative effects of the nearby north-south axis road.

From 1960 to 1965 the then new avenue Na Petřinách in Prague 6 District was axially closed by the building of the Institute of Macromolecular Chemistry of the Czechoslovak Academy of Sciences designed by Karel Prager. The main seven-storey three-aisled building with laboratories and study rooms is connected to a perpendicular three-storey wing with administrative, social and technical rooms and an entrance hall, opposite which is an annex with a large lecture hall. The structure is of reinforced concrete cast on site, with hollow partitions and suspended steel curtain walls including windows and strips of transparent glass. Characteristic features are the vertical aluminium strips between windows

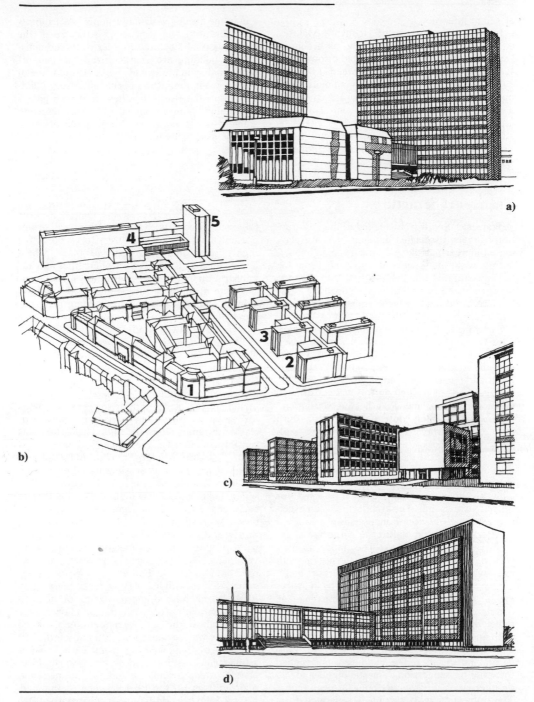

a) **Faculty of Architecture and Faculty of Civil Engineering**
c) **Faculty of Electrical Engineering and Faculty of Mechanical Engineering**
d) **Institute of Macromolecular Chemistry**

b) **Czech Technical University, Dejvice:** 1 parts constructed between the two world wars, 2 Faculty of Electrical Engineering, 3 Faculty of Mechanical Engineering, 4 Faculty of Civil Engineering, 5 Faculty of Architecture

at 120 m intervals.

In the industrial zone of Hostivař—Malešice a building designed by a team of architects headed by Edvard Kos for the Radioisotope Research Institute was built between 1972 and 1974. In front of the four-storey administration building is a low structure with a kitchen and a dining-hall, while behind the central building are two five-aisled laboratory wings linked by a two-storey manufacturing and distribution hall. There are green plots in front of the complex and in the atrium, with water pools and sculptural decoration. The supporting structure of the buildings is of steel, the façades of the administration building are characterized by strips of dethermal windows and white-painted metal panels, while the façade of the laboratory building and of the workshops has red-brown panels in the aluminium suspended wall. An interesting element is the sculptural form of the chimney and the associated piping.

Transport Structures

Transport and travel have led to the construction of many associated buildings that are playing an increasing role and have become important points in the town- and landscape. From the railway stations built in the mid-19th century, these constructions have developed towards modern road and railway transport buildings and airports.

Air transport was developing in this country after World War I and, as a result, a modern civil airfield was constructed northwest of Prague near the road to Slaný. From 1931 to 1934 an arrivals and departures building, used also for post, storage, and air-traffic control was constructed along with three hangars, a heating station and a group of dwelling-houses in the south-eastern part of the airfield. It was designed by Adolf Benš, Kamil Roškot and Vojtěch Kerhart who had been awarded the first prize in a competition for the project. The airport was of international standard, but it could not keep pace with growing demand and is now used for official visitors only. The architecture is an excellent example of Czech Functionalism.

After World War II Ruzyně Airport was extended and modernized. The modernization started by extending the runway system with runways up to 4.3 km long. A new airport building was constructed, with a hall 100 by 70 m, for passengers and for all services, such as luggage handling, post and goods. The building was constructed after a competition that was held in 1958 and that was won by a group of architects, namely Karel Bubeníček, Karel Filsak, Jiří Louda and Jan Šrámek. The building was designed for 1,400 passengers on domestic flights and 900 on international flights per hour (at peak times). The domestic flights section is separated from that for international flights by a block of rooms for airport services with restaurants above. There are also waiting-rooms and snack bars followed by covered boarding ramps. Other important buildings are the three-storey block for flight crews, and the technical block which houses all the air-traffic control facilities and administration units in its eleven storeys. The forms are quite plain, both outside and inside, and the colours and structures of the building materials are exposed.

A goods railway station was built between 1933 and 1936 in the east end of Žižkov District to a technical plan by Miroslav Chlumecký and an architectural design by Vladimír Weiss and Karel Caivas. On Jana Želivského Street is a three-storey building, No. 2200, which is followed by two rows of four-storey storehouses for railway consignments, parcels and other articles, with ramps along the rails. The station was sensibly situated on the main road traffic axis from Záběhlice through Vršovice and Žižkov to Libeň, which made it possible to supply all the left-bank districts of Prague with goods.

The building of a new main station for Prague had been discussed for some twenty-five years before its realization could begin. Even its location was discussed and argued, as several sites were proposed, such as the surroundings of Invalidovna (Disabled Soldiers' Hospital) and the road intersection U Bulhara. It was even suggested that the original Art Nouveau building by Fanta be demolished and that a station beneath the north-south axis road be built, or a new building above the rails. A competition of invited architects was organized in 1970 and on the basis of its results as well as of some earlier studies a final plan was prepared by Josef Bočan, Josef Danda, Alena Šrámková and Jan Šrámek, and realized from 1973 to 1979. The new station hall, 120 by 50 m, was designed for a capacity of 210 thousand passengers a day. With the north-south axis road above it, the hall has two storeys used for both arrivals and departures. It also contains

Transport Structures

a)

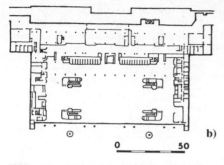

b)

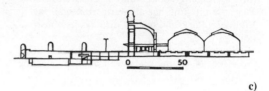

c)

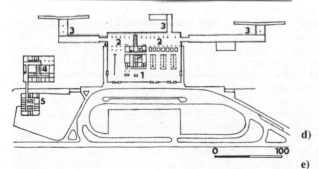

d)

e)

a) b) c) **Main Station hall**
d) e) **Ruzyně Airport hall:** 1 passenger clearance hall,

2 waiting-room, 3 boarding galleries, 4 crew rooms,
5 technical block

entrances to the Underground. The main entrance for pedestrians is from Vrchlický Park, passenger cars can arrive at the sides of a forecourt, or can use the car-park for 130 cars and 6 buses on the roof of the hall; people using municipal buses can enter through entrances at the bus stops. In the front part of the hall there are booking-offices, in the rear part left-luggage and other offices, and the hall is flanked by various services and shops. In the part under the axis road, which can be reached through two corridors for arriving passengers and where one corridor for departures starts, there is a waiting-room with timetables and an entrance to the historic building by Fanta with restaurants, waiting-rooms, reading-rooms, and a children's room. The new building has a robust front wall facing Vrchlický Park and openly displays its construction.

The principal concept of the hall is based on the effect of a long glass wall and a projecting terrace roof, with two glass cylinders surmounted with domes in front of the front wall. The monumental scale of the interior with a structure supported by two rows of pillars fully complies with the architectural postulates of the early 1980s.

A solution to the urgent parking problem seemed to be the cooperative large-scale multi-storey car-parks constructed in the 1970s in Prague 4, Pankrác, Milevská Street, and Prague 10, Malešice. In both cases short ramps were used to connect the garage floors with a difference of level of half the height of each floor. The six to eight-storey car-park of Malešice was designed by Jaroslav Celý and Antonín Průšek and its parking spaces can accommodate some 1,400 small and medium-size cars. The concrete prefabricated structure has a curtain-wall made of vertical bands of corrugated iron sheets alternating with narrower strips of glass and with vent holes in their recesses.

Sports Structures

Physical training and sports have always been very popular in this country and there have been many important international achievements in this field. After the Second World War they came into the hands of the state. Before, the construction of respective facilities depended on the economic strength of the particular sports clubs. After the war, in the late 1940s and, in particular, as of 1967 sports facilities were systematically built.

The Spartakiad Stadium on Strahov Hill, No. 100, has a long history that started with the levelling of former quarries here in 1925. A competition took place in 1930 and the winning project by Alois Dryák, Ferdinand Balcárek and Karel Kopp then became a basis of the large sports complex with the Sokol Stadium in the middle, smaller sports stadiums to the west, and the small Army Stadium to the north, all with earth stands and with permanent grandstands only in the central part and in the corners. Access roads were built from Pohořelec and Hřebenky, which were later enlarged and equipped with parking areas. After the war, in 1948, concrete grandstands were built in the great stadium on its south and north sides, and major parts of the west and east stands were constructed. In 1961, the east stand of the Spartakiad Stadium was reconstructed to a design by František Cubr, Viktor Formáček, Stanislav Franc, Luděk Hanf, Josef Hrubý and Jaroslav Kandl, the sports stadium was enlarged, and eleven pavilions of students' hostels for 5,000 students were built at the east edge of the complex, which were used during the Spartakiads as dressing-rooms. In addition, there was a dining-room for students, a pavilion with shops and services, and a health centre. In the late 1960s, the east stands were totally reconstructed to plans by Oliver Honke-Houfek, Zdeněk Kuna and Zdeněk Stupka, and below them three gymnasia and a swimming-pool were created. The Evžen Rošický Sports Stadium was rebuilt in 1978 for the European Athletics Championships, and a new stadium called "Přátelství" (Friendship) was built west of it, while in the northern part a sports hall designed by Petr Kutnar and Svatopluk Zeman was constructed which introduced modern features into the Strahov complex.

In the last twenty years other technically well-equipped sports stadiums have been built, for example the A.C. Sparta Stadium on Letná Square by Cyril Mandel, where new steel stands were added to the concrete west stand from the 1930s (made in collaboration with Vladimír Syrovátka), the Dukla Praha Stadium at Juliska with a grandstand covered by a steel roof, and the large sports complex of Slavia IPS in Vršovice District. An interesting feature here is the roof of the winter stadium with a structure carried by bars diagonally suspended from tall towers and anchored outside the building. A combination of

Sports Structures

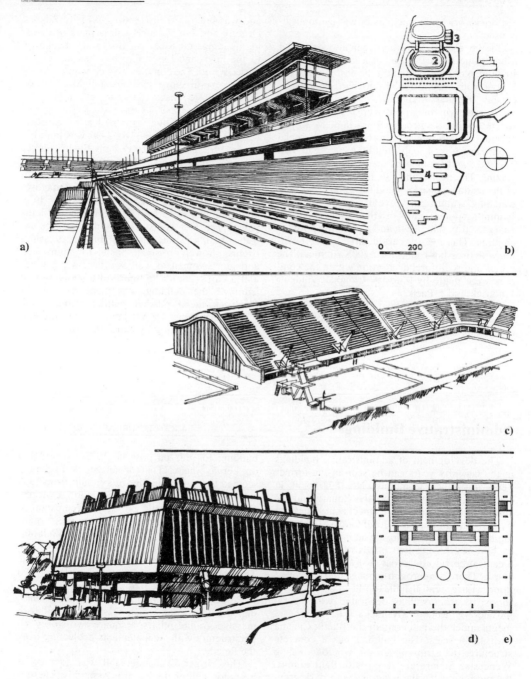

a) b) **Spartakiad Stadium:** 1 Spartakiad Stadium, 2 E. Rošický Stadium, 3 Sports Hall, 4 Students' hostels

c) **swimming stadium, Podolí**
d) e) **Slavia VŠ gymnasium, Na Folimance**

(323)

red brickwork and white plaster was symbolically used.

On the site of a former cement works and a limestone quarry in Podolí a large swimming stadium, No. 74, was built on the east bank of the Vltava from 1960 to 1965 by Richard Podzemný, Gustav Kuchař and Juraj Domič. There is a covered swimming-pool with a stand for 700 spectators, dressing-rooms for swimmers, a gymnasium, a catering establishment and social rooms, and a roof supported by concrete arches. The west and south sides of the hall have triple glazing. The roof of the hall, facing the hill north of the stadium, bears a stand for 4,500 spectators watching water sports events in two open-air swimming-pools, and in the background is a large sun-bathing lawn and a paddling pool for children. There is a separate three-storey building with dressing-rooms for 2,200 swimmers. The reliefs and sculptural decoration within the complex were made by Miloslav Chlupáč, Vladimír Janoušek and J. Pacík.

The natural bathing lake Džbán in the sunny and beautiful environment of Vokovice Valley crossed by a dam covers an area of 12 hectares and was created from 1966 to 1971 by Zdeněk Drobný and Jan Talacko. Three pairs of dressing-buildings for 8,000 visitors form a backdrop to the lawn and the stone "beaches" under the Šárka Wood. The complex also contains a diving tower, several sports grounds, a children's playground, three snack bars, a restaurant, and a parking area for 800 cars.

Under the Baroque walls of Karlov a sports hall for Slavia VŠ Praha, No. 2490, was built between 1972 and 1976 to designs by Jiří Siegel. From a square plan of 40 by 40 m a glass mass rises in the form of a truncated pyramid. It is supported by a steel framed structure and encloses a sports hall with a playing area of 15 by 30 m and a stepped stand for 600 spectators and journalists. The first two storeys contain a large entrance hall, a gymnasium, a clubroom, dressing-rooms, showers, a small hostel for sportsmen and sportswomen, as well as offices, a snack bar and a cloakroom. The figure of a sportsman in front of the building was made by Zdeněk Němeček, the suspended sculpture representing a basket and ball by Vladimír Preclík, the emblem on the building by Karel Pekárek.

The development of administrative buildings in the last fifty years can be seen in the former Fénix Insurance Company, No. 802, built in 1927—1928 between Wenceslas Square and the streets Krakovská and Ve smečkách to designs by Bedřich Ehrmann and Josef Gočár. The building has five storeys enclosing an inner courtyard, each storey having two bands of offices along a central corridor, and has two receding storeys above. There is a through-passage on the ground floor with a central hall, top-lit and lined with shops; its front wall is decorated with figural mosaics by Rudolf Kremlička. The two basements under the hall contain the Blaník Cinema with 1,000 seats. The building has a concrete structure, the strips under the windows facing Wenceslas Square are faced with light granite, the piers between the windows with dark granite, while the walls facing both streets are lined with ceramic tiles.

After the liberation of Czechoslovakia in May 1945 a suitable hall building was sought to house the National Assembly (Parliament) until a new building for this purpose could be constructed on Letná Square. The former Stock Exchange seemed the most suitable choice, built from 1936 to 1938 by Jaroslav Rössler and no longer necessary under the new political circumstances. A competition of invited architects was organized in 1966 for the redevelopment and adaptation of the building and of its surroundings, where a block of houses was to be demolished. The competition was won by Karel Prager and he was invited to prepare the final project.

Prager suggested adding to the existing building, the façade of which was articulated with massive granite pillars, a square two-storey superstructure with steel elements projecting from the façade.

The former Exchange Hall was adapted as a session hall of the Federal Assembly. There is a new restaurant for M.P.s adjoining the building in the south, towards Vinohradská Street, the steel superstructure contains Federal Assembly offices, while in the east, towards the main railway station, an additional building was attached

Administrative Buildings

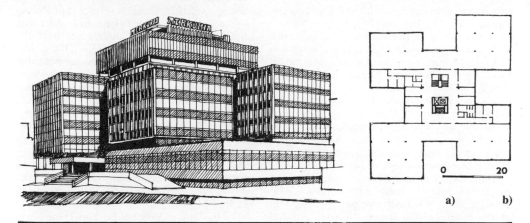

a)   b)

0   20

c)   d)

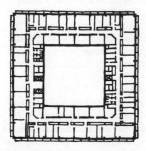

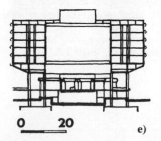

0   20   e)

f)

a) b) **Merkuria**
c) **Federal Assembly**
d) **Children's Book Shop**
e) f) **Koospol**

(325)

Administrative Buildings

that contains service rooms for the neighbouring Smetana Theatre. In front of the Federal Assembly Building is a tall steel pylon as well as, on the side facing Vinohradská Street, the sculpture called "Nuclear Age" by Vincenc Makovský from the Czechoslovak pavilion at the 1958 World Exhibition in Brussels.

The superstructure and the redevelopment of the Federal Assembly Building are examples of an unsuitable architectural solution to the problem of how modern architecture should be integrated in its historic surroundings, which here mostly date from the 19th century.

The publishing house Albatros, which has specialized in children's books, built in 1966—1968 an eight-storey administrative building, No. 342, at the corner of the streets Národní and Na Perštýně designed by Stanislav Franc and Luděk Hanf. The ground floor and the inner mezzanine floor contain a bookshop, and in the basement are a theatre hall and a lecture room. For the first time in Prague a fully glazed curtain-wall with an aluminium structure was used.

From 1967 to 1969, a building of the Merkuria Foreign Trade Company and of the Czechoslovak Chamber of Commerce designed by Vlastibor Klimeš, Eva Růžičková, Vratislav Růžička and Milan Vašek was built next to the Barikádníků (Barricade Fighters) Bridge in Holešovice District. The building is formed by four five- and six-storey prisms containing offices on an 18 by 18 m plan at the corners of the central part. This central part houses the vertical communications and is two floors higher. The ground floor contains an entrance hall, ceremonial, technical and social rooms, while the upper floors enclose hall-type offices, separate rooms for managers, lounges and accounts rooms. The total capacity of the building is 700 employees. The management rooms and those of the board of directors are on the top floors. The building has a prefabricated concrete skeleton and aluminium curtain-walls with rich vertical articulation. Of the many buildings from the 1960s where industrial prefabrication and suspended façade panels were used the Merkuria Building is the most successful, reminiscent of the functional architecture of the 1920s.

The Soviet trade representation complex includes four dwelling-houses, a round exhibiton hall, No. 1054, and a three-storey administrative building, No. 1027, along the crescent of Rooseveltova Street in Prague's Bubeneč District. The administrative building is three aisles wide, the structure is of transverse reinforced concrete frames cast on site, with brackets on both sides. The entrance hall contains a spiral staircase passing through all floors. The external cladding has a steel structure with light infill panels covered with a glass mosaic and stone prisms. The complex, designed by Vladimír Leníček, Lumír Holuša and Jiří Kulišťák and built in 1962—1964, is in harmony with the surrounding villas. Next to the building, a circular exhibition pavilion was constructed in 1972—1975 to designs by Vratislav Růžička, Boris Rákosník and Vladimír Mošna.

The building of Koospol Foreign Trade Company on E. Beneše Avenue in Vokovice District was designed by Vladimír Fencl, Stanislav Franc and Jan Nováček and built between 1974 and 1977. The building is a five-storey cube, 60 by 60 m, supported at a height of 11.4 m above the entrance by a reinforced concrete slab with four supports and projecting 14.4 m on each side, which is also the depth of the three-aisled office block enclosing an inner atrium 28.8 by 28.8 m The height of the building is 30 m and its capacity is 1,000 employees. The elongated ground floor contains an entrance hall, service and social rooms, and catering facilities. Attached at a right angle to it is the single-storey wing of the computer centre, power plant and Tuzex shop on E. Beneše Avenue with an adjoining parking area for 300 cars and a garage. The cube façades are clearly articulated with horizontal concrete elements. The surroundings of the house are laid out in the style of a modern French park.

Several administrative buildings were constructed in the 1970s on the street front: in Revoluční Street the eight-storey Unicop Building by Jaroslav Mayer, in Nekázanka Street the Omnipol Foreign Trade Company Building by Zdeněk Kuna, Zdeněk Stupka, Milan Valenta and Jaroslav Zdražil, with unusually designed interiors, furniture and walls. Both buildings have a concrete structure cast on site, the façade is fully glazed with reflective glass, being plain in Unicop and with oriel-like articulation in Omnipol.

For information about the Kovo, Motokov and other tower buildings see page 335.

Hotels

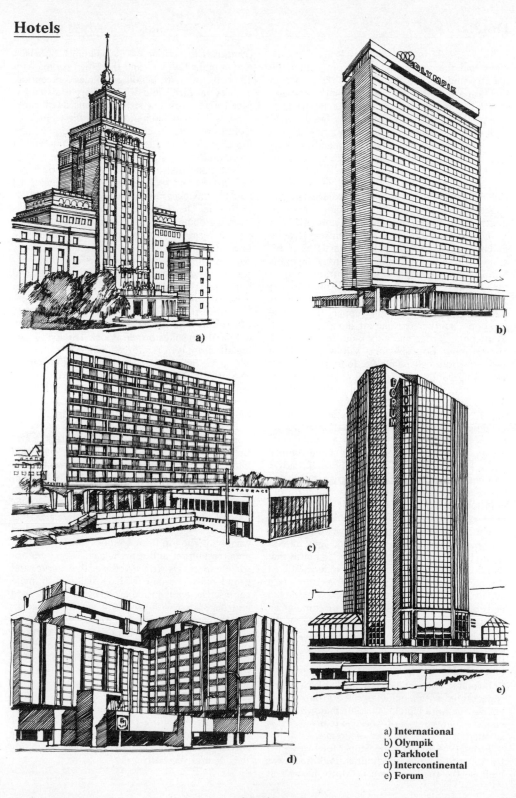

a) International
b) Olympik
c) Parkhotel
d) Intercontinental
e) Forum

Hotels

Since the early Middle Ages Prague has always had many visitors, both from within the country and abroad. As transport developed in the 19th and 20th centuries traffic increased and travel became gradually accessible to the general public. In the 1950s the existing hotels could no longer accommodate all the visitors and tourists nor did they meet modern demands. Consequently, new accommodation and catering facilities had to be constructed.

On Družba Square at the end of Jugoslávských partyzánů Street in Dejvice District the huge hotel International commanding the valley under Baba Hill was built between 1952 and 1956 to a plan prepared by František Jeřábek and a team of workers of the Military Design Institute. In the centre of the symmetrical layout is a fourteen-storey tower with an entrance hall on the ground floor and clubrooms on the first floor. The hotel has 100 single and twin rooms as well as 21 suites on the upper floors; the top floors contain a restaurant and a café, as well as a winter garden and a look-out terrace at the highest point. Both six-storey side wings contain 144 two-room cells while the four-storey courtyard wing contains restaurants, cafés, clubrooms and a reception hall. The total capacity of the hotel is 650 beds, the total volume of the building is 110,000 m³. The rich decoration of the hotel, which was conceived in the then official style of "socialist realism", is the work of a number of artists, such as Max Švabinský, Cyril Bouda, Alois Fišárek, Josef Novák, Irena and Ludvík Kodym, and others; they were responsible for the reliefs above the entrance, the sgraffito decoration on the façade, the mosaics, frescoes, tapestries and carpets in the interiors.

The Jalta Hotel in the upper part of Wenceslas Square was built in 1954 to designs by Antonín Tenzer on the site of an older house that had been demolished. Unlike the older hotels in this part of the city all the rooms for visitors face Wenceslas Square; there are 96 rooms with 140 beds on six floors. The ground floor contains an elevated terrace café which is followed by the hotel lounge with a free-standing curving staircase and a restaurant in the connecting part witg the courtyard wing which houses the kitchen. Upstairs are a café, meeting-rooms and reception rooms. The stone façade made of travertine is decorated with mouldings and a group of caryatids. The Jalta Hotel is the only major building conceived in the style of "socialist realism" that is situated in the historic core of Prague.

From 1964 to 1971 the Stop Motel designed by Alena Šrámková and Jindřich Pulkrábek was built on the road to Plzeň in Motol District. It comprises three four-storey buildings, of which two contain 129 two- and three-bed rooms with 220 beds; the third building includes a reception, a snack bar (grill), and offices. There is also a garage for 103 cars. The structure consists of transverse walls; seen from outside are the white horizontals of concrete ceilings and the ceramic facing of the outer walls. The neighbouring part of the motel was designed by Milan Rejchl.

The Parkhotel in Prague 7 District, built between 1964 and 1967 to designs by Zdeněk Edel and Jiří Lavička, ranks among the largest hotels in Prague. The twelve-storey main building rises from a sloping site at Dukelských hrdinů Street, with a reception lounge and a day bar on the ground floor which is connected to a two-storey wing with a restaurant, a café and meeting-rooms. In spite of its architectural qualities and purity of style the building is an example of de-urbanizing intervention in the historic 19th century town plan of the district. There is a total of 229 rooms with 378 beds (with extra beds even 607) and ten suites on ten floors. The load-bearing structure is of reinforced concrete with cross walls, the façade consists of metal infill panels. The artistic decoration of both the exterior and the interior is by Václav Bejček, Josef Klimeš, Karel Hladík, Ivana Dědičová, Věra Drnková-Zářecká, among other sculptors and artists.

Another large modern hotel in Prague is the Intercontinental designed by Karel Filsak, Karel Bubeníček, František Cubr and Jan Šrámek, and built from 1968 to 1974 on the Old Town bridge-head of Svatopluk Čech Bridge. The hotel consists of three five- to seven-storey buildings with hotel rooms while the ground floor contains a hotel lounge with a reception area, cafés, restaurants, a meeting-room, a bar, and a conference hall. The top floor contains a luxury panoramic restaurant and a night bar. The system of social spaces is conceived so that large and grand halls alternate with closed and intimate rooms. The walls inside are artistically designed and decorated with works of art, in particular, with paintings by František Ronovský. The exterior of the building is characterized by verticals of exposed concrete and window bays, combined with a ceramic wall cladding. The hotel has 356 rooms and 52 suites with a total of 825 beds, the social rooms contain 1,500 seats. *The Intercontinental Hotel as well as the department store Kotva were attempts at integrating modern architecture into the historic Old Town. In spite of the great size of the hotel the problem could be solved by dividing the mass and by articulating the façades vertically.*

By the southern bridgehead of the Nuselský Bridge the Hotel Forum was built, which is a tower building of polygonal plan with 27 storeys. The building has a steel structure with suspended walls, with a metal outer skin, and its construction was completed in 1988. The hotel was designed by Jaroslav Trávníček and has 568 suites with 1135 beds as well as many social and sports rooms. *The vertical mass of the hotel was intended to be a counterbalance to the huge horizontal mass of the Palace of Congresses. In the overall townscape, however, and particularly in the general vistas of the town it appears too big, and together with other high buildings in Pankrác it has considerably spoiled the scale of the town and its southern skyline.*

For information about the Panorama Hotel see page 335.

Department Stores

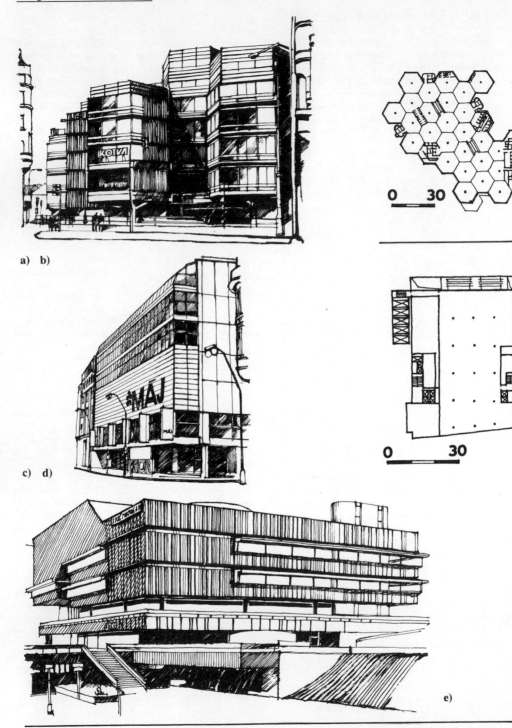

a) b)

c) d)

e)

a) b) **Kotva**   c) d) **Máj**   e) **Home Furnishings Store**

Department Stores

Social and economic changes and the need for more efficient trade with a reduced number of workers in the network of shops led both to the modernization of existing shopping facilities and to the construction of new shops on the new housing estates and of large department stores in the centre of Prague.

The Czechoslovak Government decided on 12th November 1954 to build new department stores in the place of houses on Wenceslas Square destroyed by the Germans during the Prague Uprising in May 1945. The five-storey House of Food at the corner of Washingtonova Street was designed by Max Gronwald, Jiří Chvalina and M. K. Řehoř and constructed from 1955 to 1957. The eight-storey House of Fashion, designed by Josef Hrubý, was built at the same time. Both buildings are situated on irregular, sloping plots. The layout of both interiors is based on the same principle: one shopping hall on each floor, corner entrances, stairs and elevators behind, storerooms and technical facilities in the basement. The reinforced concrete framework made it possible in both cases to use large windows in the façades which are vertically articulated, clad in travertine, and decorated with stone reliefs above the entrance. However, if compared with department stores from the pre-war period, such as Perla, Bílá labuť, etc., nothing new was developed in their concept and they both fully conform to the classicizing concept of the "socialist realism".

Smaller stores, supermarkets and shopping centres with foodstuffs and industrial goods were built in the 1960s and 1970s in the centres of Prague's housing estates, such as the Petřiny Store in Petřiny District, the Šárka Store on Červený vrch (Red Hill), the Ládví Store in Ďáblice District, the Prior in Prosek, the Centrum in Spořilov, the Vltava in Modřany, the Zdar in Jižní Město (South Town), etc. Other shopping facilities are under construction.

The department store Máj on Národní (National) Avenue was built by the Swedish company ABO between 1973 and 1975 to a design by John Eisler, Miroslav Masák and Martin Rajniš. In the attempt to make the orientation inside the building as easy as possible the architects did not pay enough attention to the fact that the store was situated at the intersection with Spálená Street, which is "faced" by a gable wall of exposed concrete. The flat façade on Národní Avenue displays continuous windows alternating with strips of white glass, and is closed on the sixth floor by a rounded surface of office windows. On the other side of the building, facing a square adjoining Spálená Street is a glass wall covering the escalator bay and with a grid structure. The easily understandable layout of the shopping spaces is underlined by the bright colours of the walls, ceilings, technical equipment and furnishings.

A totally different concept was chosen for the largest department store in Prague, Kotva, which was designed by Věra and Vladimír Machonin and built between 1971 and 1975 by the Swedish company S.I.A.S. between náměstí Republiky (Square of the Republic) and the streets Králodvorská and Rybná. The store has 2,000 workers and some 75,000 customers every day. The six- and seven-storey building has hexagonal flat ceilings made of cast reinforced concrete, supported by pillars, and with starlike inclined struts. The four shopping floors are connected by escalators and painted in different colours; the top floor contains a large restaurant with a terrace. There are three basements with offices, storerooms, technical facilities and garages for 330 cars. The building is articulated both in its plan and vertically, and the façades are mostly glazed with brown dethermal glass, the parapets being made of "tombak" alloy while elsewhere exposed concrete has been used.

The department store "Domov" on Budějovice Square in Prague 4 District, which specializes in furniture and other accessories for the home, was designed by Věra Machoninová in 1969 and constructed from 1972 to 1981. The steel framework with truss girders of 14.4 m span carries six selling floors with a third of the area of each floor displaced by half the storey height, and with escalators and stairs at the points where the level changes. This solution improved circulation inside the building. The exterior is characterized by alternating strips of metal sheeting (korten) and projecting windows. The mass of the building is enlivened with rounded towers for the emergency stairs and an elliptical cinema on the roof, both made of exposed concrete.

Palace of Congresses

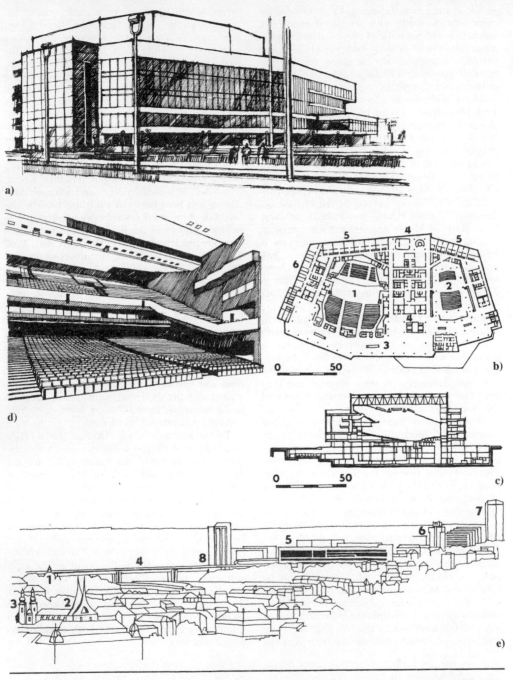

a) b) c) d) **Palace of Congresses:** 1 Congress Hall, 2 Social Hall, 3 foyer, 4 meeting-rooms, 5 cloakrooms, 6 offices

e) **Palace of Congresses in the panorama of Prague:** 1 Church of Our Lady and St. Charles the Great, 2 monastery Na Slovanech, 3 Church of St. John na Skalce, 4 Nusle Bridge, 5 Palace of Congresses, 6 Centrotex, 7 Motokov, 8 Hotel Forum

Palace of Congresses

A number of important cultural and artistic establishments were constructed in Prague in the late 19th and the early 20th centuries, which were joined between the two world wars by one new facility only, namely the SVU Mánes House, No. 250, built by Otakar Novotný in 1930 on the site of the earlier Šítkovské Mills on the bank of the Vltava.

In the new social situation after the Second World War new buildings were built in the new suburbs for cultural and social activities. From 1957 to 1961 a four-storey social centre MARS designed by Jiří Siegel was built in Vršovice District, with a large conference hall, clubrooms, a restaurant and a café, and in the subsequent years similar "houses of culture" with cinemas were constructed in the housing estates Novodvorská, Ďáblice, Bohnice, and other new residential areas.

In 1975 the Government decided to build a palace of congresses (Palác kultury, literally Palace of Culture) which was completed in 1980. Consequently, Prague obtained an excellent social and cultural centre where congresses, symposia and concerts for large audiences could be organized.

A competition of invited architects was organized and the first prize was awarded to the entry prepared by a team of architects of the Military Design Institute headed by Jaroslav Mayer, Antonín Vaněk and Josef Karlík. The building is a monoblock of irregular heptagonal plan with entrances, cloakrooms, restaurants and foyers, three storeys high, concentrated on the north side, i.e., the side facing the city. There are galleries offering beautiful views of the town. The southern part of the building contains offices and dressing-rooms for artists, while in the middle of the block is the large Congress Hall and the smaller Social Hall, as well as many meeting-rooms and rehearsal rooms on several floors. The first basement contains a car-park for 835 cars and 46 coaches, technical facilities, staff catering establishments, while in the second basement the power plant, the heating and ventilation facilities, the kitchens and storerooms are concentrated.

The Congress Hall, which is also intended for concerts, films and performance arts has 1852 seats on the main floor and 991 on the balcony. To improve the acoustics for concerts, the ceiling can be lowered. When this is done, the number of seats is reduced to 2,071. The stage is adjustable using a system of hydraulics. The front wall contains an organ by the sculptor Kočiš.

The seats in the hall have air-conditioning and translation equipment built in.

The Social Hall is suitable for concerts and symposia, and also for receptions and balls. It can seat 800 to 1,200 people in the parterre and on two galleries. The floor can be either raised or level. There are bridges for lighting, vertically adjustable, inside the hall. The curtain was made by Martin Sladký. The Small Hall on the ground floor has a special foyer, a cloakroom and a snack bar, and can accommodate 440 spectators or 340 people sitting at tables. There is also another hall, called the Chamber Hall, on the fourth floor for an audience of 200, with a glazed wall and a view of Prague. The Conference Hall on the fifth floor has 60 to 200 seats at tables. The restaurants, the café, the clubrooms and the night club can accommodate a total of 1,700 visitors. In addition, there is a day bar connected to the look-out terrace, a Youth Club, and several snack bars.

The architectural concept of the exterior followed the principle of expressing the internal function of the building by technically perfect means. The curtain wall is made of reinforced concrete panels, with an exposed structured surface of white cement. Also the interiors are solved according to their function: the walls of the foyers and corridors are characterized by the tints of brown and grey colour of the plastic materials and the stones used for facing and flooring; the halls, meeting-rooms and restaurants have walls and floors covered with materials of bright colours, whose effect is increased by the interesting furniture, decorative details, metal and glass objects, and by some 150 works of fine art, such as engravings, tapestries, paintings, sculptures and reliefs made by Jan Bauch, Josef Brož, Cyril Bouda, Mikuláš Bazovský, Ludovít Fulla, Jaroslav Gruss, František Jiroudek, Radomír Kolář, Stanislav Libenský, Klára Patakiová, Rudolf Riedelbauch, Ludvika Smrčková, Karel Souček, and other artists. The curtain in the Congress Hall was made by Alois Fišárek, the look-out terrace in front of the building is adorned with an allegorical statue by Jan Hána. *In spite of the ambitious attempt to create a new, lively cultural centre for Prague here, this goal has not been reached. The building is too far away from the centre to be able to play this role. The building also had a negative impact on the townscape. Its huge unarticulated body on an open site on the edge of the Nusle Valley totally commands the surrounding small-scale buildings in the "foreground" and optically changes the relationships in the skyline of Prague.*

Skyscrapers in Prague

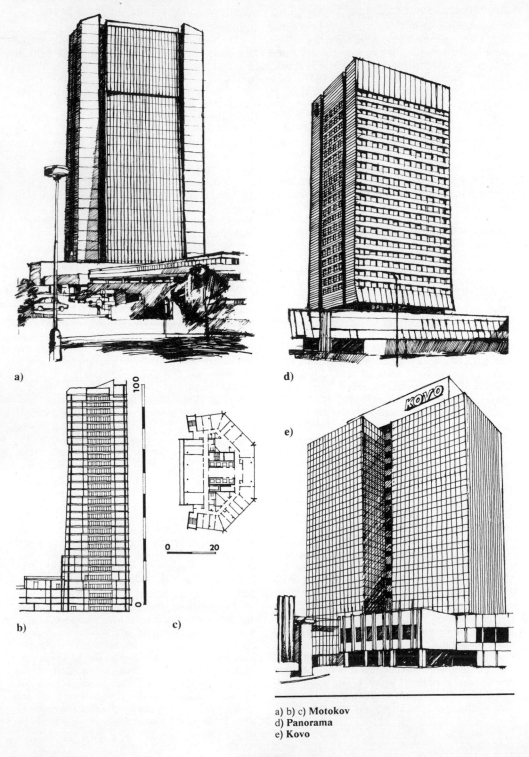

a) b) c) **Motokov**
d) **Panorama**
e) **Kovo**

Multi-storey administrative buildings and hotels were made possible by modern construction technologies and technical progress, and proved useful as early as the beginning of this century. However, the aesthetic value of the townscape of Prague means that we should be careful about showing any great sympathy for the plans that emerged in the 1930s suggesting the construction of such tall buildings in the historic core of the town or its periphery. Such buildings require a high-capacity of traffic, which was impossible in Prague until the underground railway was built. The bridge over the Nusle Valley with an Underground tunnel created the conditions needed for making Pankrác a site for high-rise buildings in Prague.

Earlier, in 1971, the tall building of the foreign trade company Strojimport was constructed to the south of the intersection of Vinohradská Street and Želivského Street. Designed by Zdeněk Kuna, Zdeněk Stupka and Oliver Honke-Houfek, the building has a two-storey base with the entrance hall, meeting-rooms, an accented session hall, and a sixteen-storey prism with office space above, with a steel construction and outer walls with alternating strips of parapets of eloxal-coated aluminium and windows of dethermal glass.

In the same year the construction of the Hotel Olympik, twenty-two storeys high, designed by Josef Polák in collaboration with Jan Zelený, Milan Rejchl and Vojtěch Šalda was completed. The frame is of reinforced concrete cast on site, the façade is clad in ceramic tiles.

The building of the foreign trade company Kovo was designed in 1974—1975 and its construction was completed in 1977. It is situated north of the Libeň Bridge in Holešovice District and was designed by Zdeněk Edel, Josef Matyáš, Luděk Štefka and Pavel Štěch. Its seventeen floors are covered with a fully glazed aluminium grid raster, filled with blue-tinted reflective glass, which contrasts with the textured exposed concrete in the communication core and the base. The bearing structure was made of prefabricated concrete parts, and the building became an interesting dominant structure commanding the Ho-

lešovice embankment and offering an interesting view of Přístavní Street.

The building of Centrotex Foreign Trade Company dominating Hrdinů Square in Prague 4 Podolí was designed in 1972 by Václav Hilský and Otakar Jurenka and its construction was completed in 1978. The building consists of a two-storey base with the entrance, and fifteen storeys of offices above. Above the base, there is a large terrace with an entrance to the vestibule of the main building and a parking area. The bearing structure is a reinforced concrete skeleton cast on site, the curtain-wall is of eloxal-coated or enamelled aluminium sheets.

On a dominant site in the middle of Pankrác area the foreign trade company Motokov constructed in 1975—1977 the tallest building in Prague so far, a 104 m high office building with 27 storeys for 1,500 employees, intended as part of a future central square of the district. The building was designed by Zdeněk Kuna, Zdeněk Stupka, Oliver Honke-Houfek, Milan Valenta and Jaroslav Zdražil, and is joined in the south to a large entrance part, articulated both horizontally and vertically, with meeting rooms, a social hall for 150 people, a dining-room and a Tuzex luxury shop. The bearing structure is of steel and encloses a vertical communication core of reinforced concrete. The five walls facing north and the oblique central part of the southern wall are characterized by fully glazed surfaces of fixed windows.

The second of the three skyscrapers planned on Pankrác Square is the 24-storey massive prism of the Panorama Hotel finished in 1983 and designed by Alois Semela and Vlado Alujevič. The building rises from a square base and has 440 hotel rooms facing all four sides with a vertical communication core in the centre. The bearing structure of the building is of reinforced concrete cast on site; the hotel tower is conceived as a system of load-bearing partition walls. The strips of continuous windows and the ochre colour of the concrete parapets are in striking contrast with the glaring glass façade of the Motokov Building.

New Bridges

a)

b)

c)

d)

a) Šverma Bridge
b) **Barricade Fighters Bridge** (Barikádníků)

c) **Nusle Bridge**
d) **Barrandov Bridge**

The City of Prague continued developing after the Second World War both in its size and in the number of inhabitants, which in the early 1960s exceeded one million. As there was full employment of all social and age categories of the population, the transportation needs were very high. Due to this and to the rising number of passenger cars and the development of municipal bus transport, the capacity of streets had to be increased. Large new roads and bridges were constructed. In some cases existing bridges were adapted, or even totally reconstructed. A very old dream came true when a bridge across the Nusle Valley was built.

The first new bridge built after the war was the Šverma Bridge which in 1951 replaced an old steel suspension bridge dating from 1865—1868, once called Francis Joseph I Bridge and later Štefánik Bridge. In 1898, the chains were replaced by ropes and in 1947 the bridge was dismantled and a provisional wooden bridge was built here instead. Then, from 1948 to 1951, a reinforced concrete bridge was constructed, 200 m long and 24 m wide, with three segmental arches above the river and two flat sections bridging the embankments. The concrete piers are clad with granite blocks. The structure was designed by Jan Fischer, the architectural realization was by Vlastislav Hofman and Otakar Širc, following their original project from 1941.

All development plans for Prague after 1948 paid much attention to the area of Pankrác which was regarded as very important for the future expansion of the town, provided, of course, it had direct communications to the centre of the town. Such plans had existed since 1903 when Jaroslav Marjanek suggested a steel arch bridge to connect Karlov with Pankrác. A number of studies were prepared and competitions held between the two world wars which suggested a suspended steel bridge (Josef Chochol—Škoda Works), a straight steel bridge with several supports (František and Vojtěch Kerhart), parabolic concrete arches (Stanislav Bechyně—Bohumír Kozák), among other solutions. Then, in the late 1950s, another competition was organized and the plan submitted by Stanislav Hubička, Svatopluk Kobr and Vojtěch Michálek was then carried out from 1965 to 1969.

The Nusle Bridge ranks among the most remarkable works of civil engineering in Prague. Almost half a kilometre long, it bridges the 40 m deep valley with a straight concrete bridge deck resting on a hollow prism, 5 by 11 m, where the Underground and distribution lines pass. The top part of this concrete casing projects, with supporting elements on both sides so that the total width of the bridge reaches 26.5 m, which is enough for six lanes of traffic and for pavements on either side. The walls of the casing are 30 to 50 cm thick, the reinforcement is made by means of prestressed cables. The five bridge spans, of which the central three are 115 m and the end spans 69 m, are supported by reinforced concrete piers, each composed of four diverging flat prisms tapering upwards. Due to its position the bridge can be seen both from the streets beneath, and as part of the general panorama of the town. We see both its massive solidity and its impressive height. In contrast to this is the human scale of a pair of atriums at the Underground station Vyšehrad on the Pankrác side of the bridge. The adjoining park terraces in front of the Palace of Congresses have fine views of the Nusle Valley and the Vltava.

The bridge called "Barikádníků" (Barricade Fighters Bridge) between Holešovice and Troja, dating from 1928, has a bold structure of reinforced concrete with arched ribs designed by František Mencl, although the more visible architectural elements were the work of Josef Chochol. It was seriously damaged during the uprising against the Nazis in May 1945. This reduced its carying capacity and, in addition, the bridge was too narrow to accommodate the traffic on the second north-south axis road passing here. Therefore, it was dismantled in 1973—1975 and on its foundations a new bridge, 200 m long, designed by Pavel Dobrovský and Jiří Trnka was built. The new bridge has a roadway twice the width of the old bridge, with pavements, but the old foundations required an unusual form of piers made of massive reinforced concrete prisms.

In 1978, the construction started on the Vltava between Braník and Barrandov of a bridge and its road links to form part of the southern section of Prague's inner ring road. This extremely difficult task, including two road junctions linked to two arterial roads on the banks of the river, was solved by Jiří Hejnic, Pavel Tripal and Karel Filsak. The final traffic system has, unlike the previous studies, fewer bridge girder structures, but, as a result, is irregularly shaped. The bridge crosses the river at a height of 15 m above the water with a total length of 200 m and at an angle of 53°.

The bridge is divided into two strips, each 20 m wide, with a total of eight traffic lanes and with two pavements. It is the widest bridge in Czechoslovakia now. Made of reinforced concrete, it has six different spans, the length of which varies from 35 to 72 m. The same piers support both halves of the bridge and they consist of three concrete prisms of increasing size one above the other. The piers bear a system of longitudinal girders and the slabs of the roadway. The first part of the bridge was put into operation in 1983 and the whole structure, including all the access ramps and connections was completed in 1988.

Underground Railway Stations

Prague became the capital of independent Czechoslovakia in October 1918 and, as a result, the number of its inhabitants rapidly increased in the subsequent years, reaching 676,000 in 1922 and even 816,000 in 1926. New districts and settlements emerged, such as Dejvice, Pankrác, the eastern part of Vršovice, Ořechovka, Spořilov, etc. The problems of municipal transport, which was provided by means of tram lines only, were further increased by the narrow streets in the historic centre of the town and by the uneven relief of the townscape with many steep slopes and curves. These problems could only be solved by building an underground railway.

The first suggestions, however, were not from the Municipal Council, but on the personal initiative of two engineers, Vladimír List and Bohumil Belada, who in 1926 submitted a study for Prague's subway system with four lines making a triangle in the centre of the city. Some years later another proposal was made which just reckoned with underground tram lines in the centre, in rather shallow tunnels that would be entered via ramps from streets. It was not until 1939 that the Municipal Council commissioned a plan for an underground railway for the city; however, the German authorities stopped the work in 1941.

The interrupted work could have been the starting point of a final plan after the liberation of the country. The new social situation led to further development of the town and the need for a better system of municipal transport became quite apparent. Instead, however, the idea of a tram subway prevailed, with 14.5 km of the total length of 119 km under the ground. The construction started in 1965, however due to a detailed analysis of its efficiency and, in particular, to the conclusions of foreign, mostly Soviet specialists, the work was interrupted in 1967 and a new decision was made: to construct an underground railway, a "metro". The first line, known as Line C, from Pankrác to Karlín was put into operation on 1st May 1974, and its second section to Holešovice was opened on 7th November 1984. The second Line A, from Dejvice to Vinohrady, has been in operation since 12th August 1978. The extensions of both lines to Jižní Město (South Town) and to the end of Vinohrady were completed on 7th November 1980 and 19th December 1980, respectively. The third line, coded B, from Smíchov to Karlín has been operating since 2nd November 1985, the extension of Line A from Vinohrady to Strašnice since 11th July 1987, that of Line B to Jihozápadní Město (Southwest Town) since 26th October 1988, and to Vysočany since 22nd November 1990. Another extension of Line C to Severní Město (North Town) is now under construction.

The Underground has not only dramatically improved municipal transport in the city, but also enriched the town's environment with fine new elements, particularly the Underground stations, which—following the example of Soviet cities—were not considered merely as practical transport facilities, but were also intended to be of considerable aesthetic value. There is an excellent lighting system, a clear system of orientation, and there are also public toilets and an air-conditioning and air-cleaning system. All this contributes to a sense of good taste and good organization.

The entrances of the stations depend on the particular conditions at ground level. In the centre of the town they have in many case been incorporated in existing or new arcades. To climb down to the station, solid granite stairs are available or, if the station is deeper than six metres below the surface, escalators have been installed in both directions. The Line C extension has stations conceived as free-standing entrance pavilions.

The ticket-halls form the first part of the stations below ground, and the space in front of the ticket-stamping machines can be entered free of charge. Attended WCs are also available. Many of these halls are lined with shops, stalls, newspaper stands, stands with flowers, souvenirs, etc. Some stations have large glass walls separating the entrance part from the turnstiles and the platforms. The ticket-halls also often form part of pedestrian underpasses enabling communication underground between several urban spaces.

Passing through the turnstiles one climbs

Underground Railway Stations

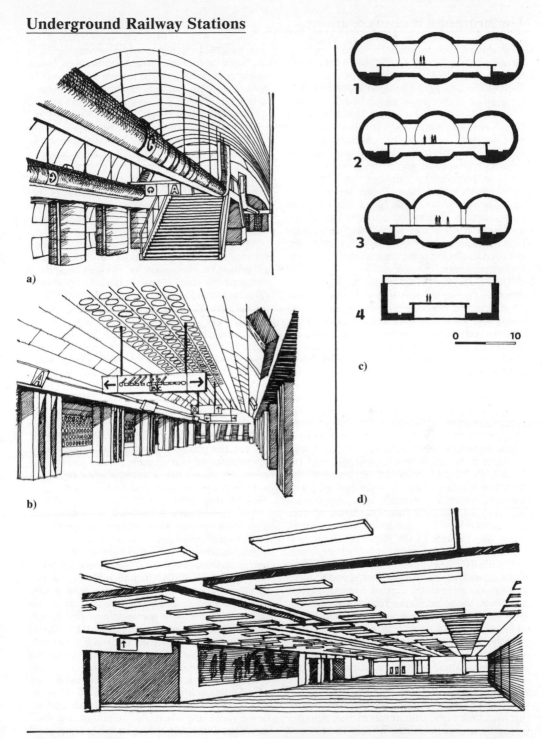

a)

b)

c)

d)

1

2

3

4

0   10

a) Můstek—Line B
b) Můstek—Line A

c) **Underground station types:** 1, 2 driven, with piers, 3
driven, with columns, 4 excavated
d) **Florenc**

down to the platform, either by means of stairs or escalators (or both), the platforms being mostly of the "island" type (i.e., with rails on both sides) and only exceptionally of the "side type" (with platforms on either side of the rails, as in the stations Vyšehrad or Hlavní nádraží). Line C was excavated and the stations here are covered with flat roofs, either without any supporting piers (Museum, Florenc), with one row of piers (Hlavní nádraží), or with two rows. At the first stage of construction the walls were mostly lined with polished stone, the extensions have stations with ceramic facing. Lighting is incorporated in illuminated ceilings. The station Vyšehrad at the south end of the Nusle Bridge offers fine views of the Vltava Valley up to Vinohrady District. At some stations there are well-shaped ventilation towers.

The character of stations on Line A is a little different due to the fact that they are in three driven tunnels, linked by wide passages, the central tunnel being used for access, with escalators, and the side tunnels containing the platforms. The walls and ceilings form one unit, made of eloxal-coated aluminium panels, of different colours in each station. An exception to this is the final station Dejvická, which has a flat ceiling and walls decorated with ceramic vertical stripes of different colours (glazed Hurdis pieces). The entrance part of Malostranská (Lesser Quarter) Station is attached to a small garden in front of the Wallenstein Riding-School.

The B Line, which forms a triangle with the lines A and C in the centre of the town and thus makes possible various combinations of travel through Prague, has strongly influenced the appearance of Prague's streets with the surface structures above its stations at Těšnov, náměstí Republiky (Square of the Republic), Wenceslas Square, Národní třída (National Avenue), Karlovo náměstí (Charles Square), and above both stations in Smíchov. Unlike the lines A and C, much demolition was needed here of unimportant old buildings, the streets were rebuilt and new station buildings were constructed; new tall blocks are also expected to be built here in the future. Construction conditions of the entrance and underground spaces were more difficult. Using the experience gained with the construction of the previous stations, tunnels of greater radius curve were driven for both the platforms and escalators which, together with the new method of lighting by means of fluorescent lamps urns improved the general effect. Walls were covered with glazed ceramic tiles, glass bricks and plates, and decorated with figural or ornamental mosaics and ceramic reliefs. Quite unusual is the sta-

tion "Anděl" in Smíchov which was designed in cooperation with the Soviet architect Lev Nikolayevich Popov. Coloured marble was used here for the flooring and wall facing, and the station is decorated with a monumental stone mosaic and bronze figural reliefs.

Chief architect of the Line C stations is Jaroslav Otruba, while Evžen Kyllar is the chief architect of lines A and B. The stations were designed by a total of 39 architects. The orientation signs were designed by Jiří Rathouský. Most stations are embellished with works of art, such as statues, reliefs, mosaics, decorative window lights and latticework, made by 27 sculptors, painters and other fine artists.

The pedestrian subways at the Underground stations had a very good precedent: the pedestrian subway in the middle of Wenceslas Square, designed by Josef Kales, Stanislav Kovář and Jaroslav Strašil and built in 1966—1968, with a total area of 50 by 80 m. There are stairs and escalators in all directions leading to pavements or arcades. Its reinforced concrete ceiling is supported by steel tubes forming a rhomboid grid. The subway is three metres high and contains glazed stands, stalls, shops, WCs and technical services. The granite flooring, marble wall-facing and good lighting make a good impression and give a sense of protection against traffic and bad weather.

The construction of Prague's underground railway has proved that even such a large-scale scheme, which was initially feared due to the concerns about historic architecture, can contribute to the renovation and presentation of ancient buildings.

The construction stimulated the activity of monument preservation bodies. In particular, constant archaeological research was carried out during the driving and excavation work. The research has brought a lot of interesting information to light. Of the "minor" findings we can mention here wells in Wenceslas Square that were discovered during the construction of the pedestrian subway in the middle of the square, and the findings at Staroměstská (Old Town) Station in Kaprova Street. Particularly interesting is the Gothic bridge found in the street Na můstku which has been incorporated in the architecture of the Underground entrance hall. This finding confirmed the aptness of the name "Na můstku" (i.e., On the Bridge), which was believed to be just a legend. The remarkable finding enlivens this highly frequented Underground station.

The Underground railway has also helped to draw attention to and enliven certain historic spaces, particularly at Malostranská (Lesser Quarter) Station, where an old exhibition pavilion from the late 1940s was demolished and, on the site of a former stable yard near the east wall of the renovated Wallenstein Riding-School, a very attractive public garden was created that has become quite popular. Its fine architecture is the work of Zdeněk Drobný and Otakar Kuča. The attractive atmosphere of the Lesser Quarter can be felt even in the escalator vestibules where replicas of Braun's allegorical statue "Hope" from Kuks Castle and of urns from Vrtba Garden were placed. In the

adjoining garden are copies of sculptures by Anton Braun from the garden of Valeč Castle.

Another benefit that the construction of the Underground has brought with it is the renovation of buildings around the stations, both in the historic centre of the town and in the suburbs. The construction accelerated the renovation of houses in the street Na můstku, around Jungmann Square, on Charles Square, at Anděl in Smíchov, and elsewhere. As a result, a symbiosis of two worlds is reached, which differ very much in time, but which support each other's existence.

National Cultural Monuments

There are forty protected historic towns in this country, of which the largest, Prague, was put on the list in 1971. The historic core covers an area of over eight square kilometres, surrounded by a protective zone of some 90 square kilometres, which makes it not only the largest town conservation area in this country in terms of size, but also due to the number and importance of the ancient buildings included.

The list of Prague's historic buildings amounts to about 2,000, of which 1,440 are in the historic core of the town. Seventeen of them have been declared national cultural monuments.

The first 33 national cultural monuments in the country were declared by the Government in 1962, and further lists followed in 1969 and 1971. The list of national cultural monuments was controversially extended on 24th February 1978 by including 32 other buildings, mostly related to the history of the revolutionary and workers' movement, anti-Nazi resistance and the liberation of the country.

Of all the national cultural monuments in Bohemia and Moravia seventeen are in Prague, i.e., almost one third, of which half date back to the Romanesque and Gothic era. The oldest national monuments include both individual buildings and whole complexes of buildings that in the course of centuries have become symbols of Prague and of the nation.

The group of medieval monuments is followed by other historic buildings and complexes which are not always directly related to the topic of

this book. Nevertheless, we mention below all the national cultural monuments in Prague. The number in brackets indicates the order in which they were put on the list:

Old Town Square with the Town-Hall, Týn Church and Kinský Palace, Prague 1, Old Town (14)

Agnes Convent, Prague 1, Old Town (56)

Charles Bridge, with towers and statues, Prague 1, Old Town (13)

Carolinum, Prague 1, Old Town (15)

Bethlehem Chapel, Prague 1, Old Town (17)

Theatre of the Estates, Prague 1, Old Town (24)

National Theatre, Prague 1, New Town (25)

National Museum, Prague 1, New Town (26)

Prague Castle with archaeological findings, Prague 1, Hradčany (1)

Bohemian Crown Jewels, Prague 1, Hradčany

Town-Hall of the New Town, Prague 2, New Town (19)

Emmaus Abbey (Na Slovanech) with the Church of Our Lady and the Chapel of SS. Cosmas and Damian, Prague 2, New Town (57)

Vyšehrad (the castle, its fortifications, and the cemetery), Prague 2, Vyšehrad (11)

National Memorial on Vítkov Hill, Prague 3, Žižkov (33)

White Mountain (battlefield, Hvězda hunting-lodge, game park), Prague 6, Liboc (22)

Memorial to Victims of Anti-Nazi Resistance, Prague 8, Kobylisy (36)

Břevnov Abbey (declared on 13 February 1991)

Literature

Only Czech literature has been used by the authors of this book. Its full list is published in the Czech version.

Main periods of the history of Prague and its architecture

Century	Rulers	Style
5—7	Early Slav settlements	pre-Romanesque
	CZECH STATE **The Přemyslids** (870—1306) (most important): **Princes** Bořivoj 870—894?	
10	Spytihněv 894—905? 915? Vratislav 905—921? Wenceslas (Saint) 921?—935 Boleslav I 935—972 Boleslav II 973—999	
11	Břetislav I 1034—55 Spytihněv II 1055—61 Vratislav II 1061—92 (in 1085 acquired the title of King for himself)	**Romanesque** 1100—1230
12	Vladislav I 1120—25 Soběslav I 1125—40 Vladislav II 1140—72 (in 1158 acquired hereditary title of King) Soběslav II 1173—78	
13	**Kings** Přemysl I, King 1197—1230 Wenceslas I 1230—53 Přemysl II Otakar 1253—78	**early Gothic** 1230—1310
	Wenceslas II 1278—1305	
14	Wenceslas III 1305—6	
	The Luxembourgs (1310—1419) John 1310—46 Charles IV 1346—78 as of 1355 Emperor of the Holy Roman Empire	**high Gothic** 1310—1440
15	Wenceslas IV, Emperor 1378—1419	

Samo Empire, late 7th century
Great Moravian Empire (830—906?)

	Bořivoj converted in the last third of 9th c.	880—890	Prague Castle founded, beginning of medieval Prague
		885	first Christian church in Prague Castle
965—966	Ibrahim Ibn Ya'qub and his report on Prague	920	St. George's Basilica in Prague Castle, first Benedictine monasteries at Prague Castle (920) and Břevnov (993)
973	bishopric in Prague coin minting at Vyšehrad unification of Czech State by the Přemyslids		
1085	Vratislav II moves to Vyšehrad	1060	Spytihněv's basilica in Prague Castle Construction of palace and a basilica to SS. Peter and Paul at Vyšehrad
1125	The first Czech chronicler dies (Cosmas)	1135	Soběslav I starts construction of stone walls and palace at Prague Castle
1140	The sovereign moves back to Prague Castle	1140	Premonstratensian monastery founded on Strahov Hill fortification of Prague Castle Judith Bridge (1158—1172) churches (rotundas) stone houses in Old Town
as of 1230	development of culture and education		convent of the Clares and monastery of the Minorites in Old Town (around 1230)
1253	expansion of Bohemia, silver mining		fortification of Old Town (started in 1231) Old-New Synagogue (1270) fortification of Prague Castle founding of Havelské Město, construction of new Gothic houses (1230—53)
1278	Přemysl Otakar II defeated by Rudolf Habsburg and killed		
1300	Bohemian coin "groš" minted		
1306	the Přemyslids die out through the assassination of Wenceslas III		
1310	John of Luxembourg occupies Prague		town-hall of the Old Town
		1333	renovation of Prague Castle
1322—29	new lands gained: Egerland, Upper Lusatia, Gorlitz	1344	archbishopric, cathedral started
		1348	university founded
1333	Charles arrives at Prague	1348	New Town of Prague
1333	renovation of Prague Castle begins	1357	Charles Bridge
		1391	Bethlehem Chapel
1394—1402	revolt of lords against Wenceslas IV		
1402	Master Jan Hus preaches in Bethlehem Chapel		
1415	Jan Hus burned alive in Constance		
1419—1434	Hussite Revolution		
1419	Lesser Town destroyed		

Century	Rulers	Style
15	George of Poděbrady, King 1458—71	**late Gothic** 1440—1530
16	**Jagiello Dynasty** (1471—1526) Vladislav II Jagiello, King 1471—1516 Louis Jagiello, King 1516—26 **The Habsburgs** (1526—1918), Emperors Ferdinand I 1526—64	**Renaissance** 1500—1580
		Mannerism 1580—1620
	Ferdinand II 1620—37	**early Baroque** 1620—1690
	Ferdinand III 1637—57 Leopold I 1657—1705	
18	Joseph I 1705—11 Charles VI 1711—40	**high Baroque** 1690—1740
	Maria Theresa, Queen 1740—80	**late Baroque** Rococo
		Baroque neo-Classicism 1740—1780
	Joseph II 1780—90	
19	Francis II 1792—1835	**neo-Classicism** 1780—1804
		Empire
	Ferdinand V 1835—48	**Romanticism** historic styles 1848—1900

	new prosperity of Prague		
1457	Unitas Fratrum established (the first reformed Church independent of Rome)		
1468	first book printed		
		1486—1502	renovation of Prague Castle Vladislav Hall
		1493	advent of Renaissance
1526	Louis killed in battle with Turks		
1526	Ferdinand I elected king of Bohemia and Hungary	1538	Royal Summer Palace Hvězda hunting lodge palaces for nobles
1541	big fire in Lesser Quarter, Hradčany and Castle		
1546—7	revolt of the Estates against the Habsburgs		
1556	Jesuits come to Prague		
1561	archbishopric restored		
	Rudolphian Prague is an important centre of culture and a seat of Imperial Court		renovation of Castle, middle-class houses town-hall of Lesser Quarter
1612	Rudolph II dies		
1618	defenestration, revolt of Bohemian Estates, beginning of Thirty Years' War		
1620	defeat of Bohemian Estates on White Mountain		
1621	execution of 27 leaders of anti-Habsburg revolt		Clementinum Wallenstein Palace
1627	property of non-Catholic nobles confiscated		Loretto construction by clergy and new nobility
	foreign nobles arrive J. A. Comenius (1630s—1660s)		fortifications of Prague Černín Palace
1648	Prague occupied by Swedish army		
1684	fire in Old Town and New Town		large-scale construction of religious buildings, such as
	peak of Baroque development of neo-Classicism War of Austrian Succession three Silesian Wars		St. Nicholas Church St. Marguerite's Church
1741—2	Bavarian occupation	1753—75	renovation of Prague Castle
1744	Upper and Lower Silesia lost (attached to Prussia)		
1773	Jesuit Order dissolved		
1775	greatest peasant uprising in Bohemia	1781	Theatre of the Estates
1781	abolition of serfdom	1786	Czech patriotic theatre "Bouda" on Horse Market (Wenceslas Square)
1782	monasteries and convents closed		
1782—1848	national rebirth		
1788	first Czech patriotic newspaper		
1799	foundation of Academy of Fine Arts	1782	Strahov Library
1805	compulsory school attendance		
1818	founding of Patriotic (National) Museum	1811—19	customs house "U hybernů", Church of the Holy Cross
1825	horse-drawn railway to Linz	1817	Karlín suburb founded
1830	Czech Cultural Foundation		tenement-houses
	early 19th century—social institutes constructed	1827—31	Kinský Summer Palace
1848	bourgeois revolution in Prague, abolition of servitude		today's Masaryk Station built, arrival of first train in 1845 (Prague—Olomouc line)

Century	**Presidents**	**Style**
19	Francis Joseph I 1848–1916	
		neo-Renaissance last third of 19th century
20	Charles I 1916–18	**Czech Cubism** 1910–1915
	CZECHOSLOVAK REPUBLIC **presidents** T. G. Masaryk 1918–35	**National Style, Rondocubism** 1920–25
		Constructivism, Functionalism 1923–37
	E. Beneš 1935–38 E. Hácha 1938–45	
	E. Beneš 1945–48	**Beginning of socialist realism**
	K. Gottwald 1948–53 A. Zápotocký 1953–57	
	A. Novotný 1957–68	**advent of International Style** 1957–70

		1854—63	Church of SS. Cyril an Methodius in Karlín
		1867—1929	completion of St. Vitus' Cathedral
1866	occupation of Prague by Prussian army	1868—83	National Theatre
		1858—62	Czech Savings Bank
1868	foundation stone of National Theatre laid	1885—90	National Museum
		1872	Czech Technical University
1874	demolition of Prague walls	1876—84	Rudolfinum
1875	first horse-drawn tram in Prague	1876	Bohemian neo-Renaissance (A. Wiehl)
1881	fire of National Theatre		
1882	Czech and German universities opened	1889	Slavín at Vyšehrad
		1891	Jubilee Exhibition in Prague
1883	reopening of National Theatre		from the end of 19th century many
1885	decision to demolish the Jewish Town in Prague, major town-planning action in 19th century		tenement houses built in Art Nouveau style
1896	electric tramline		new construction in the Old Town, early 20th century (corner of Old Town Square)
	end of Habsburg Empire	1905—11	Community House
		1899	Peterka House, Wenceslas Square
		1901—9	today's Main Station built
		1911—12	house "At the Black Mother of the Lord"
		1911—13	houses under Vyšehrad
1918			
	end of World War I	1921—25	Legiobanka building
	creation of Czechoslovak Republic	1923—25	Adria di Sicurta
1920	Greater Prague Act	1920—35	renovation of Prague Castle
		1927—30	Mánes Building
		1924—28	Fair Palace
		1926—35	Municipal Transport Company Building
		1929—34	Pension Institute
		1932	Baba housing estate
	Beginning of modern protection of ancient monuments	1924—32	renovation of Černín Palace
		1928—49	Renovation of Clementinum
		1920—35	renovation of Prague Castle and its gardens
		1937	Glass Palace, Dejvice
1938	Munich Diktat		
1939	German occupation, Protectorate of Bohemia and Moravia		
1945	liberation of Prague	1946	construction of first housing estate Solidarita-Spořilov
1948	Communist coup d'état	1946—54	postwar renovation of Prague
		1948—52	monuments: Belvedere, Ball-Game Court, Riding-Hall at Prague Castle
		1950—53	reconstruction of Bethlehem Chapel, renovation of Emmaus Monastery and Strahov Abbey
		1949—65	Carolinum
		1958	Brussels Expo 58 Pavilion
		1967	construction of Underground begins
			construction of panel-based housing estates

Century	Presidents	Style
20		renovation of Prague's monuments continues
	L. Svoboda 1968–75	
		New trends in architecture 1971–83
	G. Husák 1975–1989	
		Postmodernism
	V. Havel 1989	

		1967—72	Federal Assembly building
		1958—76	renovation of Agnes Convent starts
		1965—81	renovation of Agnes Convent continues, rebuilding of central part of Prague Castle renovation of King's Way begins town-hall of the Old Town
1968	"Prague Spring", A. Dubček occupation of Czechoslovakia by Warsaw Pact armies		
1974—80	more communities attached to Prague whose territory now is 49,688 ha	1965—81	New department stores:
		1970—75	Máj
		1972—77	renovation of Main Station of Prague
		1975—77	first skyscrapers in Prague (Motokov)
		1970—83	renovation and completion of National Theatre
		1967—85	construction of Underground lines A, B ČKD Building
		1977	Koospol
		1975—81	Palace of Congresses
		1978	rebuilding in Prague's suburbs Vinohrady, Žižkov construction of Czech National Council (Diet) in the Lesser Quarter
1989	November Revolution		
1989	end of Communist rule in Czechoslovakia		
1991	General Czechoslovak Exhibition in Prague		

CONTENTS